VOL. 27
VIZ Media Edition

Story and Art by
RUMIKO TAKAHASHI

English Adaptation/Gerard Jones
Translation/Kaori Inoue
Touch-up Art & Lettering/Bill Schuch
Cover and Interior Design & Graphics/Yuki Ameda
Editor/Avery Gotoh
Supervising Editor/Michelle Pangilinan

Managing Editor/Annette Roman
Editorial Director/Elizabeth Kawasaki
Editor in Chief, Books/Alvin Lu
Editor in Chief, Magazines/Marc Weidenbaum
Sr. Director of Acquisitions/Rika Inouye
Sr. VP of Marketing/Liza Coppola
Exec. VP of Sales & Marketing/John Easum
Publisher/Hyoe Narita

Printed in Canada.

Published by VIZ Media, LLC
P.O. Box 77010
San Francisco, CA 94107

VIZ Media Edition
10 9 8 7 6 5 4 3 2
First Printing, July 2004
Second Printing, January 2007

www.viz.com

store.viz.com

Ranma ½

VOL. 27 VIZ Media Edition

STORY & ART BY
RUMIKO TAKAHASHI

STORY THUS FAR

The Tendos are an average, run-of-the-mill Japanese family—on the surface, that is. Soun Tendo is the owner and proprietor of the Tendo Dojo, where "Anything-Goes Martial Arts" is practiced. Like the name says, anything goes, and usually does.

When Soun's old friend Genma Saotome comes to visit, Soun's three lovely young daughters—Akane, Nabiki, and Kasumi—are told that it's time for one of them to become the fiancée of Genma's teenage son, as per an agreement made between the two fathers years ago. Youngest daughter Akane—who says she hates boys—is quickly nominated for bridal duty by her sisters.

Unfortunately, Ranma and his father have suffered a strange accident. While training in China, both plunged into one of many "cursed" springs at the legendary martial-arts training ground of Jusenkyo. These springs transform the unlucky dunkee into whoever—or whatever—drowned there hundreds of years ago.

Henceforth, a splash of cold water turns Ranma's father into a giant panda, and Ranma becomes a beautiful, busty young woman. Hot water reverses the effect...but only until next time. As it turns out, Ranma and Genma aren't the only ones to take the Jusenkyo plunge—and it isn't long before they meet several other members of the Jusenkyo "cursed."

Although their parents are still determined to see Ranma and Akane marry and carry on the training hall, Ranma seems to have a strange talent for accumulating surplus fiancées...and Akane has a few stubbornly determined suitors of her own. Will the two ever work out their differences, get rid of all these "extra" people, or will they just call the whole thing off? What's a half-boy, half-girl (not to mention all-girl, angry girl) to do...?

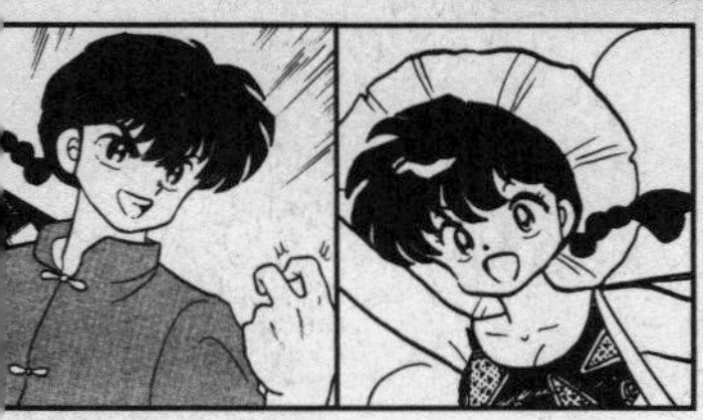

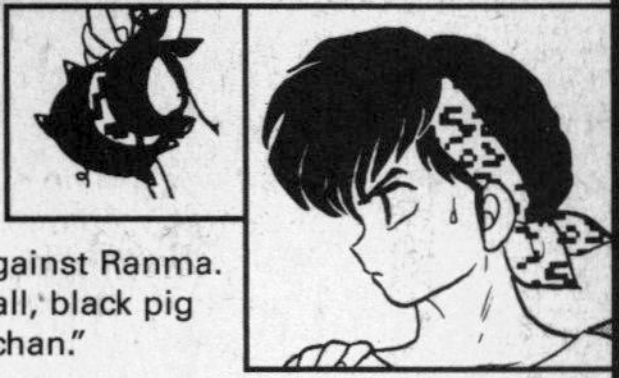

RYOGA HIBIKI
Melancholy martial artist with no sense of direction, a hopeless crush on Akane, and a stubborn grudge against Ranma. Changes into a small, black pig Akane's named "P-chan."

RANMA SAOTOME
Martial artist with far too many fiancées, and an ego that won't let him take defeat. Changes into a girl when splashed with cold water.

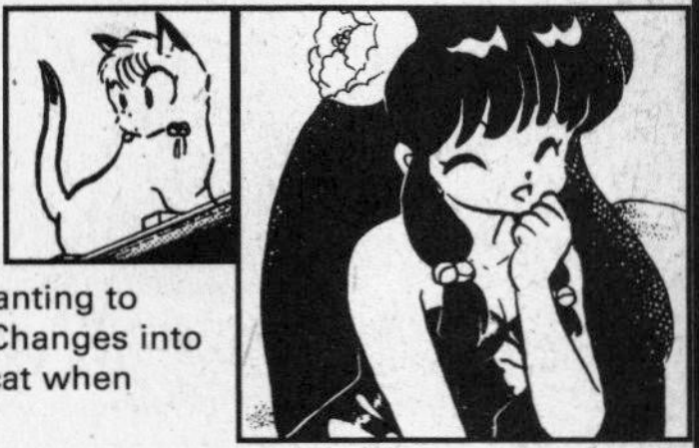

SHAMPOO
Chinese-Amazon warrior who's gone from wanting to kill Ranma to wanting to marry him. Changes into a cute kitty cat when splashed.

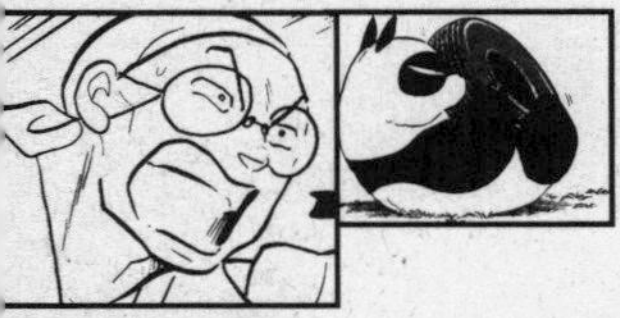

GENMA SAOTOME
Ranma's lazy father, who left his wife and home years ago with his young son (Ranma) to train in the martial arts. Changes into a panda.

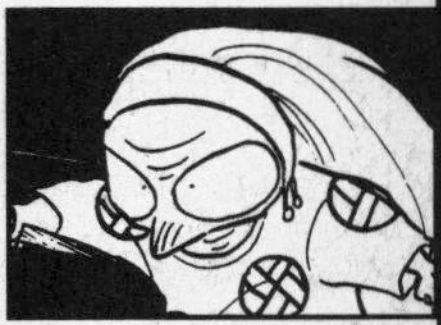

COLOGNE
Shampoo's great-grandmother, a martial artist, and matchmaker.

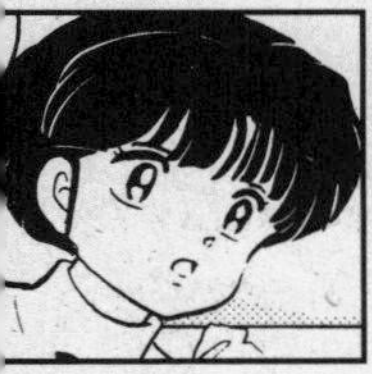

AKANE TENDO
Martial artist, tomboy, and Ranma's reluctant fiancée. Has no clue how much Ryoga likes her, or what relation he might have to her pet black pig, P-chan.

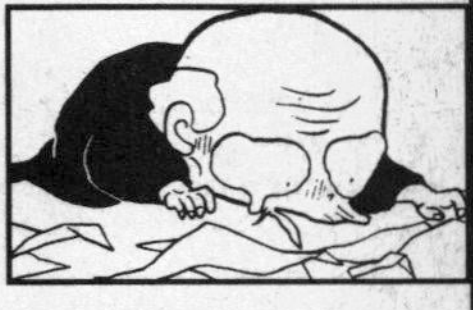

HAPPOSAI
Martial arts master who trained both Genma and Soun. Also a world-class panty raider and pervert.

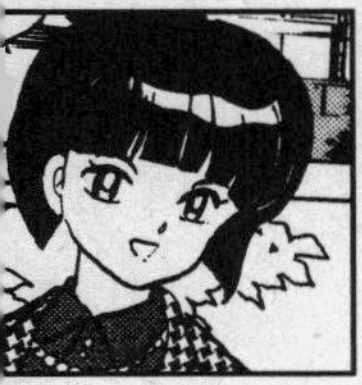

NABIKI TENDO
Middle Tendo daughter whose love of money is almost legendary. Never makes a move without first considering all the angles.

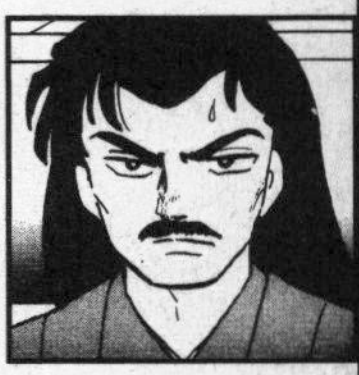

SOUN TENDO
Head of the Tendo household and owner of the Tendo Dojo. Best friends with Genma.

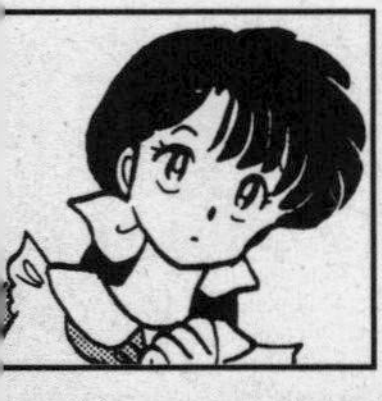

KASUMI TENDO
Eldest Tendo daughter and the family's home-maker. Has an ongoing friendship with Dr. Tofu—a practitioner of the traditional healing arts—who gets absolutely wacky whenever Kasumi is around.

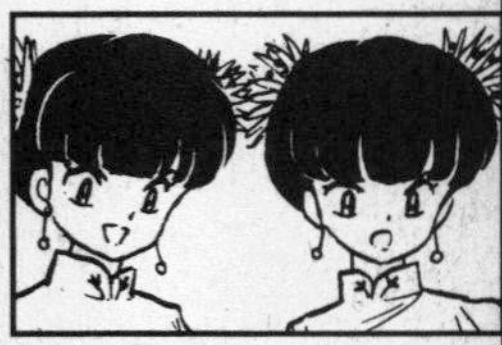

PINK and LINK
Twin sisters from a Chinese Amazon village. Known for playing pranks, the duo has come to seek revenge against Shampoo... and her "husband," Ranma!

CONTENTS

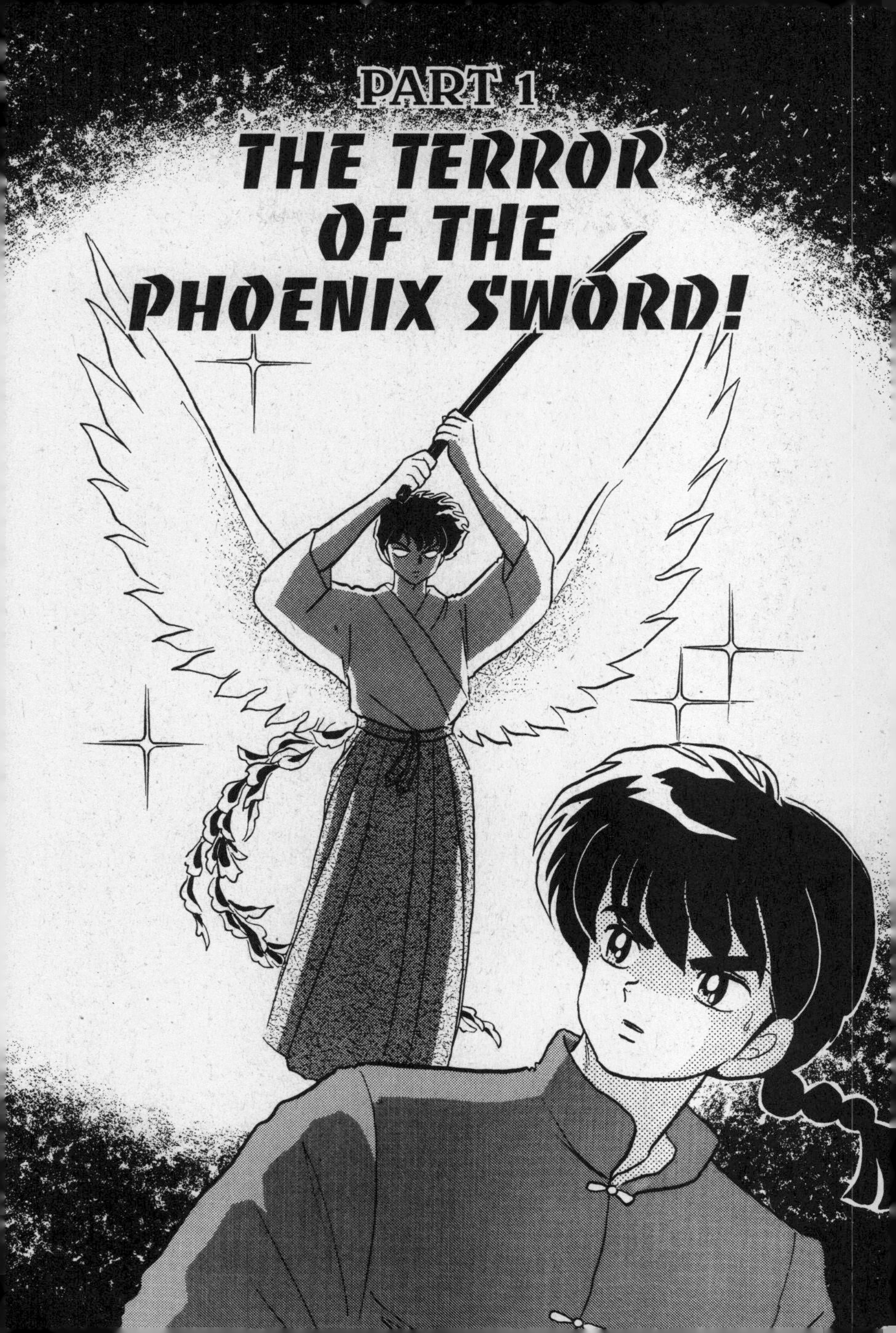
PART 1
THE TERROR OF THE PHOENIX SWORD!

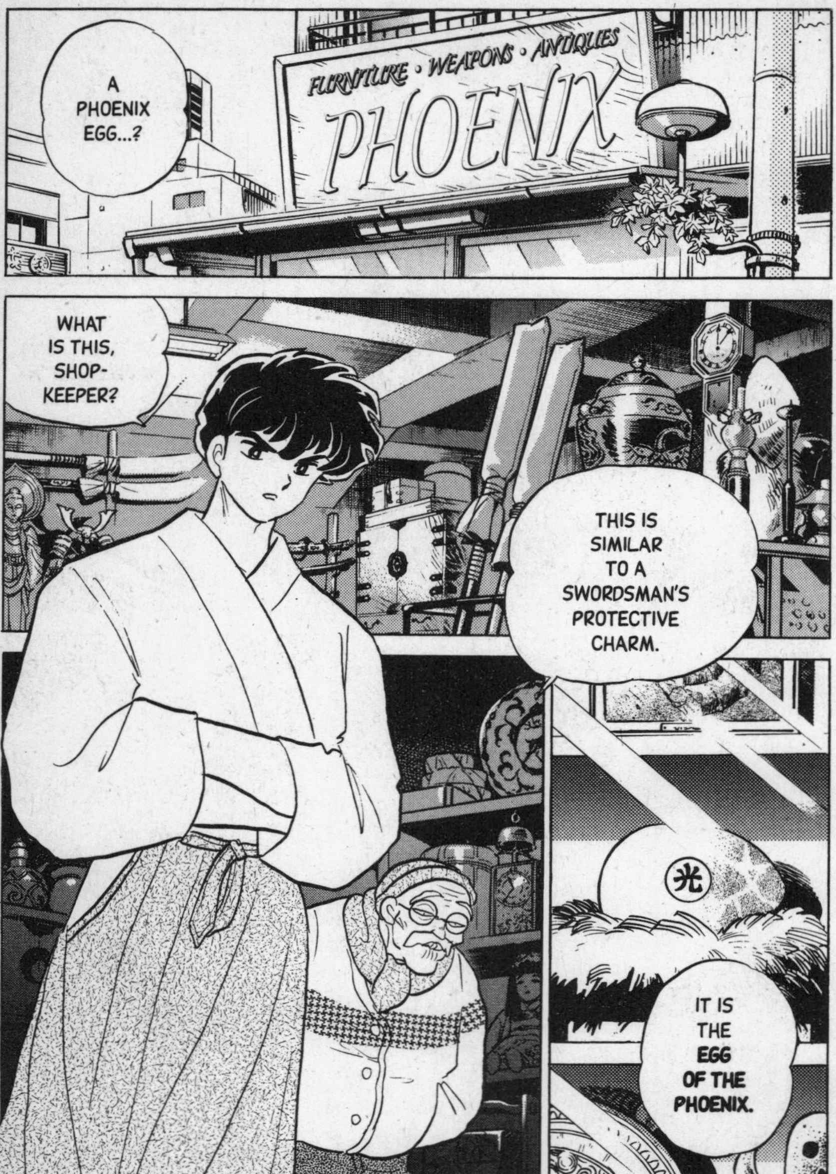
A PHOENIX EGG...?
FURNITURE • WEAPONS • ANTIQUES
PHOENIX
WHAT IS THIS, SHOP-KEEPER?
THIS IS SIMILAR TO A SWORDSMAN'S PROTECTIVE CHARM.
光
IT IS THE EGG OF THE PHOENIX.

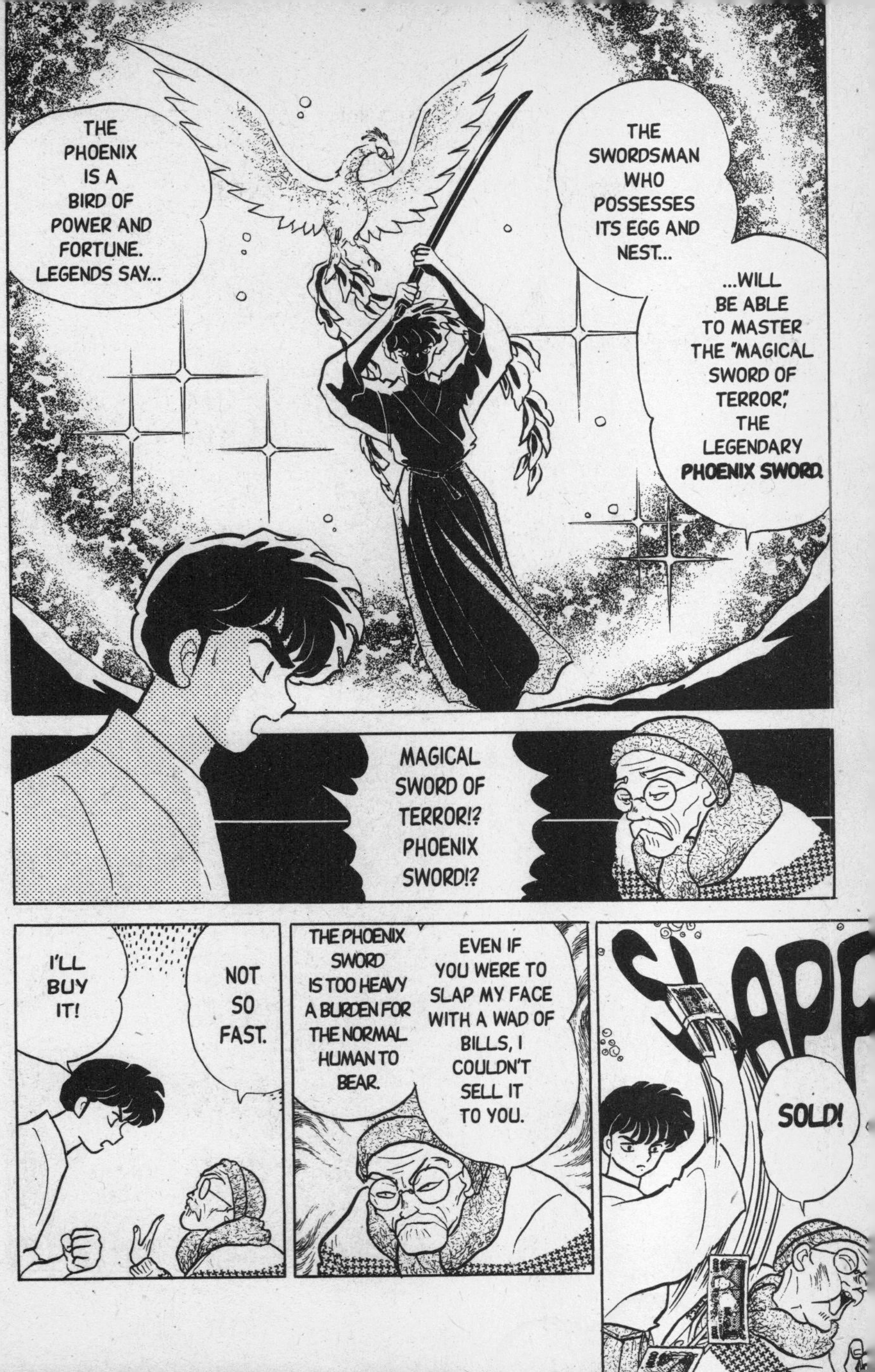
THE PHOENIX IS A BIRD OF POWER AND FORTUNE. LEGENDS SAY...
THE SWORDSMAN WHO POSSESSES ITS EGG AND NEST...
...WILL BE ABLE TO MASTER THE "MAGICAL SWORD OF TERROR," THE LEGENDARY PHOENIX SWORD.
MAGICAL SWORD OF TERROR!? PHOENIX SWORD!?
I'LL BUY IT!
NOT SO FAST.
THE PHOENIX SWORD IS TOO HEAVY A BURDEN FOR THE NORMAL HUMAN TO BEAR.
EVEN IF YOU WERE TO SLAP MY FACE WITH A WAD OF BILLS, I COULDN'T SELL IT TO YOU.
SOLD!

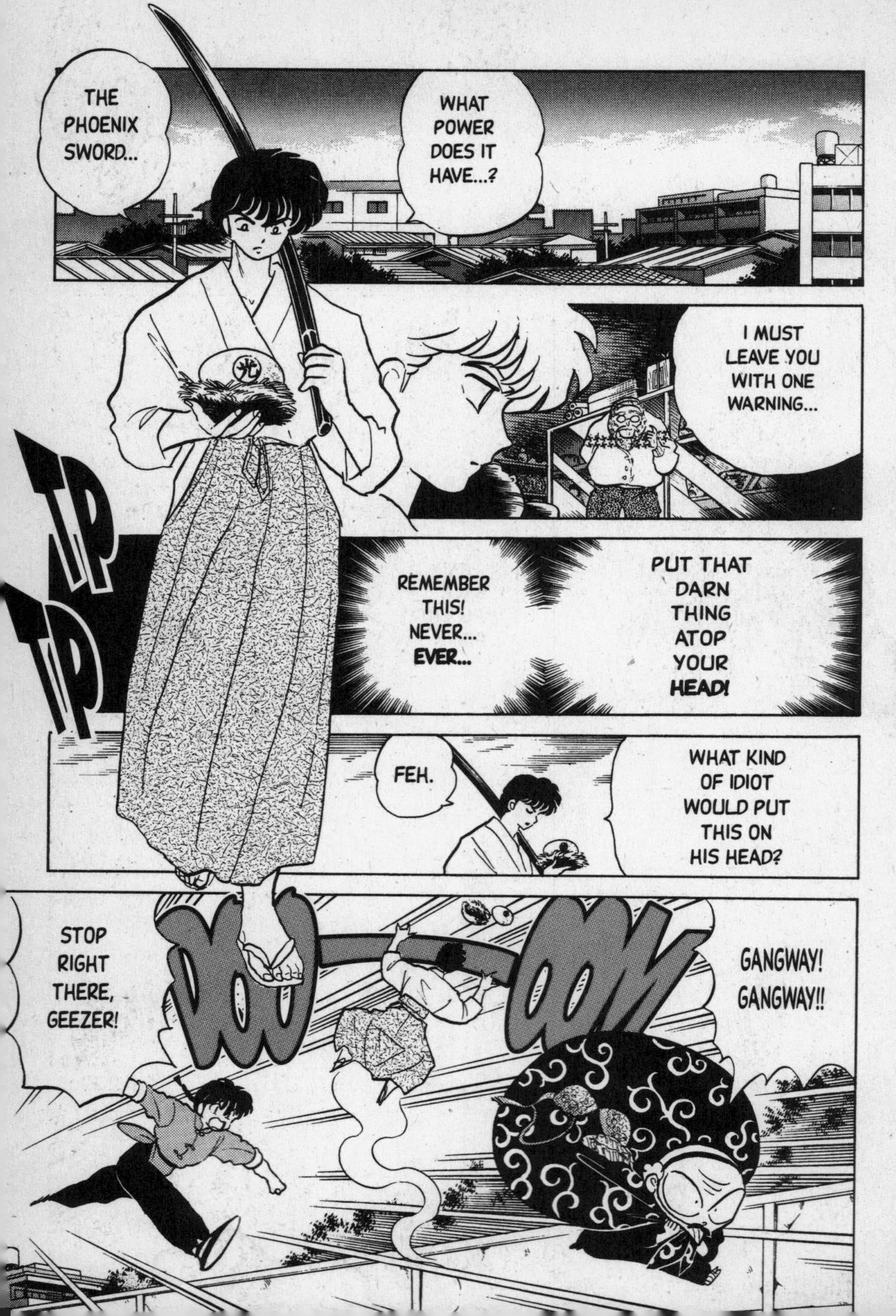
THE PHOENIX SWORD...
WHAT POWER DOES IT HAVE...?
I MUST LEAVE YOU WITH ONE WARNING...
TIP TIP
REMEMBER THIS! NEVER... EVER...
PUT THAT DARN THING ATOP YOUR HEAD!
FEH.
WHAT KIND OF IDIOT WOULD PUT THIS ON HIS HEAD?
STOP RIGHT THERE, GEEZER!
GANGWAY! GANGWAY!!

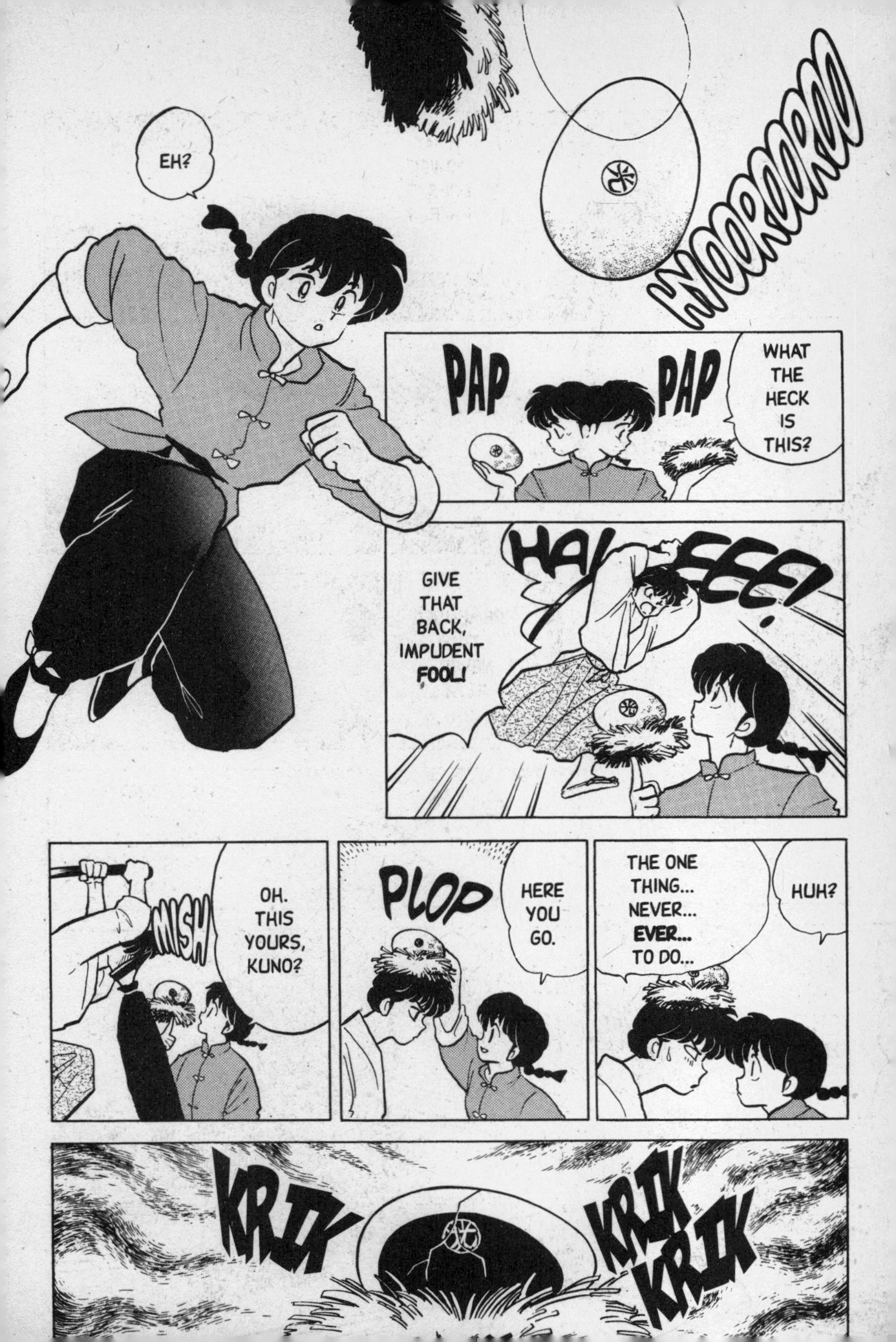
EH?
WOOROOROO
PAP
PAP
WHAT THE HECK IS THIS?
HAIEEE!
GIVE THAT BACK, IMPUDENT FOOL!
MISH
OH. THIS YOURS, KUNO?
PLOP
HERE YOU GO.
THE ONE THING... NEVER... EVER... TO DO...
HUH?
KRIK
KRIK KRIK

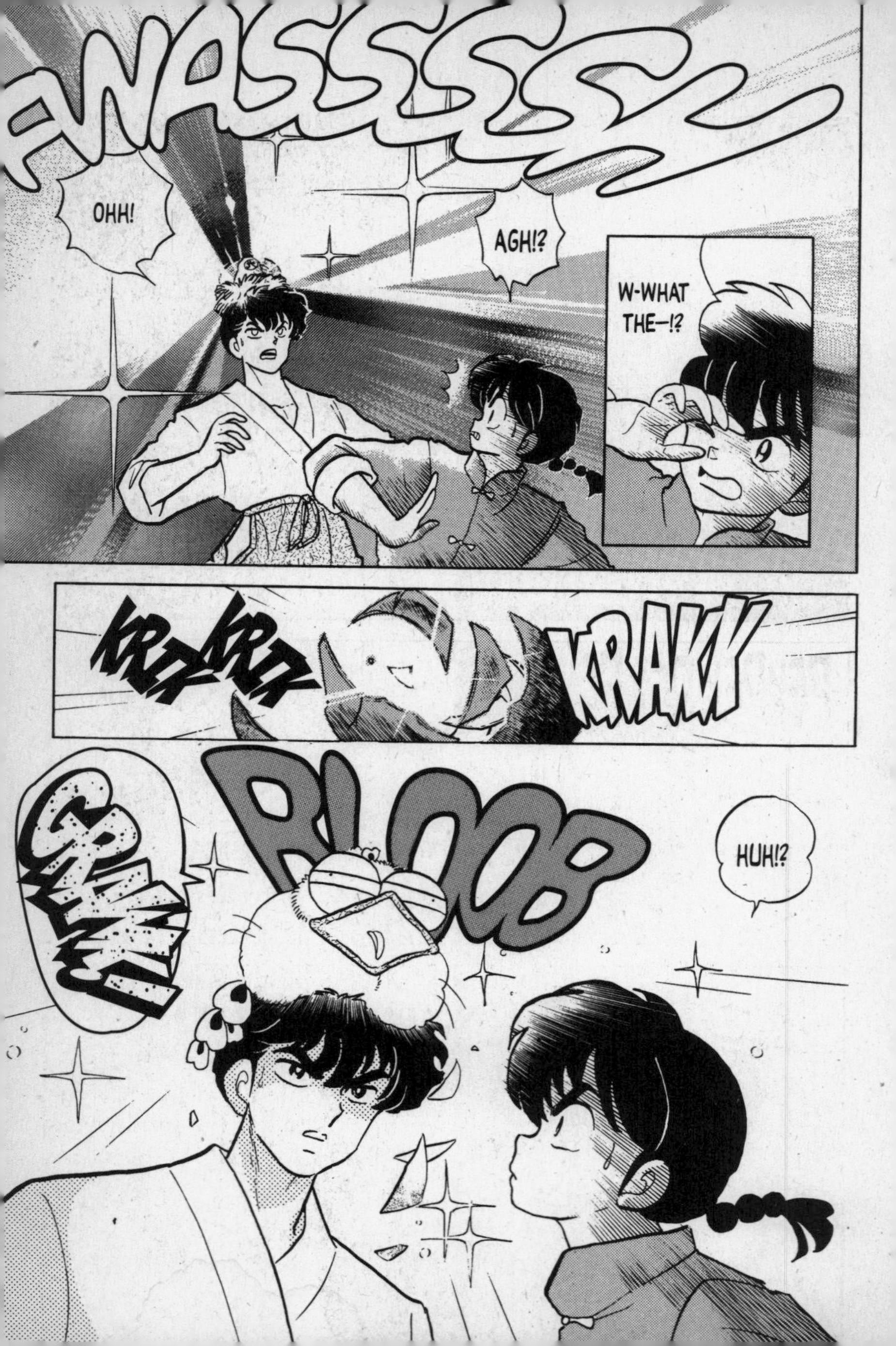
FWASSSSH
OHH!
AGH!?
W-WHAT THE—!?
KRIK KRIK
KRAKK
GRWWW
BLOOB
HUH!?

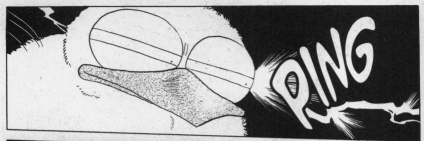

RING

PEK PEK PEK PEK PEK

OW!?
OW
OW
OW
OW!!

WHAT'S
THE
BIG
IDEA!?

YAAH!
B-BLINDED!

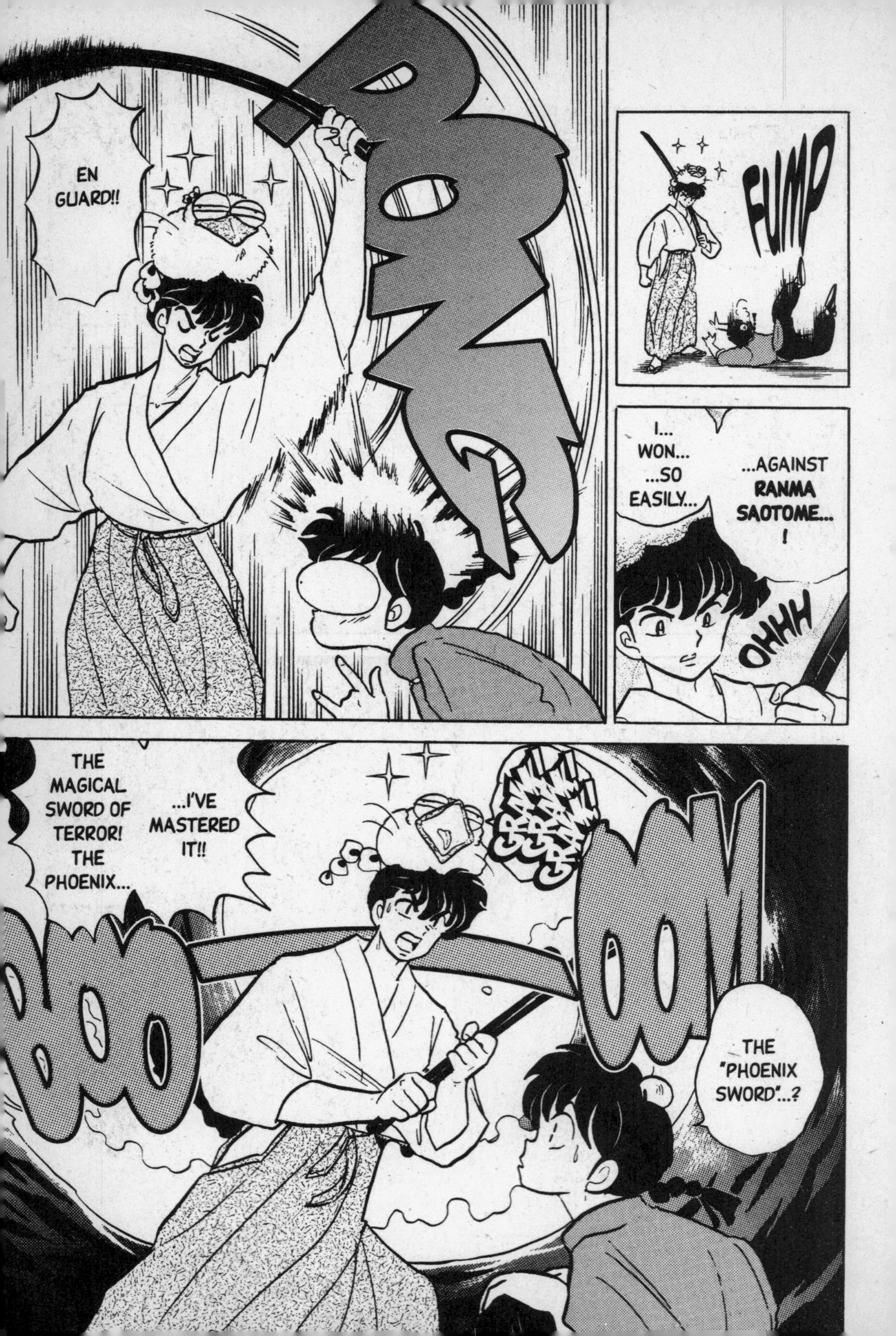
EN GUARD!!
BAM
FUMP
I... WON... ...SO EASILY...
...AGAINST RANMA SAOTOME... !
OHHH
THE MAGICAL SWORD OF TERROR! THE PHOENIX...
...I'VE MASTERED IT!!
BOOOOM
THE "PHOENIX SWORD"...?

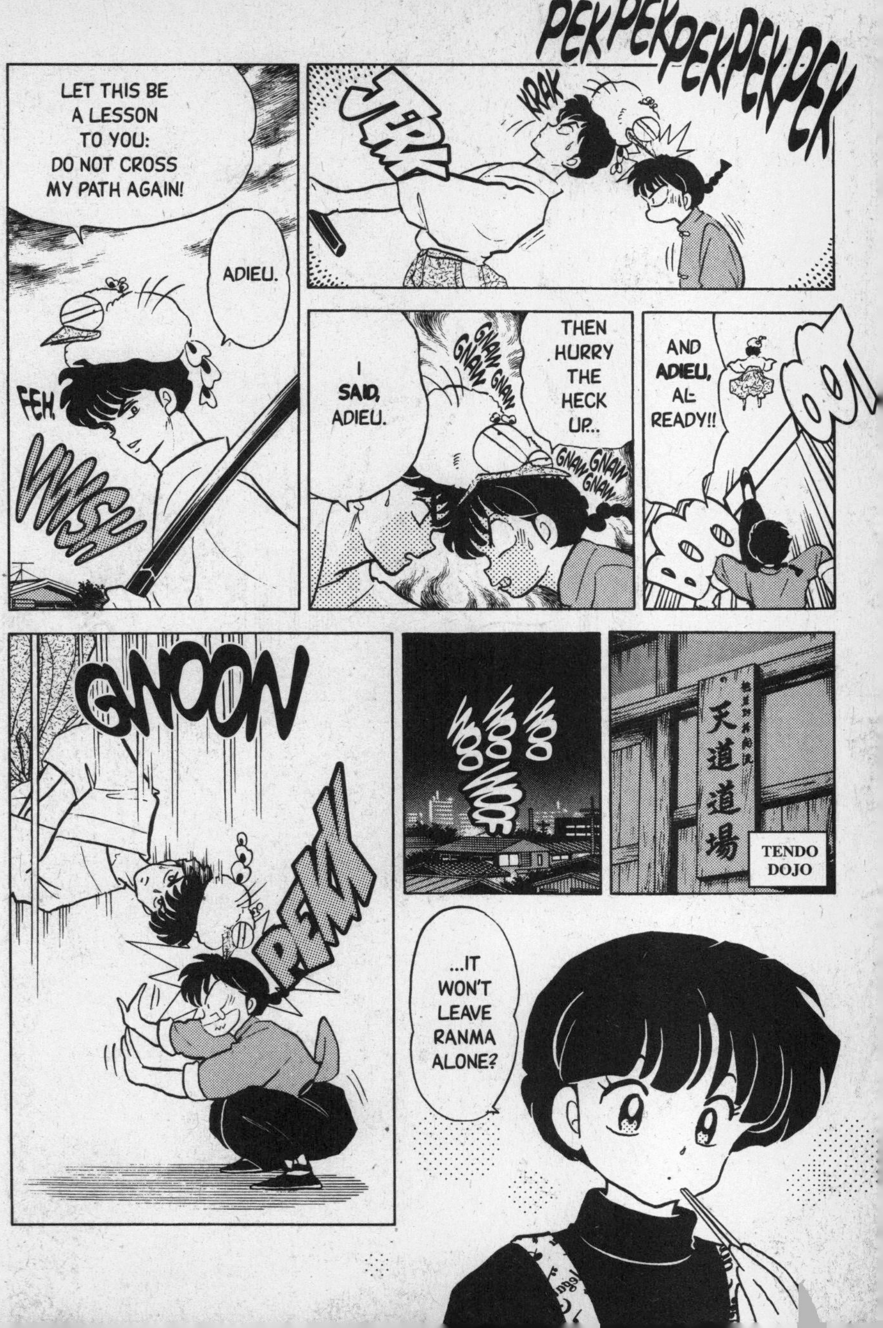
LET THIS BE A LESSON TO YOU: DO NOT CROSS MY PATH AGAIN!
ADIEU.
FEH.
VWISH
PEK PEK PEK PEK PEK PEK
JERK
KRAK
I SAID, ADIEU.
GNAW GNAW GNAW GNAW
THEN HURRY THE HECK UP...
GNAW GNAW GNAW GNAW
AND ADIEU, AL-READY!!
GNOON
PEKK
WOO WOO WOO WOOF
天道道場
TENDO DOJO
...IT WON'T LEAVE RANMA ALONE?

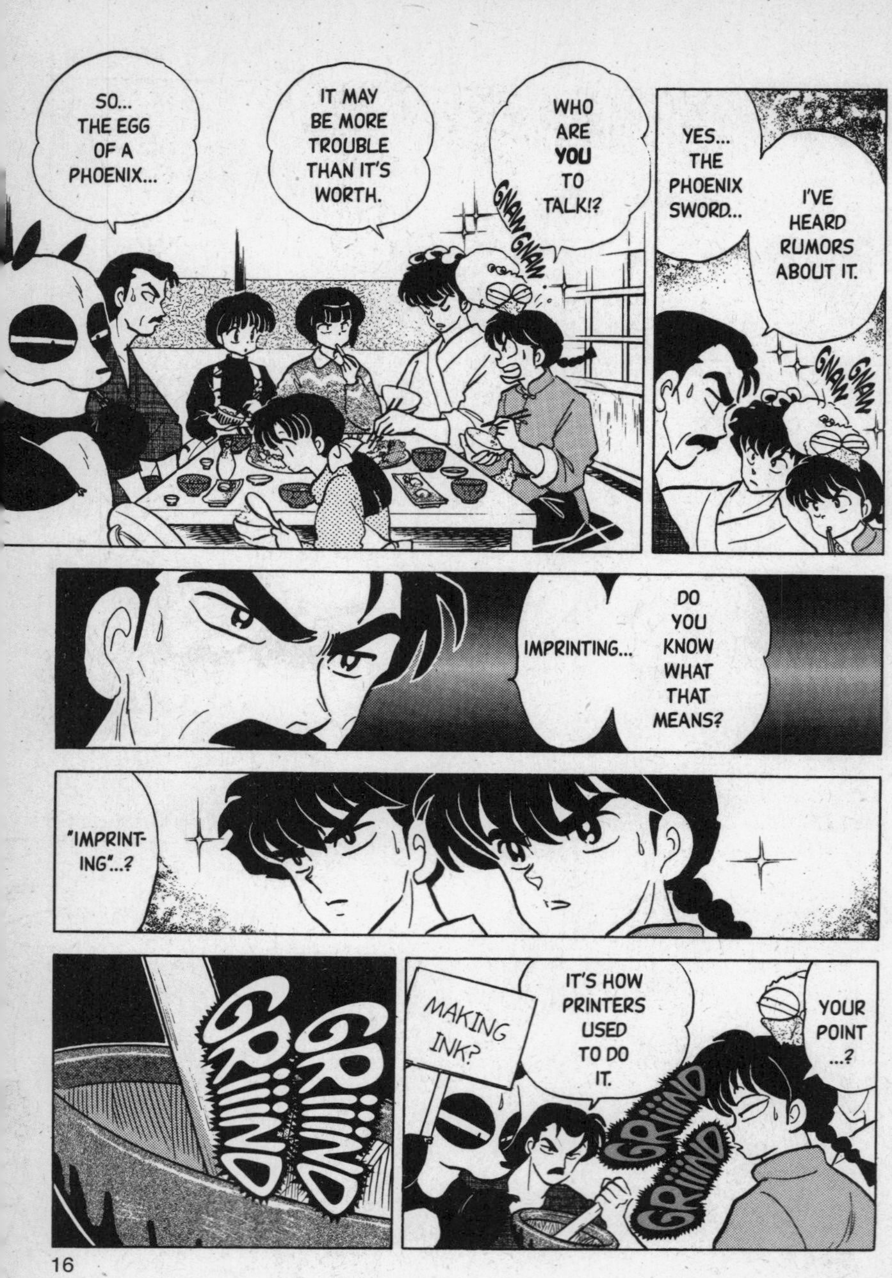

SO... THE EGG OF A PHOENIX...
IT MAY BE MORE TROUBLE THAN IT'S WORTH.
WHO ARE YOU TO TALK!?
GNAW GNAW GNAW
YES... THE PHOENIX SWORD...
I'VE HEARD RUMORS ABOUT IT.
GNAW GNAW
IMPRINTING...
DO YOU KNOW WHAT THAT MEANS?
"IMPRINT-ING"...?
GRIIIND GRIIIND
MAKING INK?
IT'S HOW PRINTERS USED TO DO IT.
YOUR POINT ...?
GRIIIND GRIIIND

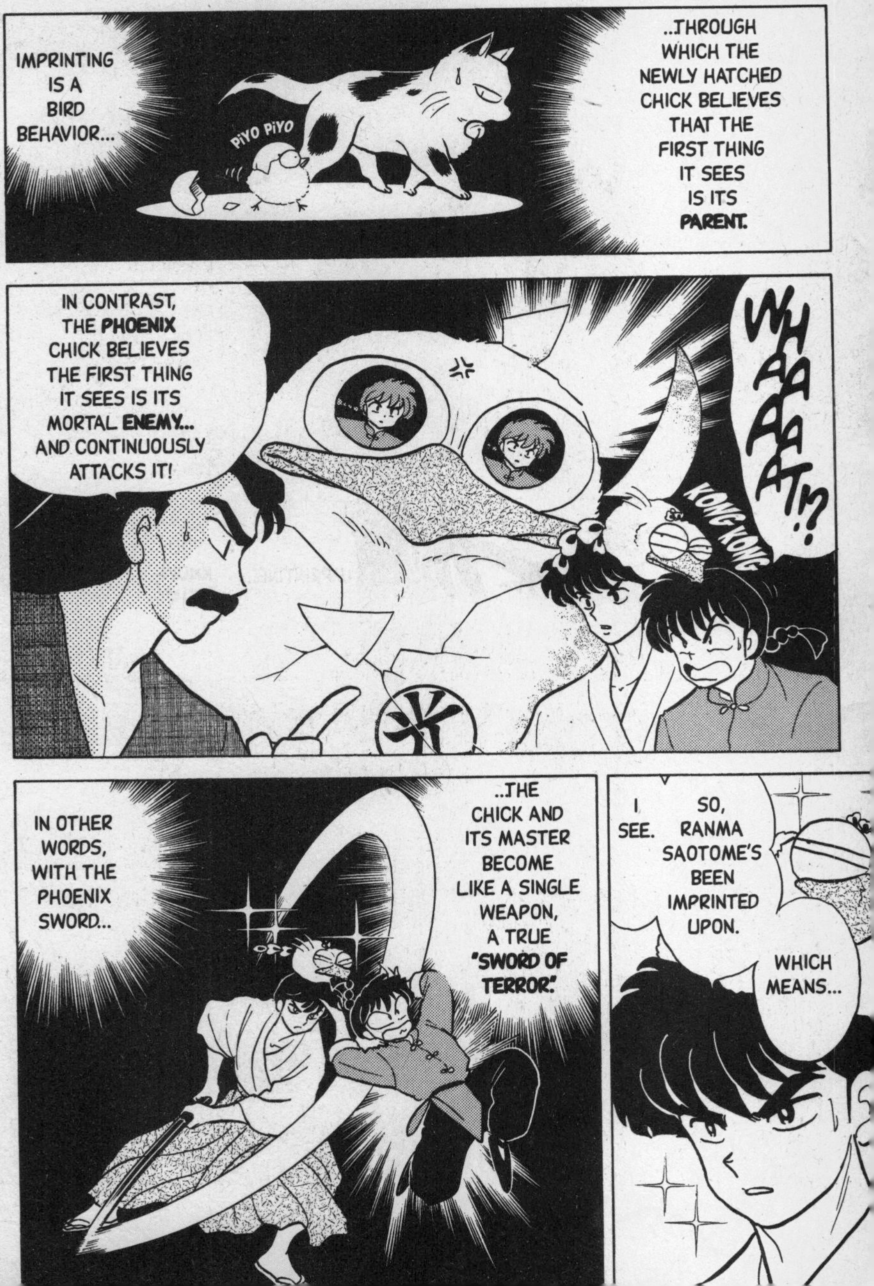
IMPRINTING IS A BIRD BEHAVIOR...
PIYO PIYO
...THROUGH WHICH THE NEWLY HATCHED CHICK BELIEVES THAT THE FIRST THING IT SEES IS ITS PARENT.
IN CONTRAST, THE PHOENIX CHICK BELIEVES THE FIRST THING IT SEES IS ITS MORTAL ENEMY... AND CONTINUOUSLY ATTACKS IT!
KONG KONG
WHAAAAAT!!?
IN OTHER WORDS, WITH THE PHOENIX SWORD...
...THE CHICK AND ITS MASTER BECOME LIKE A SINGLE WEAPON, A TRUE "SWORD OF TERROR."
I SEE.
SO, RANMA SAOTOME'S BEEN IMPRINTED UPON.
WHICH MEANS...

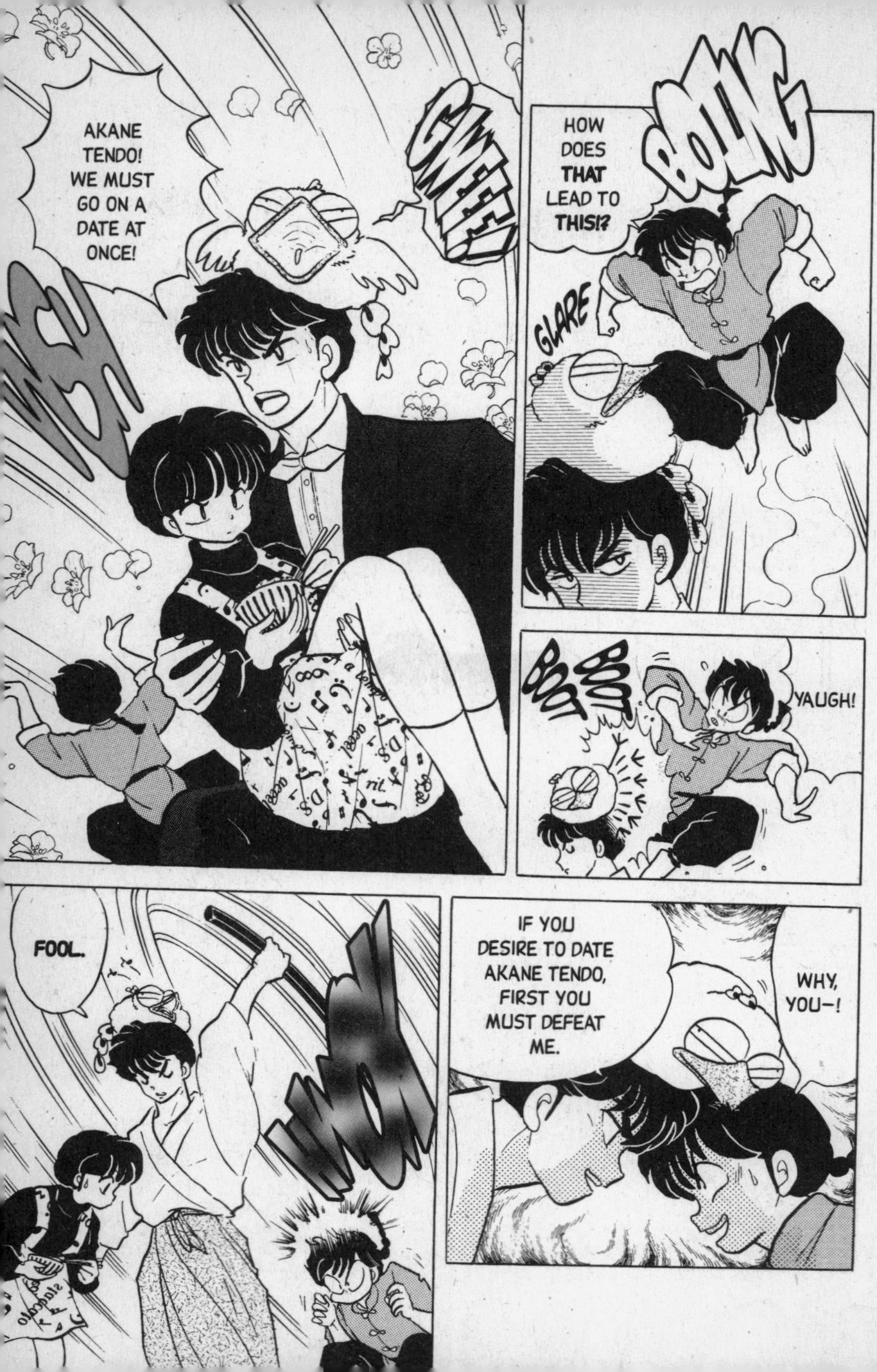
AKANE TENDO! WE MUST GO ON A DATE AT ONCE!
HOW DOES THAT LEAD TO THIS!?
BOING
GLARE
BOOT
BOOT
YAUGH!
FOOL.
IF YOU DESIRE TO DATE AKANE TENDO, FIRST YOU MUST DEFEAT ME.
WHY, YOU—!

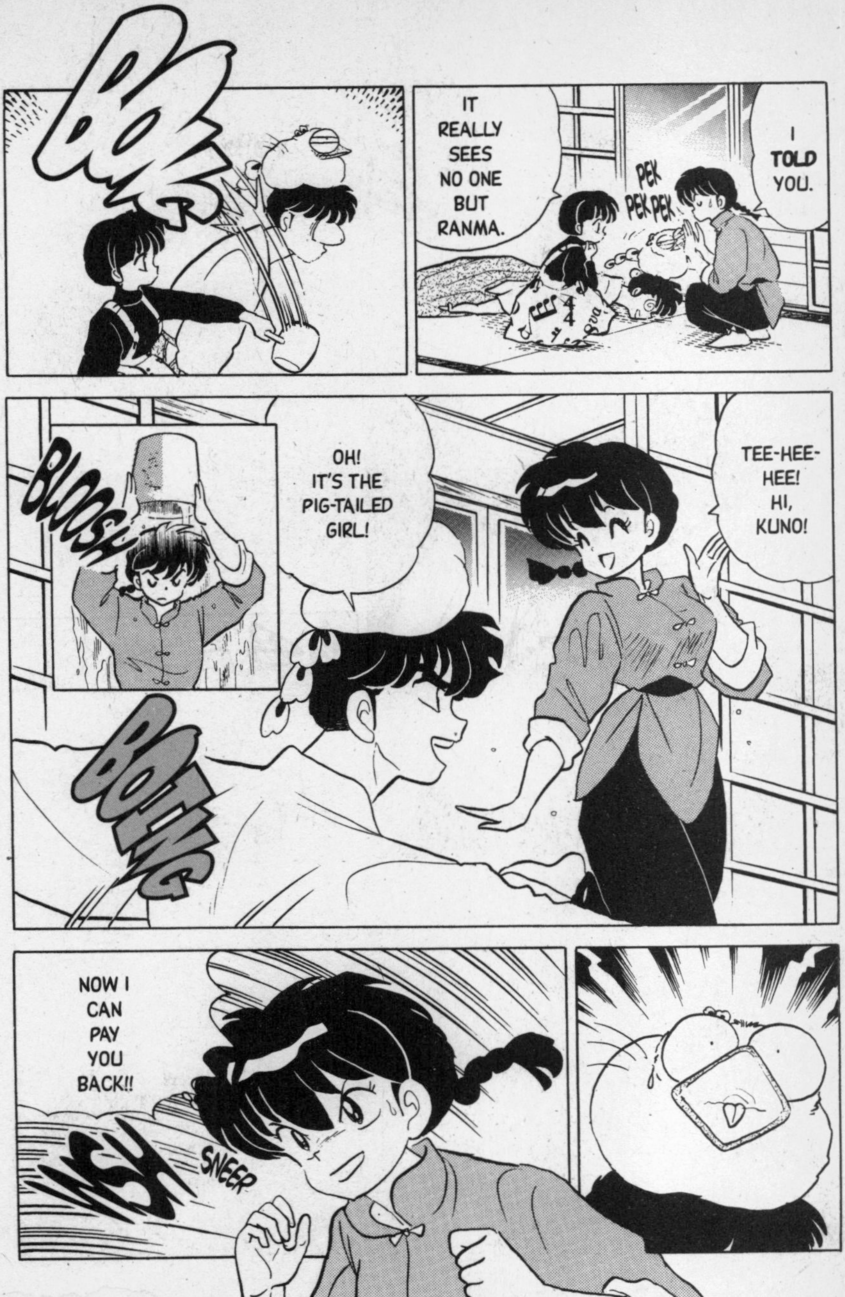
BONG
IT REALLY SEES NO ONE BUT RANMA.
PEK PEK PEK
I TOLD YOU.
BLOOSH
OH! IT'S THE PIG-TAILED GIRL!
BOING
TEE-HEE-HEE! HI, KUNO!
NOW I CAN PAY YOU BACK!!
SNEER

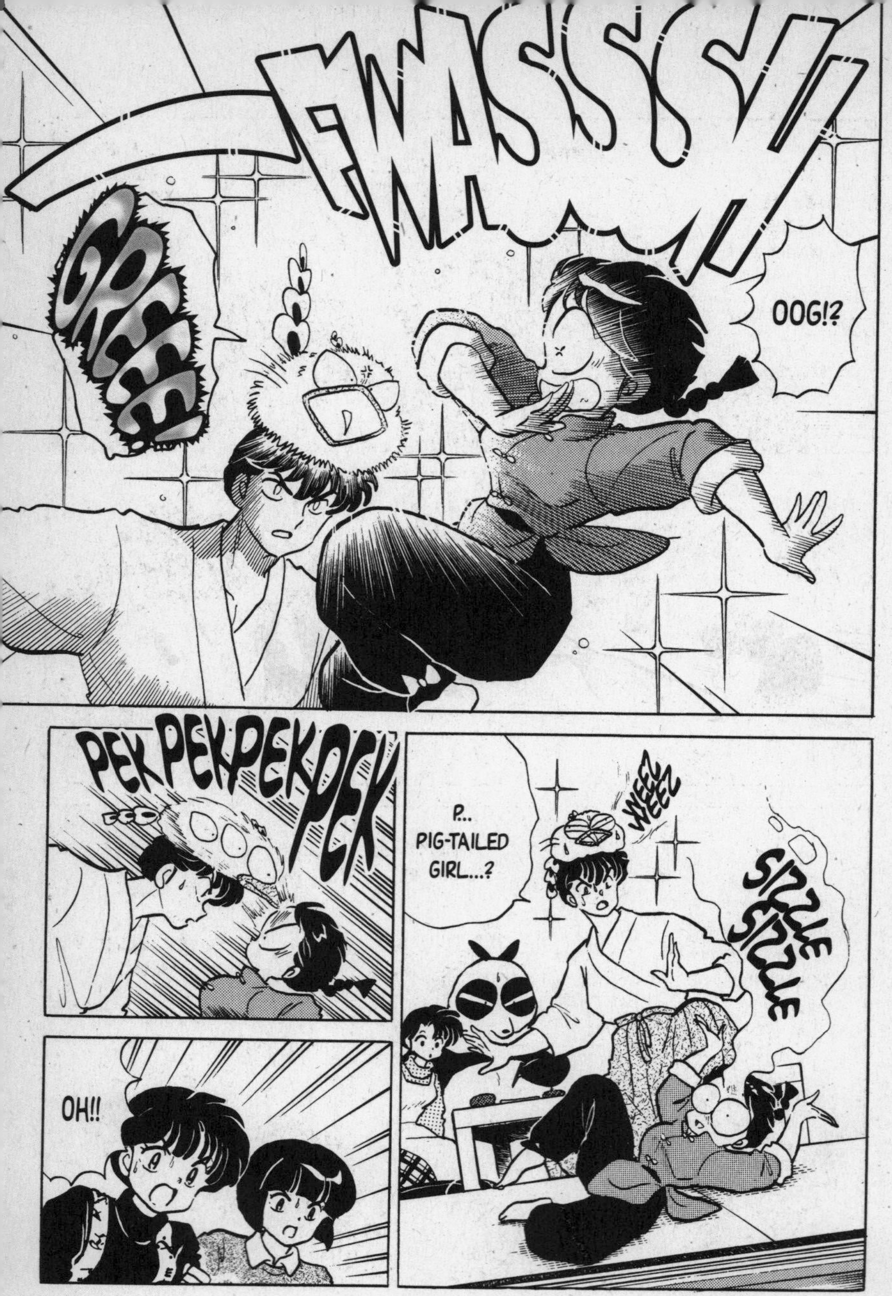
OOG!?
PEK PEK PEK PEK PEK
P... PIG-TAILED GIRL...?
WEEZ WEEZ
SIZZLE SIZZLE
OH!!

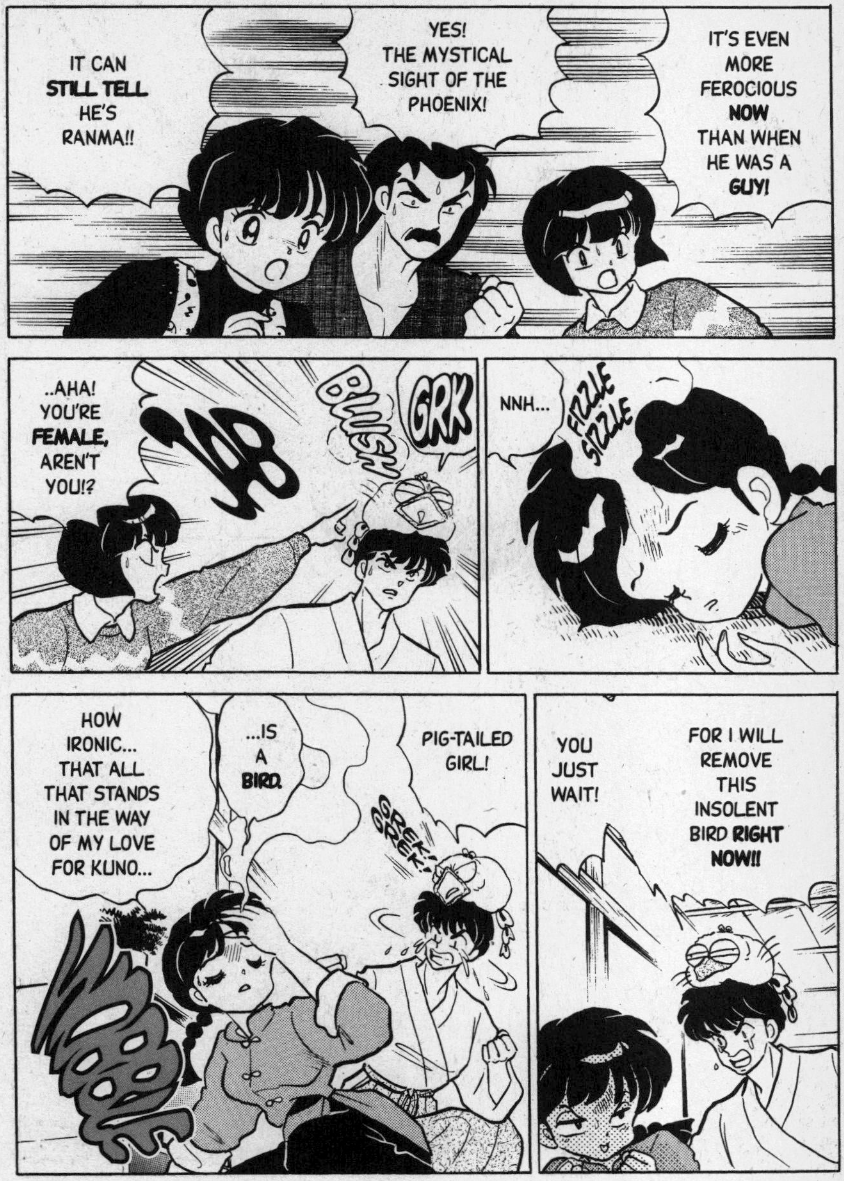
IT CAN STILL TELL HE'S RANMA!!
YES! THE MYSTICAL SIGHT OF THE PHOENIX!
IT'S EVEN MORE FEROCIOUS NOW THAN WHEN HE WAS A GUY!
..AHA! YOU'RE FEMALE, AREN'T YOU!?
BLUSH
GRK
NNH...
FIZZLE SIZZLE
HOW IRONIC... THAT ALL THAT STANDS IN THE WAY OF MY LOVE FOR KUNO...
...IS A BIRD.
PIG-TAILED GIRL!
GREK! GREK!
YOU JUST WAIT!
FOR I WILL REMOVE THIS INSOLENT BIRD RIGHT NOW!!

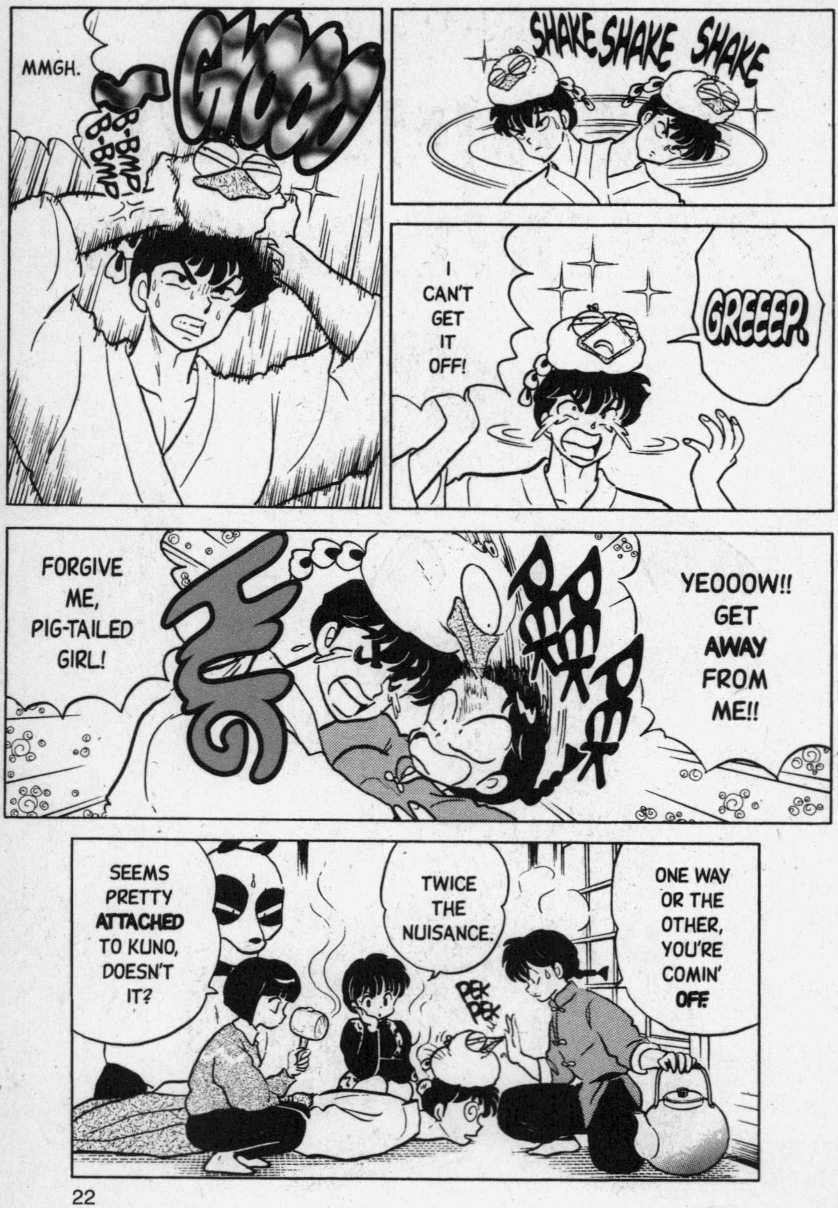
MMGH.
B-BMP! B-BMP!
SHAKE SHAKE SHAKE
I CAN'T GET IT OFF!
GREEEP.
FORGIVE ME, PIG-TAILED GIRL!
YEOOOW!! GET AWAY FROM ME!!
SEEMS PRETTY ATTACHED TO KUNO, DOESN'T IT?
TWICE THE NUISANCE.
PEK PEK
ONE WAY OR THE OTHER, YOU'RE COMIN' OFF.

PART 2

THE IMMORTAL PHOENIX SWORD

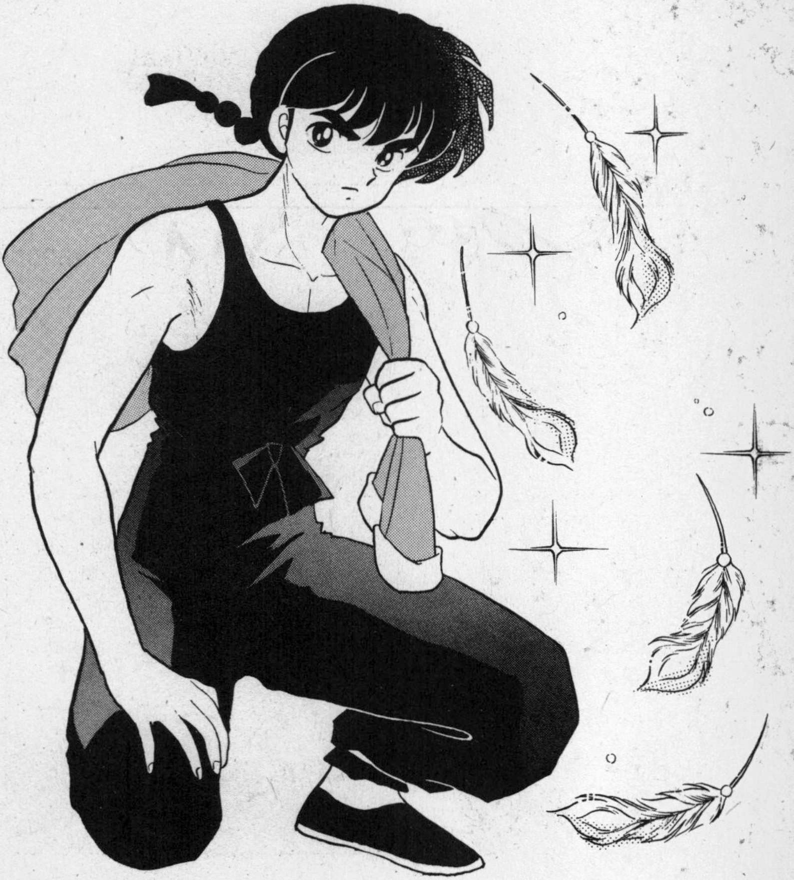

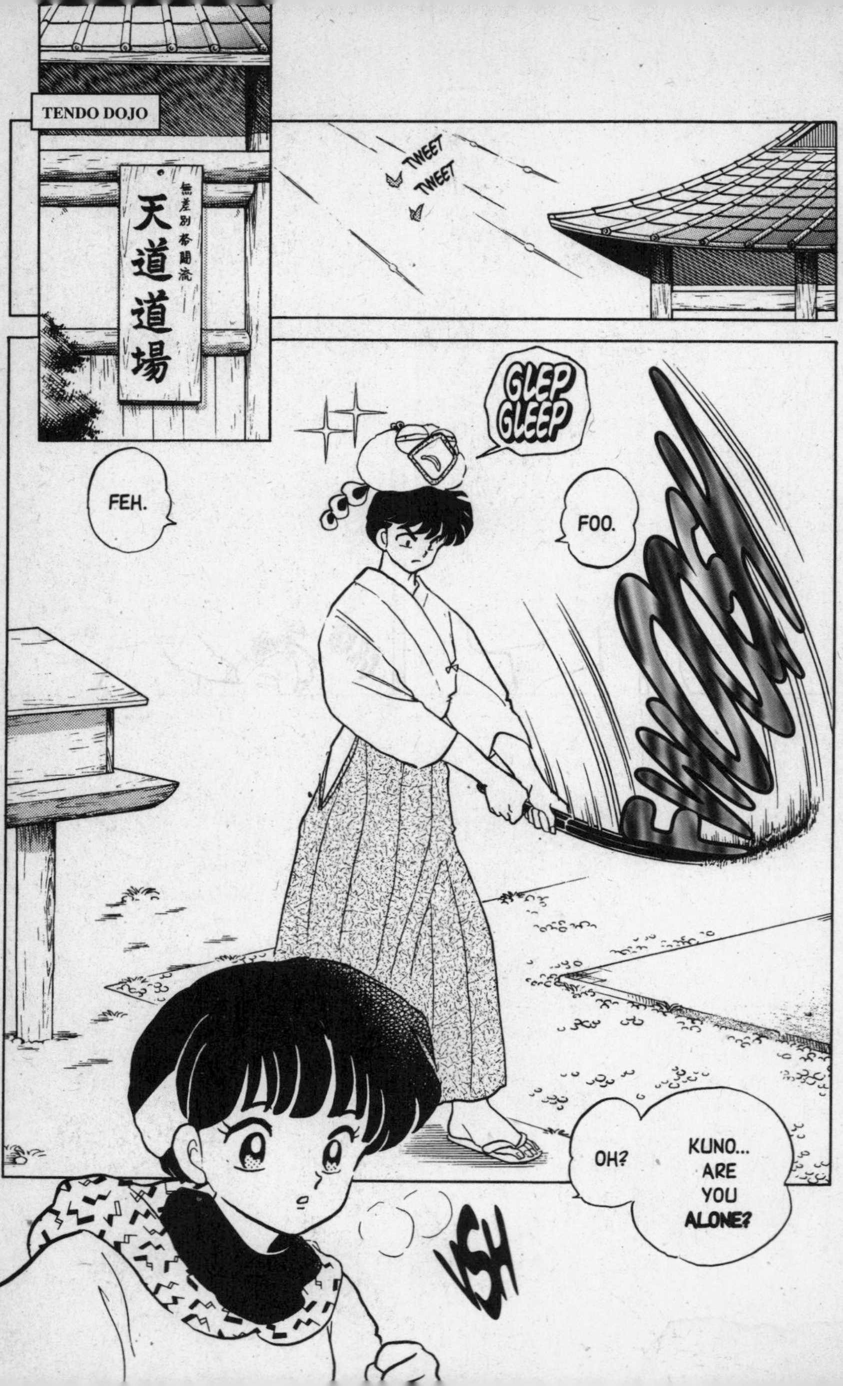
TENDO DOJO
無差別格闘流
天道道場
TWEET
TWEET
FEH.
GLEP GLEEP
FOO.
OH?
KUNO... ARE YOU ALONE?
VSH

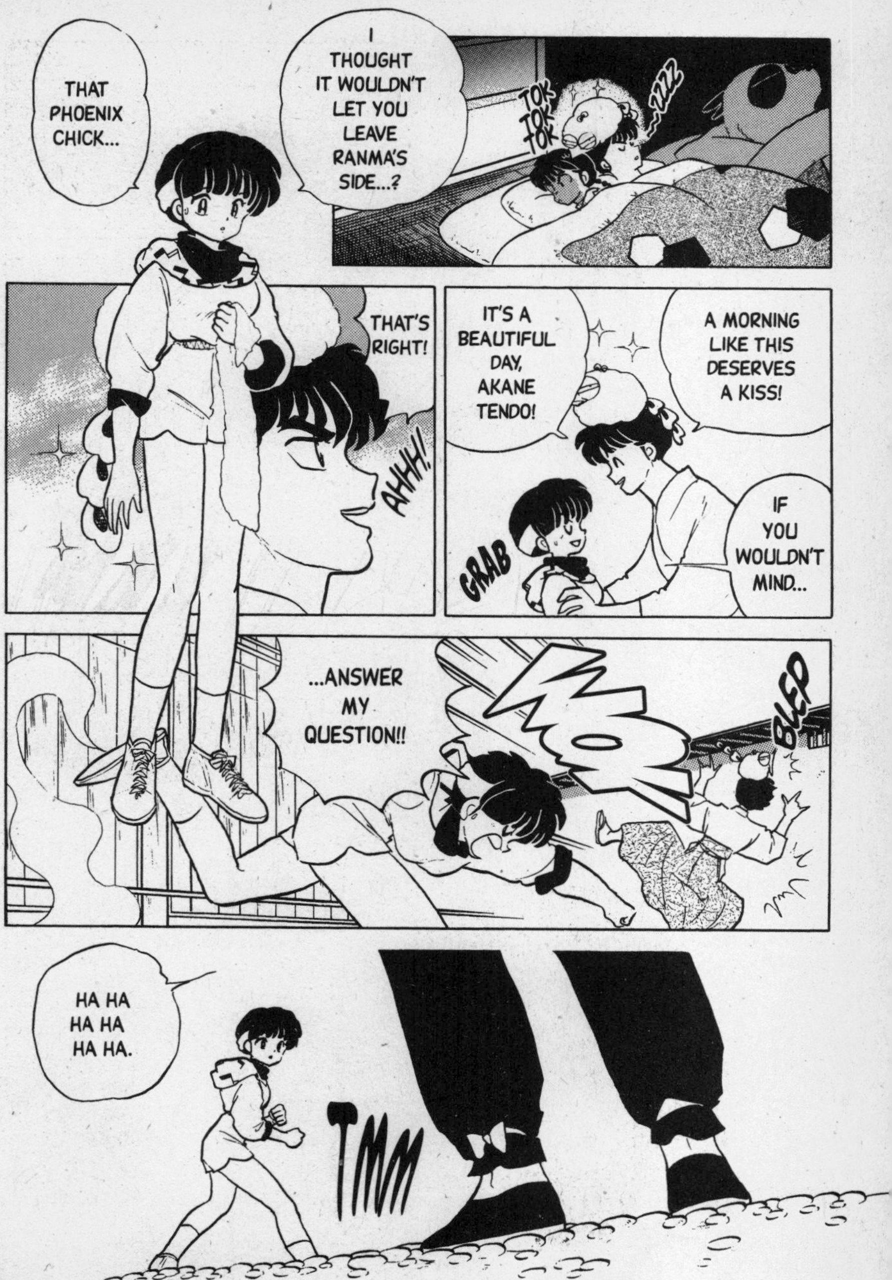
THAT PHOENIX CHICK...
I THOUGHT IT WOULDN'T LET YOU LEAVE RANMA'S SIDE...?
TOK TOK TOK
ZZZZ
THAT'S RIGHT!
AHHH!
IT'S A BEAUTIFUL DAY, AKANE TENDO!
A MORNING LIKE THIS DESERVES A KISS!
IF YOU WOULDN'T MIND...
GRAB
...ANSWER MY QUESTION!!
BLEP
HA HA HA HA HA HA.
TMM

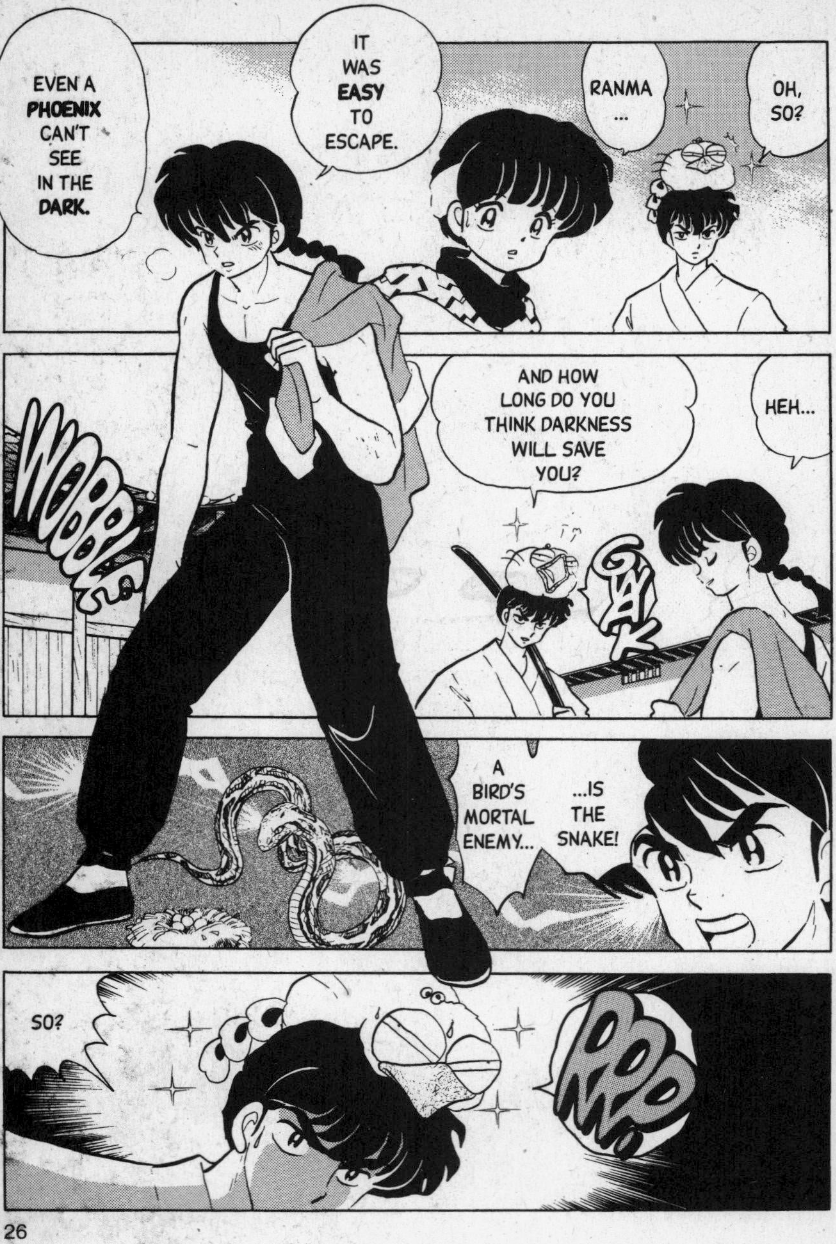
EVEN A PHOENIX CAN'T SEE IN THE DARK.
IT WAS EASY TO ESCAPE.
RANMA ...
OH, SO?
WOBBLE
AND HOW LONG DO YOU THINK DARKNESS WILL SAVE YOU?
GAK
HEH...
A BIRD'S MORTAL ENEMY...
...IS THE SNAKE!
SO?

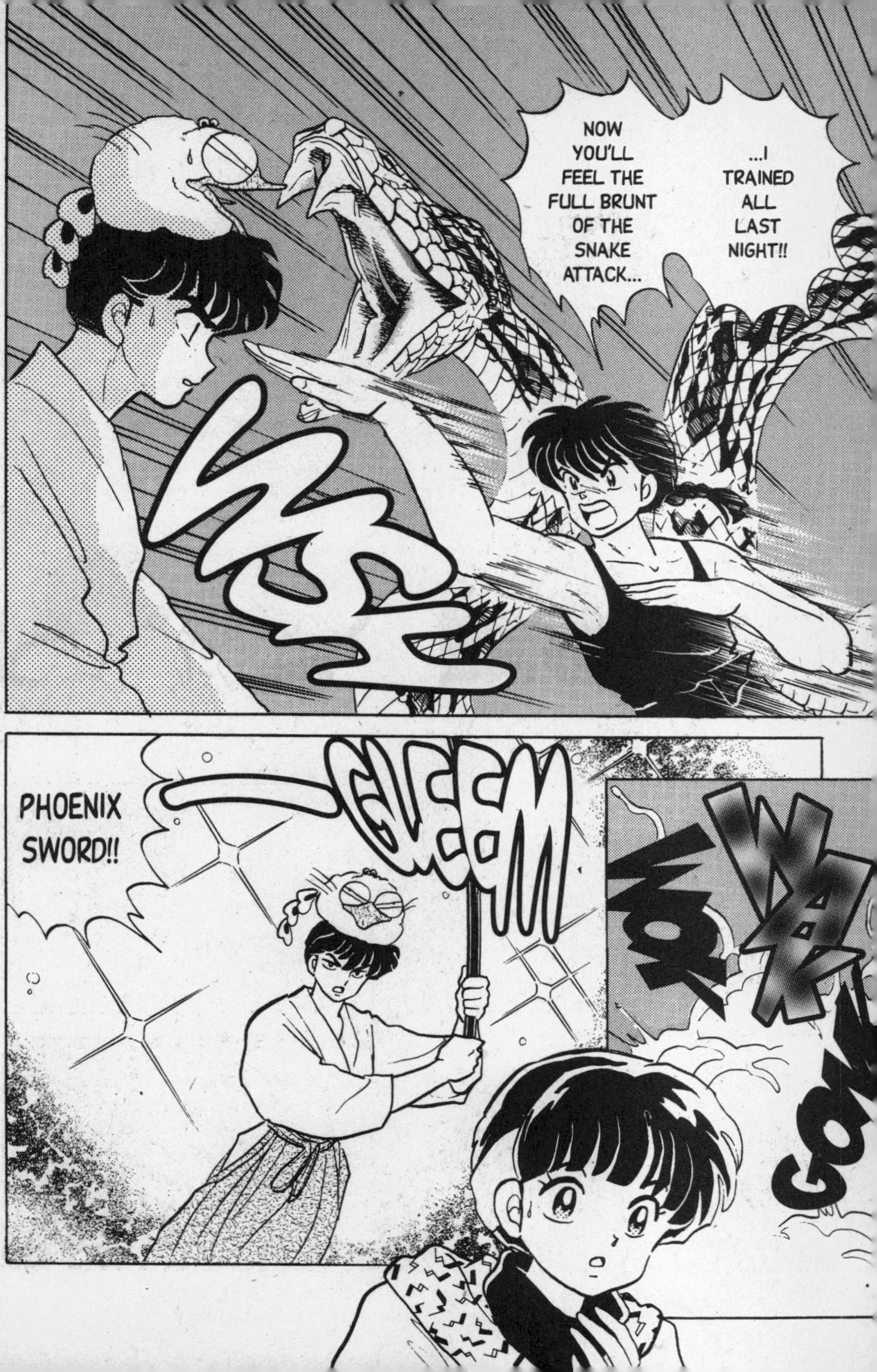
NOW YOU'LL FEEL THE FULL BRUNT OF THE SNAKE ATTACK...
...I TRAINED ALL LAST NIGHT!!
WSH
PHOENIX SWORD!!
GLEEM

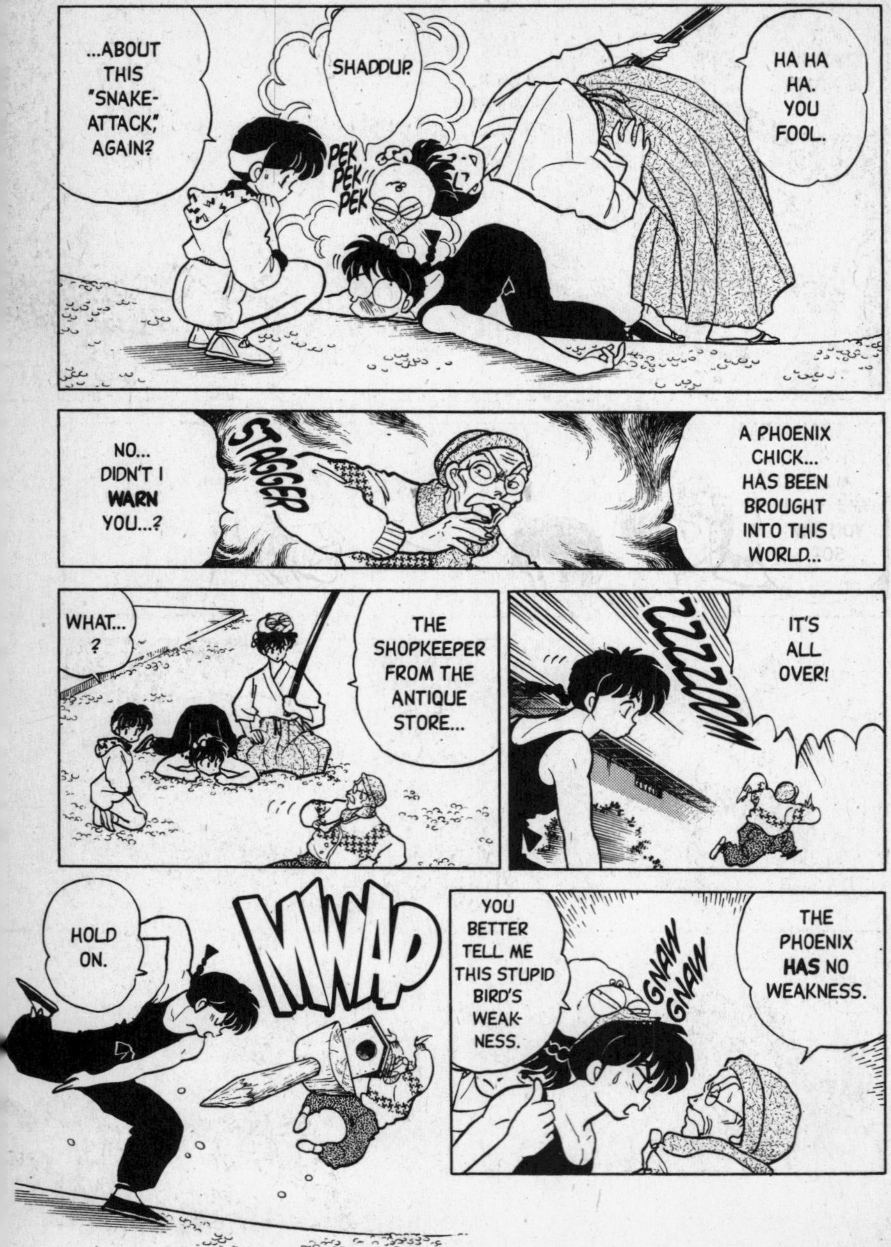

...ABOUT THIS "SNAKE-ATTACK," AGAIN?
SHADDUP.
PEK PEK PEK
HA HA HA. YOU FOOL.
NO... DIDN'T I **WARN** YOU...?
STAGGER
A PHOENIX CHICK... HAS BEEN BROUGHT INTO THIS WORLD...
WHAT... ?
THE SHOPKEEPER FROM THE ANTIQUE STORE...
ZZZZOOOM
IT'S ALL OVER!
HOLD ON.
MWAP
YOU BETTER TELL ME THIS STUPID BIRD'S WEAK-NESS.
GNAW GNAW
THE PHOENIX **HAS** NO WEAKNESS.

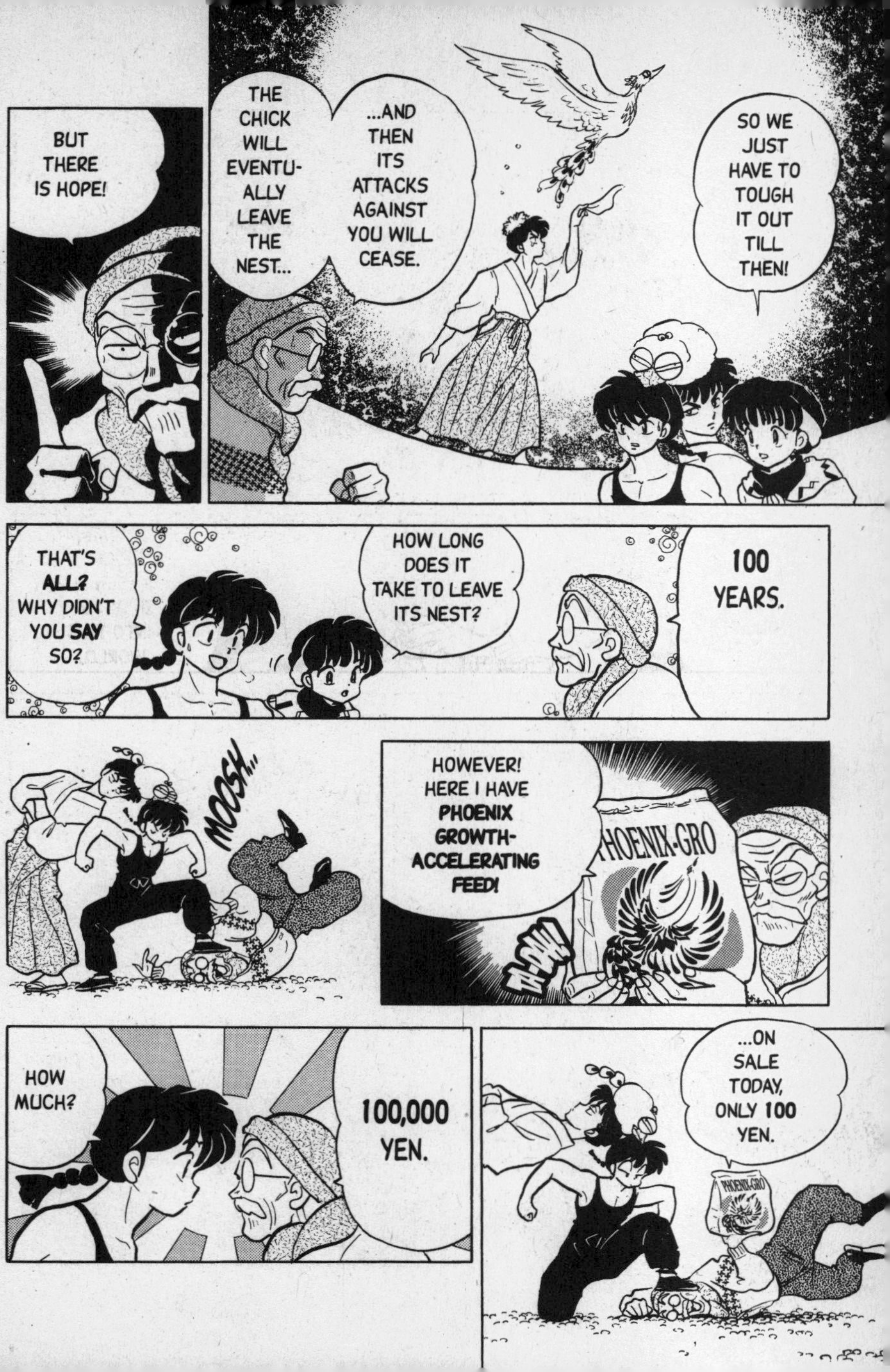
BUT THERE IS HOPE!
THE CHICK WILL EVENTU-ALLY LEAVE THE NEST...
...AND THEN ITS ATTACKS AGAINST YOU WILL CEASE.
SO WE JUST HAVE TO TOUGH IT OUT TILL THEN!
THAT'S ALL? WHY DIDN'T YOU SAY SO?
HOW LONG DOES IT TAKE TO LEAVE ITS NEST?
100 YEARS.
MOOSH...
HOWEVER! HERE I HAVE PHOENIX GROWTH-ACCELERATING FEED!
PHOENIX-GRO
HOW MUCH?
100,000 YEN.
...ON SALE TODAY, ONLY 100 YEN.
PHOENIX-GRO

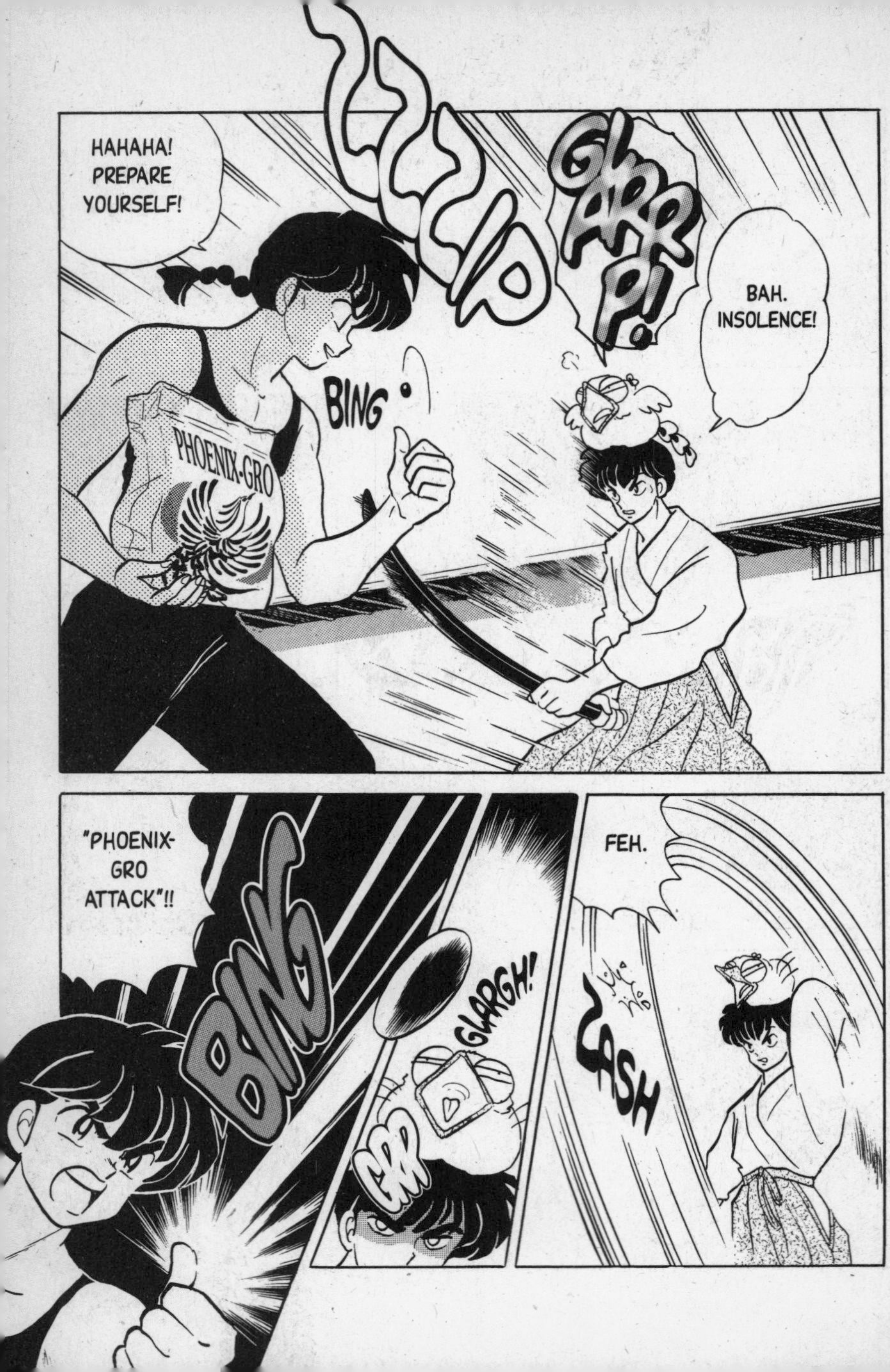
HAHAHA! PREPARE YOURSELF!
ZZZIP
PHOENIX-GRO
BING
BAH. INSOLENCE!
"PHOENIX-GRO ATTACK"!!
BING
GLARGH!
FEH.

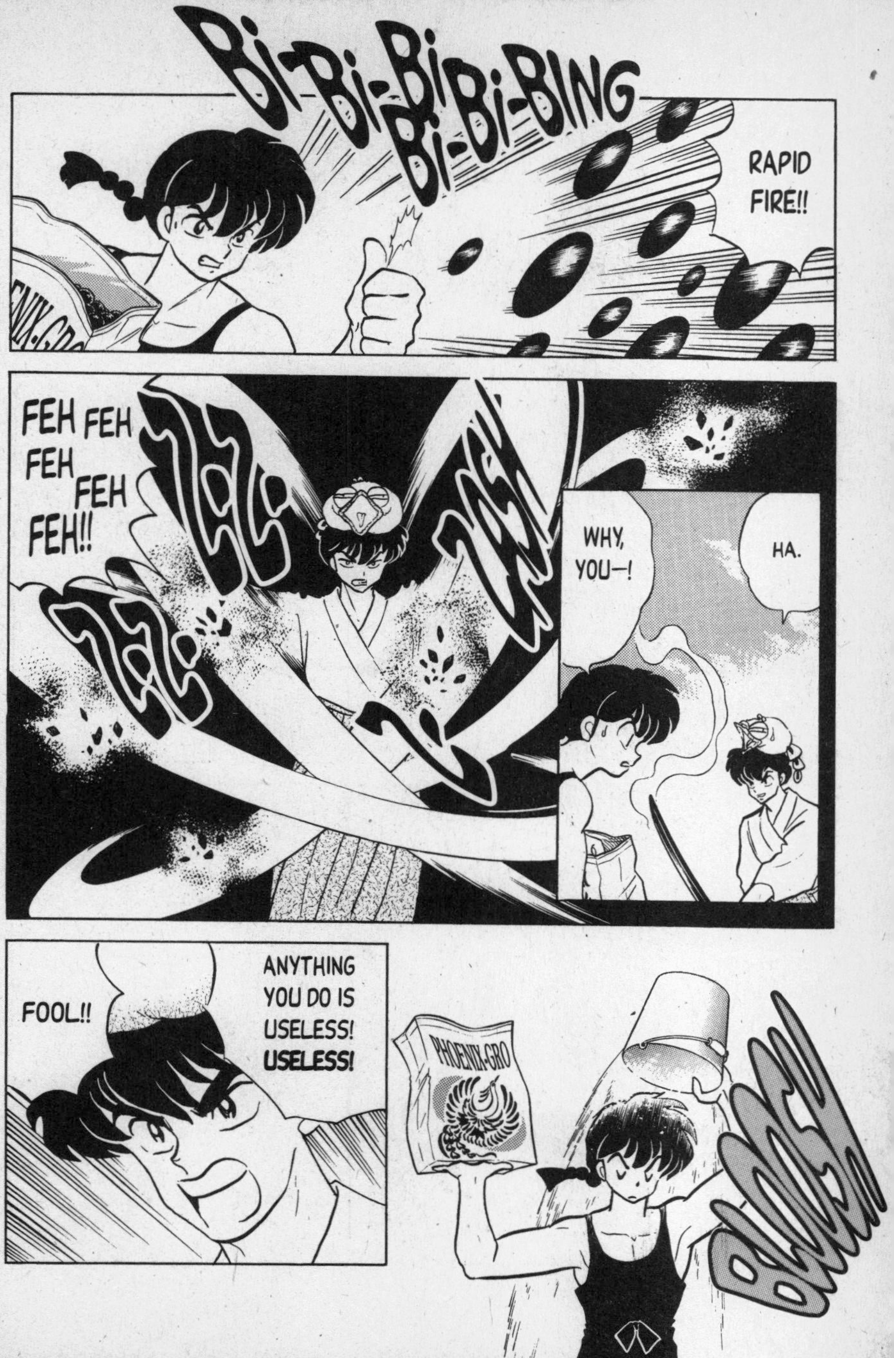
BI-BI-BI
BI-BI-BING
RAPID FIRE!!
FEH FEH FEH FEH FEH!!
WHY, YOU—!
HA.
FOOL!!
ANYTHING YOU DO IS USELESS! USELESS!
PHOENIX-GRO

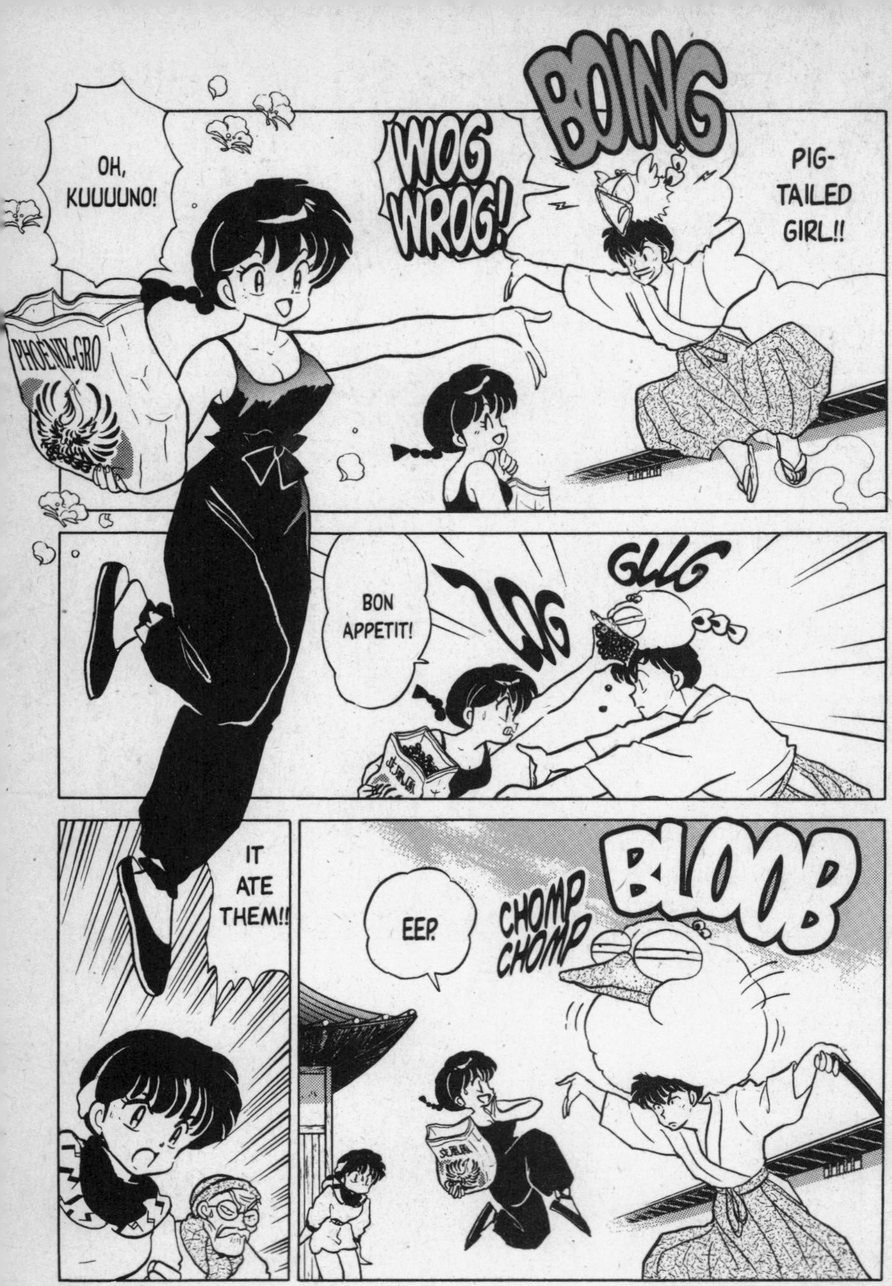
OH, KUUUUNO!
WOG WROG!
BOING
PIG-TAILED GIRL!!
PHOENIX-GRO
BON APPETIT!
IT ATE THEM!!
EEP.
CHOMP CHOMP
BLOOB

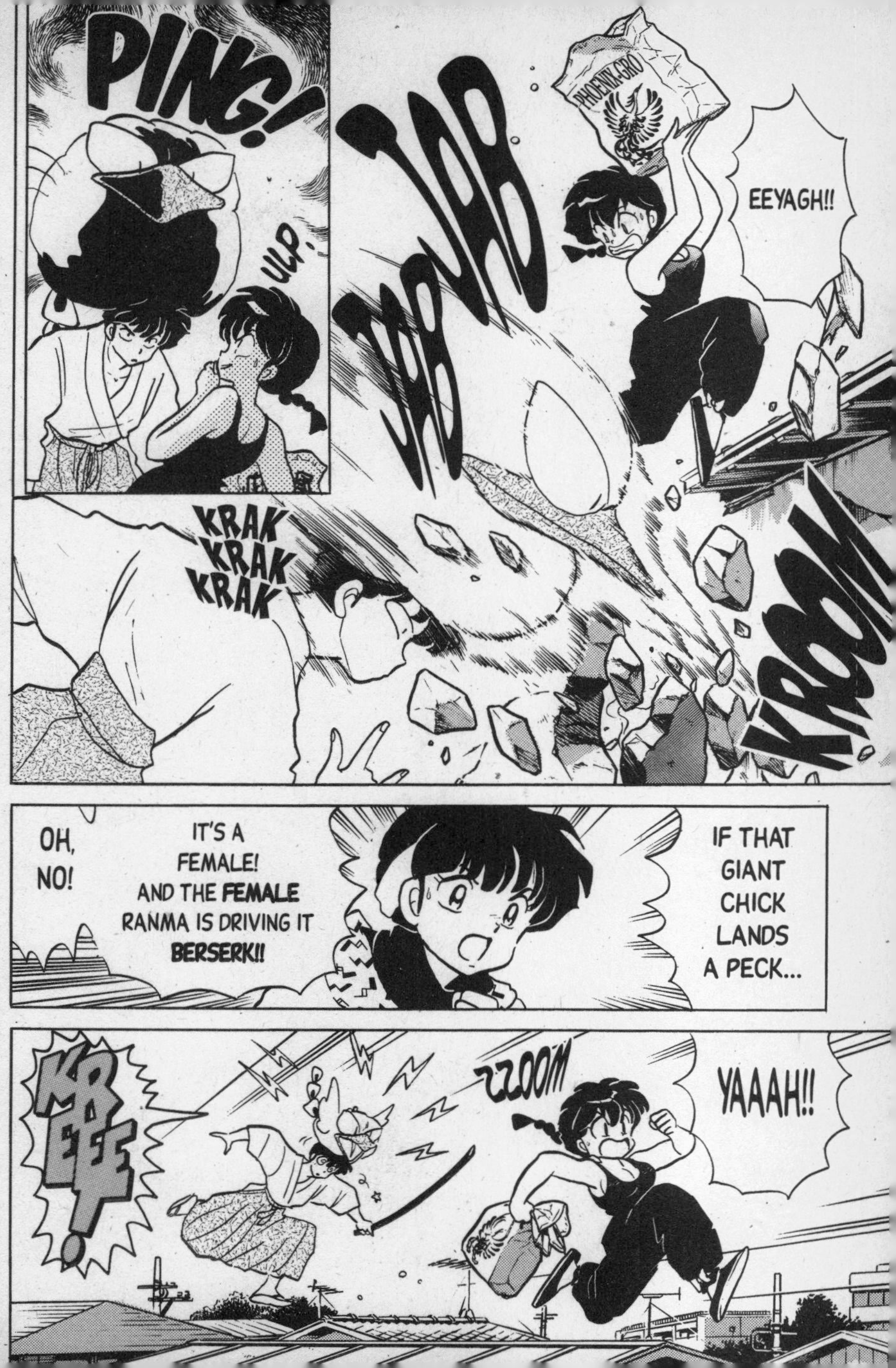
PING!
ULP
EEYAGH!!
PHOENIX-GRO
KRAK
KRAK
KRAK
KROOM
OH, NO!
IT'S A FEMALE! AND THE FEMALE RANMA IS DRIVING IT BERSERK!!
IF THAT GIANT CHICK LANDS A PECK...
ZZOOM
YAAAH!!

RANMA! HOT WATER!

CREEK

GONG GONG

ZOOSH

VWOO

RANMA SAOTOME! WHERE DID YOU COME FROM!?

AGH!

SHOOT! THE PHOENIX- GRO...

PSHOOO

LET'S DO SOME AEROBICS!

SCATA SCAT

JBLIC PARK

DON'T LITTER

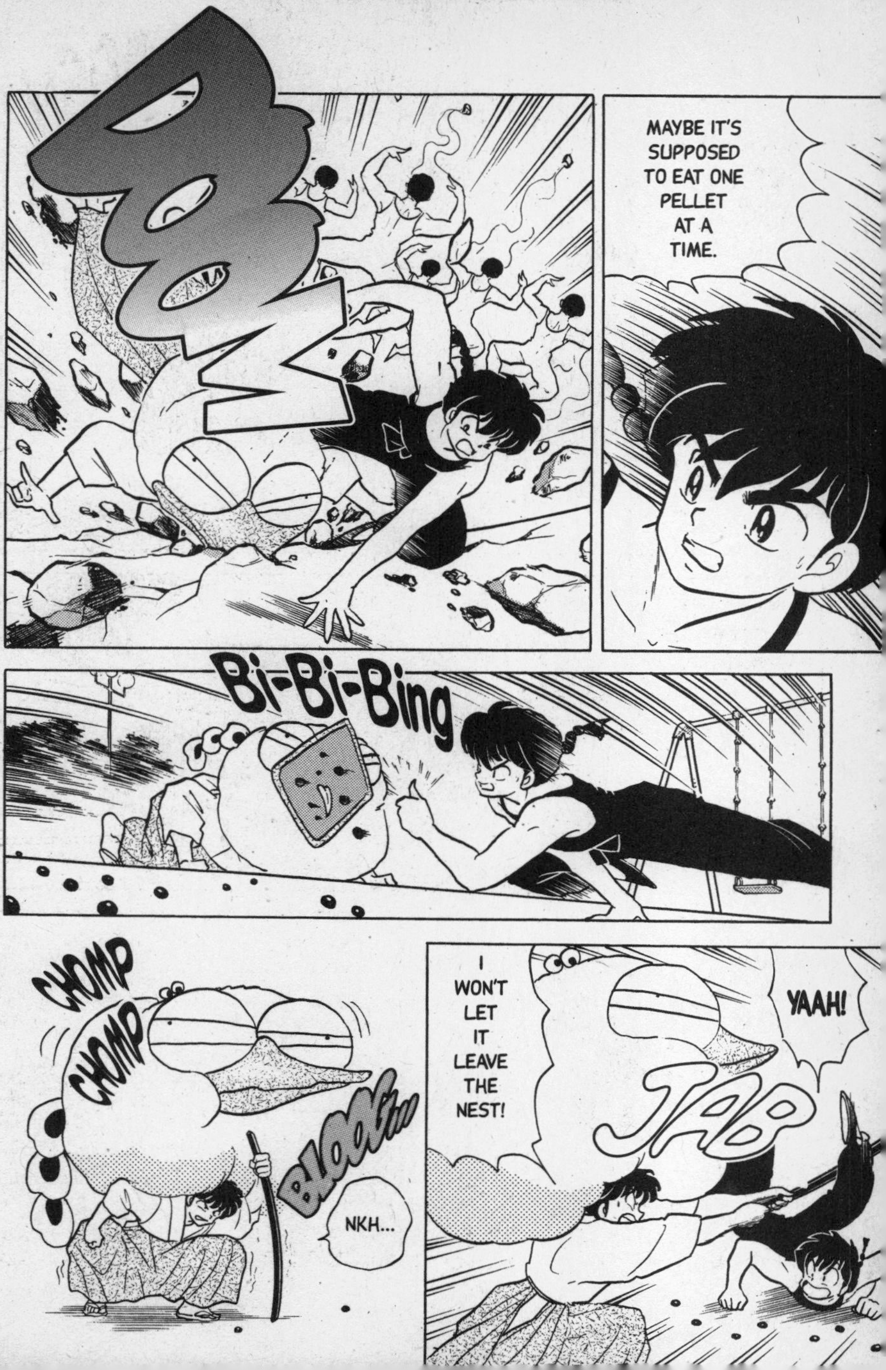
BOOM
MAYBE IT'S SUPPOSED TO EAT ONE PELLET AT A TIME.
Bi-Bi-Bing
CHOMP
CHOMP
NKH...
I WON'T LET IT LEAVE THE NEST!
YAAH!
JAB

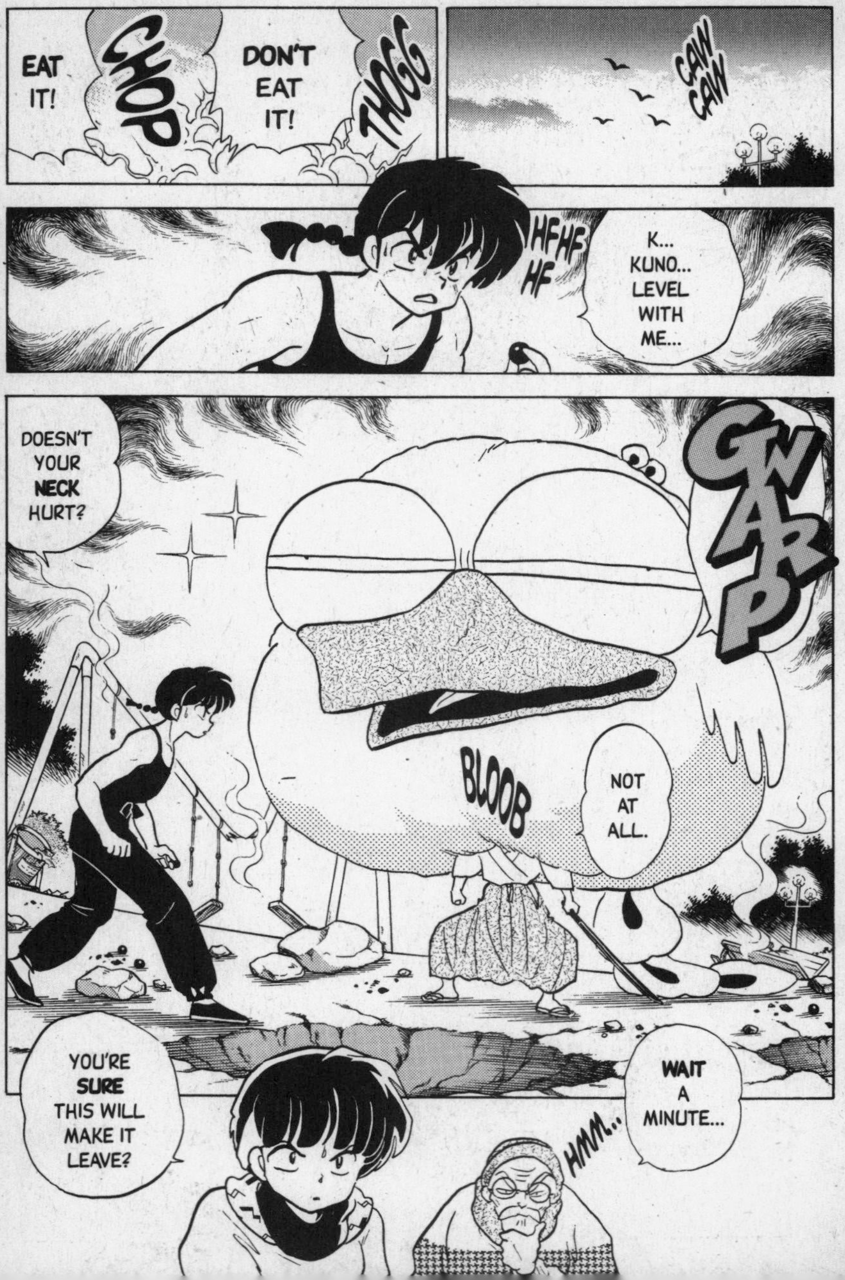
EAT IT!
CHOP
DON'T EAT IT!
THOGG
CAW CAW
HFHF HF
K... KUNO... LEVEL WITH ME...
DOESN'T YOUR NECK HURT?
GNARP
BLOOB
NOT AT ALL.
YOU'RE SURE THIS WILL MAKE IT LEAVE?
HMM..
WAIT A MINUTE...

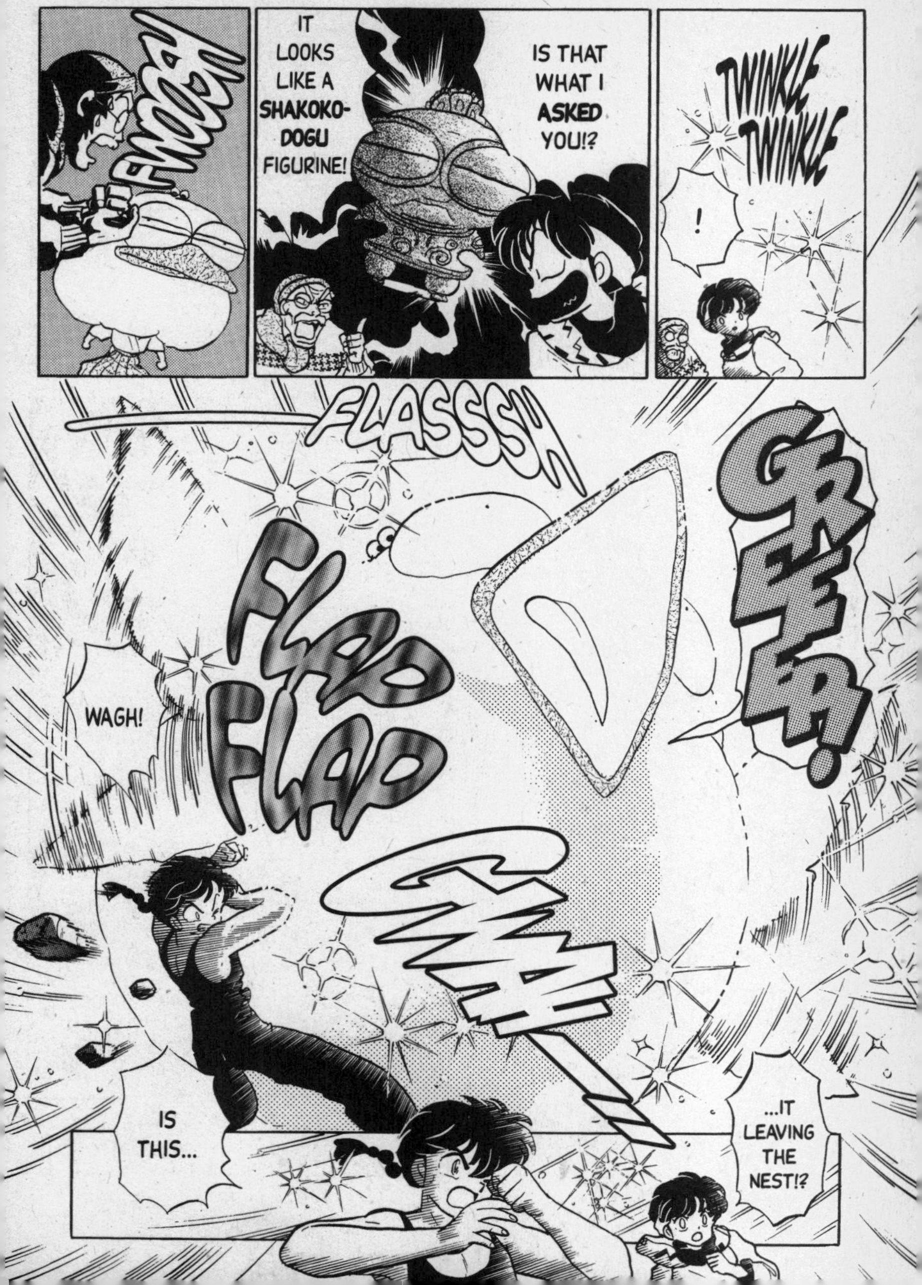

WHOOMP
IT LOOKS LIKE A SHAKOKO-DOGU FIGURINE!
IS THAT WHAT I ASKED YOU!?
TWINKLE TWINKLE
!
FLASSSH
WAGH!
FLAP FLAP
GREEEK!
CHNK
IS THIS...
...IT LEAVING THE NEST!?

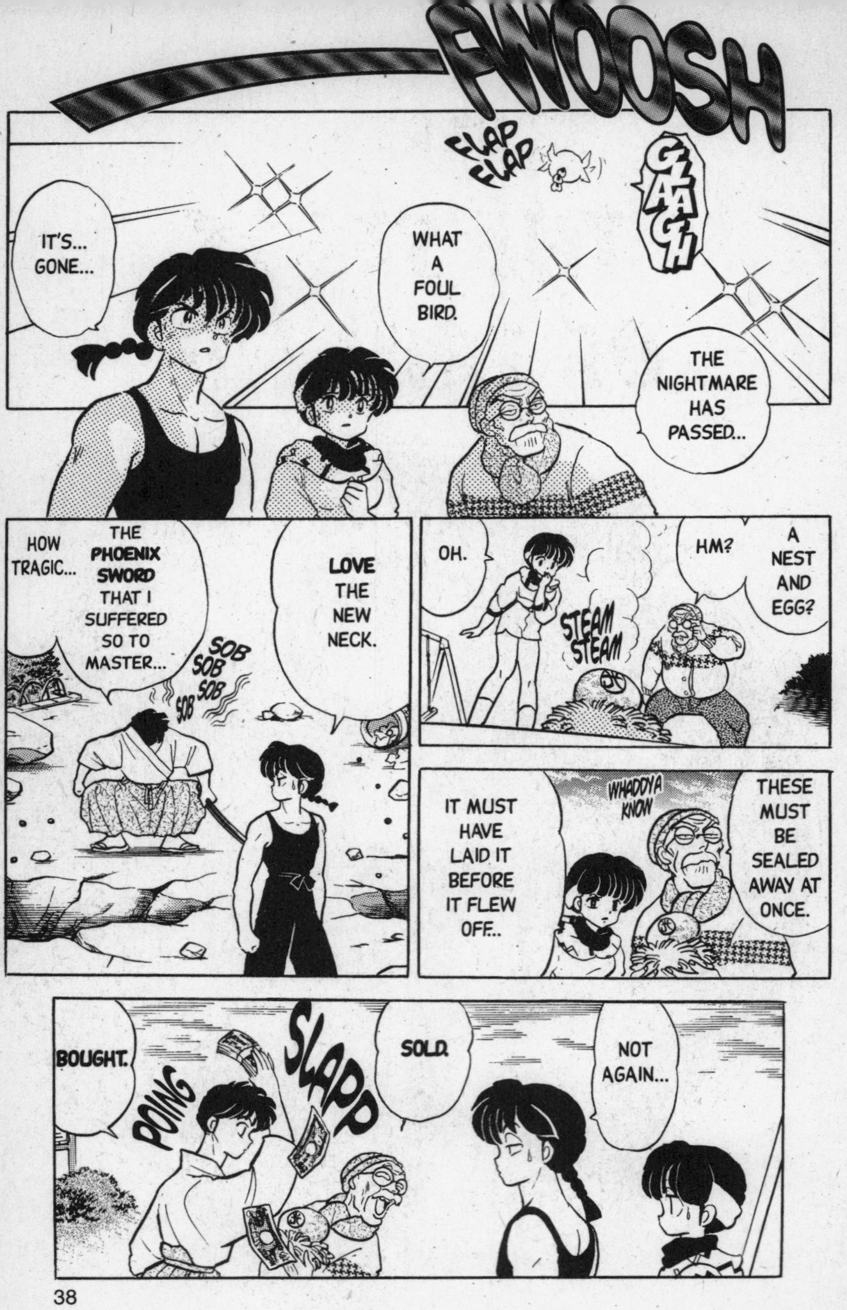
FWOOSH
FLAP FLAP
GLAAGH
IT'S... GONE...
WHAT A FOUL BIRD.
THE NIGHTMARE HAS PASSED...
HOW TRAGIC...
THE **PHOENIX SWORD** THAT I SUFFERED SO TO MASTER...
SOB SOB SOB SOB
LOVE THE NEW NECK.
OH.
STEAM STEAM
HM?
A NEST AND EGG?
IT MUST HAVE LAID IT BEFORE IT FLEW OFF...
WHADDYA KNOW
THESE MUST BE SEALED AWAY AT ONCE.
BOUGHT.
POING
SLAPP
SOLD.
NOT AGAIN...

PART 3

THE SEEDS OF TRAGEDY

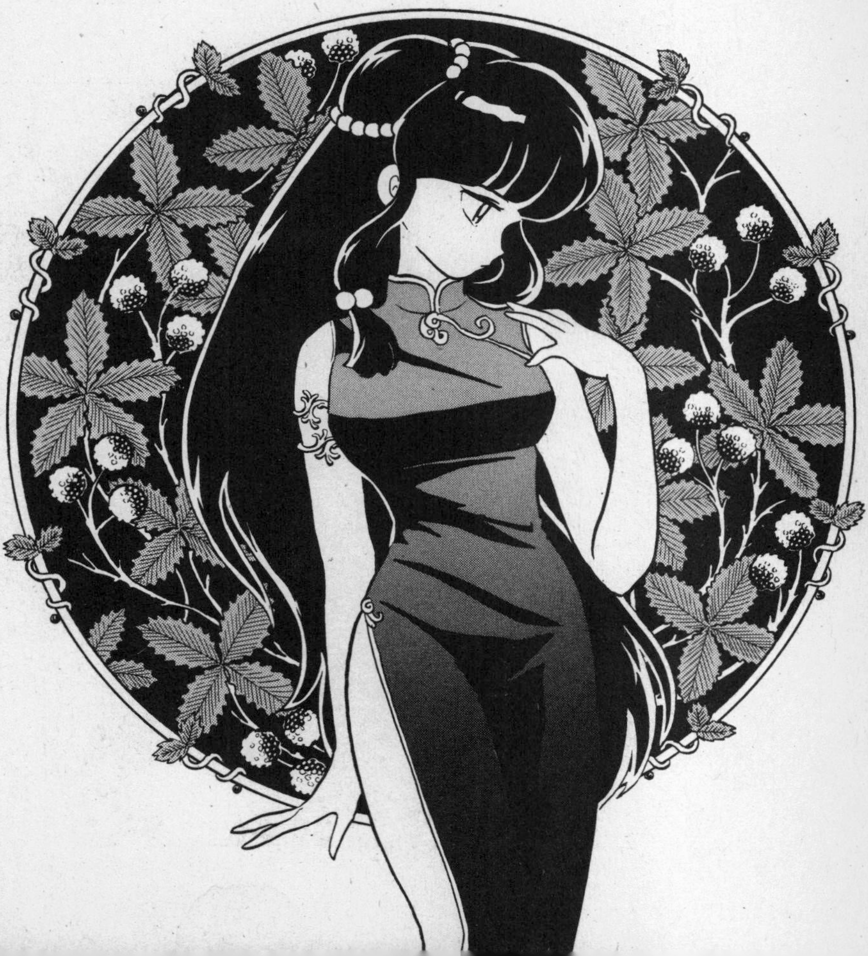

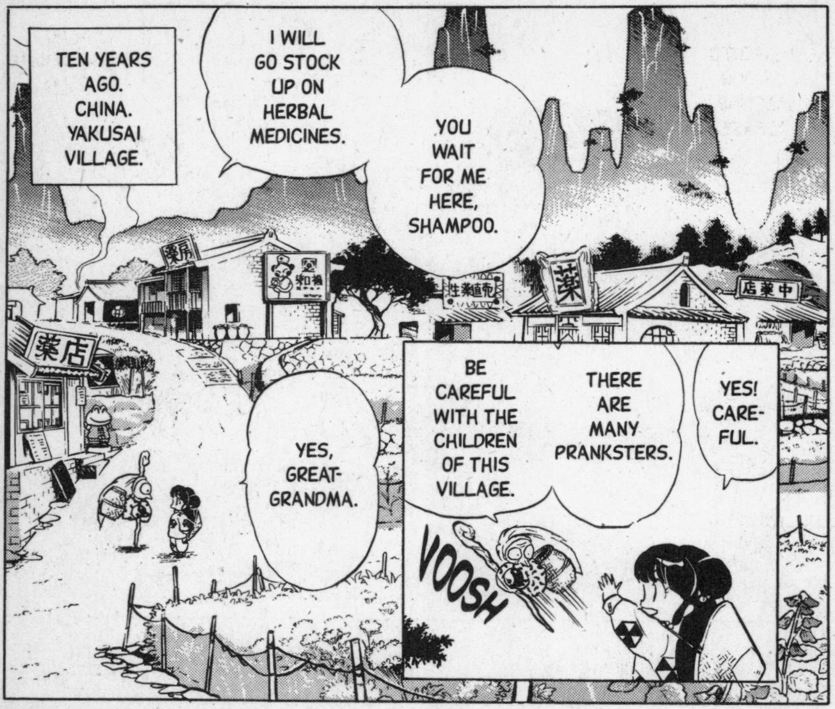
TEN YEARS AGO. CHINA. YAKUSAI VILLAGE.
I WILL GO STOCK UP ON HERBAL MEDICINES.
YOU WAIT FOR ME HERE, SHAMPOO.
YES, GREAT-GRANDMA.
BE CAREFUL WITH THE CHILDREN OF THIS VILLAGE.
THERE ARE MANY PRANKSTERS.
YES! CARE-FUL.
VOOSH

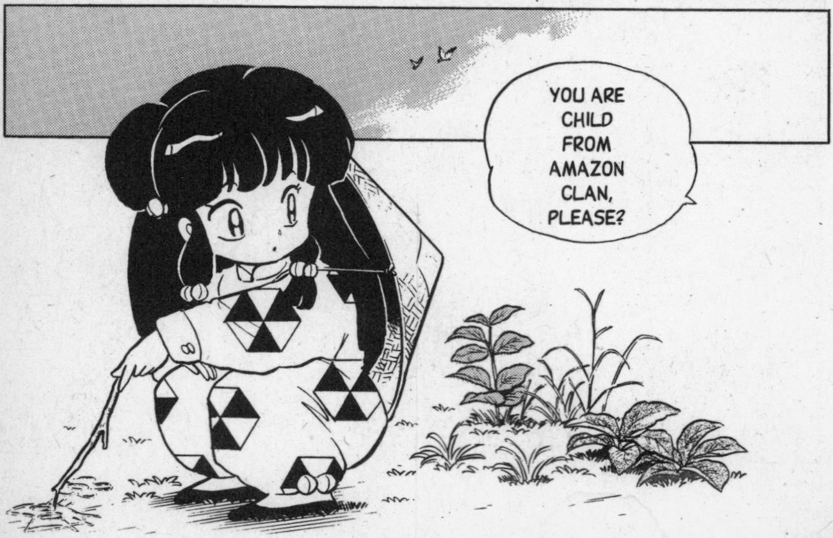
YOU ARE CHILD FROM AMAZON CLAN, PLEASE?

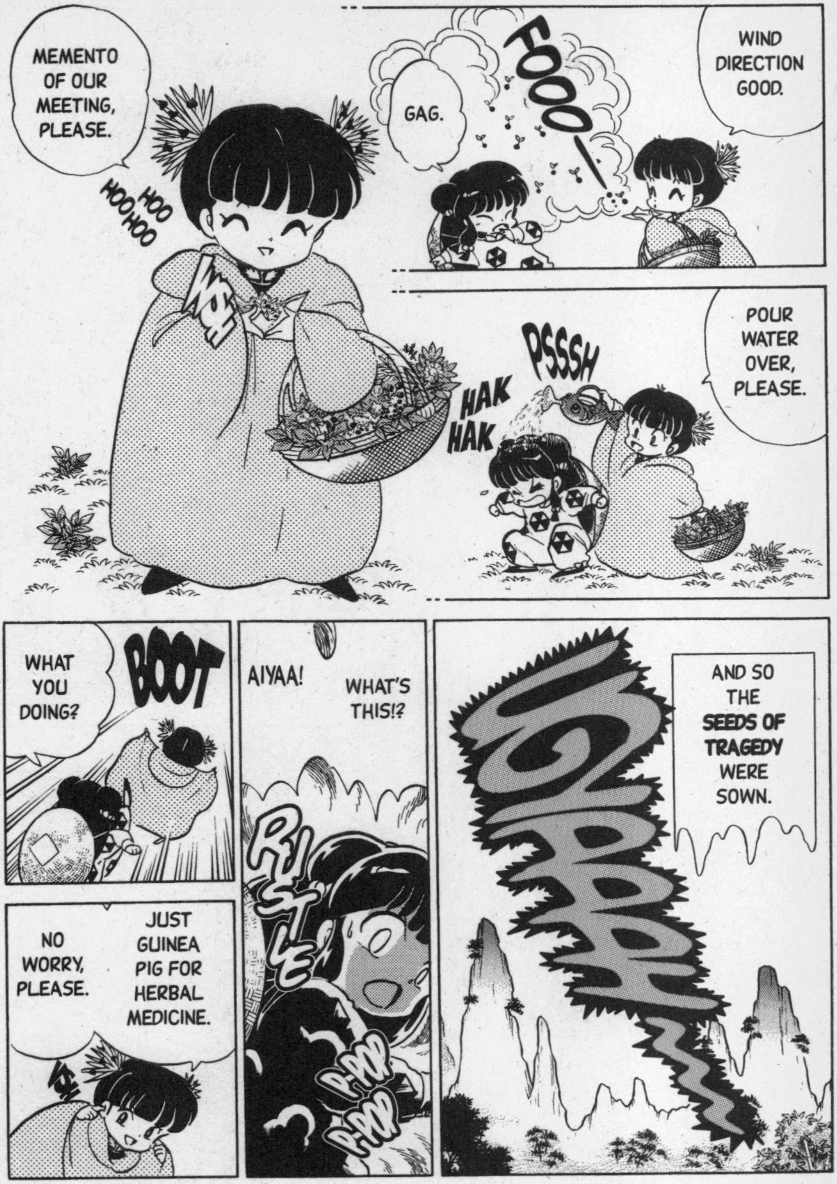
MEMENTO OF OUR MEETING, PLEASE.
HOO HOO HOO
GAG.
FOOO!
WIND DIRECTION GOOD.
PSSSH
HAK HAK
POUR WATER OVER, PLEASE.
WHAT YOU DOING?
BOOT
NO WORRY, PLEASE.
JUST GUINEA PIG FOR HERBAL MEDICINE.
AIYAA!
WHAT'S THIS!?
RUSTLE
P-POP
P-POP
AND SO THE **SEEDS OF TRAGEDY** WERE SOWN.

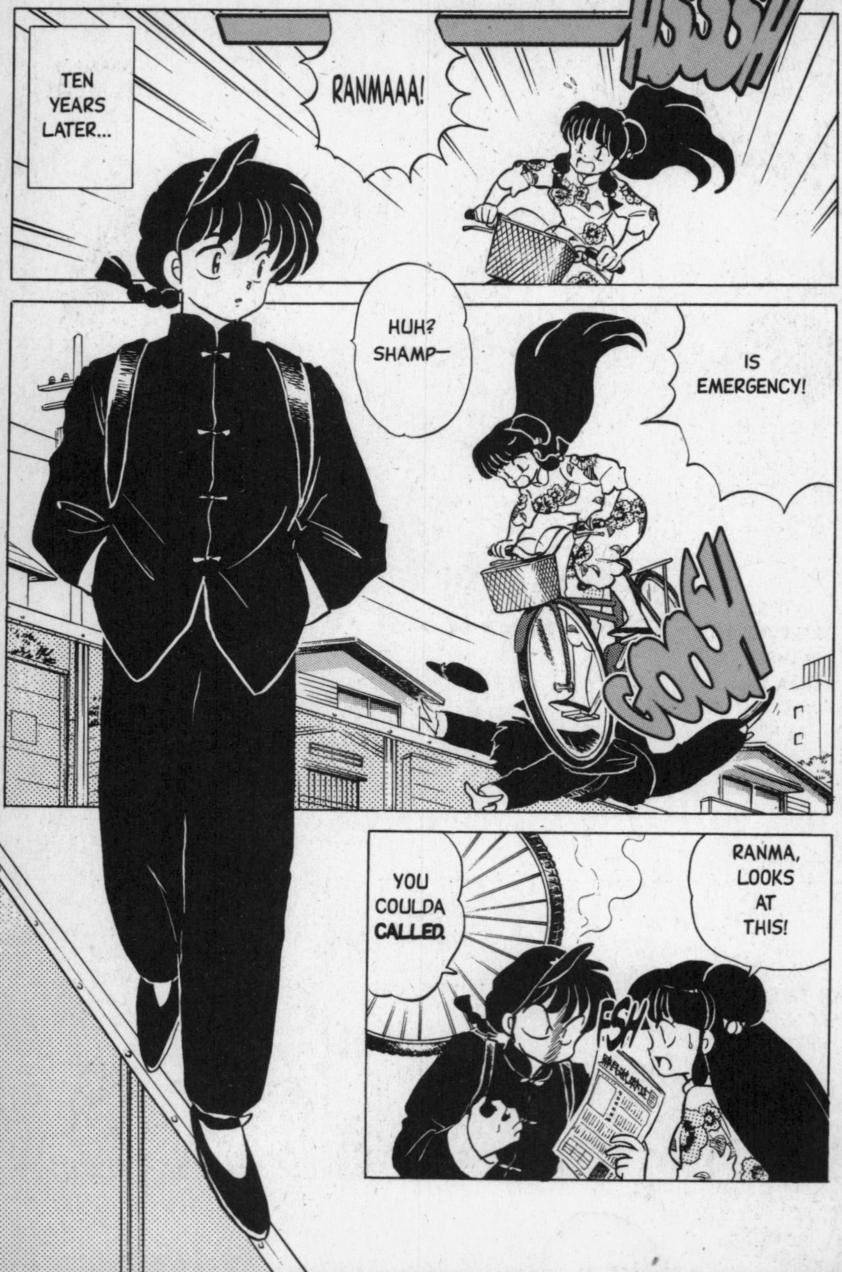
TEN YEARS LATER...
RANMAAA!
HSSSH
HUH? SHAMP—
IS EMERGENCY!
YOU COULDA CALLED.
FSH
RANMA, LOOKS AT THIS!

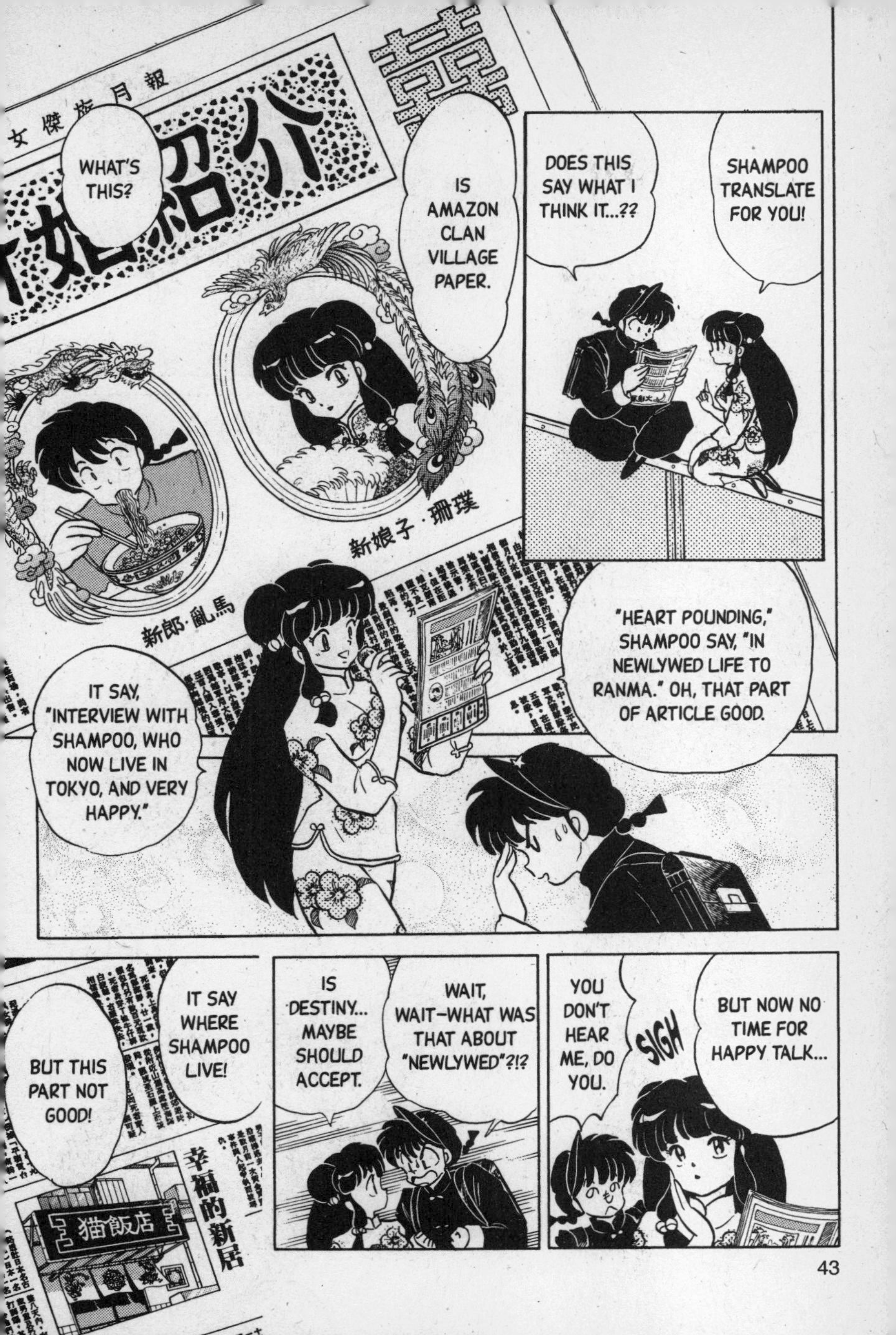
女傑族月報
WHAT'S THIS?
IS AMAZON CLAN VILLAGE PAPER.
新郎·亂馬
新娘子·珊璞
DOES THIS SAY WHAT I THINK IT...??
SHAMPOO TRANSLATE FOR YOU!
IT SAY, "INTERVIEW WITH SHAMPOO, WHO NOW LIVE IN TOKYO, AND VERY HAPPY."
"HEART POUNDING," SHAMPOO SAY, "IN NEWLYWED LIFE TO RANMA." OH, THAT PART OF ARTICLE GOOD.
IT SAY WHERE SHAMPOO LIVE!
BUT THIS PART NOT GOOD!
幸福的新居
猫飯店
IS DESTINY... MAYBE SHOULD ACCEPT.
WAIT, WAIT—WHAT WAS THAT ABOUT "NEWLYWED"?!?
YOU DON'T HEAR ME, DO YOU.
SIGH
BUT NOW NO TIME FOR HAPPY TALK...

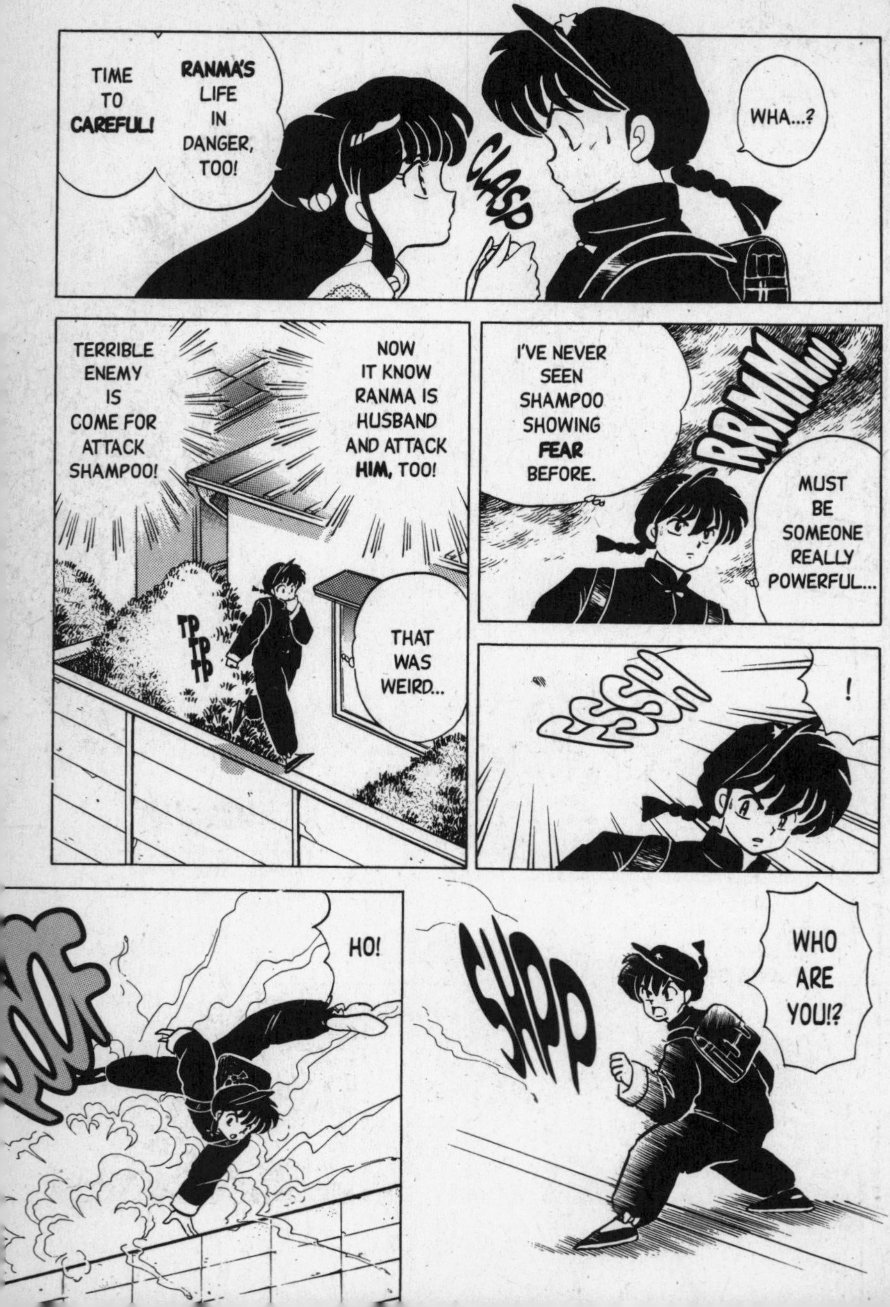

TIME TO CAREFUL!
RANMA'S LIFE IN DANGER, TOO!
CLASP
WHA...?
TERRIBLE ENEMY IS COME FOR ATTACK SHAMPOO!
NOW IT KNOW RANMA IS HUSBAND AND ATTACK HIM, TOO!
TP TP TP
THAT WAS WEIRD...
I'VE NEVER SEEN SHAMPOO SHOWING FEAR BEFORE.
MUST BE SOMEONE REALLY POWERFUL...
FSSH
!
HO!
SHPP
WHO ARE YOU!?

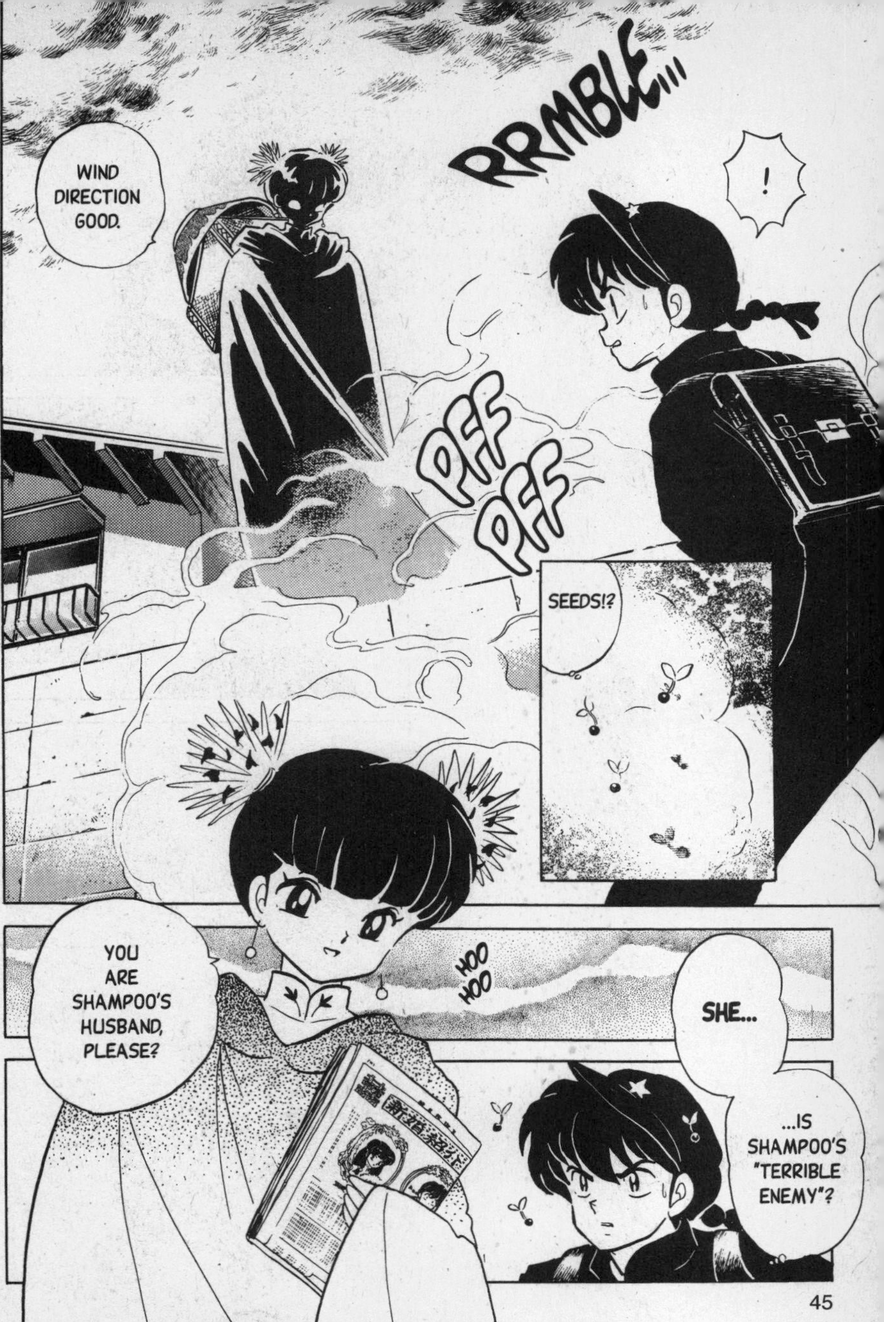
!
RRMBLE...
WIND DIRECTION GOOD.
PFF PFF
SEEDS!?
YOU ARE SHAMPOO'S HUSBAND, PLEASE?
HOO HOO
SHE...
...IS SHAMPOO'S "TERRIBLE ENEMY"?

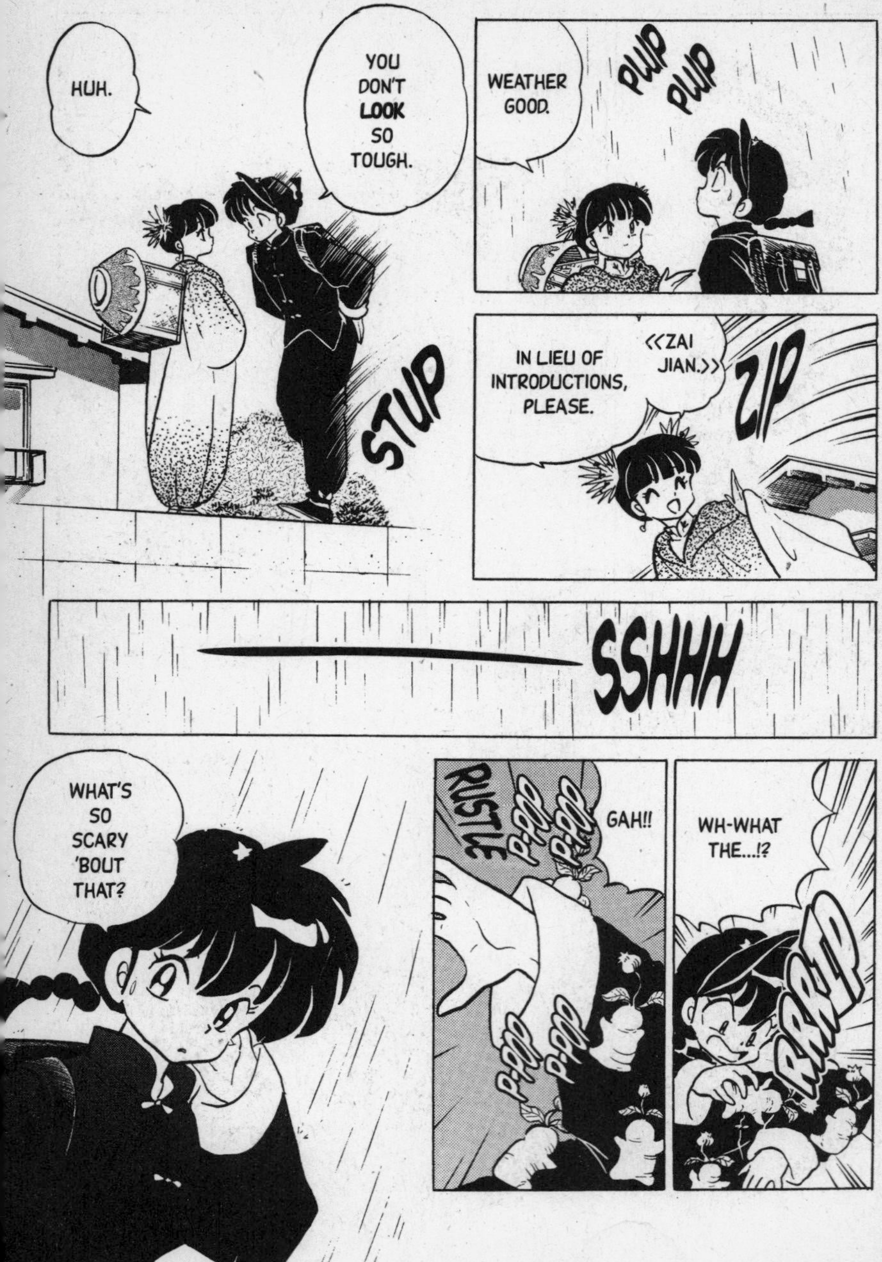
HUH.
YOU DON'T LOOK SO TOUGH.
STUP
WEATHER GOOD.
PWP PWP
IN LIEU OF INTRODUCTIONS, PLEASE.
<<ZAI JIAN.>>
ZIP
SSHHH
WHAT'S SO SCARY 'BOUT THAT?
RUSTLE
p-pop p-pop
GAH!!
p-pop p-pop
WH-WHAT THE...!?
RRRIP

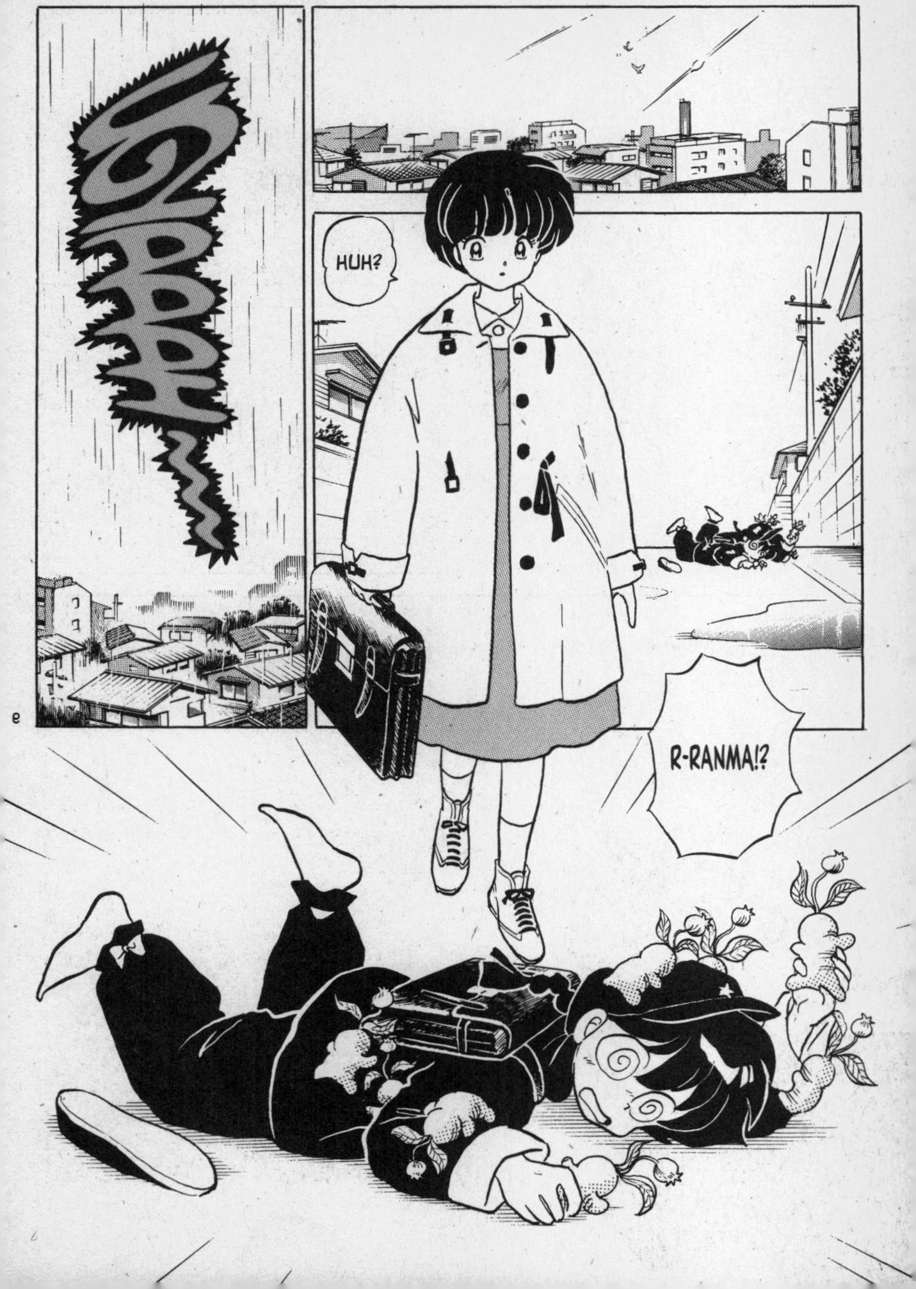
HUH?
R-RANMA!?

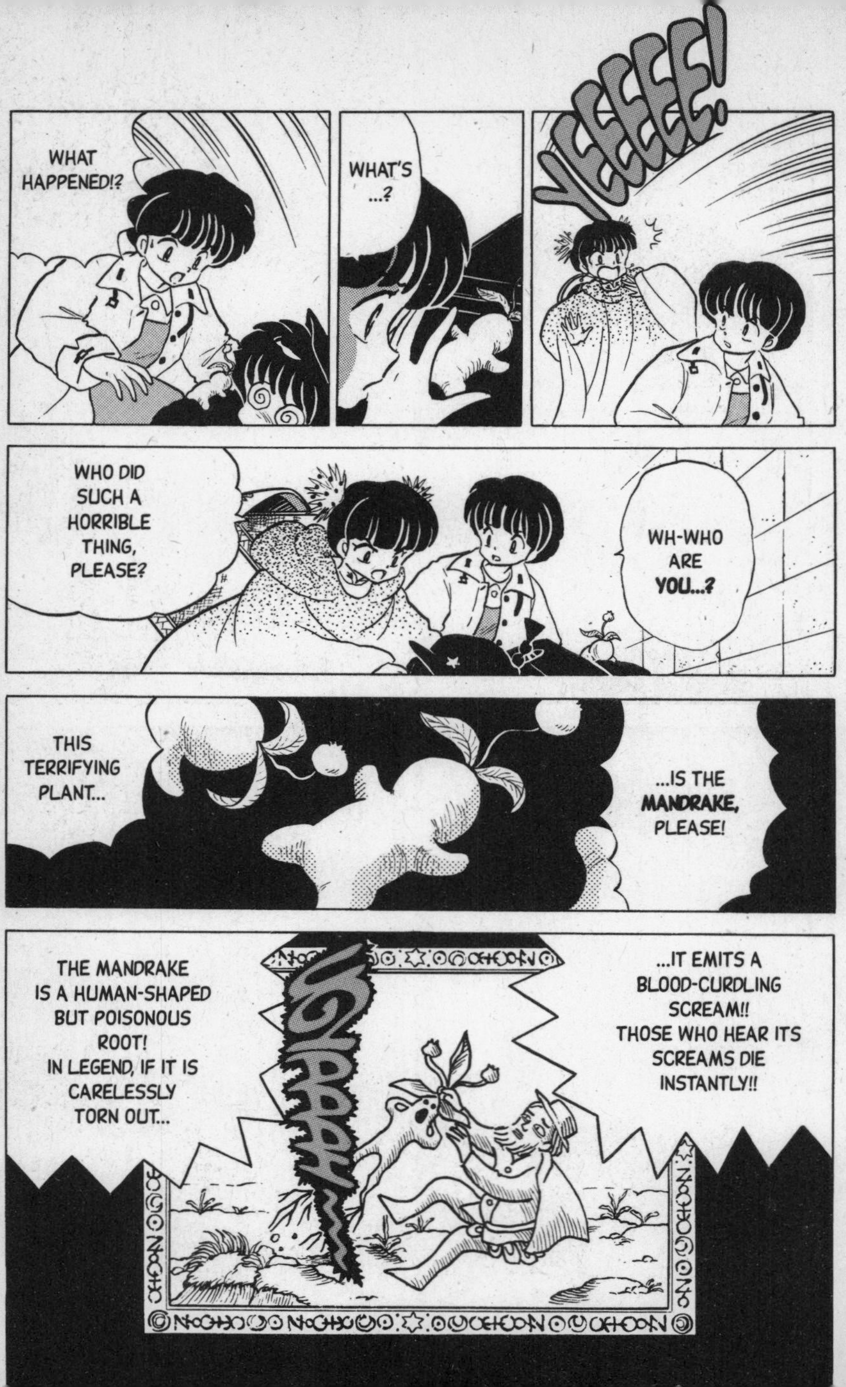
WHAT HAPPENED!?
WHAT'S ...?
YEEEEE!
WHO DID SUCH A HORRIBLE THING, PLEASE?
WH-WHO ARE YOU...?
THIS TERRIFYING PLANT...
...IS THE MANDRAKE, PLEASE!
THE MANDRAKE IS A HUMAN-SHAPED BUT POISONOUS ROOT! IN LEGEND, IF IT IS CARELESSLY TORN OUT...
...IT EMITS A BLOOD-CURDLING SCREAM!! THOSE WHO HEAR ITS SCREAMS DIE INSTANTLY!!

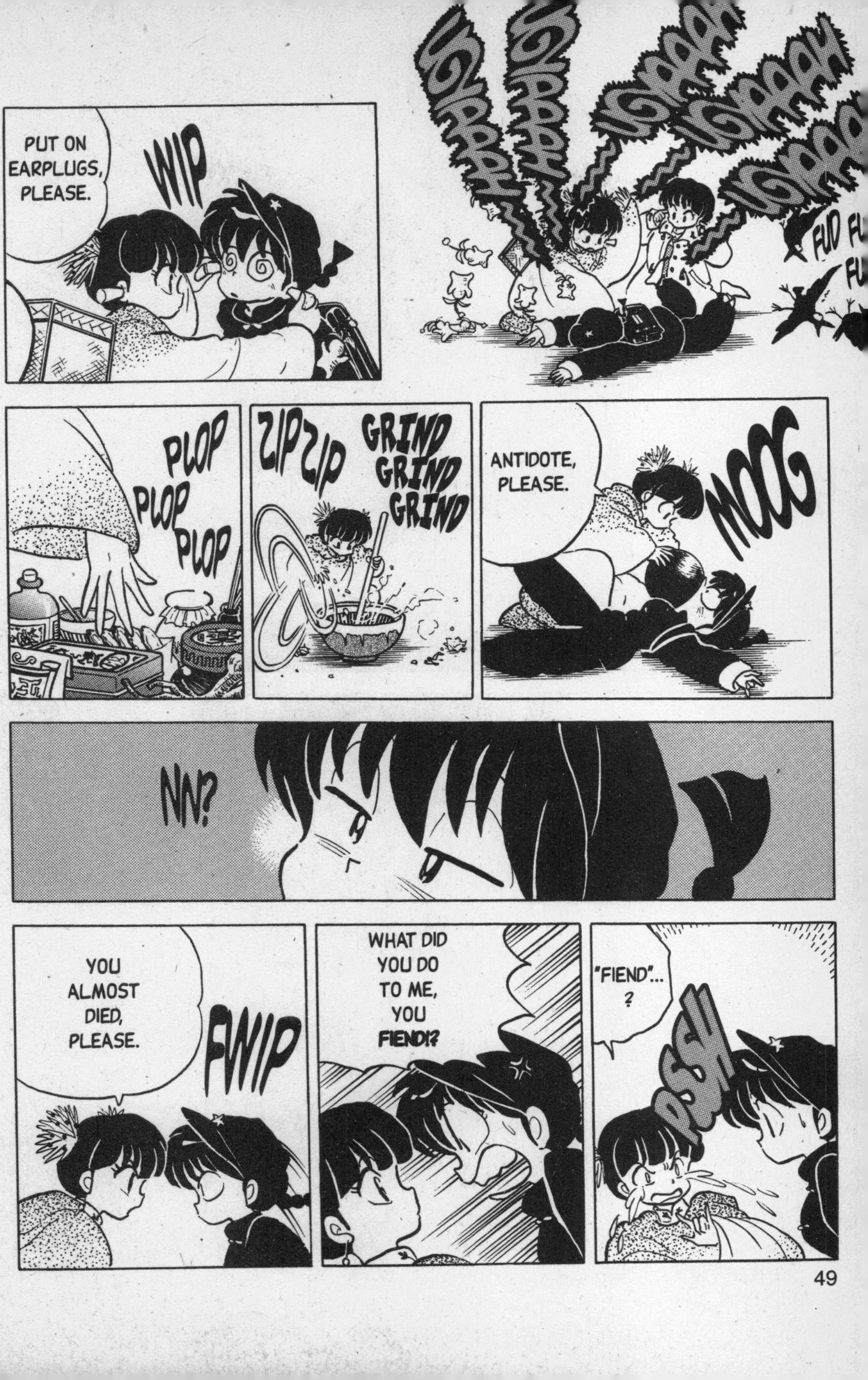

PUT ON EARPLUGS, PLEASE.
WIP
GYAAAH!
GYAAAH!
GYAAAAH!
FUD
PLOP PLOP PLOP
ZIP ZIP
GRIND GRIND GRIND
ANTIDOTE, PLEASE.
MOOG
NN?
YOU ALMOST DIED, PLEASE.
FWIP
WHAT DID YOU DO TO ME, YOU **FIEND!?**
"FIEND"...?

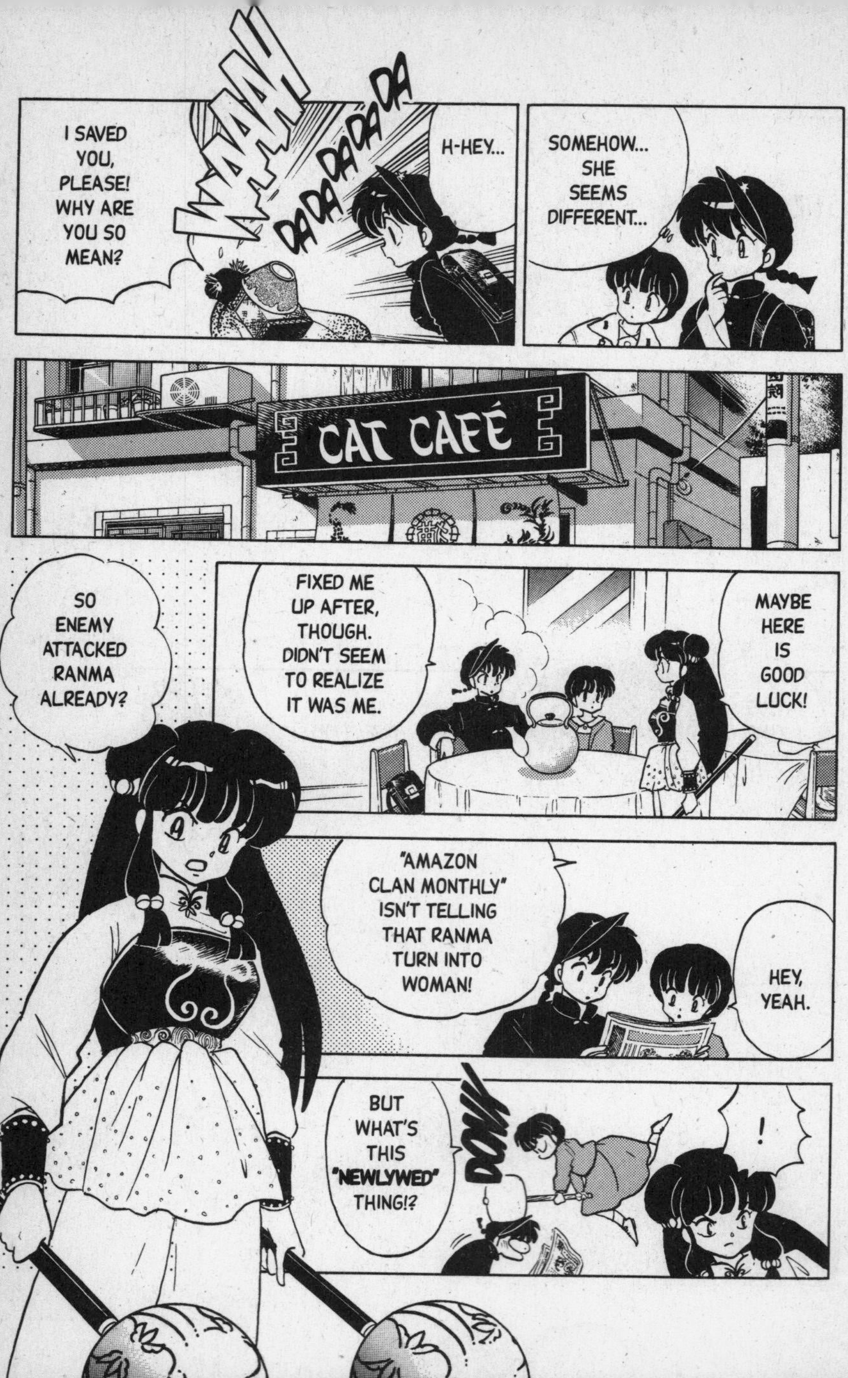

I SAVED YOU, PLEASE! WHY ARE YOU SO MEAN?
WAAAH
DA DA DA DA DA
H-HEY...
SOMEHOW... SHE SEEMS DIFFERENT...
CAT CAFÉ
SO ENEMY ATTACKED RANMA ALREADY?
FIXED ME UP AFTER, THOUGH. DIDN'T SEEM TO REALIZE IT WAS ME.
MAYBE HERE IS GOOD LUCK!
"AMAZON CLAN MONTHLY" ISN'T TELLING THAT RANMA TURN INTO WOMAN!
HEY, YEAH.
BUT WHAT'S THIS "NEWLYWED" THING!?
DOW
!

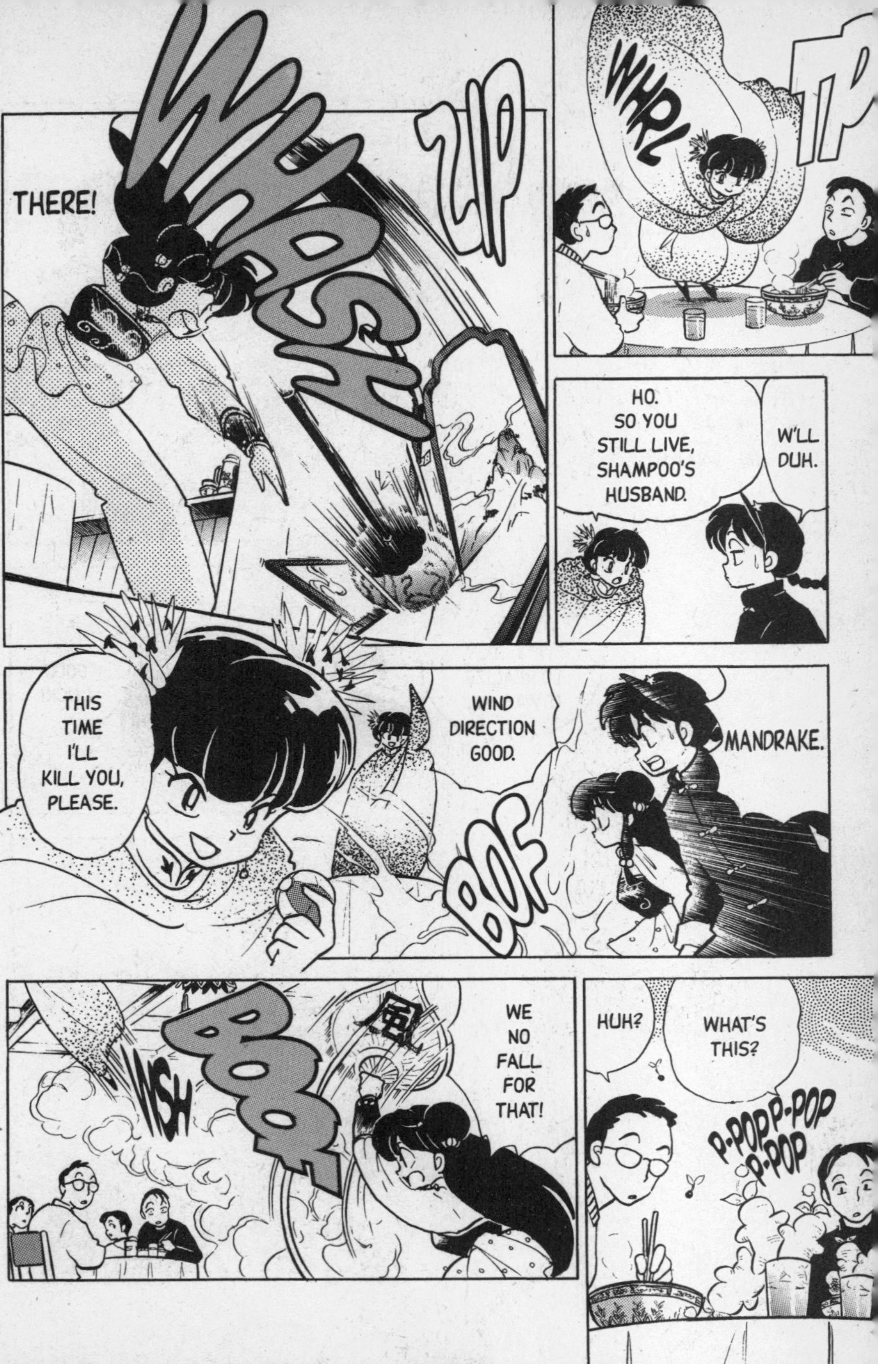
TP
WHRL
HO. SO YOU STILL LIVE, SHAMPOO'S HUSBAND.
W'LL DUH.
ZIP
WHASH
THERE!
MANDRAKE.
WIND DIRECTION GOOD.
BOF
THIS TIME I'LL KILL YOU, PLEASE.
WHAT'S THIS?
HUH?
P-POP P-POP P-POP
WE NO FALL FOR THAT!
BOOM
WSH

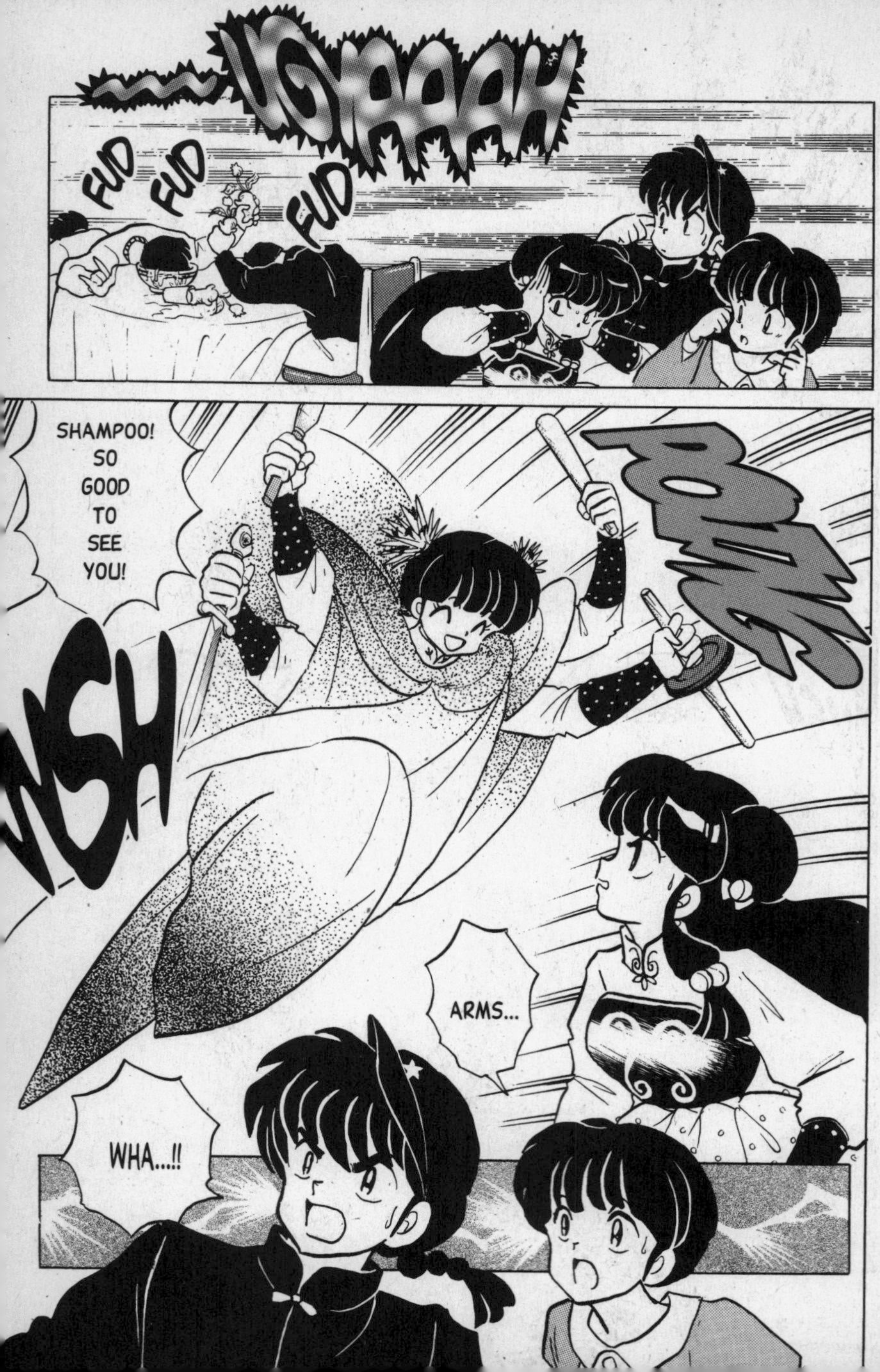
UGAAAH
FUD FUD FUD
SHAMPOO! SO GOOD TO SEE YOU!
ARMS...
WHA...!!

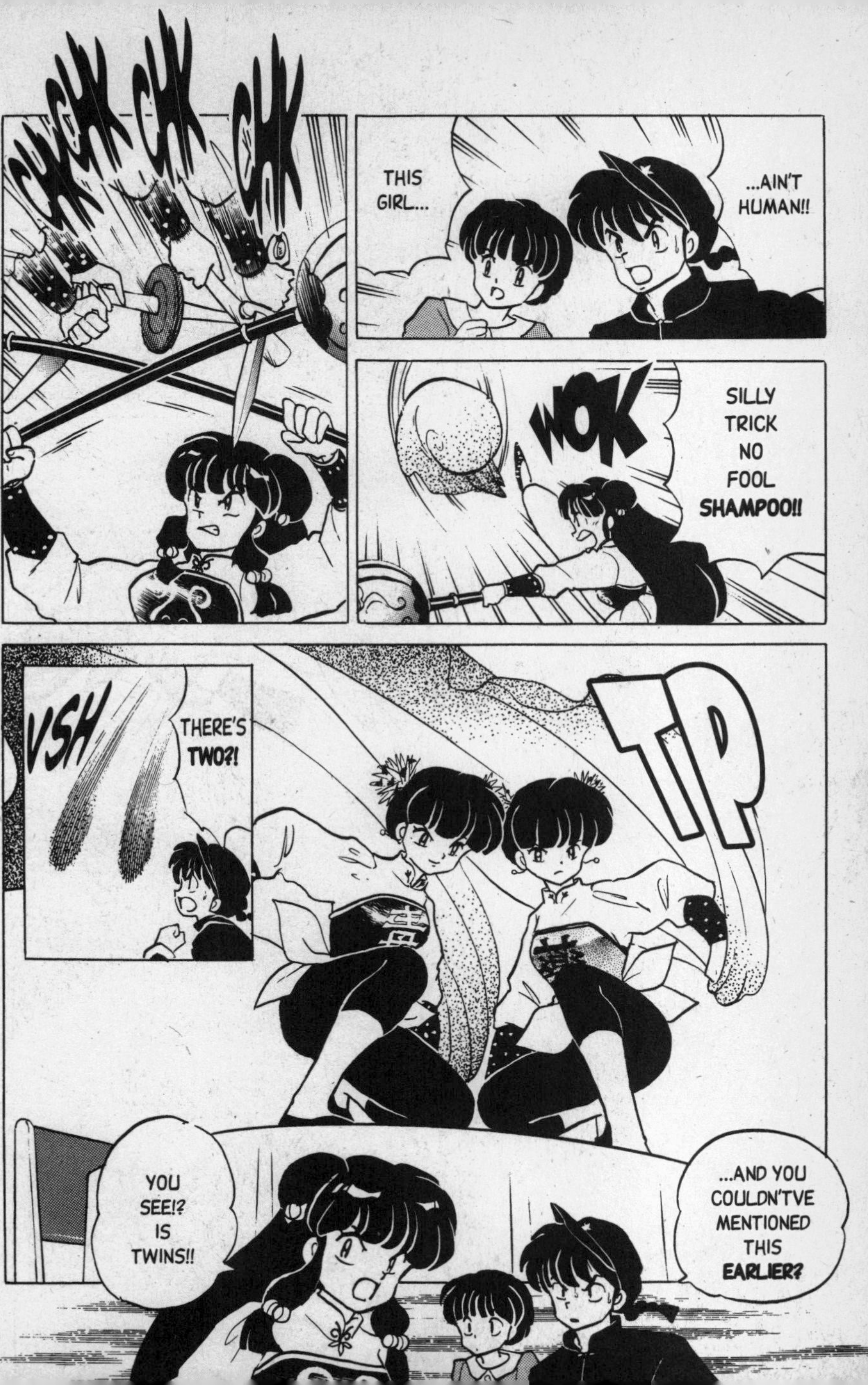
CHCHCHK CHK CHK
THIS GIRL...
...AIN'T HUMAN!!
WOK
SILLY TRICK NO FOOL SHAMPOO!!
VSH
THERE'S TWO?!
TIP
YOU SEE!? IS TWINS!!
...AND YOU COULDN'TVE MENTIONED THIS EARLIER?

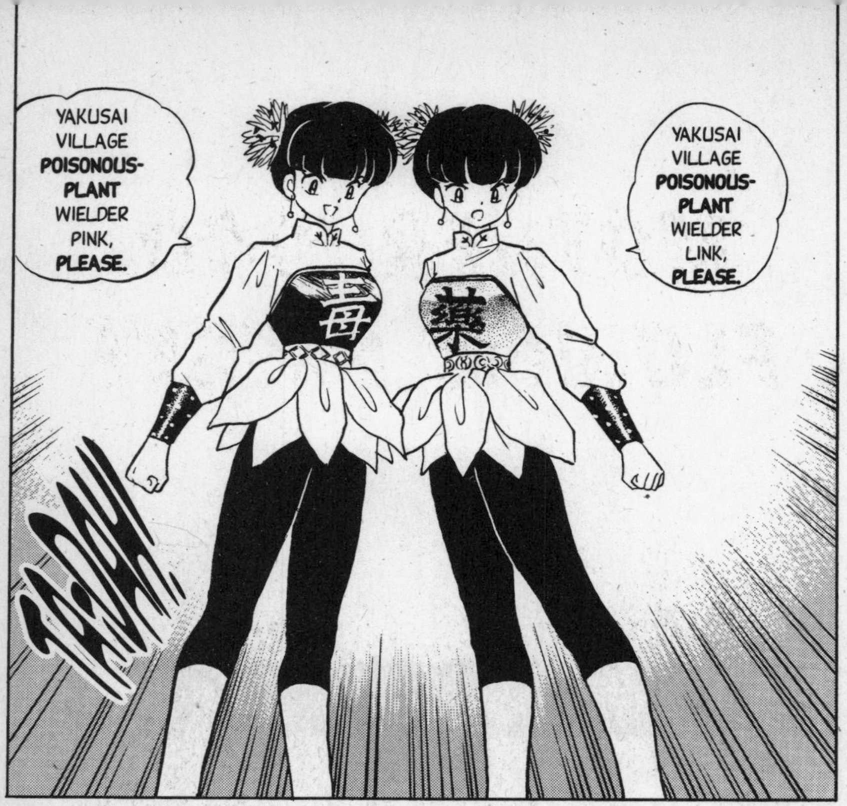
YAKUSAI VILLAGE **POISONOUS-PLANT** WIELDER PINK, **PLEASE.**
YAKUSAI VILLAGE **POISONOUS-PLANT** WIELDER LINK, **PLEASE.**

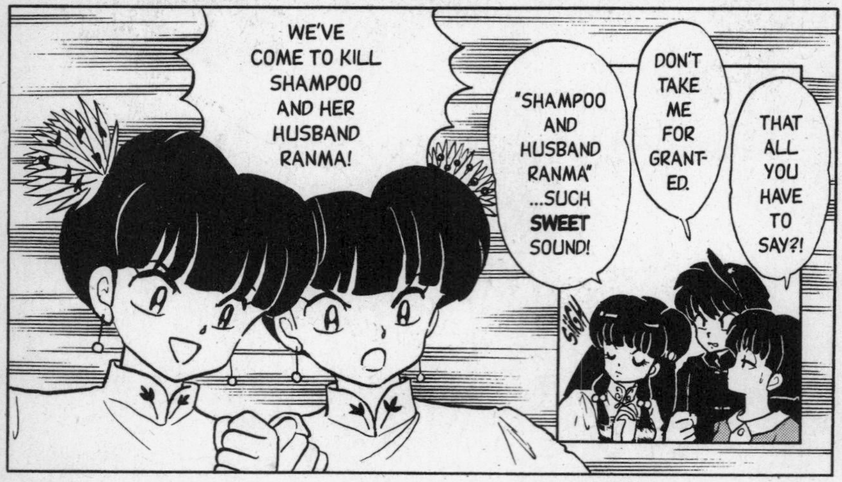
WE'VE COME TO KILL SHAMPOO AND HER HUSBAND RANMA!
"SHAMPOO AND HUSBAND RANMA" ...SUCH **SWEET** SOUND!
SIGH
DON'T TAKE ME FOR GRANT-ED.
THAT ALL YOU HAVE TO SAY?!

PART 4

MOTHERHOOD FLOWER, PLEASE

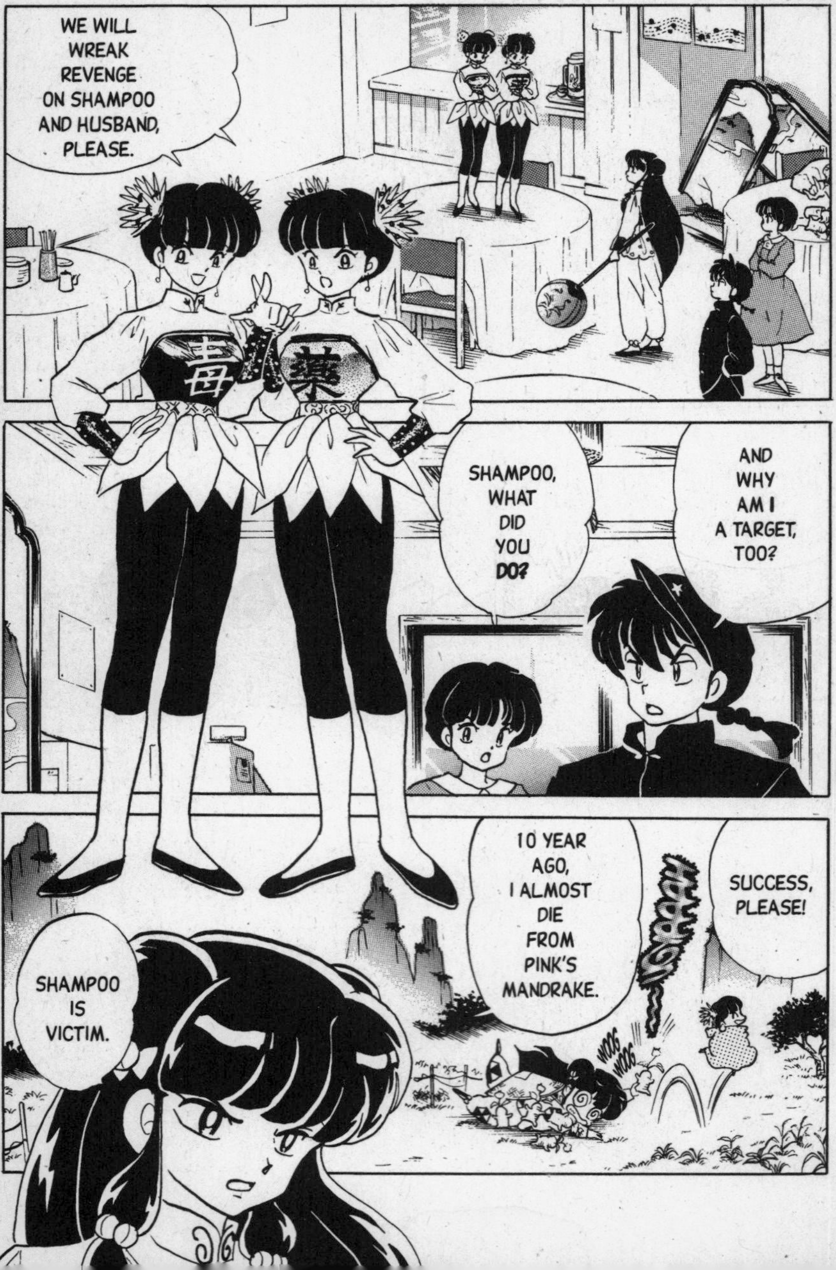
WE WILL WREAK REVENGE ON SHAMPOO AND HUSBAND, PLEASE.
SHAMPOO, WHAT DID YOU DO?
AND WHY AM I A TARGET, TOO?
SHAMPOO IS VICTIM.
10 YEAR AGO, I ALMOST DIE FROM PINK'S MANDRAKE.
WOOG
WOOG
SUCCESS, PLEASE!

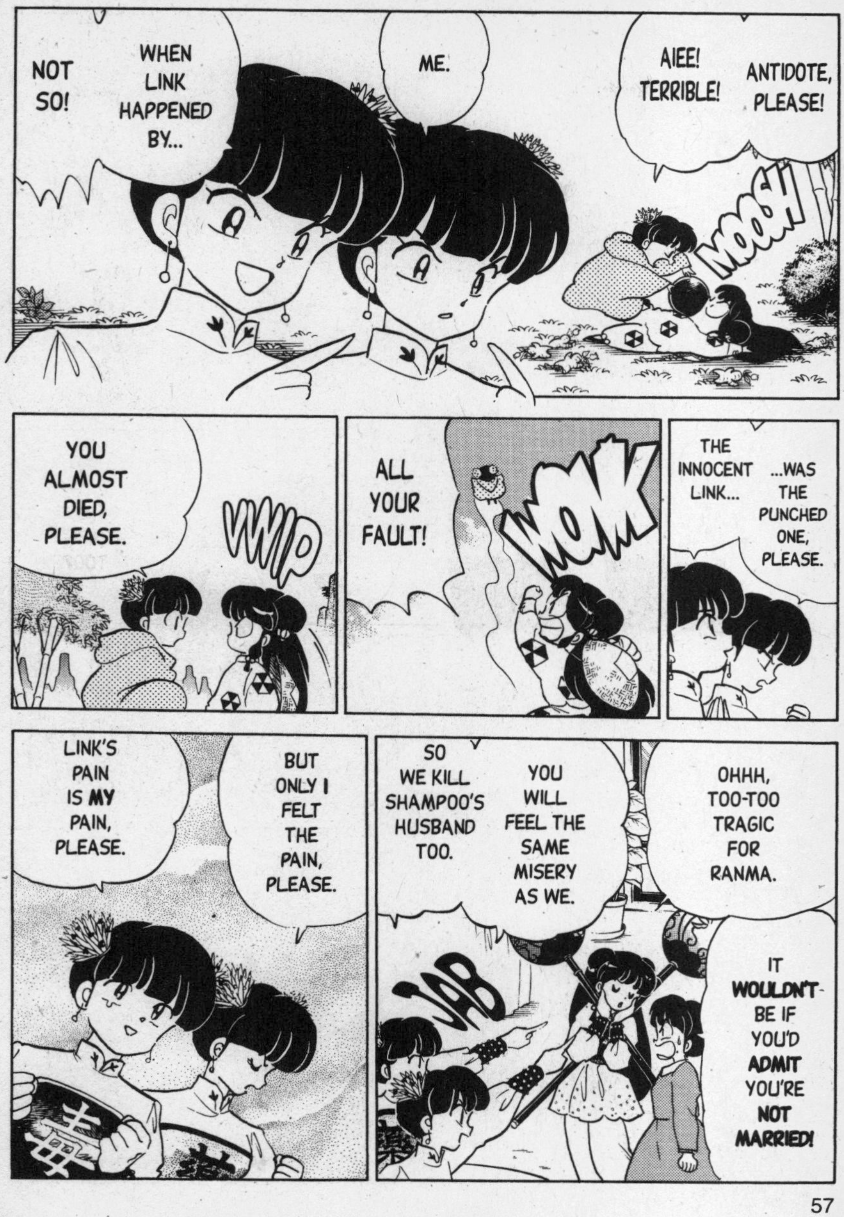
NOT SO!
WHEN LINK HAPPENED BY...
ME.
AIEE! TERRIBLE!
ANTIDOTE, PLEASE!
MOOSH
YOU ALMOST DIED, PLEASE.
VWIP
ALL YOUR FAULT!
WOK
THE INNOCENT LINK...
...WAS THE PUNCHED ONE, PLEASE.
LINK'S PAIN IS **MY** PAIN, PLEASE.
BUT ONLY I FELT THE PAIN, PLEASE.
SO WE KILL SHAMPOO'S HUSBAND TOO.
YOU WILL FEEL THE SAME MISERY AS WE.
OHHH, TOO-TOO TRAGIC FOR RANMA.
JAB
IT **WOULDN'T** BE IF YOU'D **ADMIT** YOU'RE **NOT MARRIED!**

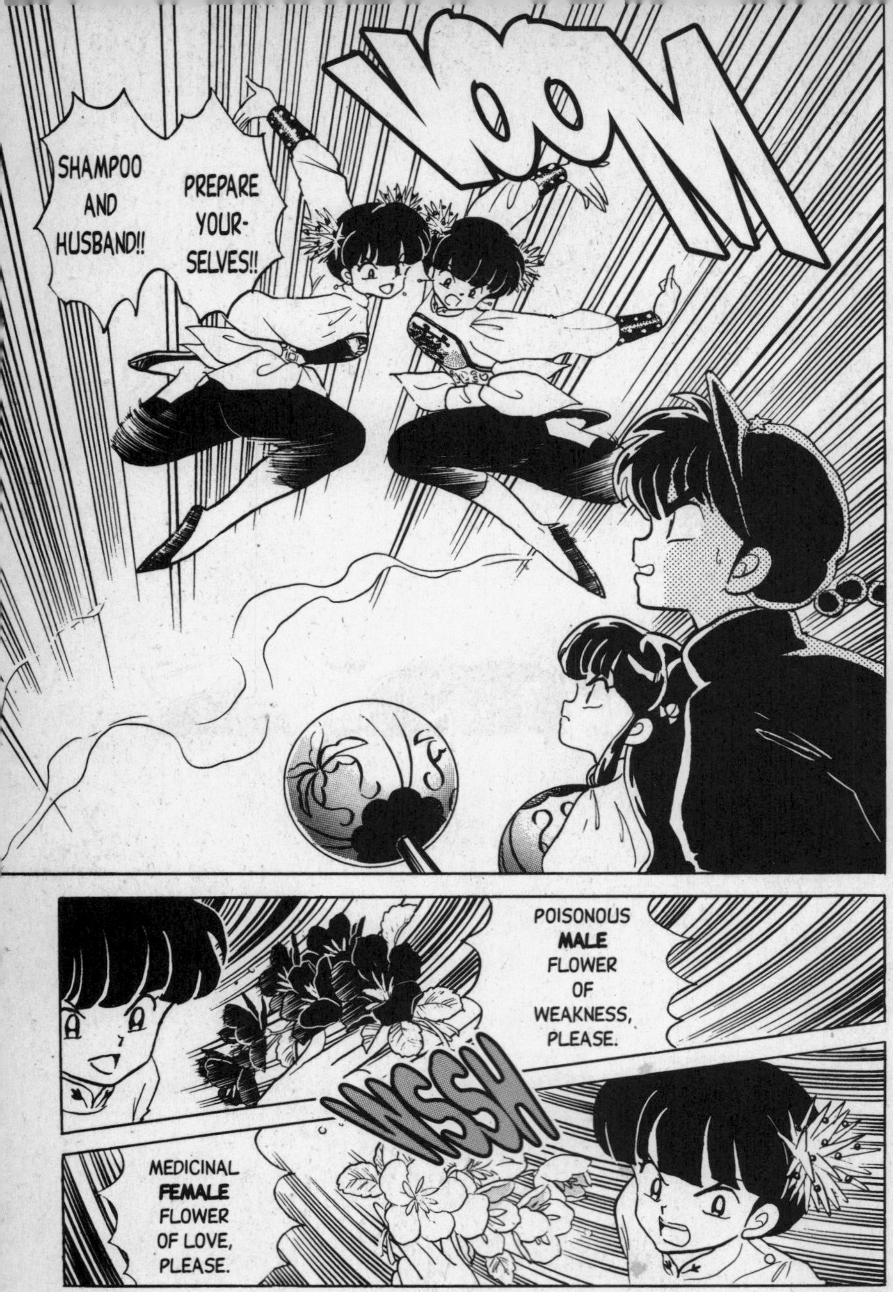
SHAMPOO AND HUSBAND!!
PREPARE YOUR-SELVES!!
VOOM
POISONOUS **MALE** FLOWER OF WEAKNESS, PLEASE.
WSSH
MEDICINAL **FEMALE** FLOWER OF LOVE, PLEASE.

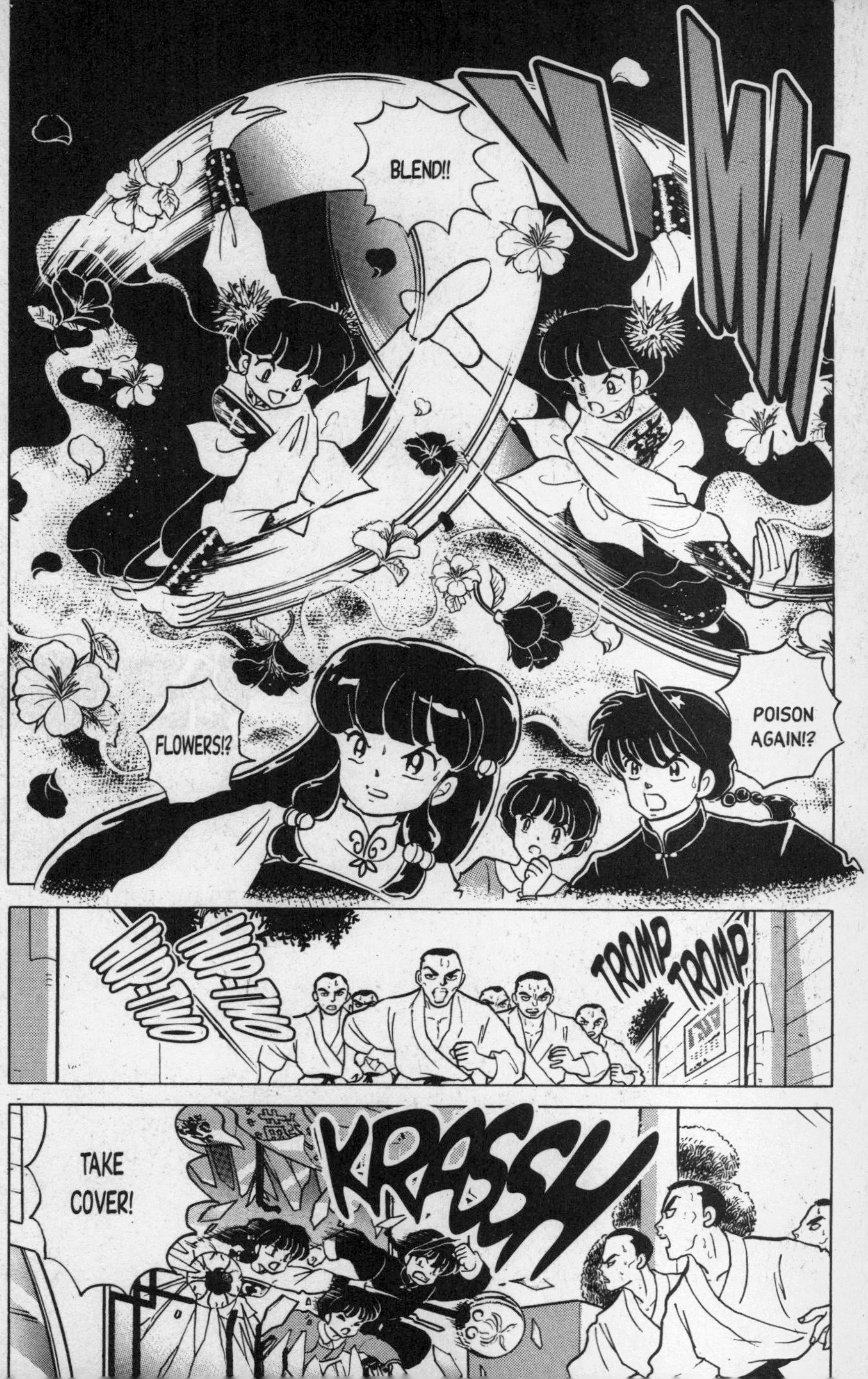
BLEND!!
VWMM
FLOWERS!?
POISON AGAIN!?
HUP TWO
HUP TWO
TROMP
TROMP
TAKE COVER!
KRASH

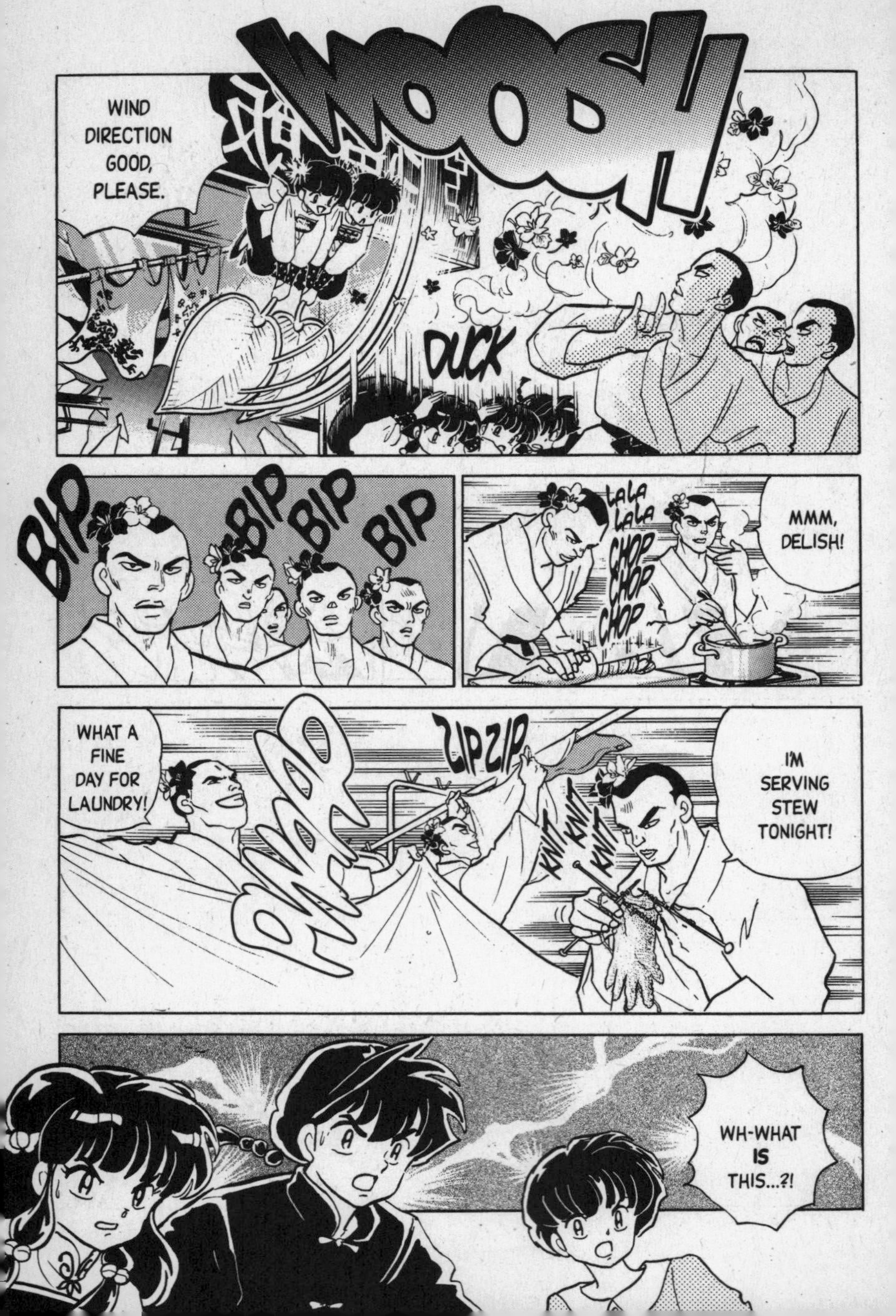
WOOSH
WIND DIRECTION GOOD, PLEASE.
DUCK
BIP BIP BIP BIP
LALA LALA
CHOP CHOP CHOP
MMM, DELISH!
WHAT A FINE DAY FOR LAUNDRY!
ZIP ZIP
KNIT KNIT KNIT
I'M SERVING STEW TONIGHT!
WH-WHAT IS THIS...?!

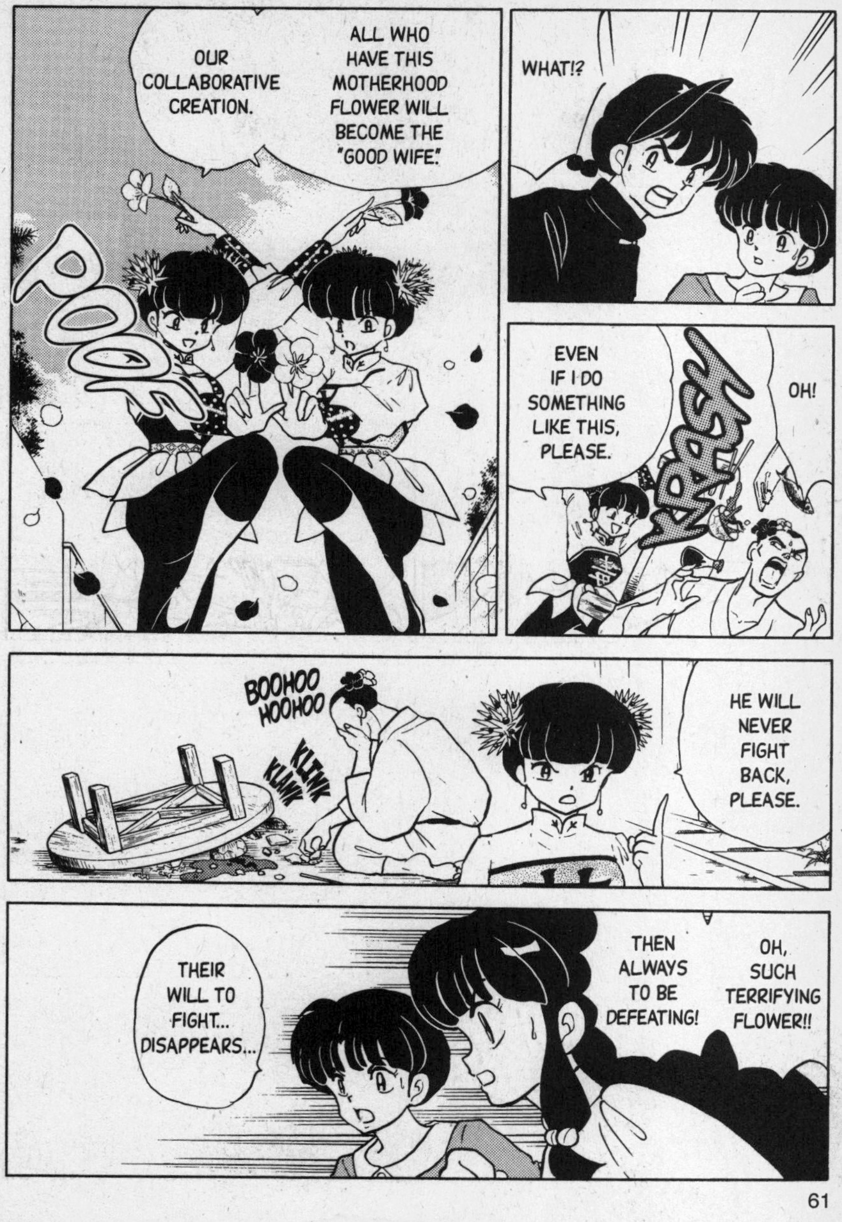
OUR COLLABORATIVE CREATION.
ALL WHO HAVE THIS MOTHERHOOD FLOWER WILL BECOME THE "GOOD WIFE."
POOF
WHAT!?
EVEN IF I DO SOMETHING LIKE THIS, PLEASE.
KRASH
OH!
BOOHOO HOOHOO
KLINK KLANK
HE WILL NEVER FIGHT BACK, PLEASE.
THEIR WILL TO FIGHT... DISAPPEARS...
THEN ALWAYS TO BE DEFEATING!
OH, SUCH TERRIFYING FLOWER!!

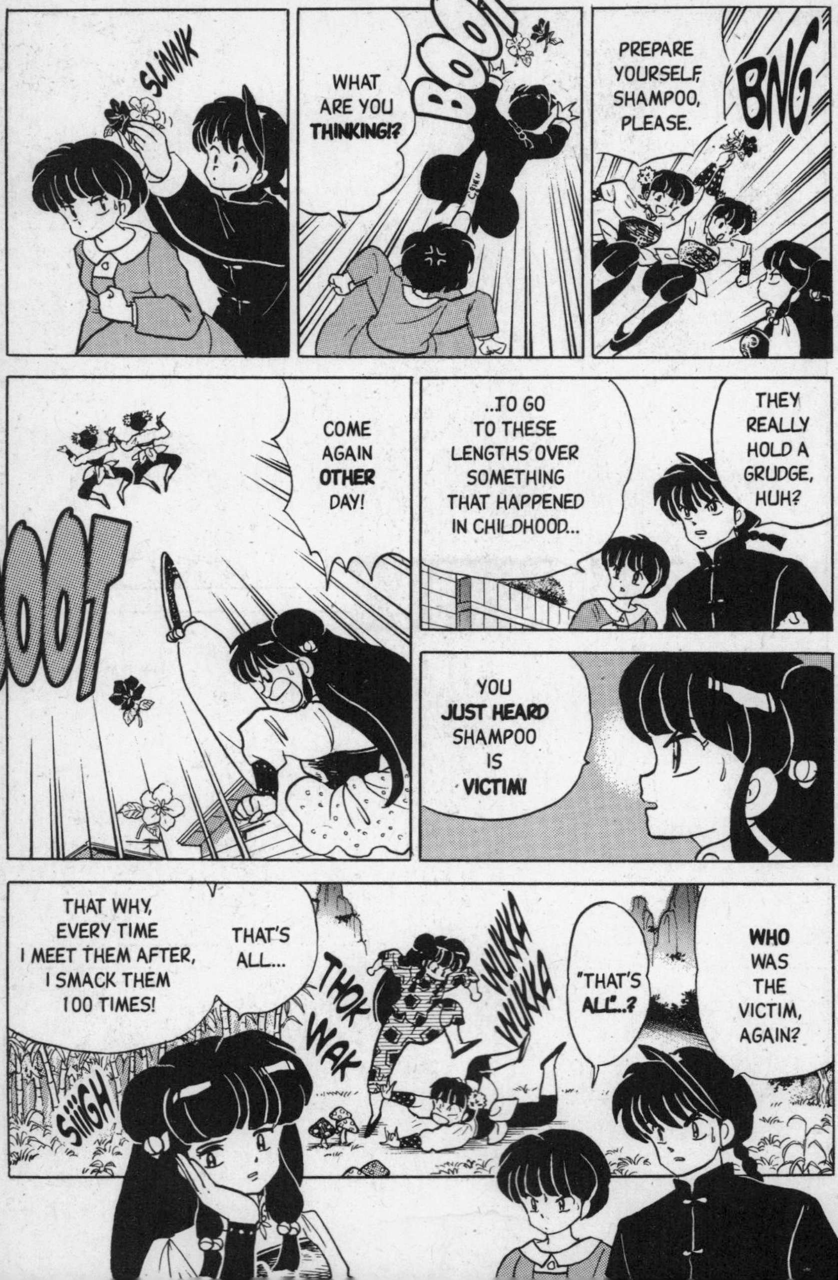
SLINNK
WHAT ARE YOU THINKING!?
BOOT
PREPARE YOURSELF, SHAMPOO, PLEASE.
BNG
COME AGAIN OTHER DAY!
BOOT
THEY REALLY HOLD A GRUDGE, HUH?
...TO GO TO THESE LENGTHS OVER SOMETHING THAT HAPPENED IN CHILDHOOD...
YOU JUST HEARD SHAMPOO IS VICTIM!
THAT WHY, EVERY TIME I MEET THEM AFTER, I SMACK THEM 100 TIMES!
THAT'S ALL...
SIIIGH
THOK
WAK
WUKKA
WUKKA
"THAT'S ALL"..?
WHO WAS THE VICTIM, AGAIN?

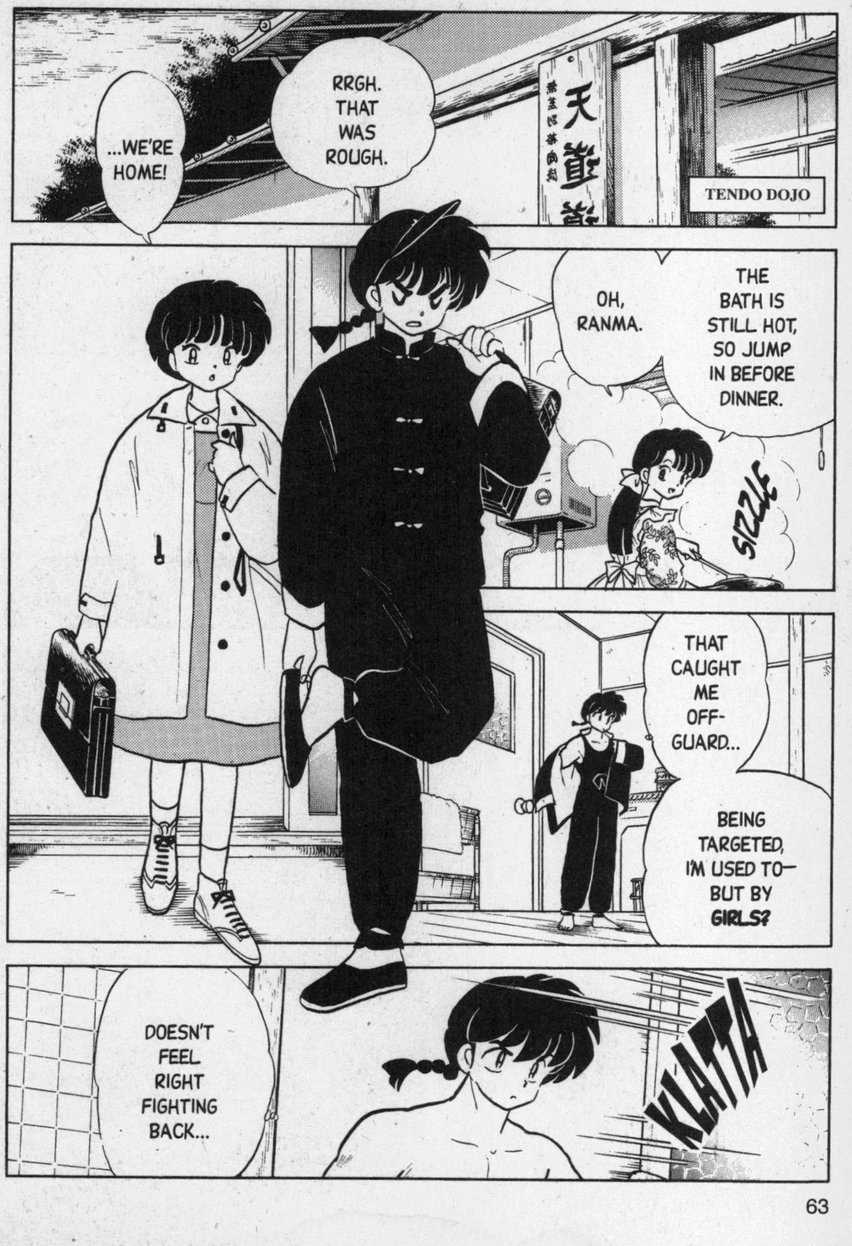
...WE'RE HOME!
RRGH. THAT WAS ROUGH.
TENDO DOJO
OH, RANMA.
THE BATH IS STILL HOT, SO JUMP IN BEFORE DINNER.
SIZZLE
THAT CAUGHT ME OFF-GUARD...
BEING TARGETED, I'M USED TO— BUT BY **GIRLS?**
DOESN'T FEEL RIGHT FIGHTING BACK...
KLATTA

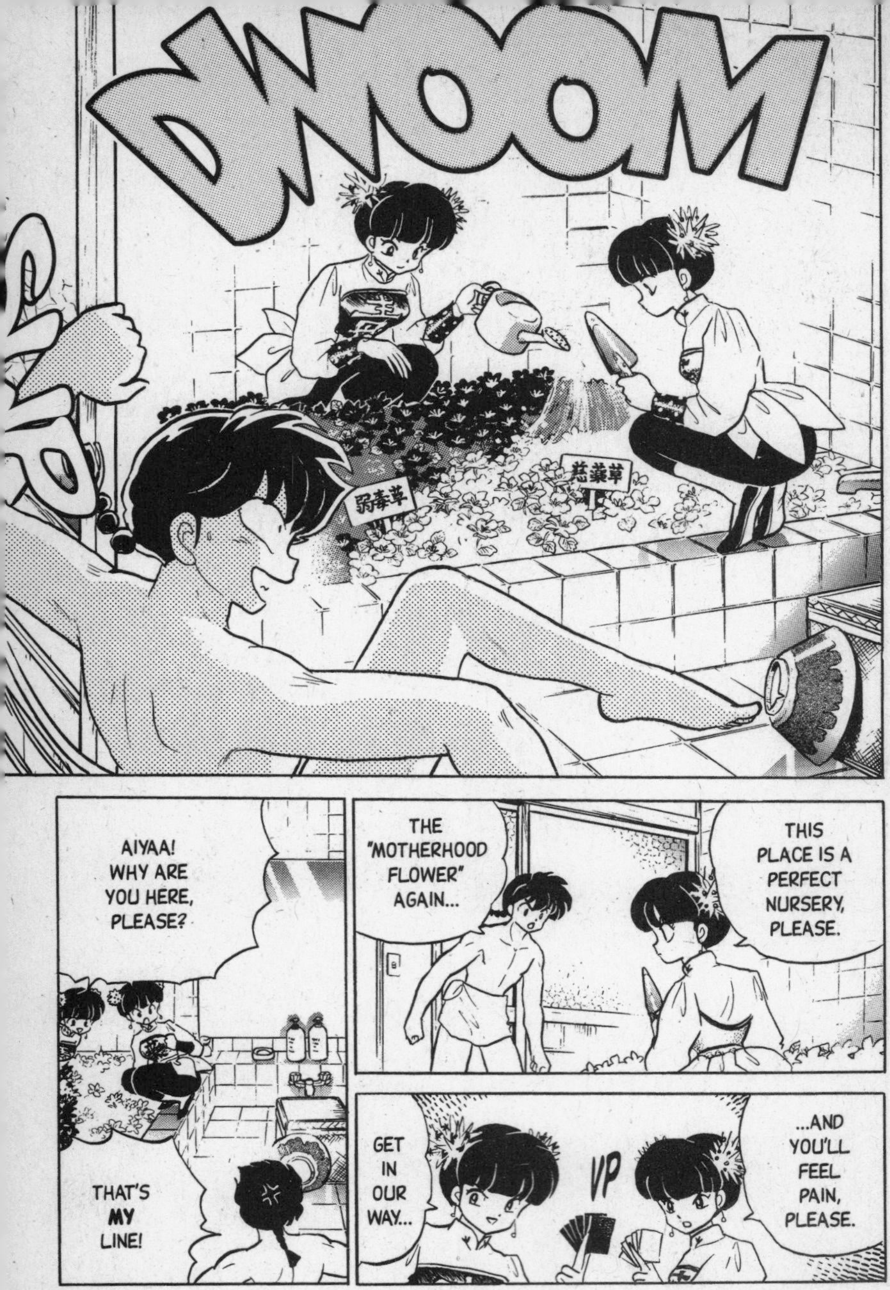
DWOOM
AIYAA! WHY ARE YOU HERE, PLEASE?
THAT'S **MY** LINE!
THE "MOTHERHOOD FLOWER" AGAIN...
THIS PLACE IS A PERFECT NURSERY, PLEASE.
GET IN OUR WAY...
VP
...AND YOU'LL FEEL PAIN, PLEASE.

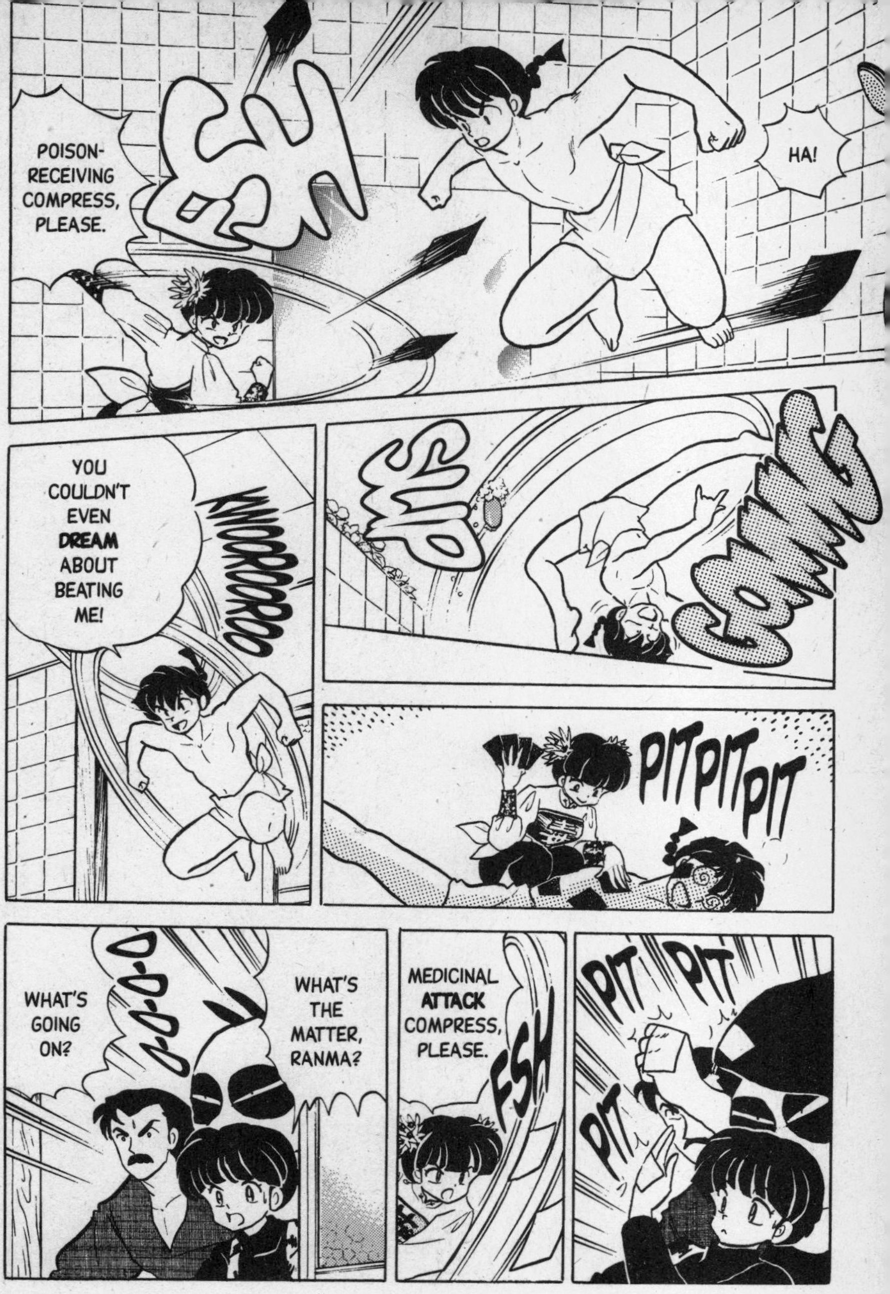
POISON-RECEIVING COMPRESS, PLEASE.
HA!
YOU COULDN'T EVEN **DREAM** ABOUT BEATING ME!
SLIP
PIT PIT PIT
WHAT'S GOING ON?
D-D-D-D
WHAT'S THE MATTER, RANMA?
MEDICINAL **ATTACK** COMPRESS, PLEASE.
FSH
PIT PIT PIT

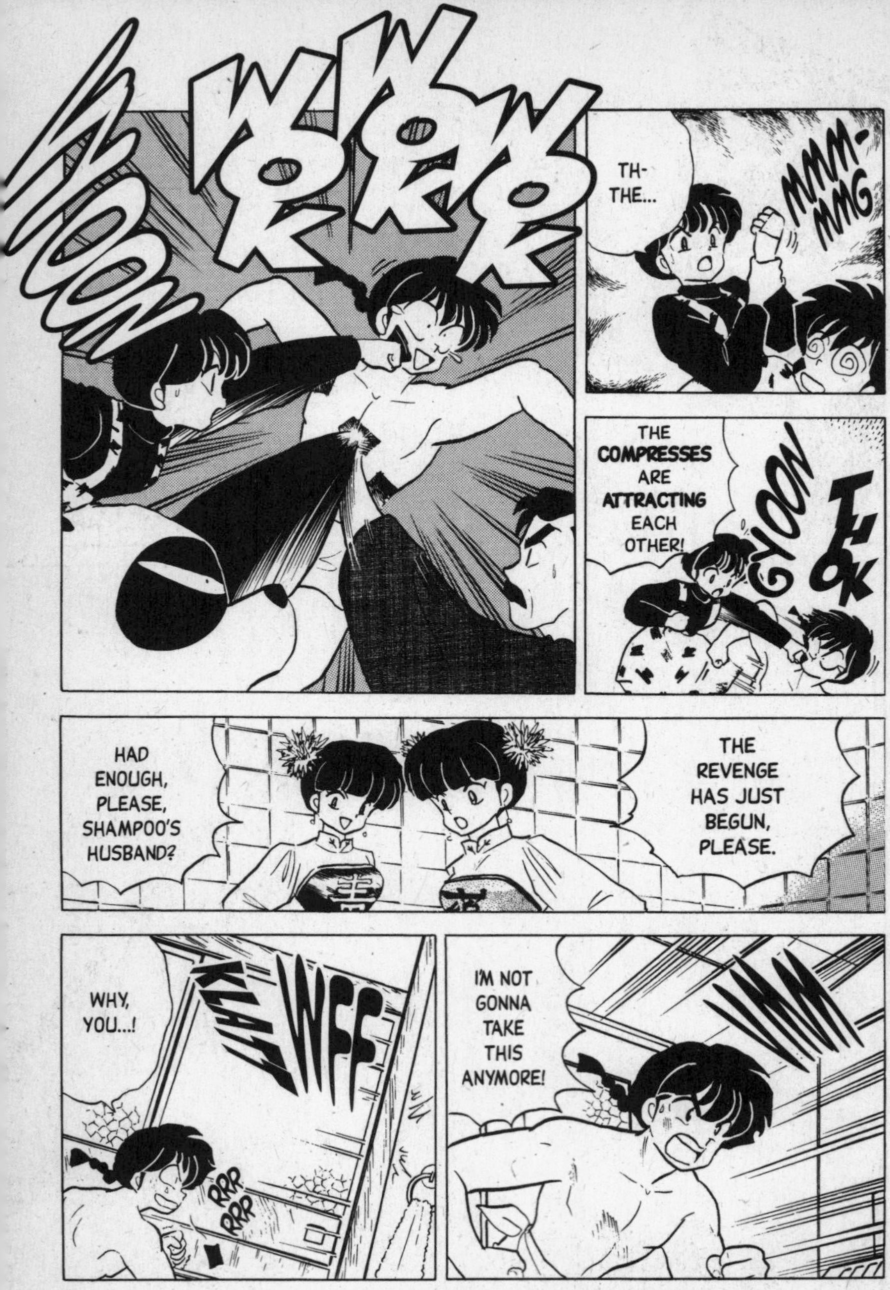
TH-
THE...
MMM-
MMG
THE COMPRESSES ARE ATTRACTING EACH OTHER!
GYOON
THOK
HAD ENOUGH, PLEASE, SHAMPOO'S HUSBAND?
THE REVENGE HAS JUST BEGUN, PLEASE.
WHY, YOU...!
RRR
RRR
I'M NOT GONNA TAKE THIS ANYMORE!

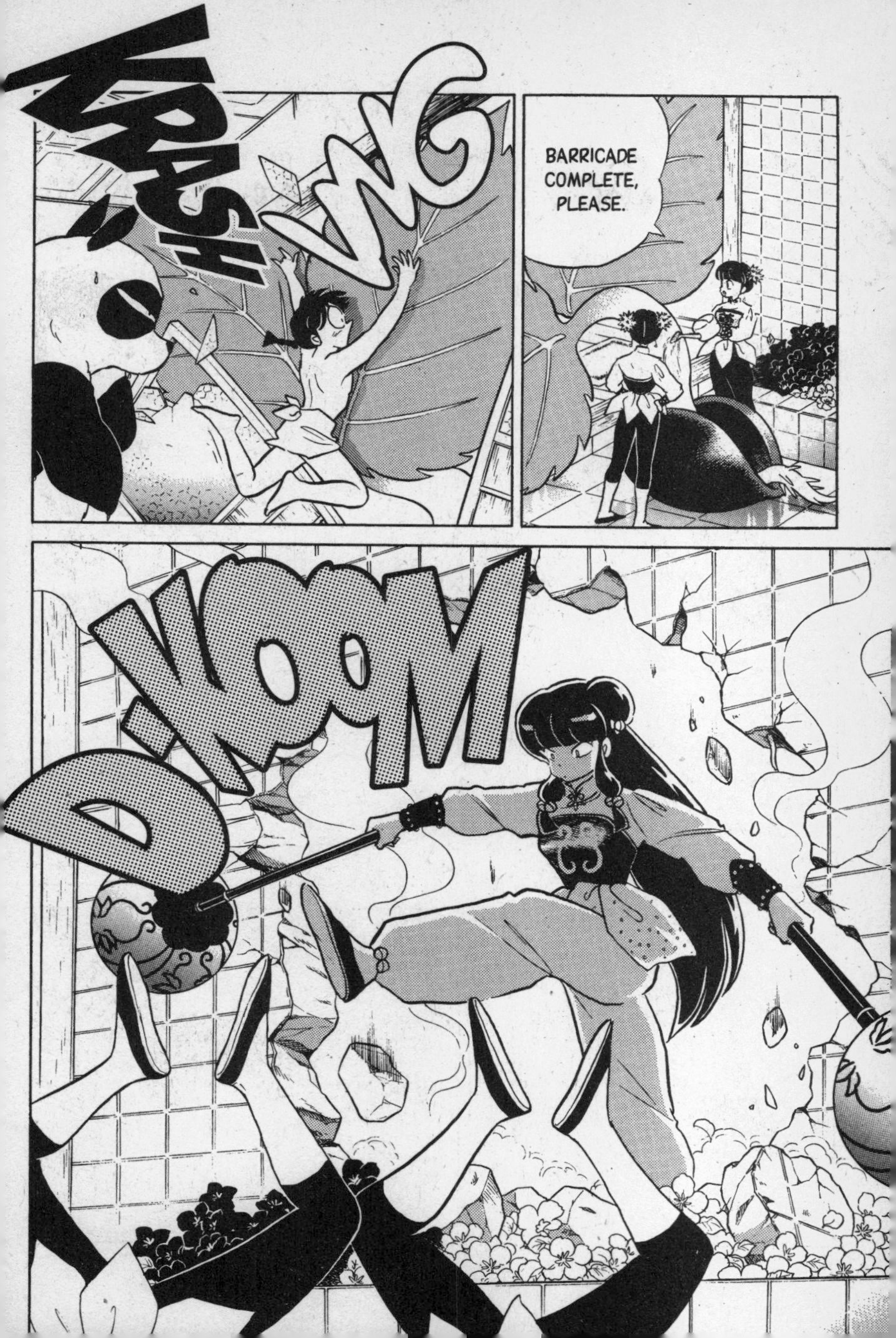
KRASH!
BARRICADE COMPLETE, PLEASE.
D-WOOM

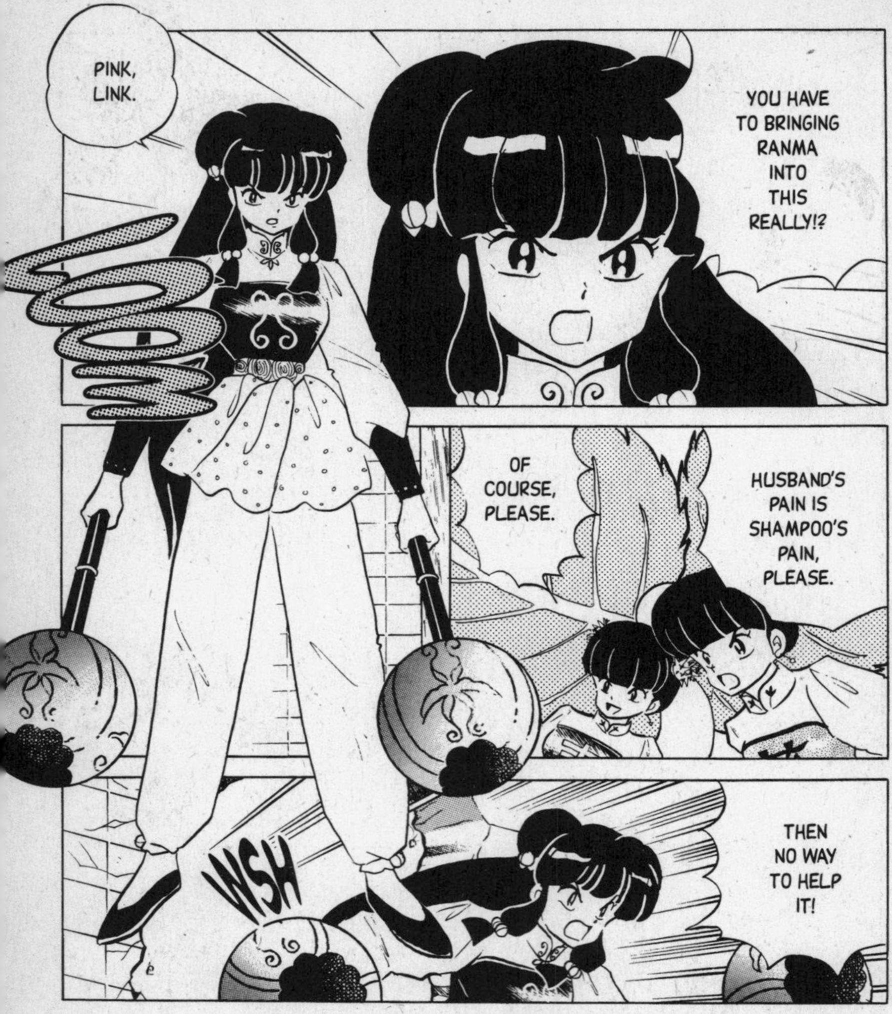
PINK, LINK.
WOOM
YOU HAVE TO BRINGING RANMA INTO THIS REALLY!?
OF COURSE, PLEASE.
HUSBAND'S PAIN IS SHAMPOO'S PAIN, PLEASE.
WSH
THEN NO WAY TO HELP IT!
LIKE A MOTH TO A FLAME, PLEASE.
TO THE MOTHERHOOD FLOWER SEED-BED, PLEASE.

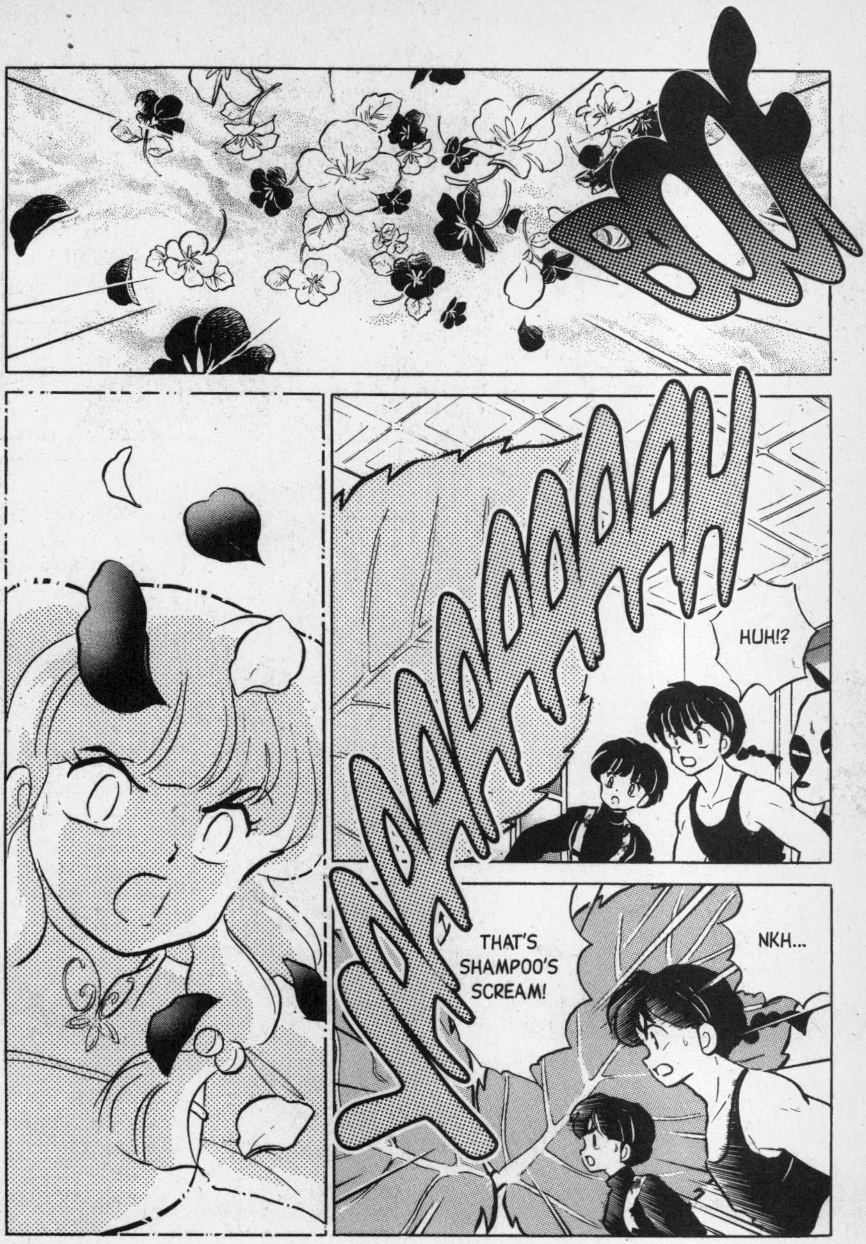
HUH!?
THAT'S SHAMPOO'S SCREAM!
NKH...

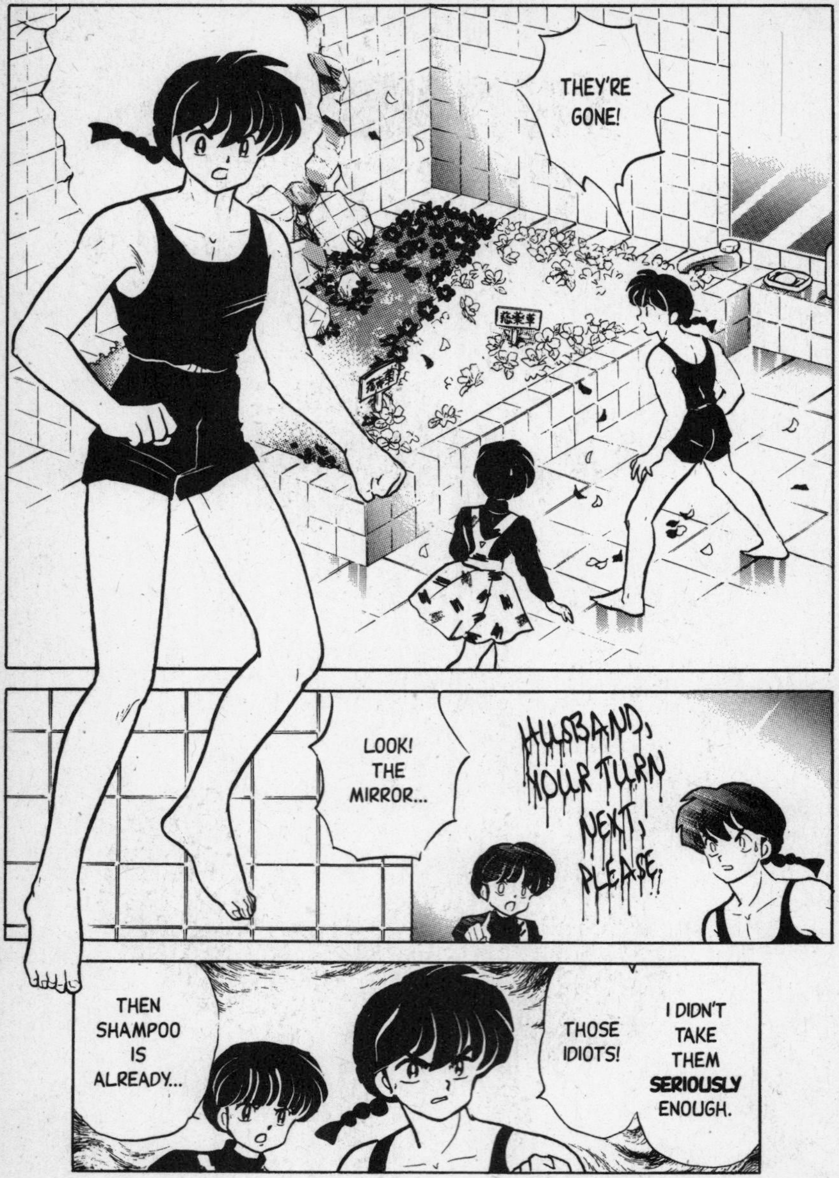
THEY'RE GONE!
LOOK! THE MIRROR...
HUSBAND, YOUR TURN NEXT, PLEASE.
THEN SHAMPOO IS ALREADY...
THOSE IDIOTS!
I DIDN'T TAKE THEM SERIOUSLY ENOUGH.

PART 5
SHAMPOO—
CAPTIVE!

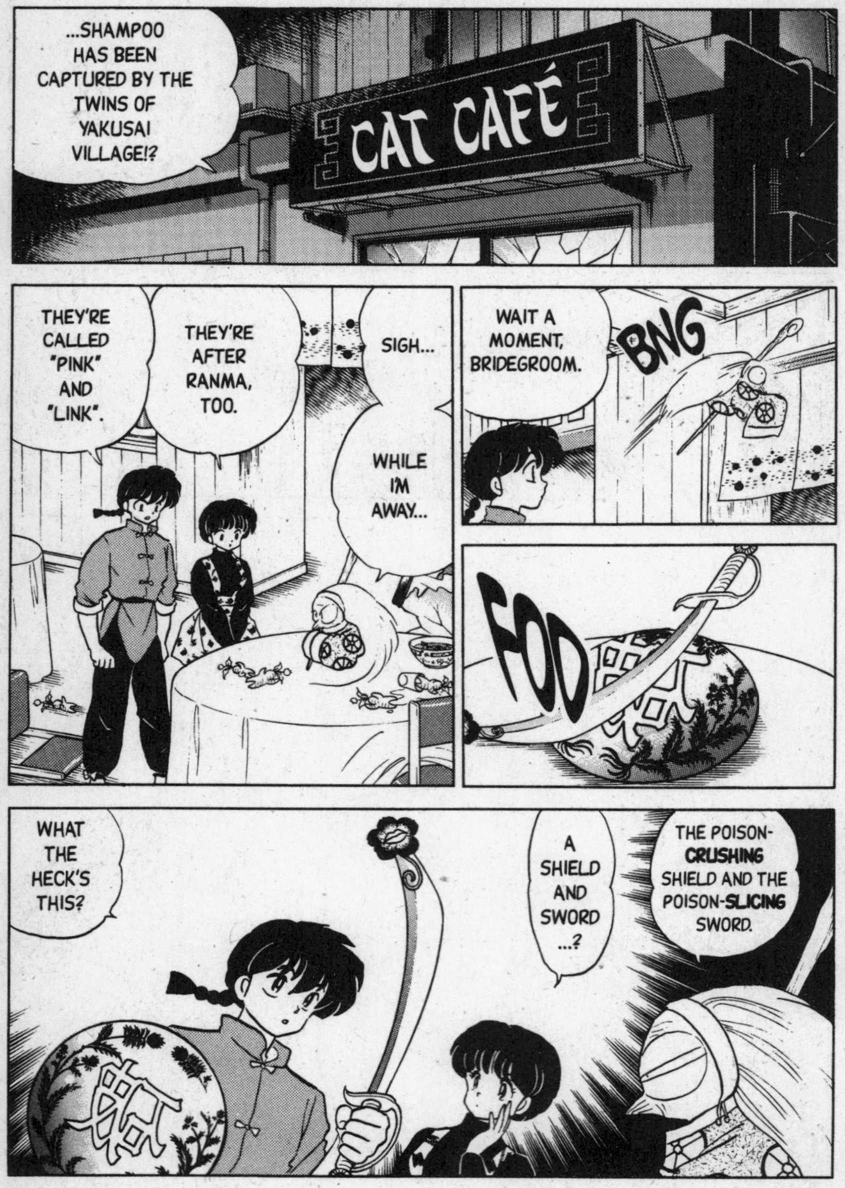
...SHAMPOO HAS BEEN CAPTURED BY THE TWINS OF YAKUSAI VILLAGE!?
CAT CAFÉ
THEY'RE CALLED "PINK" AND "LINK".
THEY'RE AFTER RANMA, TOO.
SIGH...
WHILE I'M AWAY...
WAIT A MOMENT, BRIDEGROOM.
BNG
FOD
WHAT THE HECK'S THIS?
A SHIELD AND SWORD ...?
THE POISON-**CRUSHING** SHIELD AND THE POISON-**SLICING** SWORD.

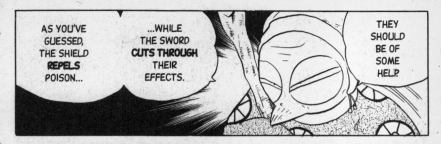

AS YOU'VE GUESSED, THE SHIELD **REPELS** POISON...

...WHILE THE SWORD **CUTS THROUGH** THEIR EFFECTS.

THEY SHOULD BE OF SOME HELP?

GRAOOOOO

HUH!?

W-WHAT IS THAT!?

YAH! OHH!

SPOTPP SPOTPP

GROOOOOO

A FLOWER!?

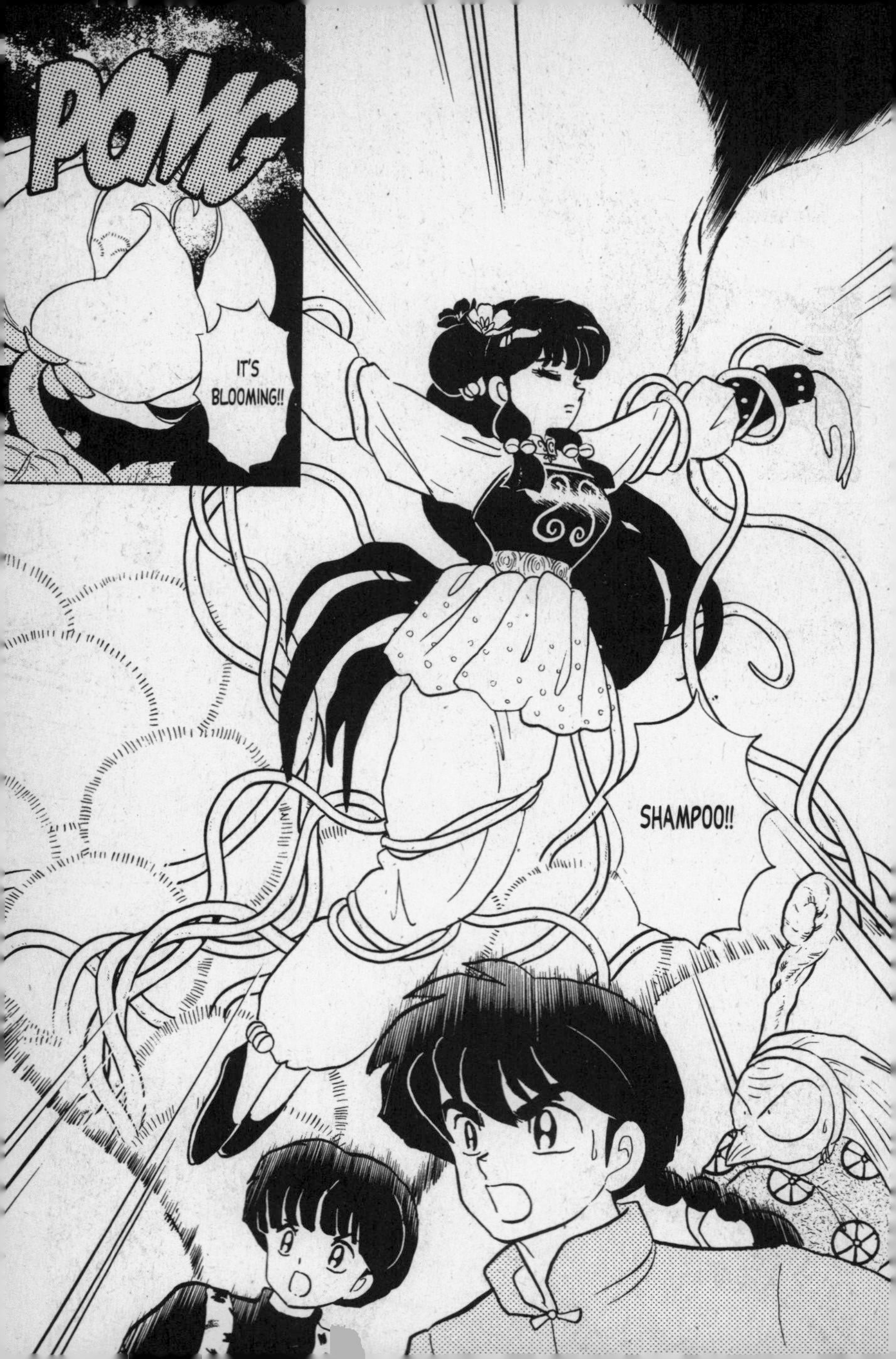
POMG
IT'S BLOOMING!!
SHAMPOO!!

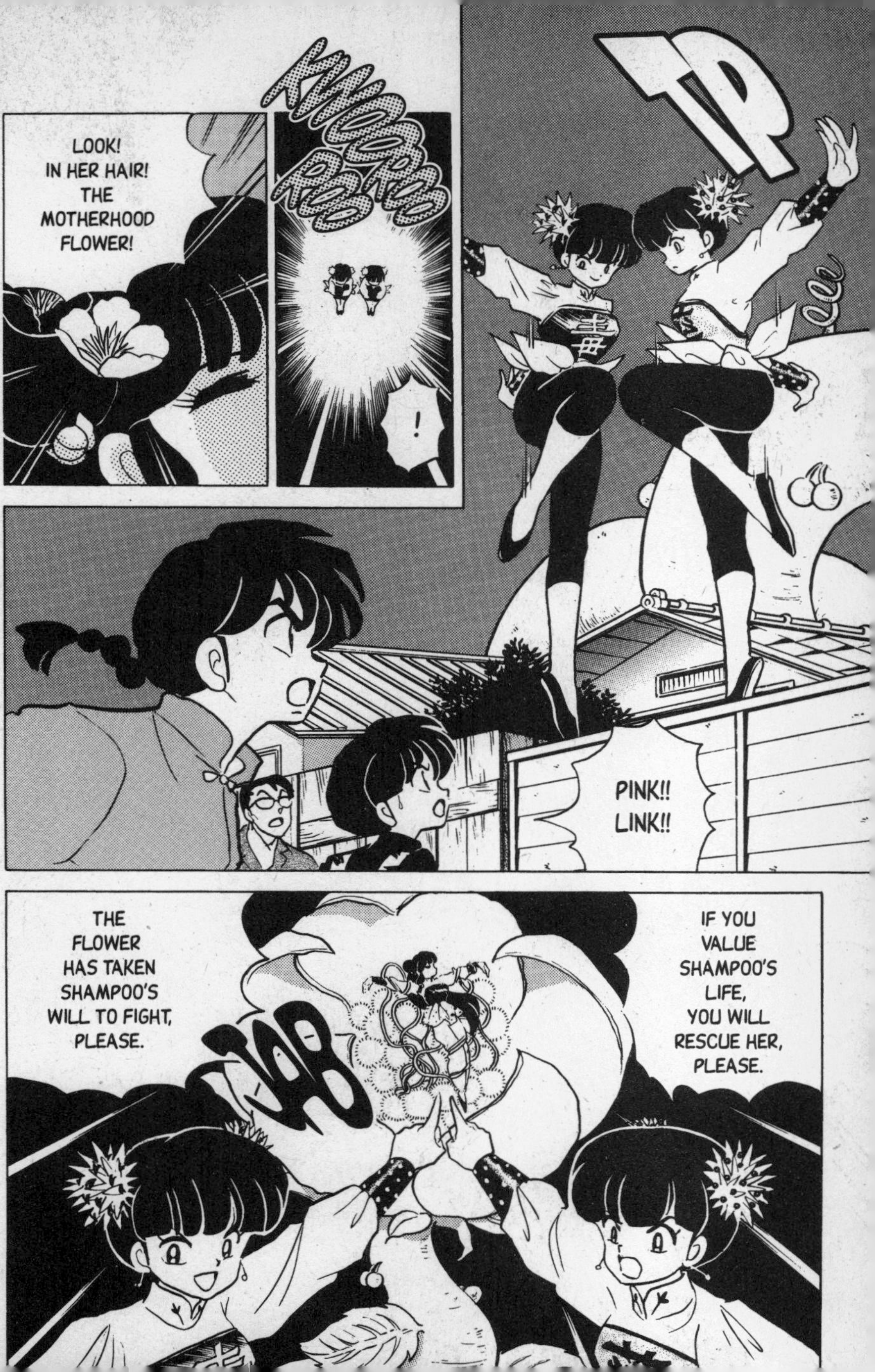

LOOK! IN HER HAIR! THE MOTHERHOOD FLOWER!
!
PINK!! LINK!!
THE FLOWER HAS TAKEN SHAMPOO'S WILL TO FIGHT, PLEASE.
IF YOU VALUE SHAMPOO'S LIFE, YOU WILL RESCUE HER, PLEASE.

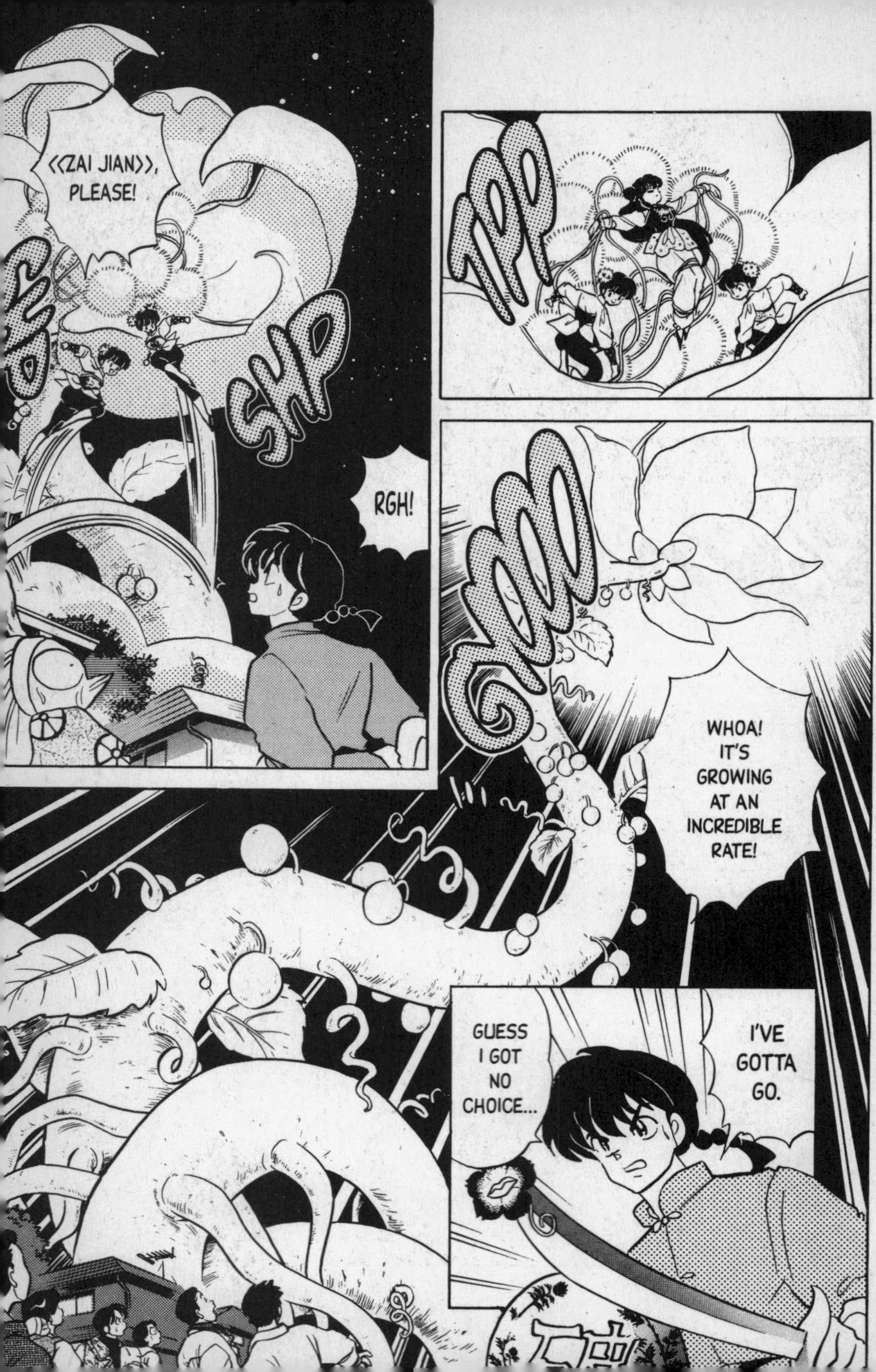

<<ZAI JIAN>>, PLEASE!
SHP
RGH!
TPP
WHOA! IT'S GROWING AT AN INCREDIBLE RATE!
GUESS I GOT NO CHOICE...
I'VE GOTTA GO.

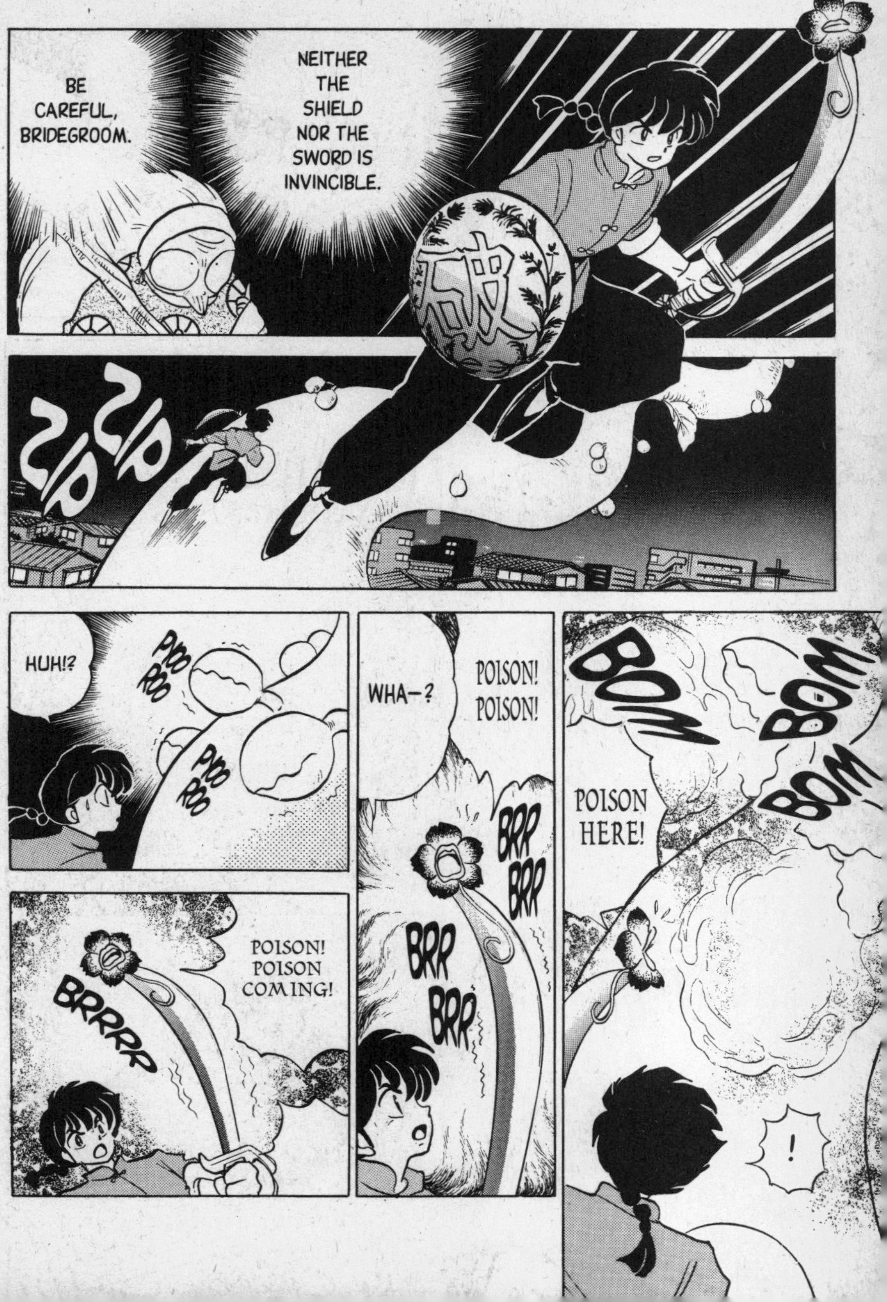

BE CAREFUL, BRIDEGROOM.
NEITHER THE SHIELD NOR THE SWORD IS INVINCIBLE.
ZIP ZIP
HUH!?
PYOO ROO
PYOO ROO
WHA—?
POISON! POISON!
BRR BRR
BRR BRR
BOM
BOM
BOM
POISON HERE!
POISON! POISON COMING!
BRRRR
!

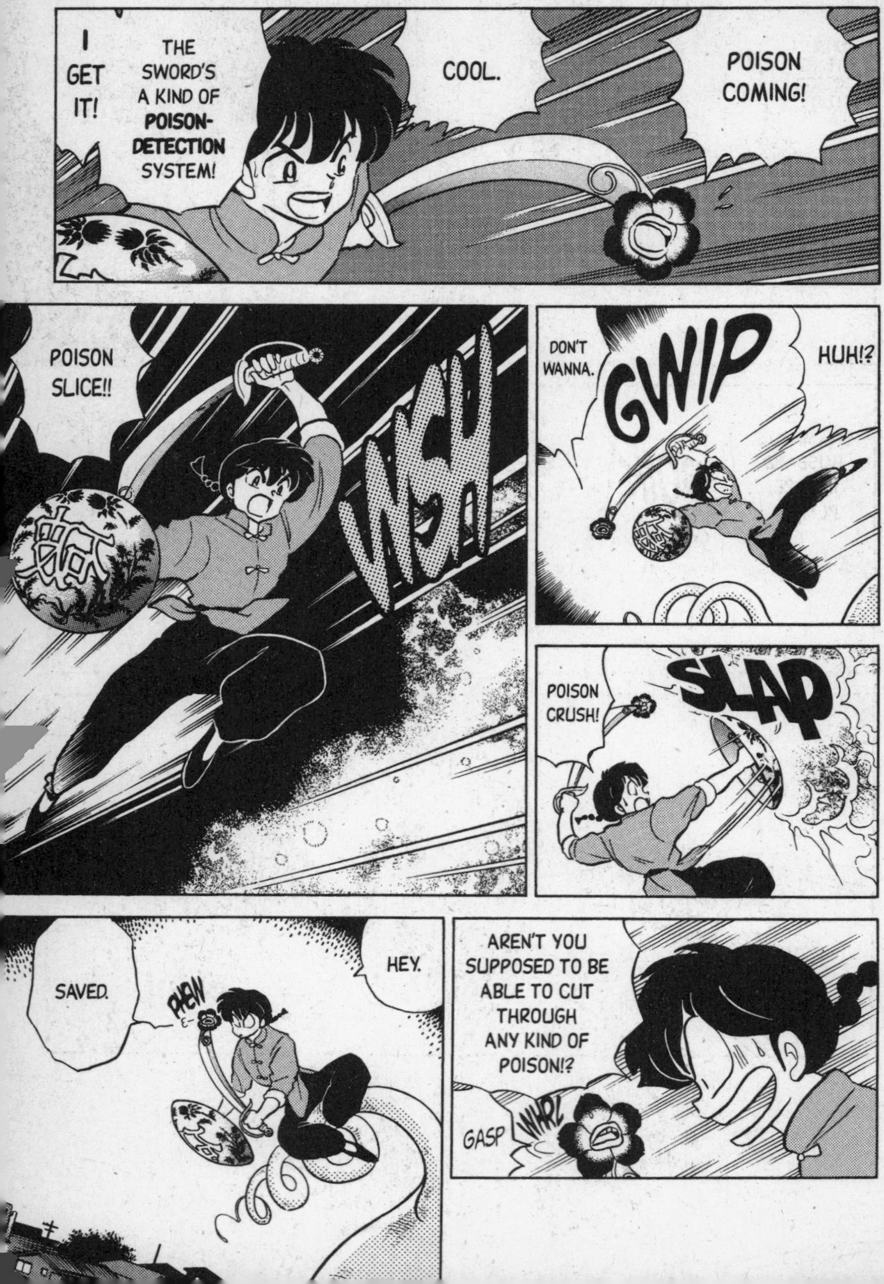
I GET IT!
THE SWORD'S A KIND OF POISON-DETECTION SYSTEM!
COOL.
POISON COMING!
POISON SLICE!!
WSH
DON'T WANNA.
GWIP
HUH!?
POISON CRUSH!
SLAP
SAVED.
PHEW
HEY.
AREN'T YOU SUPPOSED TO BE ABLE TO CUT THROUGH ANY KIND OF POISON!?
GASP
WHRL

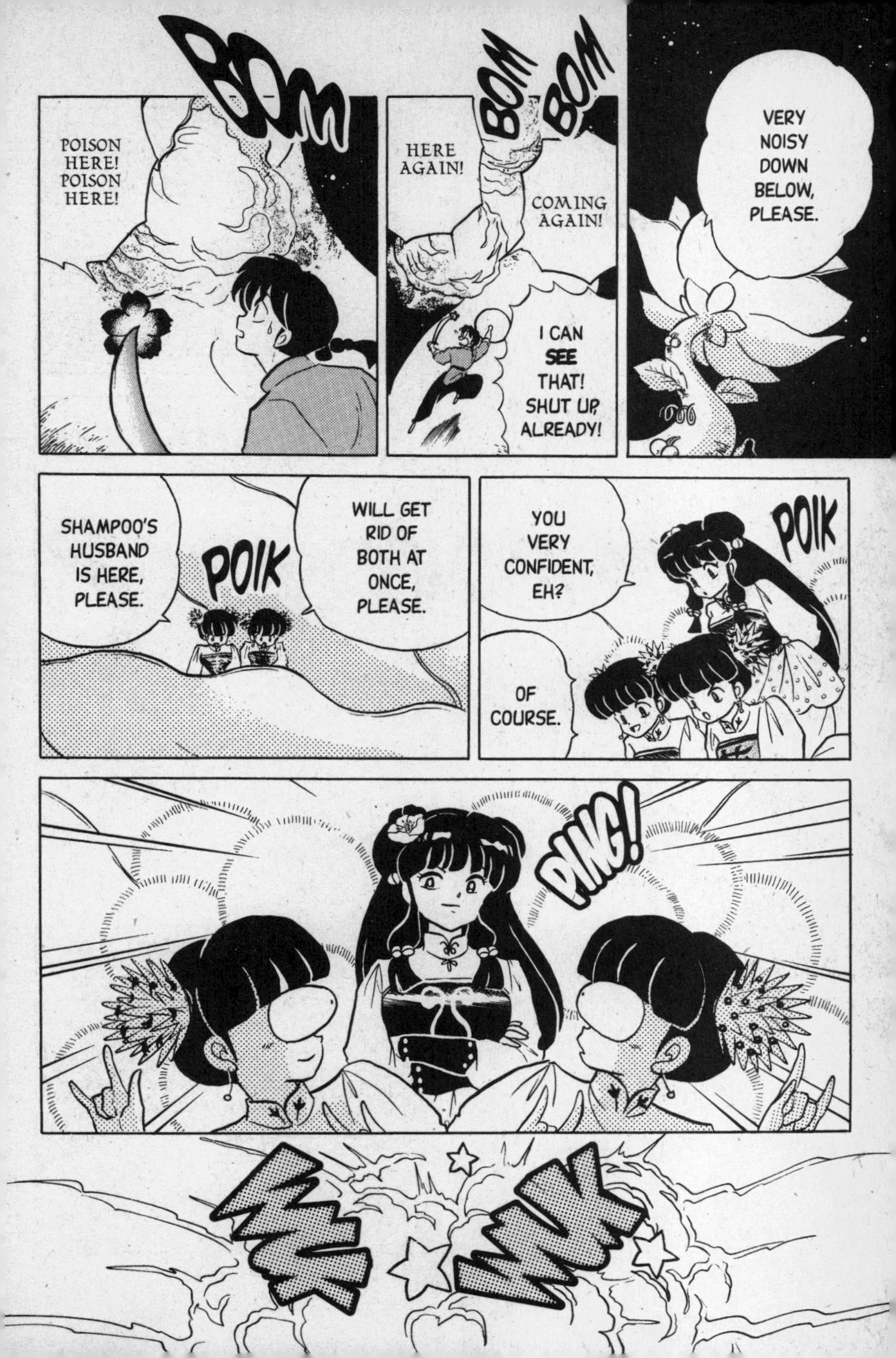
BOM
POISON HERE! POISON HERE!
BOM
BOM
HERE AGAIN!
COMING AGAIN!
I CAN SEE THAT! SHUT UP, ALREADY!
VERY NOISY DOWN BELOW, PLEASE.
SHAMPOO'S HUSBAND IS HERE, PLEASE.
POIK
WILL GET RID OF BOTH AT ONCE, PLEASE.
YOU VERY CONFIDENT, EH?
POIK
OF COURSE.
PING!
WHAK
WHAK

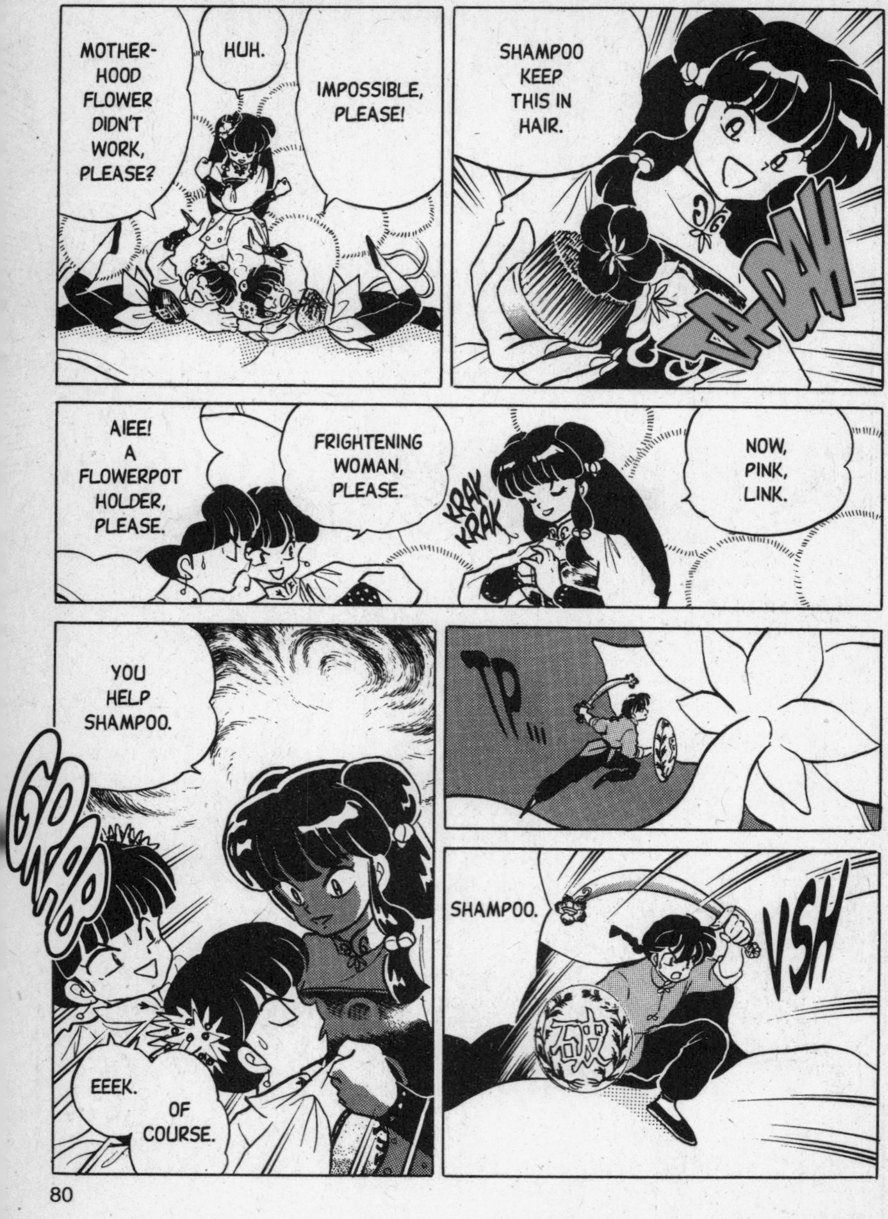

MOTHER-HOOD FLOWER DIDN'T WORK, PLEASE?
HUH.
IMPOSSIBLE, PLEASE!
SHAMPOO KEEP THIS IN HAIR.
TA-DAH
AIEE! A FLOWERPOT HOLDER, PLEASE.
FRIGHTENING WOMAN, PLEASE.
KRAK KRAK
NOW, PINK, LINK.
YOU HELP SHAMPOO.
GRAB
EEEK.
OF COURSE.
TP...
SHAMPOO.
VSH

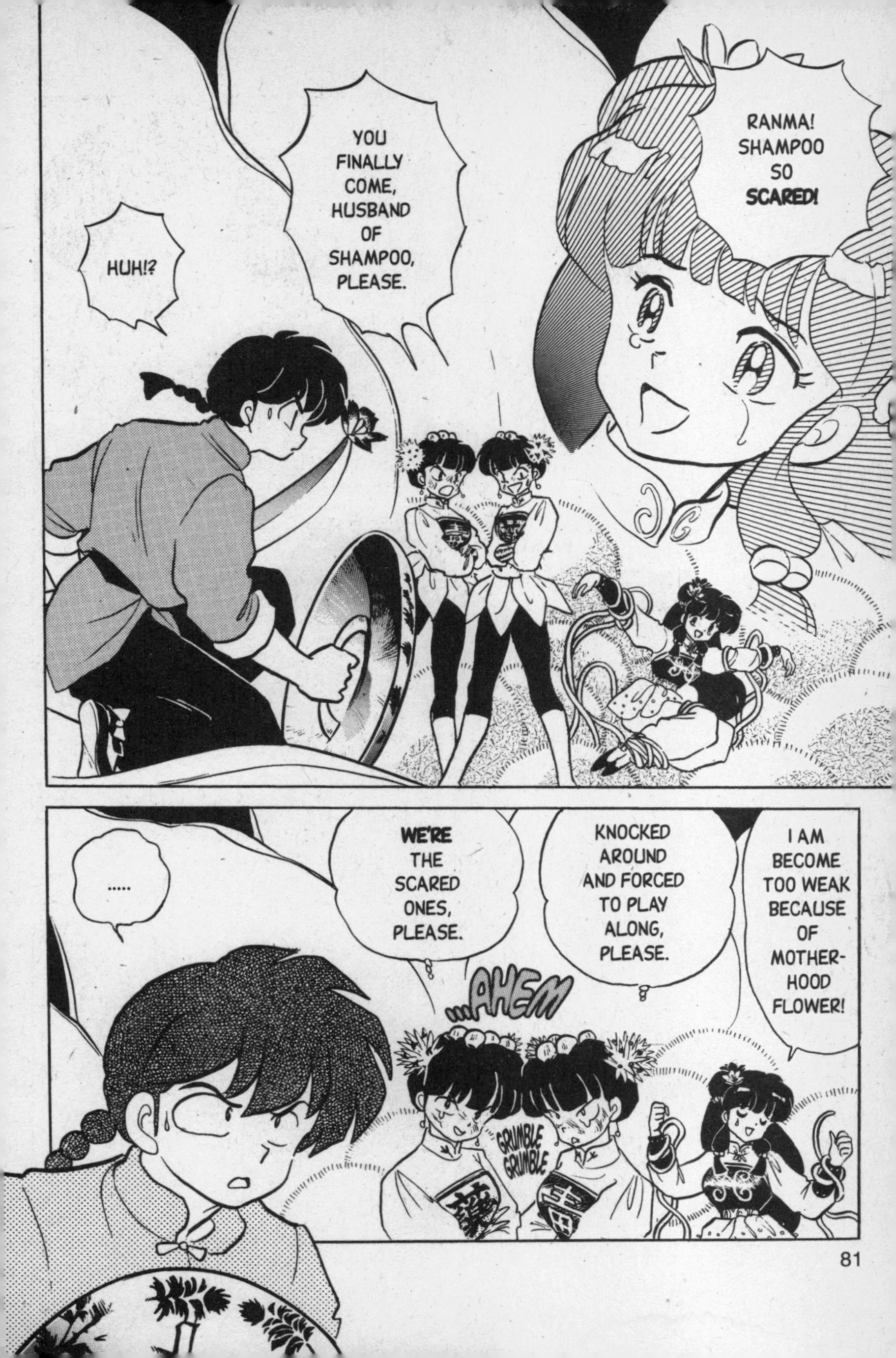
HUH!?
YOU FINALLY COME, HUSBAND OF SHAMPOO, PLEASE.
RANMA! SHAMPOO SO **SCARED!**
.....
WE'RE THE SCARED ONES, PLEASE.
KNOCKED AROUND AND FORCED TO PLAY ALONG, PLEASE.
...AHEM
I AM BECOME TOO WEAK BECAUSE OF MOTHER-HOOD FLOWER!
GRUMBLE GRUMBLE

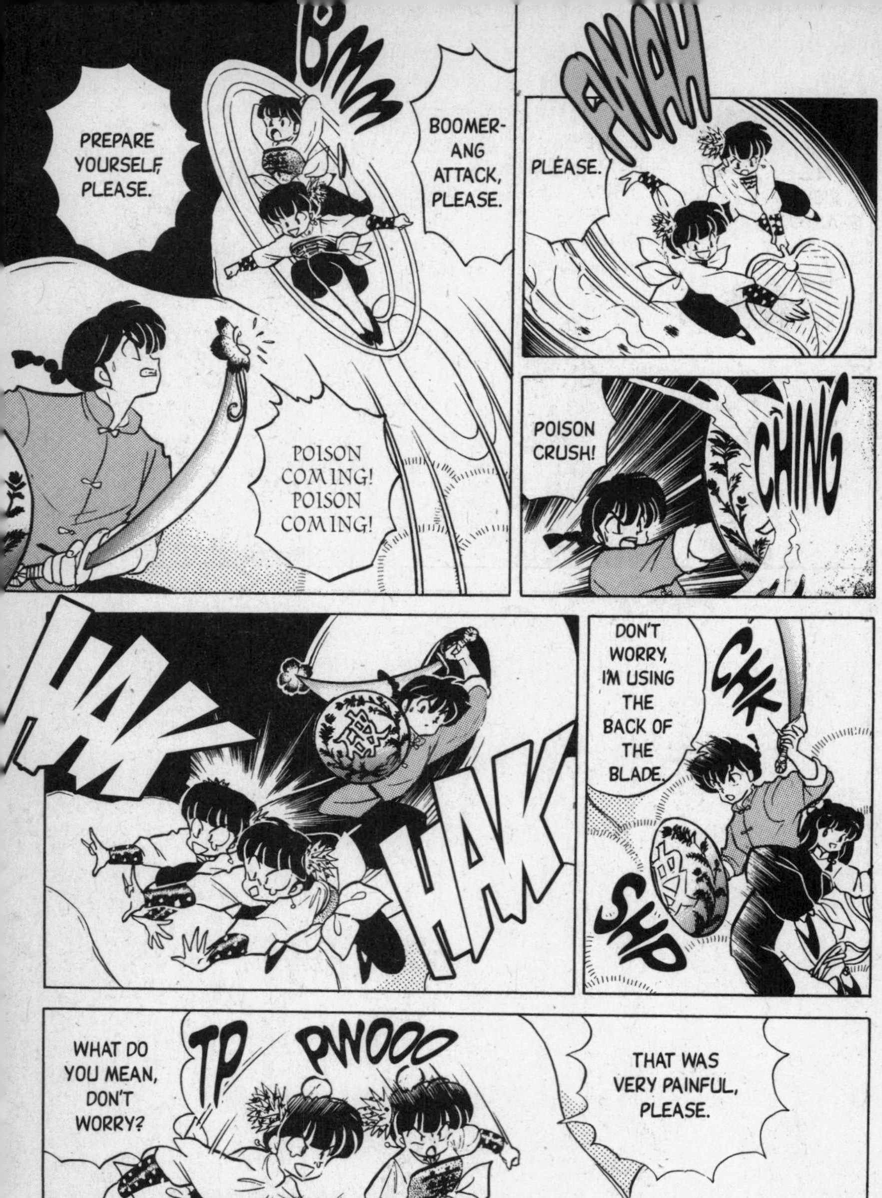
PREPARE YOURSELF, PLEASE.
BMM
BOOMER-ANG ATTACK, PLEASE.
POISON COMING! POISON COMING!
PWAH
PLEASE.
POISON CRUSH!
CHING
HAK
HAK
DON'T WORRY, I'M USING THE BACK OF THE BLADE.
CHK
SHP
WHAT DO YOU MEAN, DON'T WORRY?
TP
PWOOO
THAT WAS VERY PAINFUL, PLEASE.

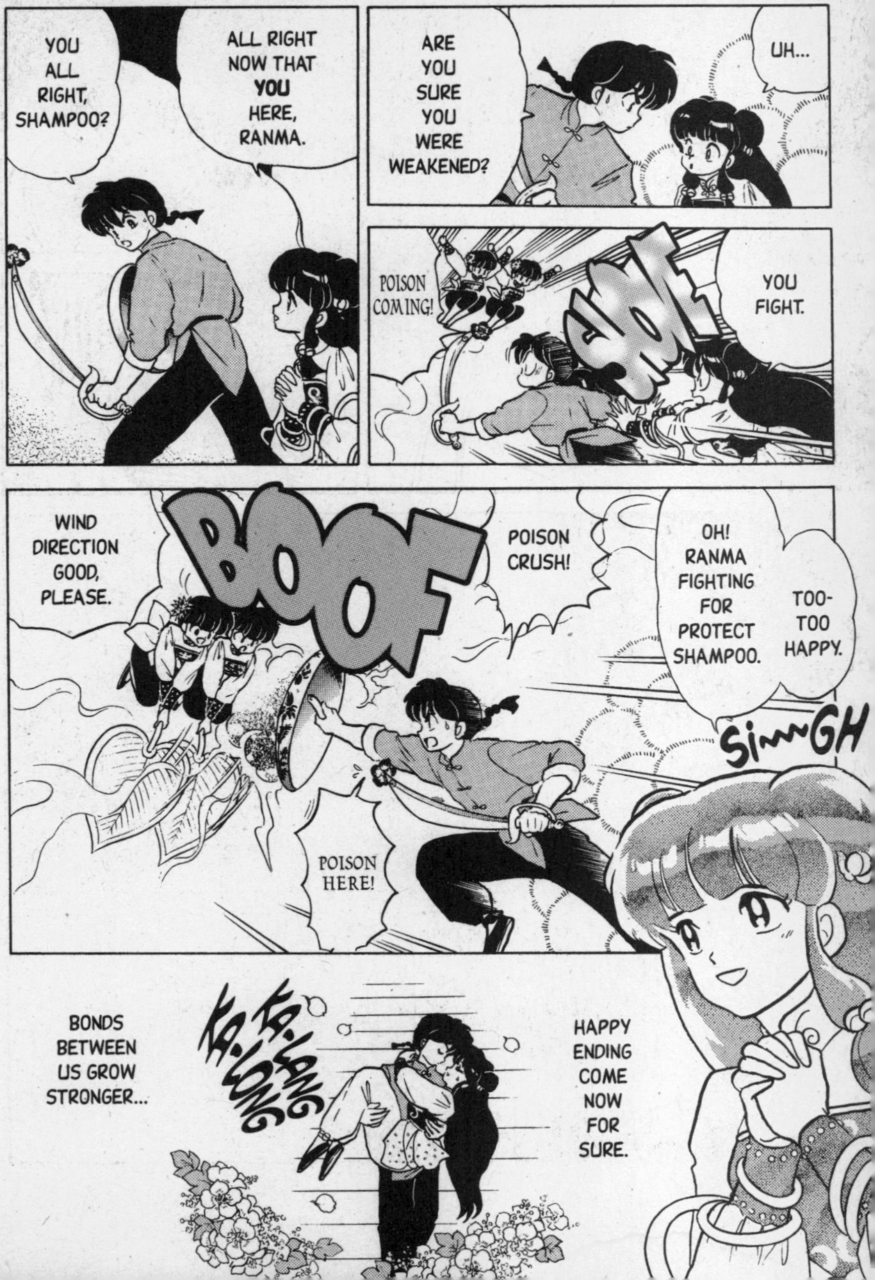
YOU ALL RIGHT, SHAMPOO?
ALL RIGHT NOW THAT **YOU** HERE, RANMA.
ARE YOU SURE YOU WERE WEAKENED?
UH...
POISON COMING!
YOU FIGHT.
WIND DIRECTION GOOD, PLEASE.
BOOF
POISON CRUSH!
OH! RANMA FIGHTING FOR PROTECT SHAMPOO.
TOO-TOO HAPPY.
POISON HERE!
Si~~GH
BONDS BETWEEN US GROW STRONGER...
KA-LANG
KA-LONG
HAPPY ENDING COME NOW FOR SURE.

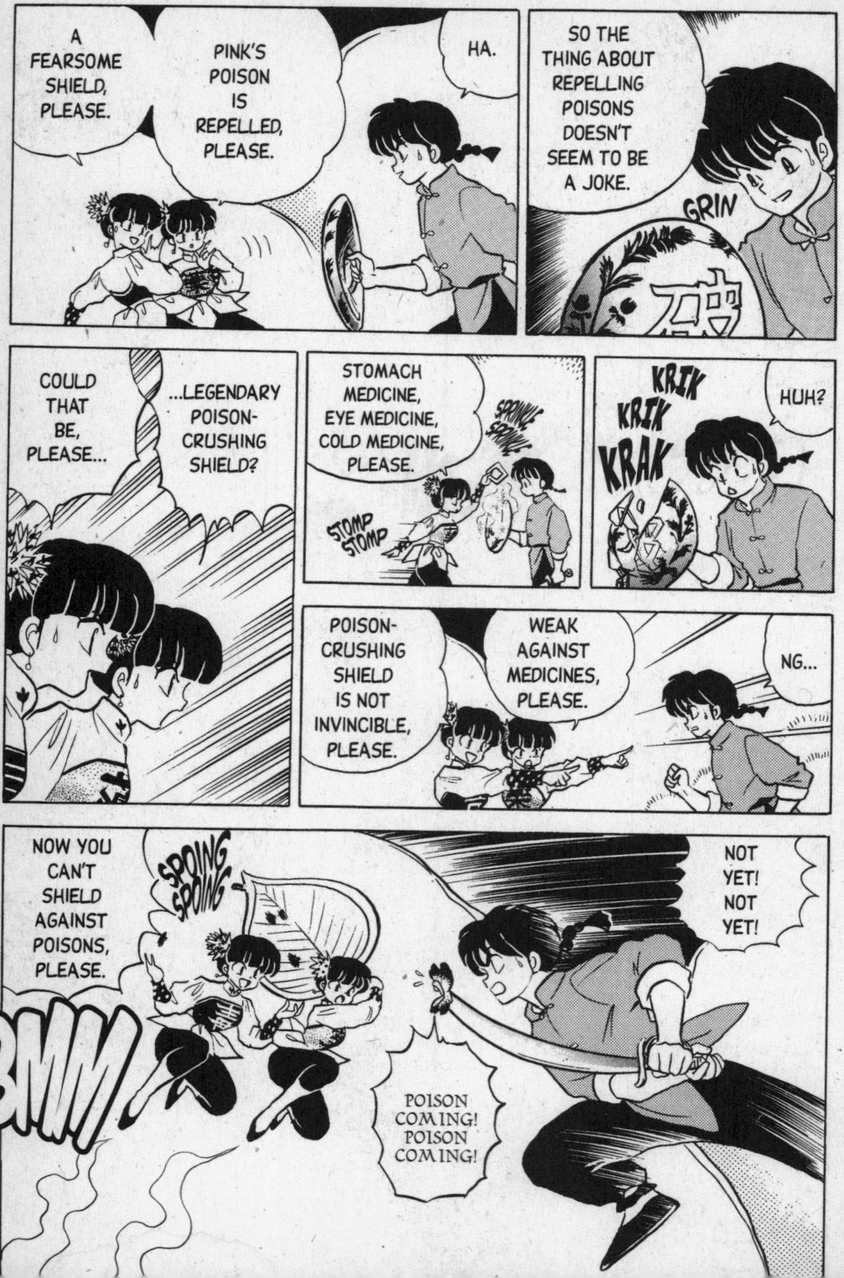
A FEARSOME SHIELD, PLEASE.
PINK'S POISON IS REPELLED, PLEASE.
HA.
SO THE THING ABOUT REPELLING POISONS DOESN'T SEEM TO BE A JOKE.
GRIN
COULD THAT BE, PLEASE...
...LEGENDARY POISON-CRUSHING SHIELD?
STOMACH MEDICINE, EYE MEDICINE, COLD MEDICINE, PLEASE.
STOMP STOMP
KRIK KRIK KRAK
HUH?
POISON-CRUSHING SHIELD IS NOT INVINCIBLE, PLEASE.
WEAK AGAINST MEDICINES, PLEASE.
NG...
NOW YOU CAN'T SHIELD AGAINST POISONS, PLEASE.
SPOING SPOING
NOT YET! NOT YET!
BMM
POISON COMING! POISON COMING!

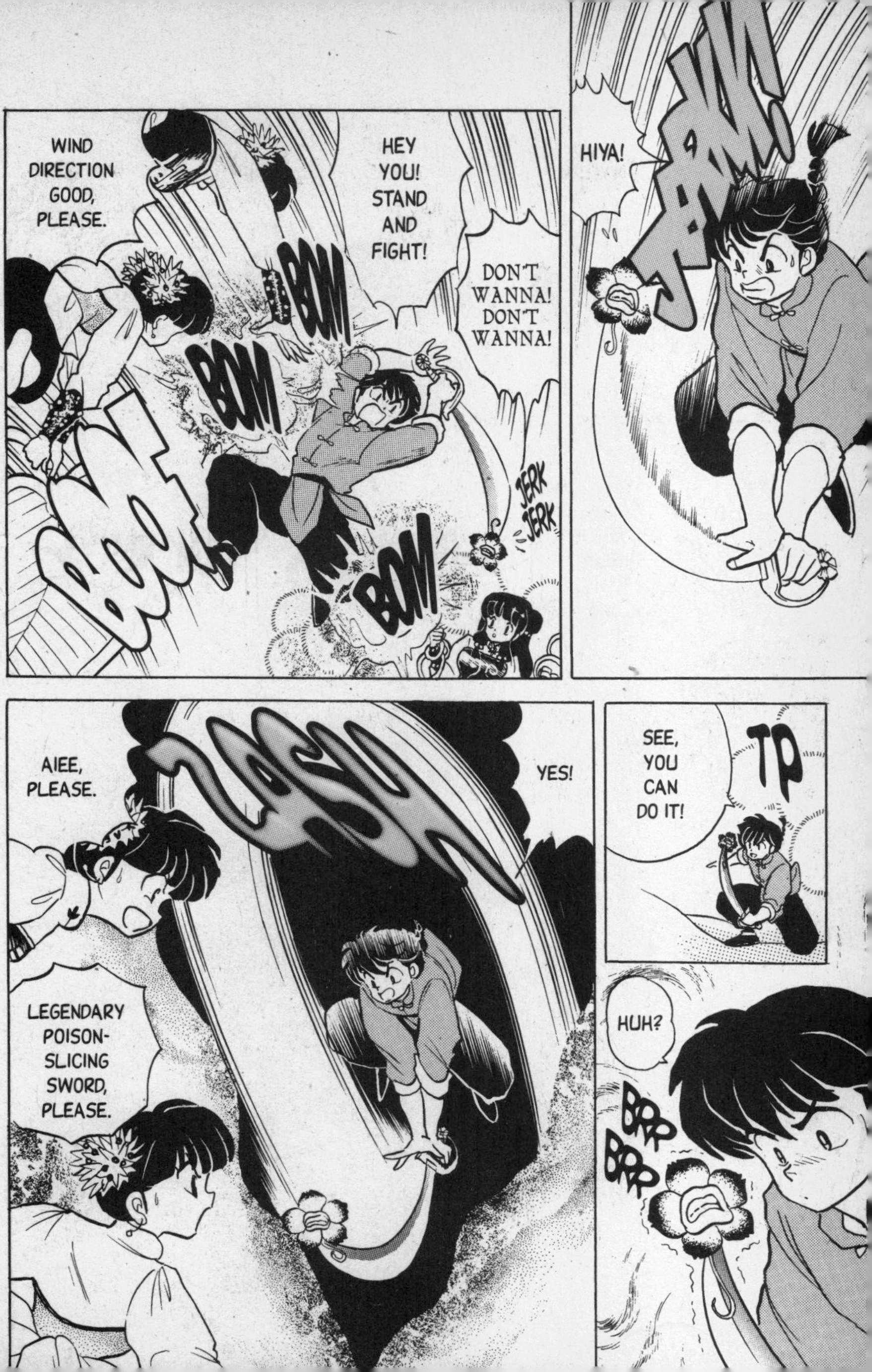
WIND DIRECTION GOOD, PLEASE.
HEY YOU! STAND AND FIGHT!
BOM
BOM
BOM
DON'T WANNA! DON'T WANNA!
JERK JERK
BOM
HIYA!
AIEE, PLEASE.
YES!
LEGENDARY POISON-SLICING SWORD, PLEASE.
SEE, YOU CAN DO IT!
TP
HUH?
BRRR BRRR

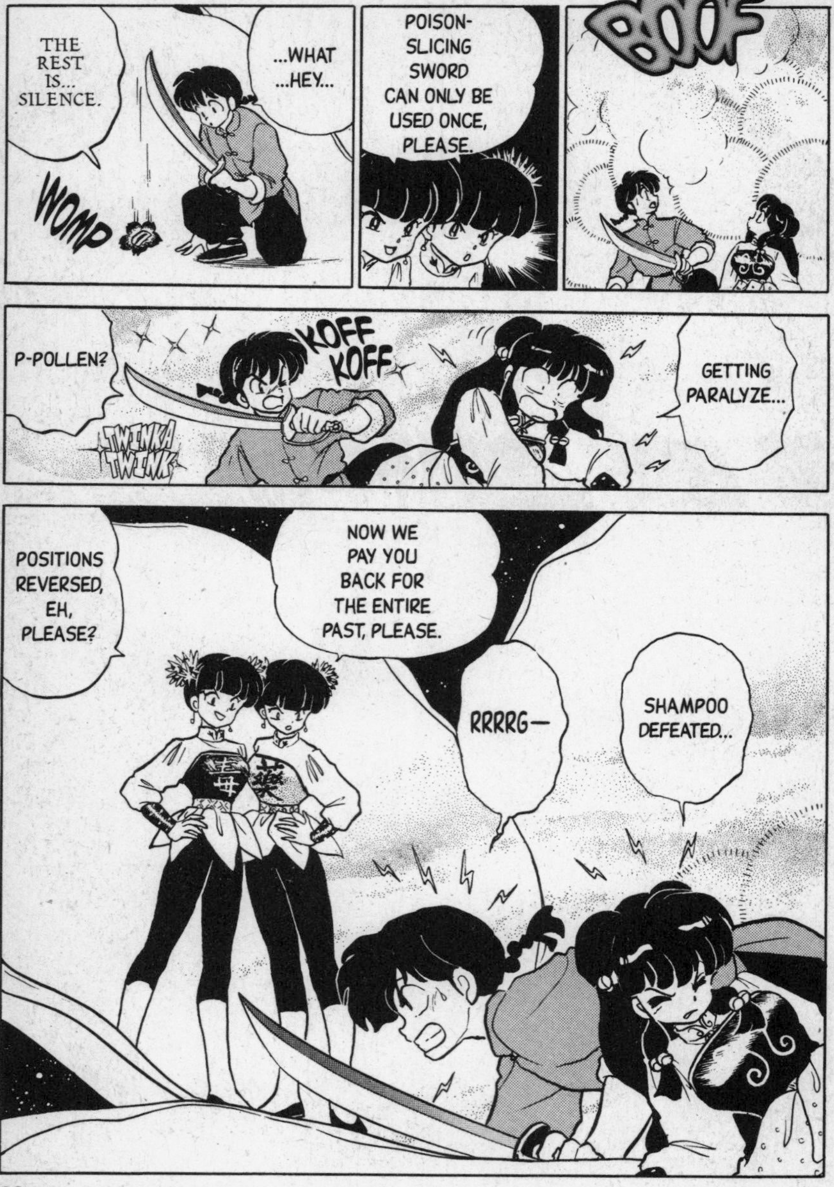
THE REST IS... SILENCE.
...WHAT ...HEY...
WOMP
POISON-SLICING SWORD CAN ONLY BE USED ONCE, PLEASE.
BOOF
P-POLLEN?
TWINKA TWINK
KOFF KOFF
GETTING PARALYZE...
POSITIONS REVERSED, EH, PLEASE?
NOW WE PAY YOU BACK FOR THE ENTIRE PAST, PLEASE.
RRRRG—
SHAMPOO DEFEATED...

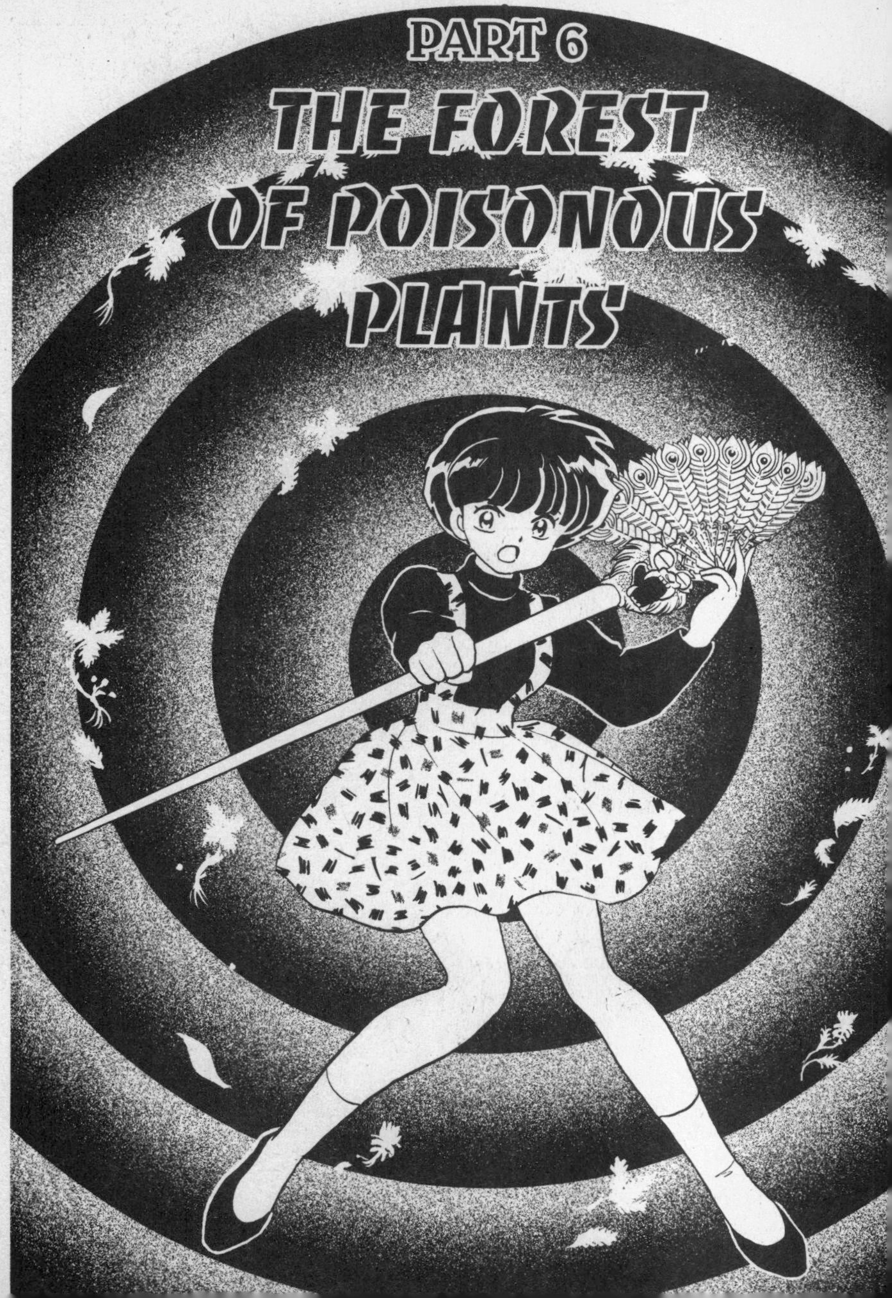
PART 6
THE FOREST OF POISONOUS PLANTS

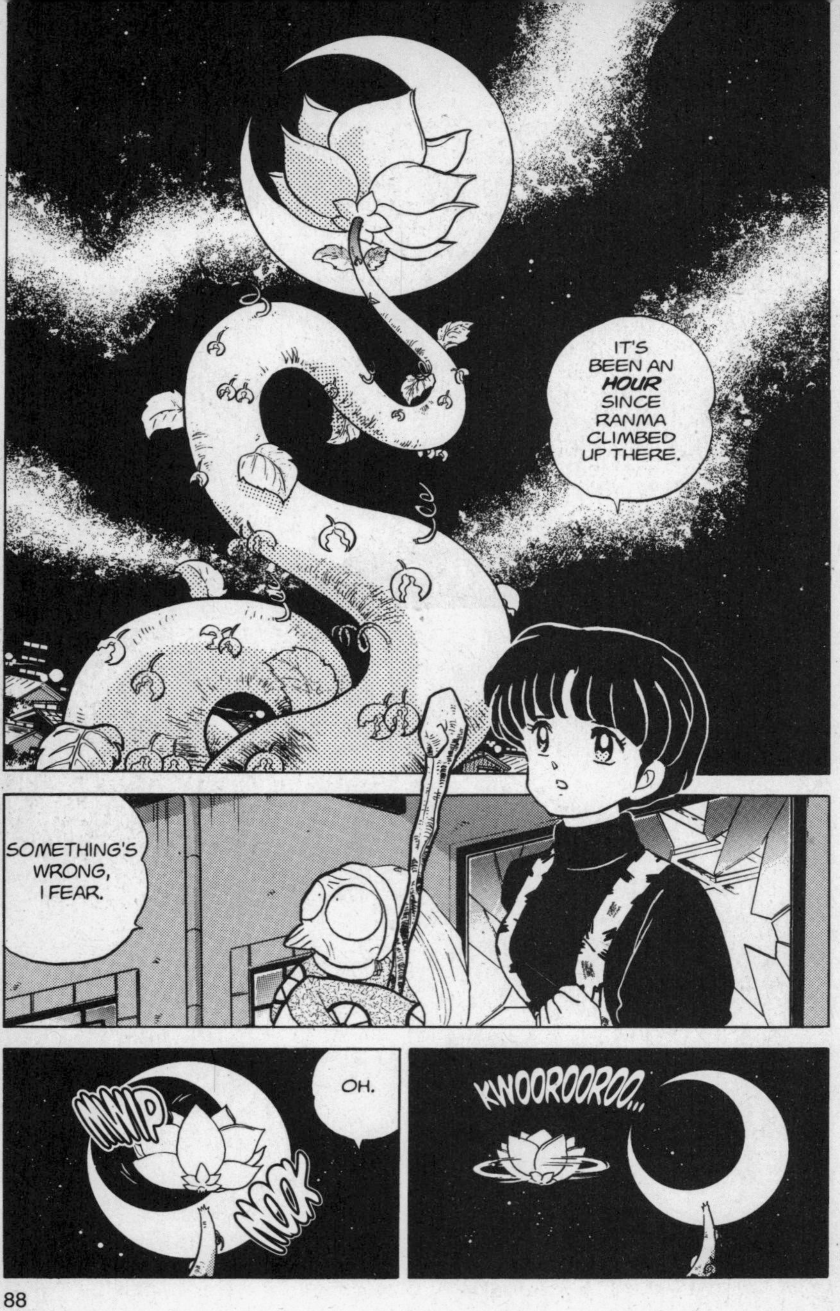
IT'S BEEN AN **HOUR** SINCE RANMA CLIMBED UP THERE.
SOMETHING'S WRONG, I FEAR.
MMIP
OH.
MOOK
KWOOROOROO...

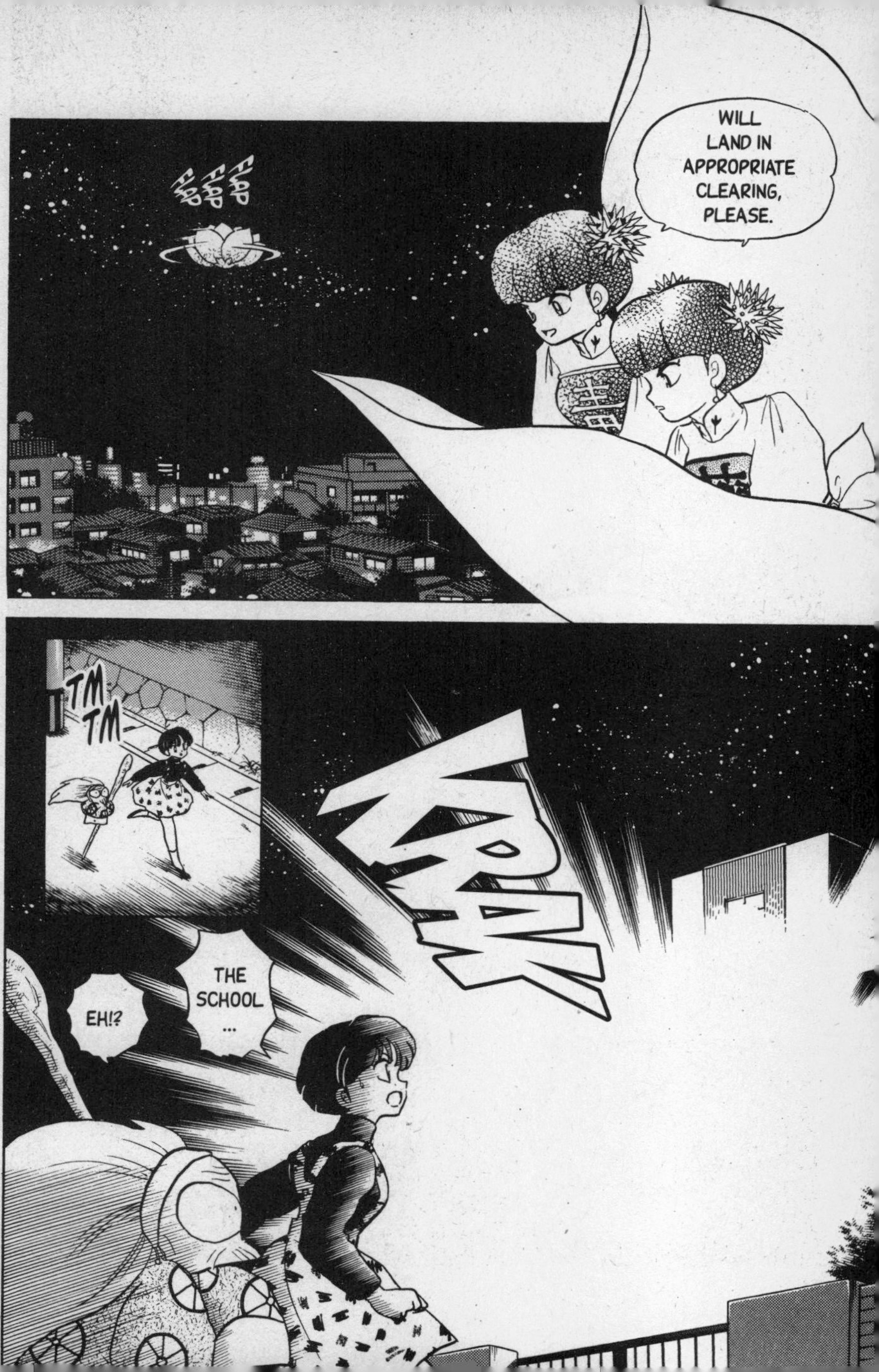

WILL LAND IN APPROPRIATE CLEARING, PLEASE.
TM TM
EH!?
THE SCHOOL ...

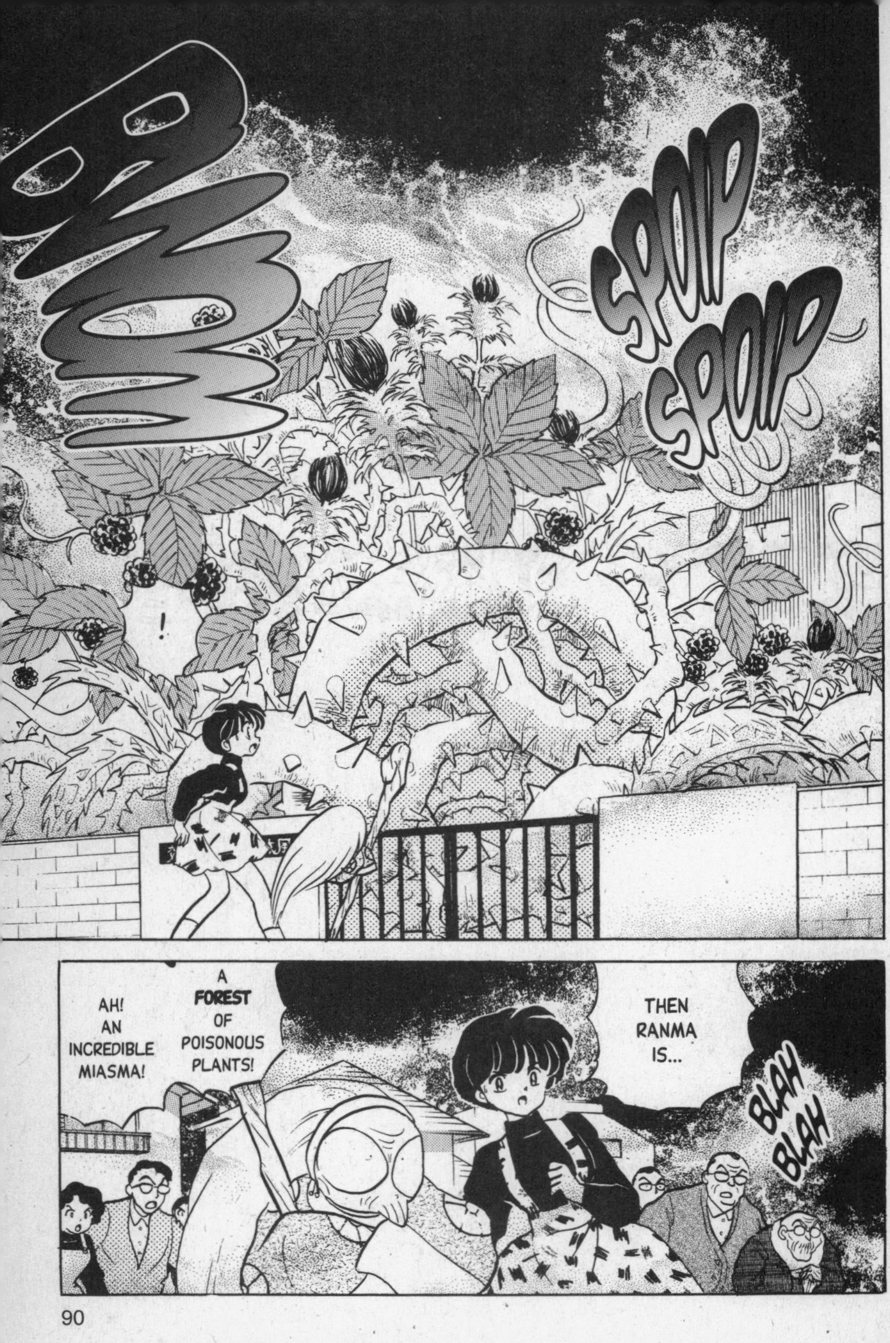
BWOM
!
SPOIP SPOIP
AH! AN INCREDIBLE MIASMA!
A **FOREST** OF POISONOUS PLANTS!
THEN RANMA IS...
BLAH BLAH

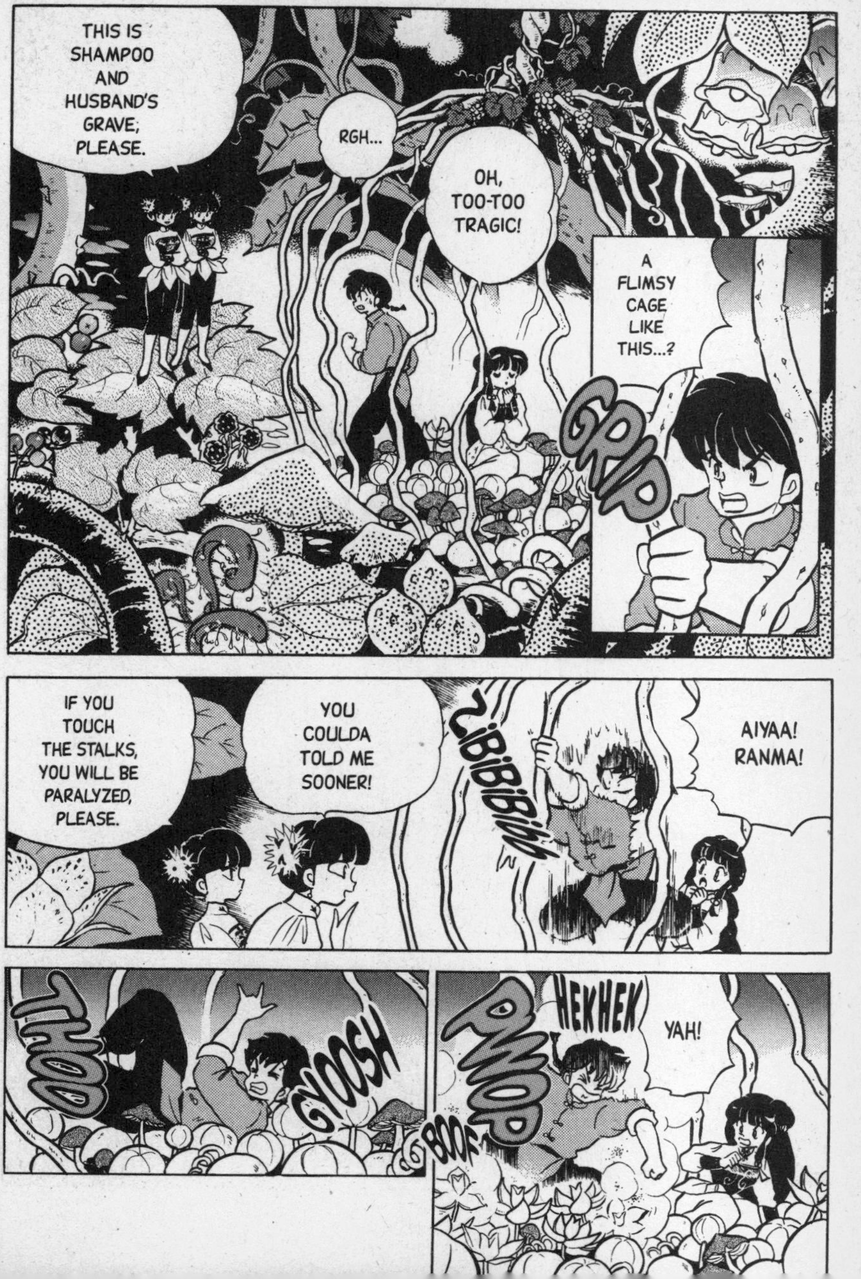
THIS IS SHAMPOO AND HUSBAND'S GRAVE; PLEASE.
RGH...
OH, TOO-TOO TRAGIC!
A FLIMSY CAGE LIKE THIS...?
GRIP
IF YOU TOUCH THE STALKS, YOU WILL BE PARALYZED, PLEASE.
YOU COULDA TOLD ME SOONER!
ZIBIBIBIBIN
AIYAA! RANMA!
THOD
GYOOSH
PWOP
HEKHEK
BOOF
YAH!

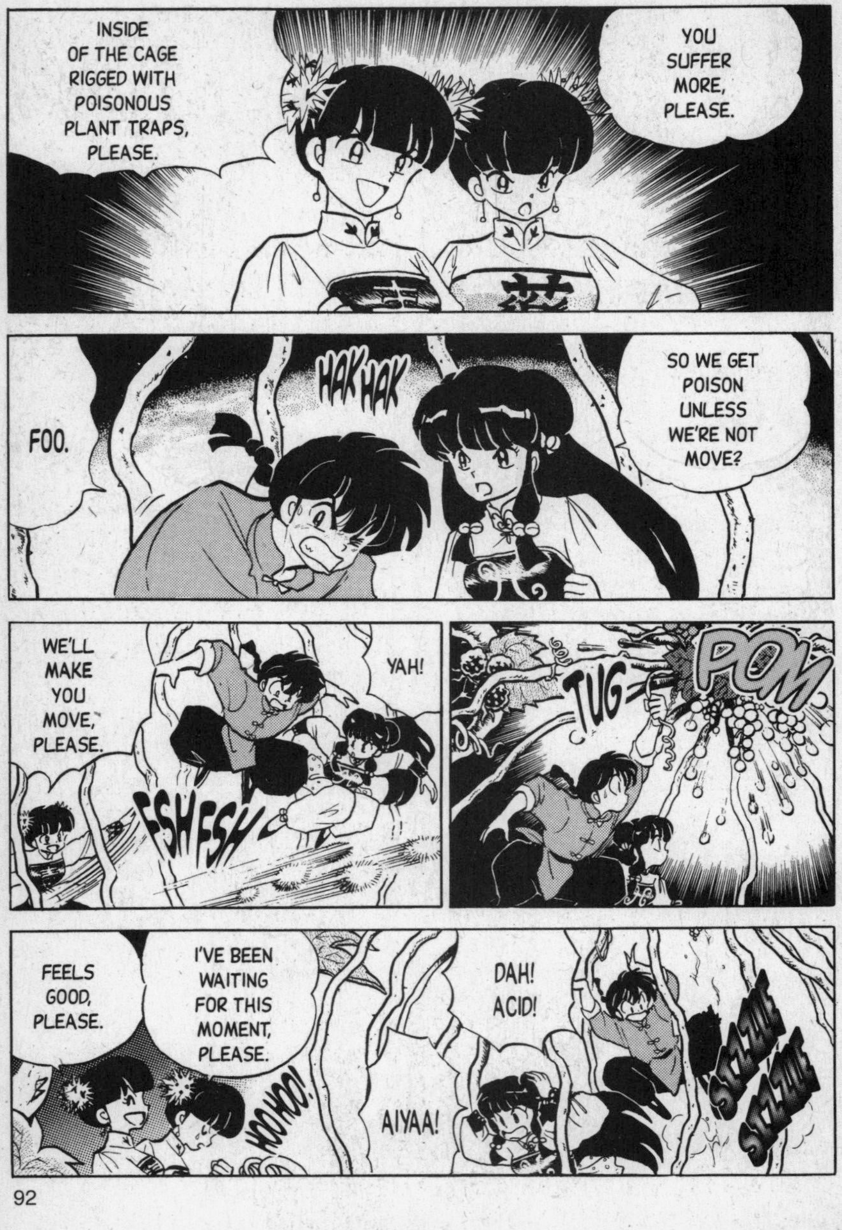
INSIDE OF THE CAGE RIGGED WITH POISONOUS PLANT TRAPS, PLEASE.
YOU SUFFER MORE, PLEASE.
FOO.
HAK HAK
SO WE GET POISON UNLESS WE'RE NOT MOVE?
WE'LL MAKE YOU MOVE, PLEASE.
YAH!
FSH FSH
TUG
POM
FEELS GOOD, PLEASE.
I'VE BEEN WAITING FOR THIS MOMENT, PLEASE.
HOO HOO!
DAH! ACID!
AIYAA!
SIZZLE SIZZLE

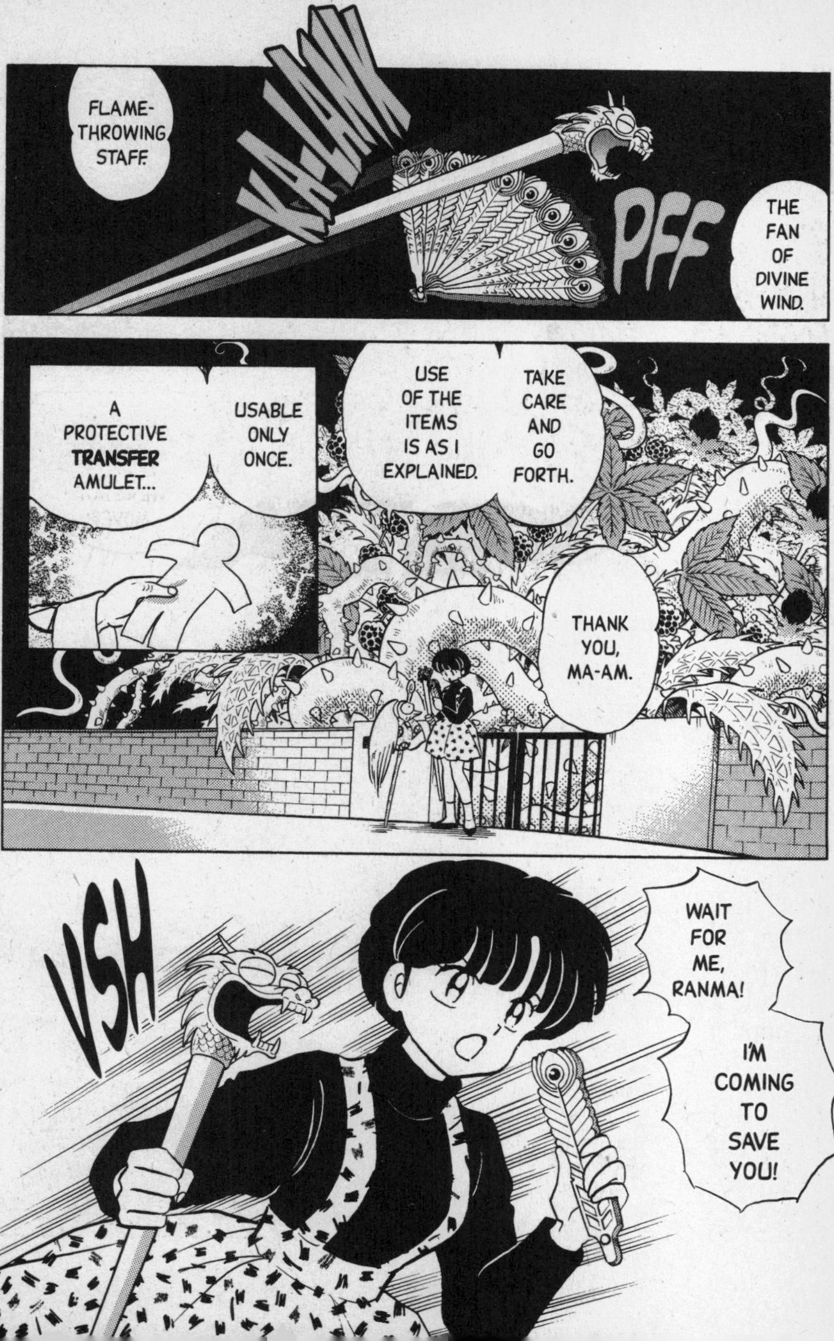
FLAME-THROWING STAFF.
VAPAM
PFF
THE FAN OF DIVINE WIND.
A PROTECTIVE **TRANSFER** AMULET...
USABLE ONLY ONCE.
USE OF THE ITEMS IS AS I EXPLAINED.
TAKE CARE AND GO FORTH.
THANK YOU, MA-AM.
VSH
WAIT FOR ME, RANMA!
I'M COMING TO SAVE YOU!

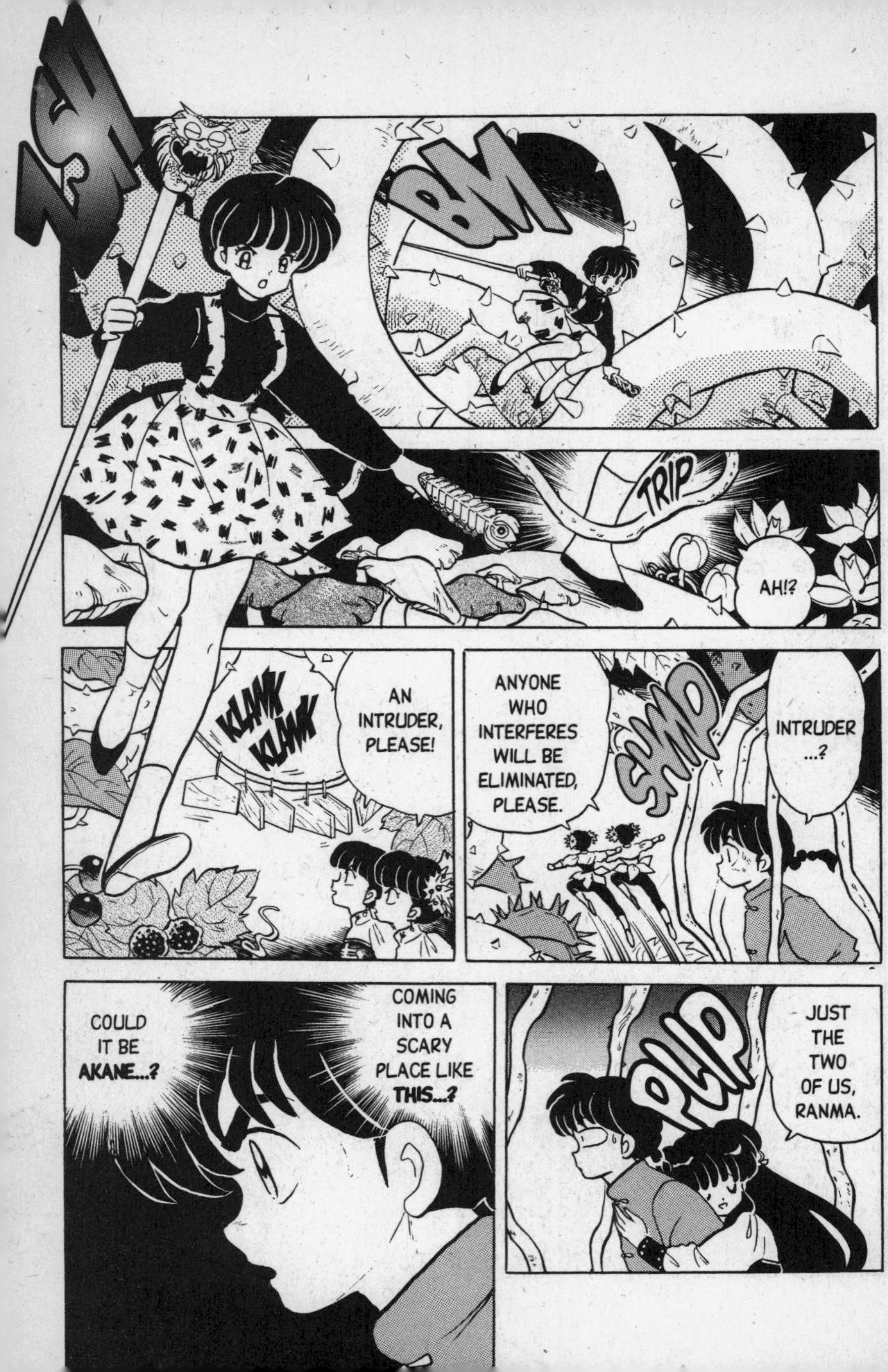
ZISH
BAM
TRIP
AH!?
KLANK KLANK
AN INTRUDER, PLEASE!
ANYONE WHO INTERFERES WILL BE ELIMINATED, PLEASE.
SWMP
INTRUDER ...?
COULD IT BE AKANE...?
COMING INTO A SCARY PLACE LIKE THIS...?
PLIP
JUST THE TWO OF US, RANMA.

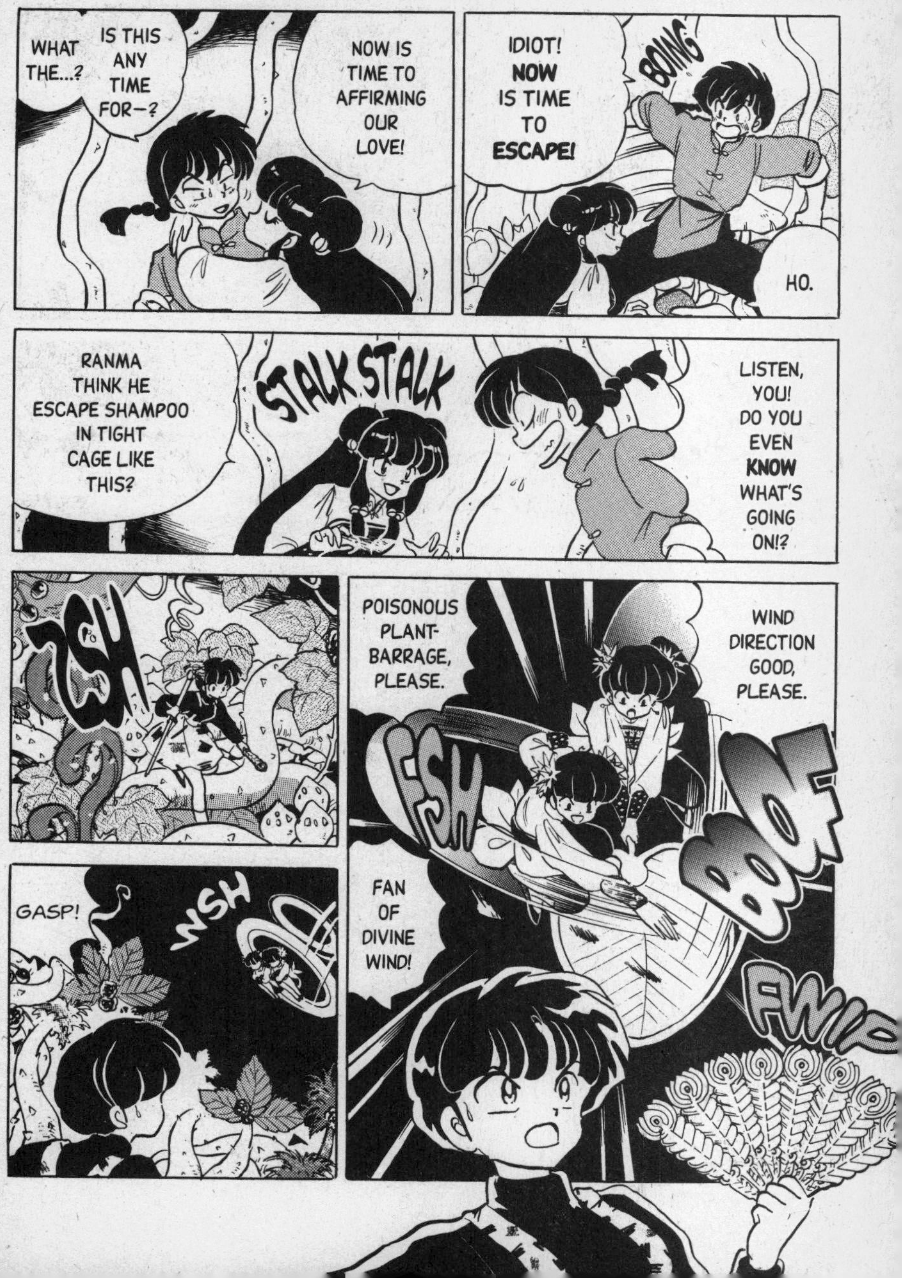
WHAT THE...?
IS THIS ANY TIME FOR—?
NOW IS TIME TO AFFIRMING OUR LOVE!
IDIOT! **NOW** IS TIME TO **ESCAPE!**
BOING
HO.
RANMA THINK HE ESCAPE SHAMPOO IN TIGHT CAGE LIKE THIS?
STALK STALK
LISTEN, YOU! DO YOU EVEN **KNOW** WHAT'S GOING ON!?
ZSH
GASP!
WSH
POISONOUS PLANT-BARRAGE, PLEASE.
WIND DIRECTION GOOD, PLEASE.
FISH
BOOF
FAN OF DIVINE WIND!
FWIP

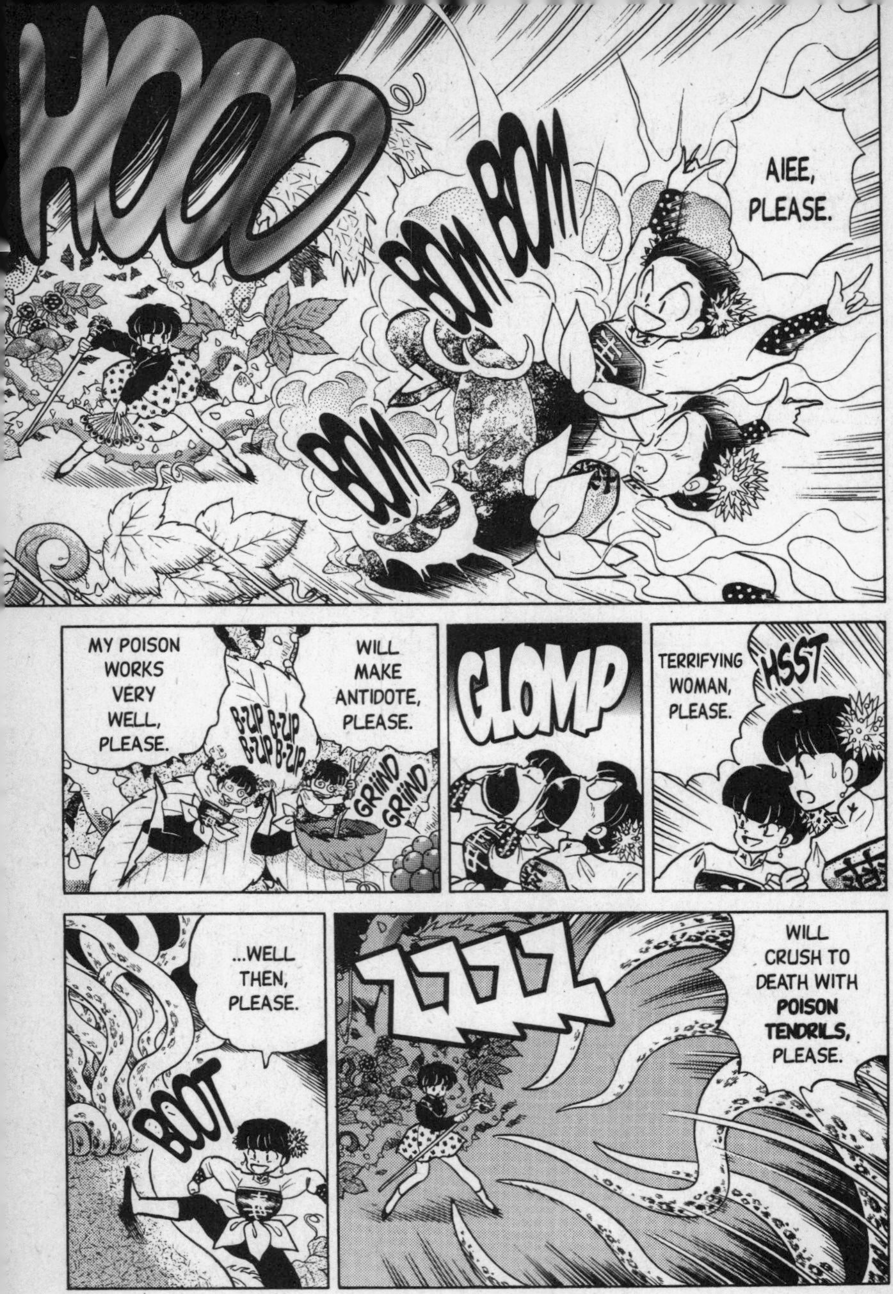
HOOO
BOM BOM BOM BOM
AIEE, PLEASE.
MY POISON WORKS VERY WELL, PLEASE.
WILL MAKE ANTIDOTE, PLEASE.
B-ZIP B-ZIP B-ZIP B-ZIP
GRIIND GRIIND
GLOMP
TERRIFYING WOMAN, PLEASE.
HSST
...WELL THEN, PLEASE.
BOOT
ZZZZ
WILL CRUSH TO DEATH WITH **POISON TENDRILS**, PLEASE.

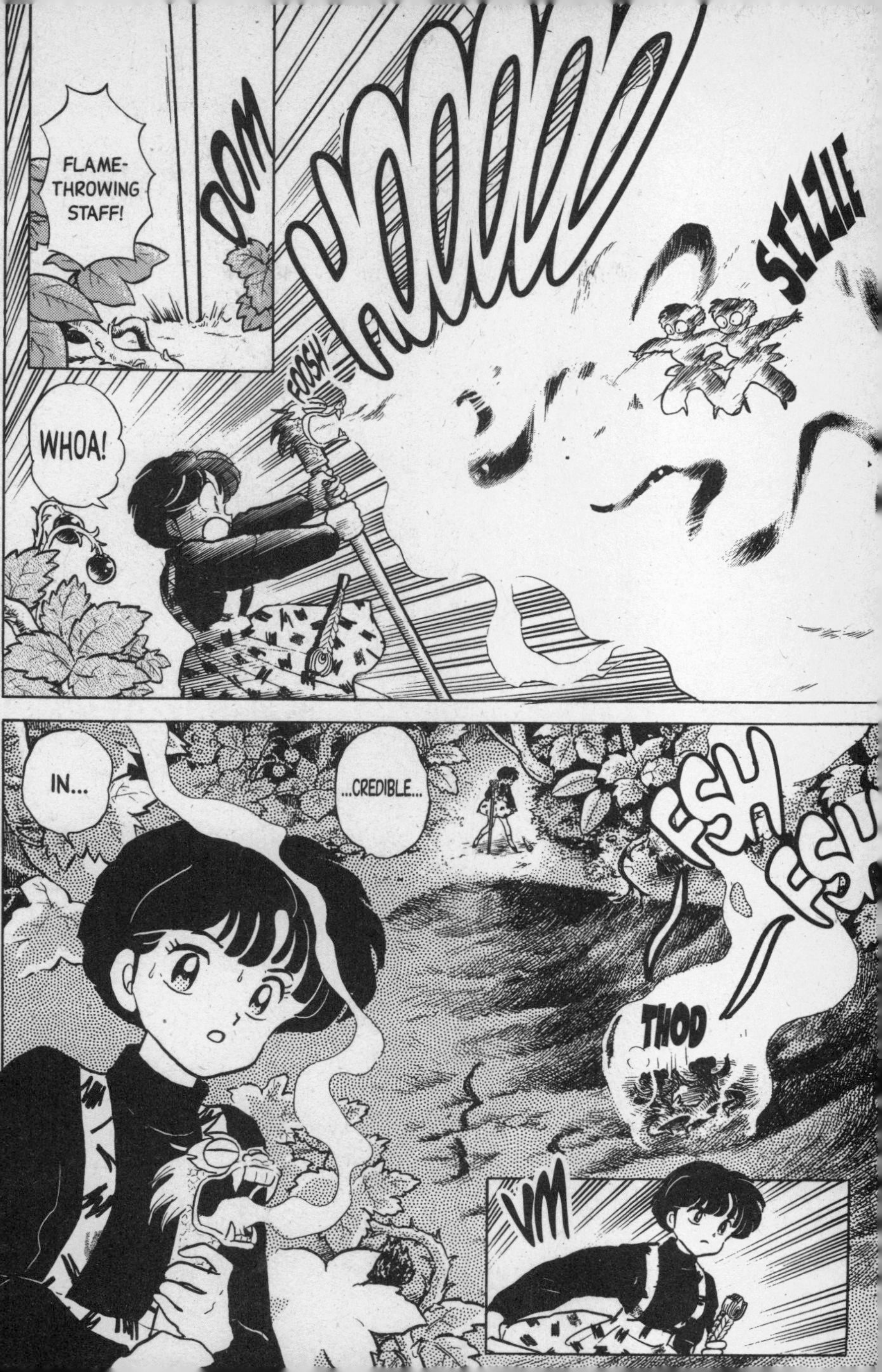
FLAME-THROWING STAFF!
DOM
FOOSH
SIZZLE
WHOA!
IN...
...CREDIBLE...
FSSH
FSSH
THOD
VM

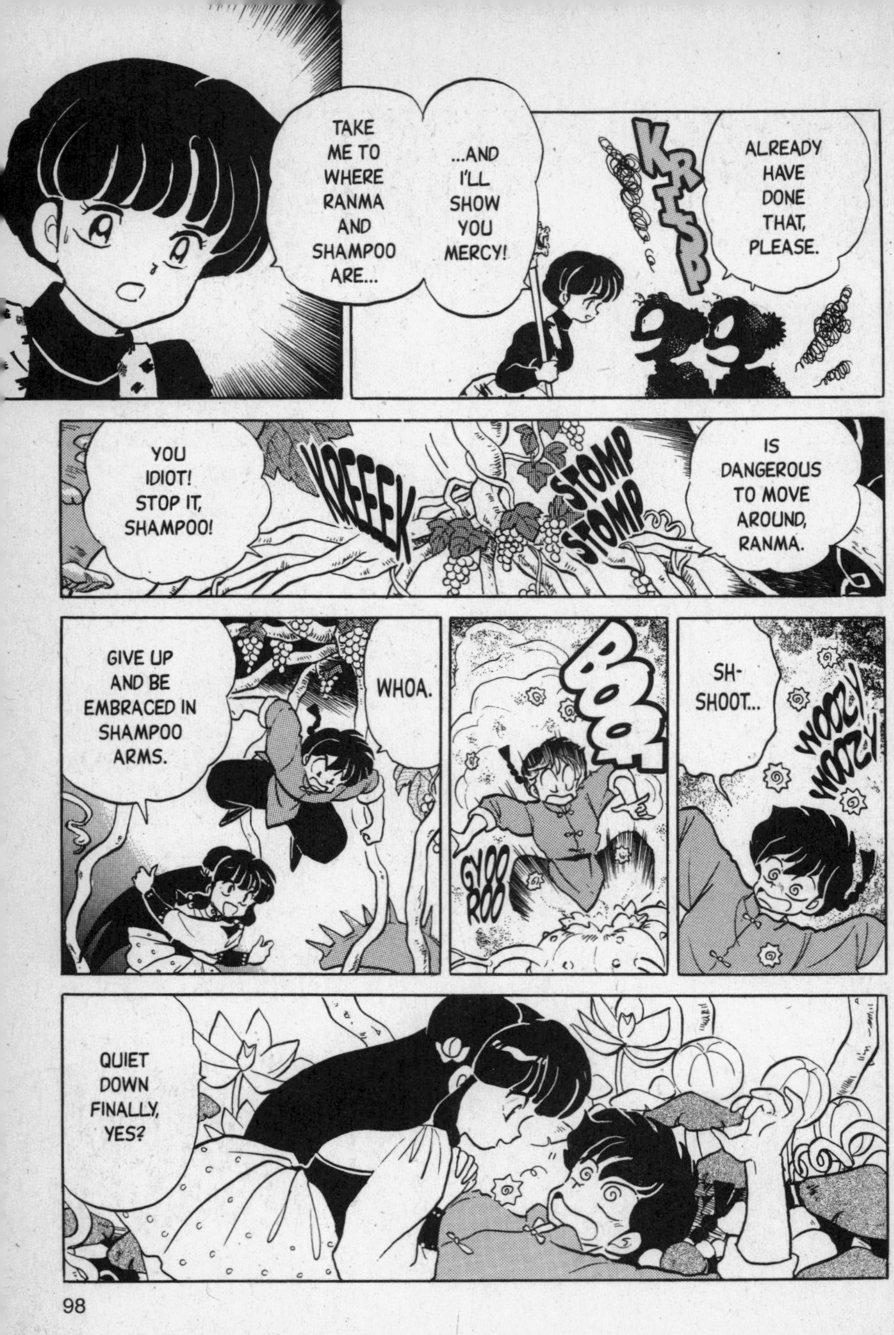
TAKE ME TO WHERE RANMA AND SHAMPOO ARE...
...AND I'LL SHOW YOU MERCY!
KRISP
ALREADY HAVE DONE THAT, PLEASE.
YOU IDIOT! STOP IT, SHAMPOO!
KREEEK
STOMP STOMP
IS DANGEROUS TO MOVE AROUND, RANMA.
GIVE UP AND BE EMBRACED IN SHAMPOO ARMS.
WHOA.
BOOOM
GYOO ROO
SH-SHOOT...
WOOZY WOOZY
QUIET DOWN FINALLY, YES?

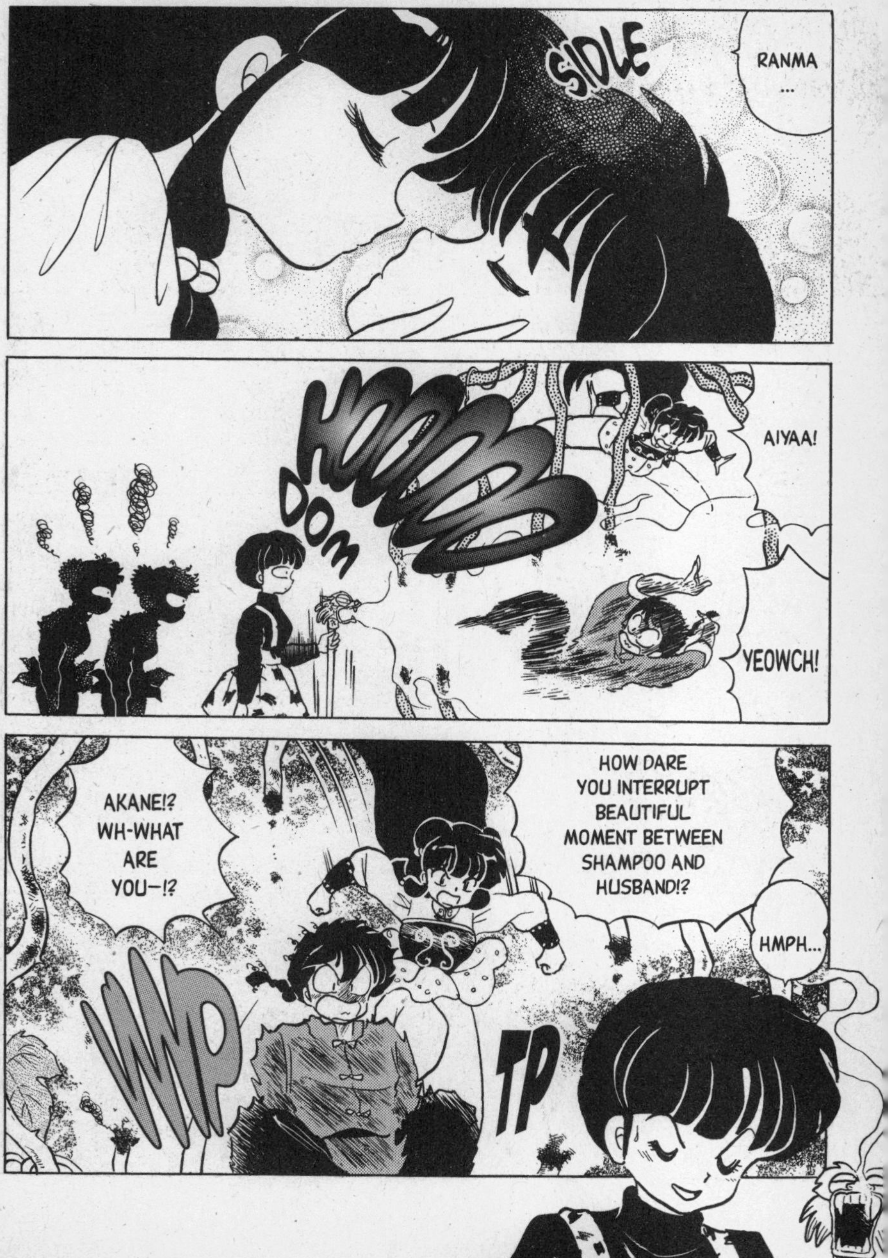
SIDLE
RANMA ...
HOOOM
DOM
AIYAA!
YEOWCH!
AKANE!? WH-WHAT ARE YOU—!?
HOW DARE YOU INTERRUPT BEAUTIFUL MOMENT BETWEEN SHAMPOO AND HUSBAND!?
HMPH...
WMP
TP

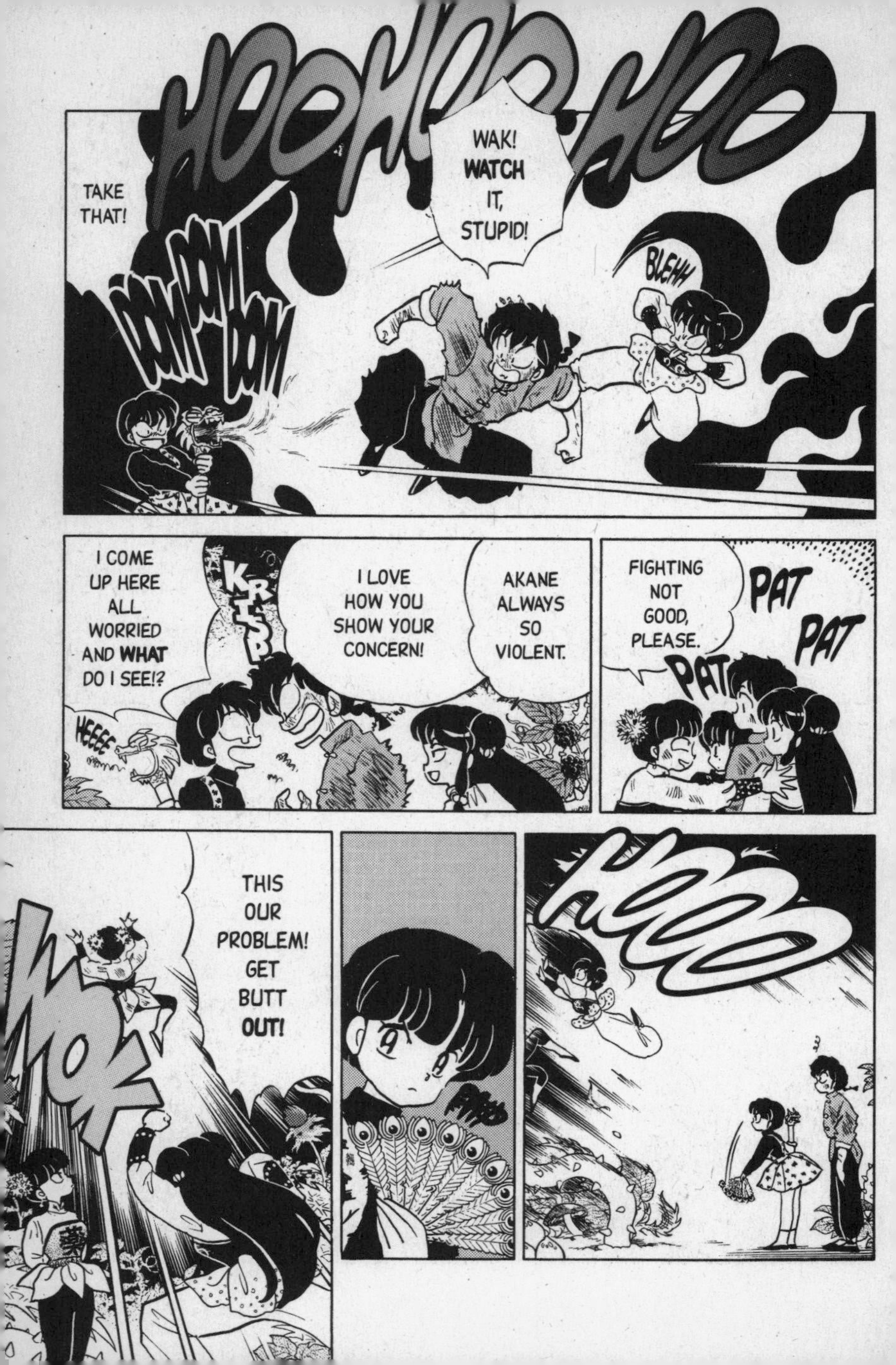
HOOHOO HOO
TAKE THAT!
WAK! WATCH IT, STUPID!
DOM DOM DOM
BLEHH
I COME UP HERE ALL WORRIED AND WHAT DO I SEE!?
HEEEE
KRISP
I LOVE HOW YOU SHOW YOUR CONCERN!
AKANE ALWAYS SO VIOLENT.
FIGHTING NOT GOOD, PLEASE.
PAT PAT PAT
THIS OUR PROBLEM! GET BUTT OUT!
WOK

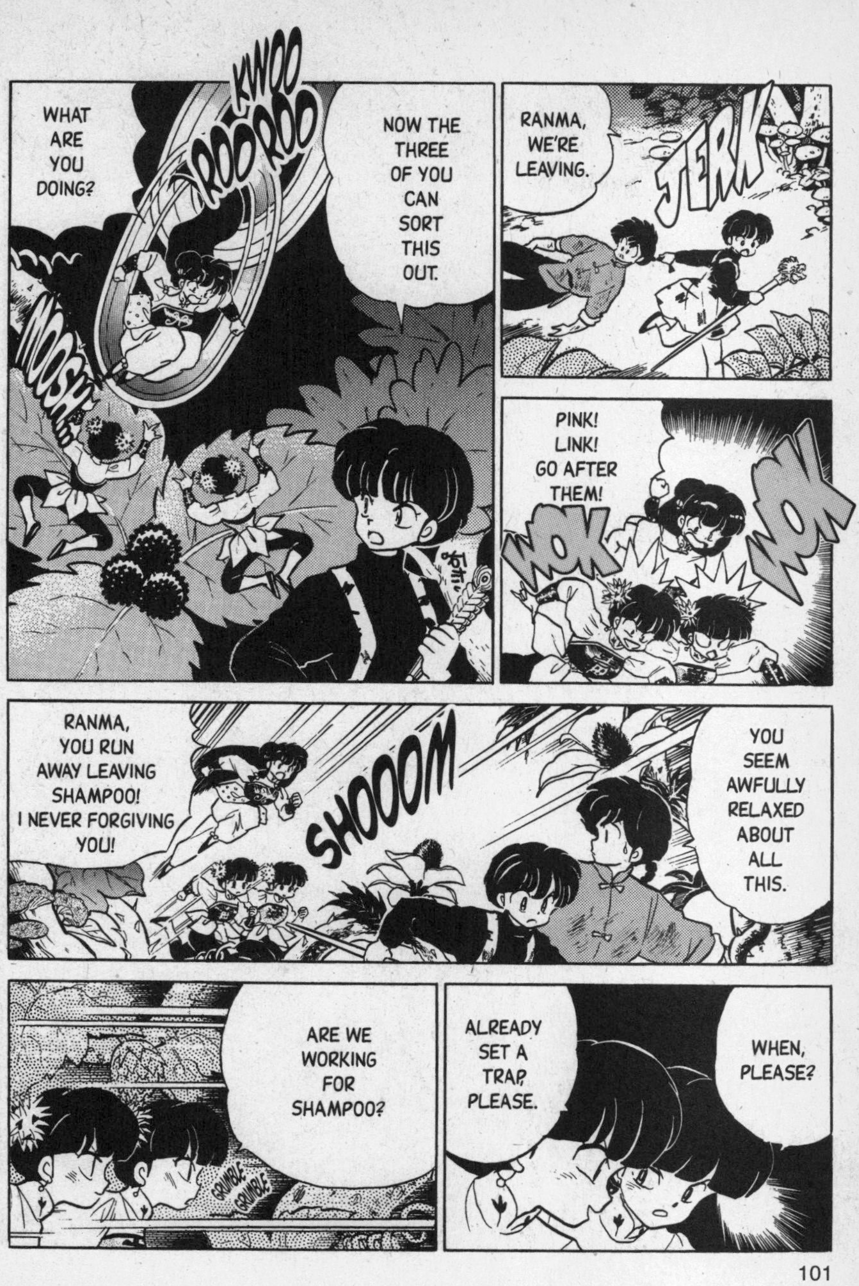
WHAT ARE YOU DOING?
KWOO ROO ROO
MOOSH...
NOW THE THREE OF YOU CAN SORT THIS OUT.
RANMA, WE'RE LEAVING.
JERK
PINK! LINK! GO AFTER THEM!
WOK
WOK
RANMA, YOU RUN AWAY LEAVING SHAMPOO! I NEVER FORGIVING YOU!
SHOOOM
YOU SEEM AWFULLY RELAXED ABOUT ALL THIS.
ARE WE WORKING FOR SHAMPOO?
GRUMBLE GRUMBLE
ALREADY SET A TRAP, PLEASE.
WHEN, PLEASE?

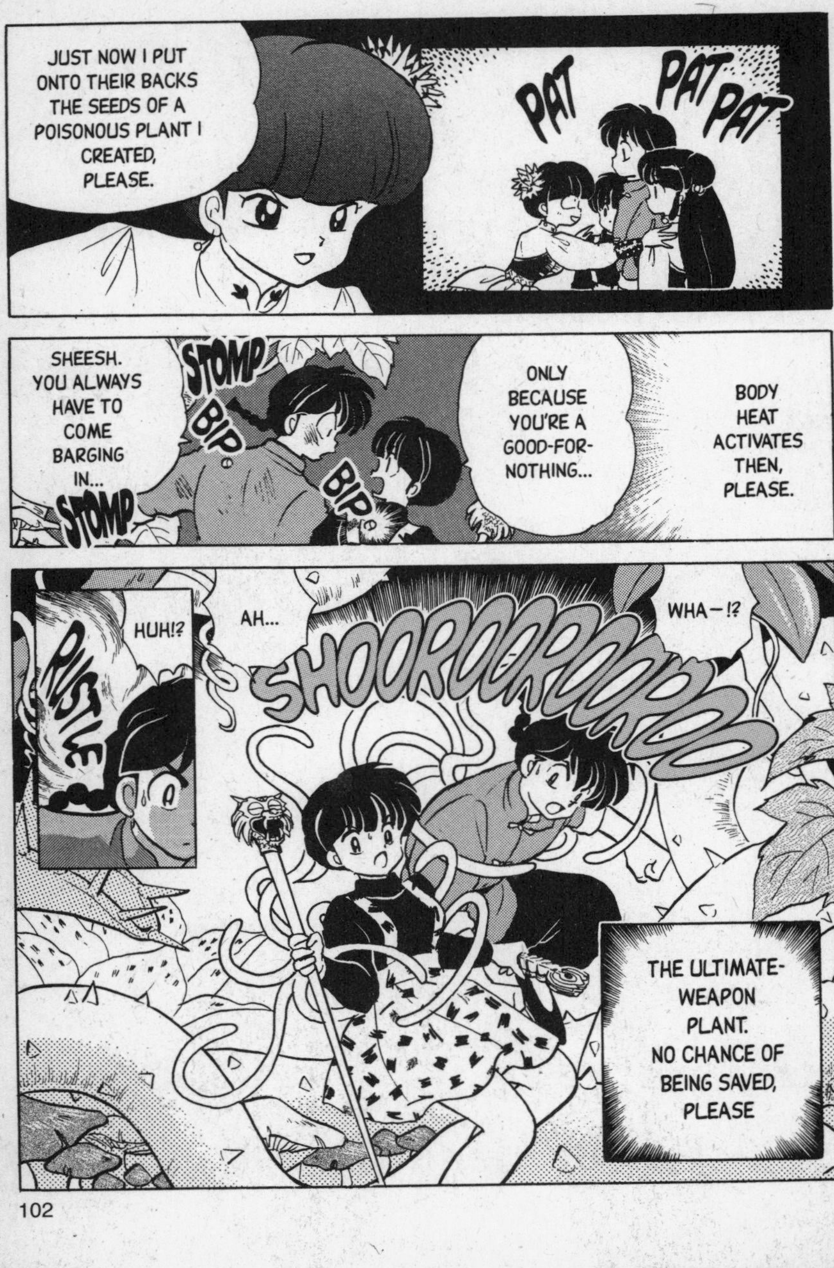
JUST NOW I PUT ONTO THEIR BACKS THE SEEDS OF A POISONOUS PLANT I CREATED, PLEASE.
PAT
PAT PAT PAT
SHEESH. YOU ALWAYS HAVE TO COME BARGING IN...
STOMP
BIP
BIP
STOMP
ONLY BECAUSE YOU'RE A GOOD-FOR-NOTHING...
BODY HEAT ACTIVATES THEN, PLEASE.
HUH!?
RUSTLE
AH...
WHA—!?
THE ULTIMATE-WEAPON PLANT. NO CHANCE OF BEING SAVED, PLEASE

PART 7

THE ULTIMATE MEDICINE

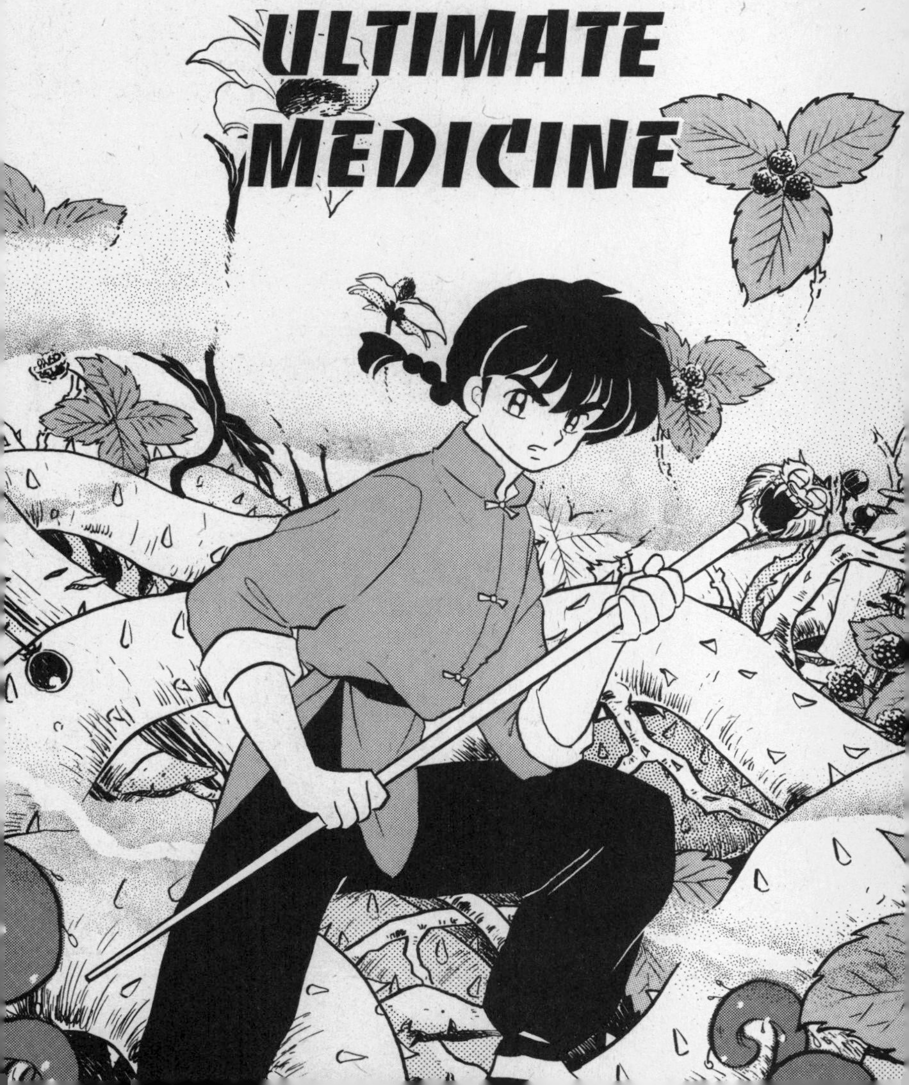

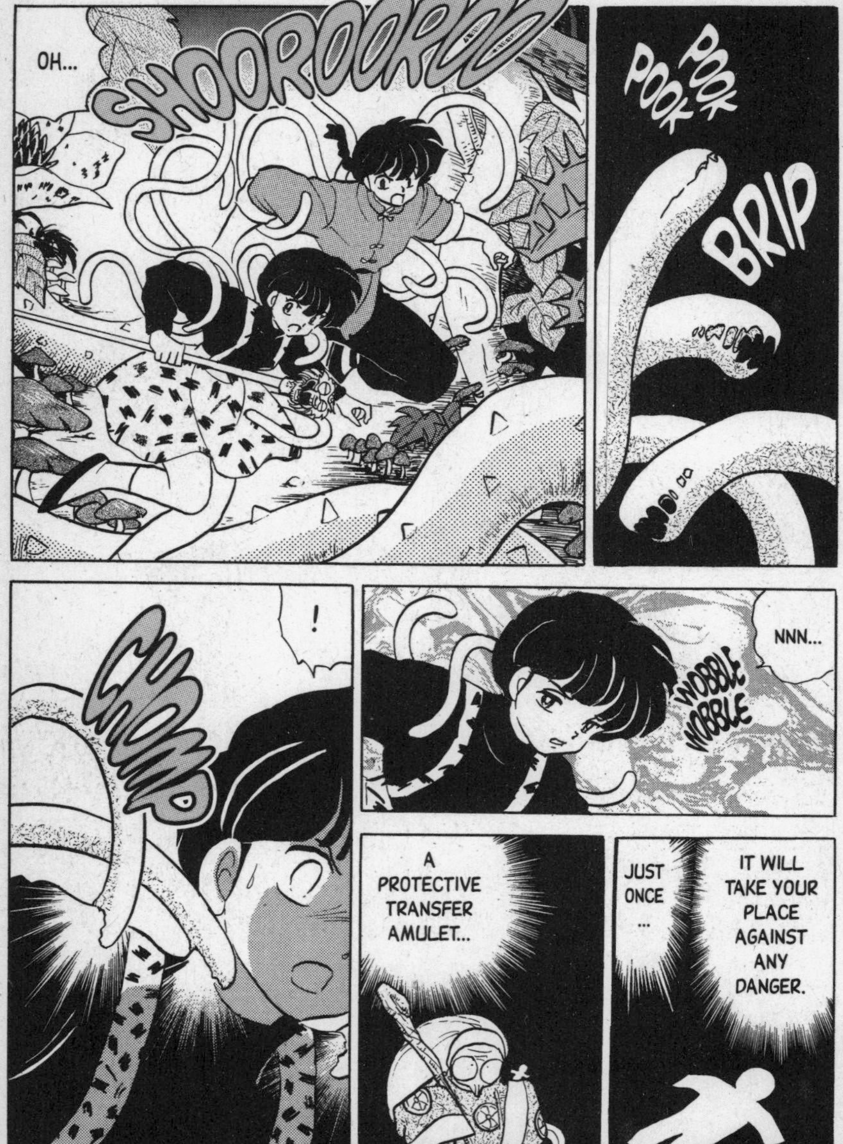
OH...
SHOOROOROO
POOK POOK
BRIP
!
CHOMP
NNN...
WOBBLE WOBBLE
A PROTECTIVE TRANSFER AMULET...
JUST ONCE ...
IT WILL TAKE YOUR PLACE AGAINST ANY DANGER.

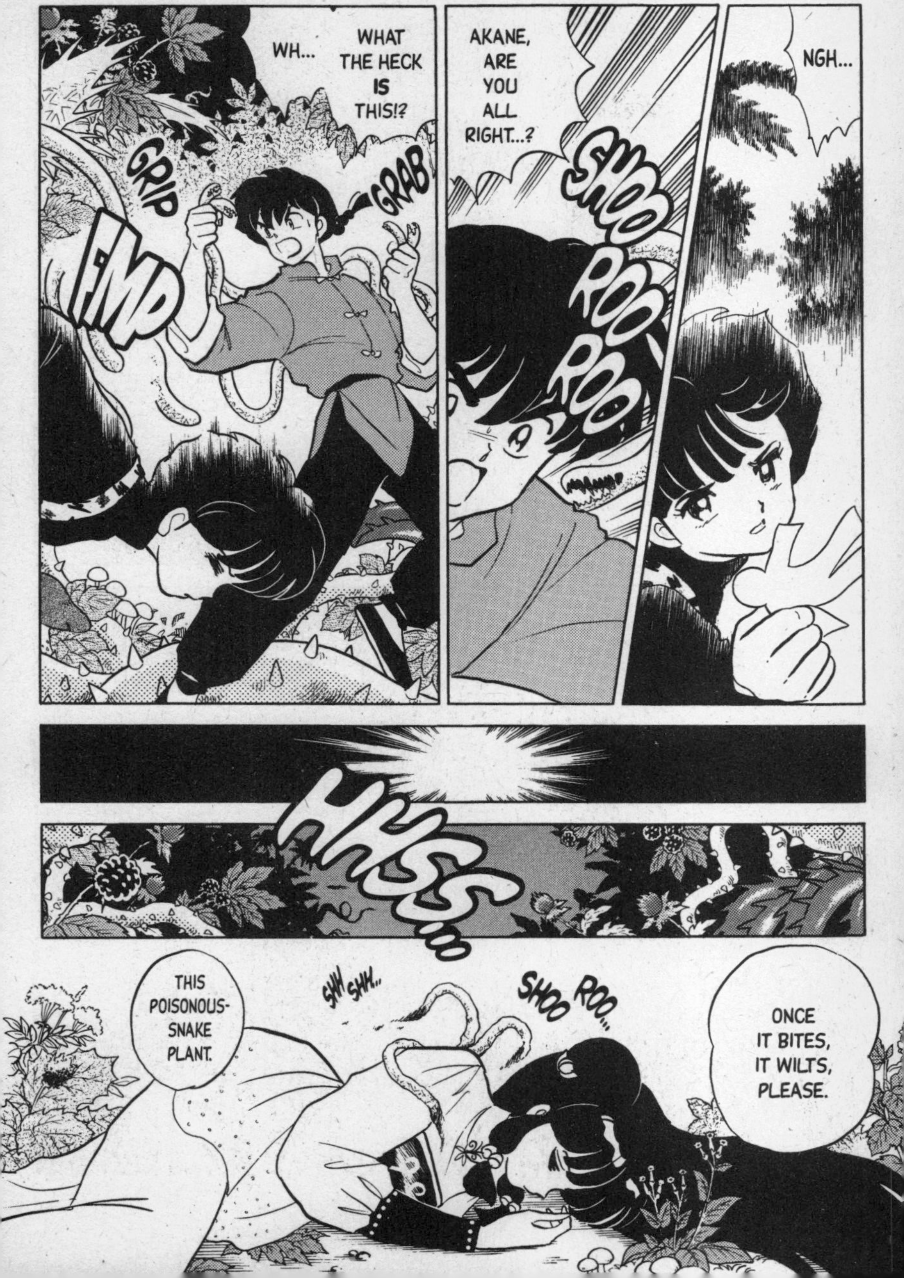
GRIP
FMP
WH...
WHAT THE HECK IS THIS!?
GRAB
AKANE, ARE YOU ALL RIGHT...?
SHOO ROO ROO ROO
NGH...
HISS...
THIS POISONOUS-SNAKE PLANT.
SHH SHH...
SHOO ROO...
ONCE IT BITES, IT WILTS, PLEASE.

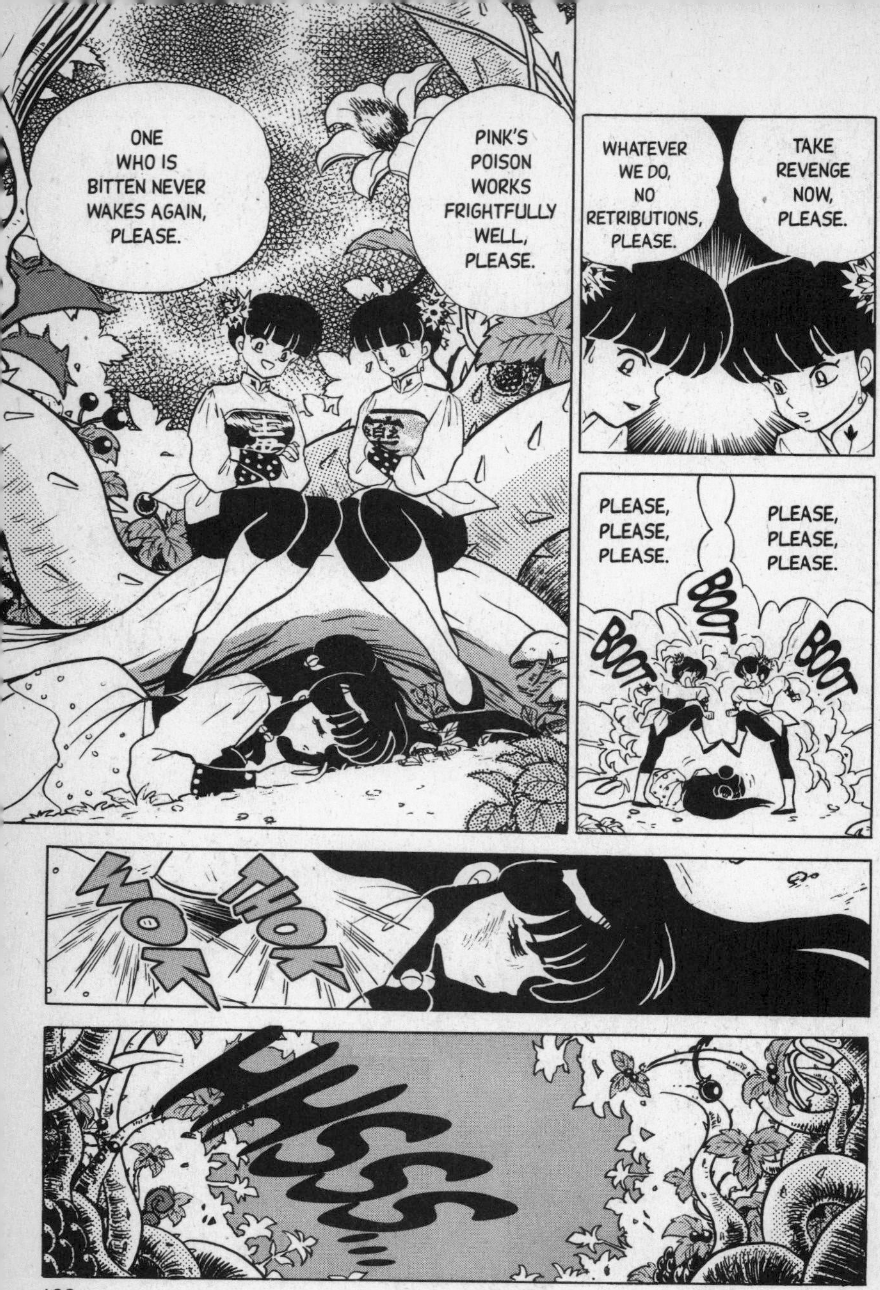
ONE WHO IS BITTEN NEVER WAKES AGAIN, PLEASE.
PINK'S POISON WORKS FRIGHTFULLY WELL, PLEASE.
WHATEVER WE DO, NO RETRIBUTIONS, PLEASE.
TAKE REVENGE NOW, PLEASE.
PLEASE, PLEASE, PLEASE.
PLEASE, PLEASE, PLEASE.
BOOT
BOOT
BOOT
WOK
THOK
HISSS

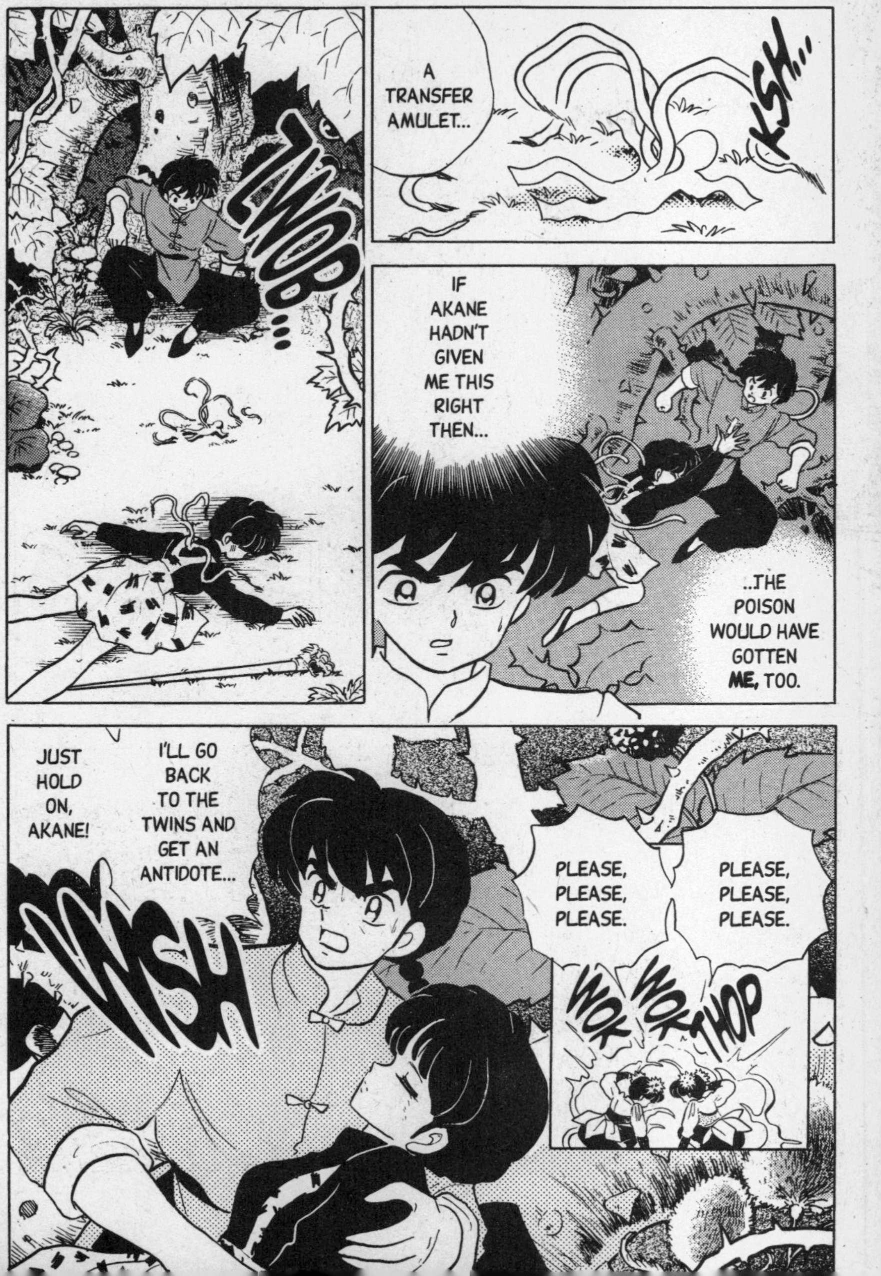
A TRANSFER AMULET...
KSH...
IF AKANE HADN'T GIVEN ME THIS RIGHT THEN...
...THE POISON WOULD HAVE GOTTEN **ME,** TOO.
JUST HOLD ON, AKANE!
I'LL GO BACK TO THE TWINS AND GET AN ANTIDOTE...
WSH
PLEASE, PLEASE, PLEASE.
PLEASE, PLEASE, PLEASE.
WOK
WOK
THOP

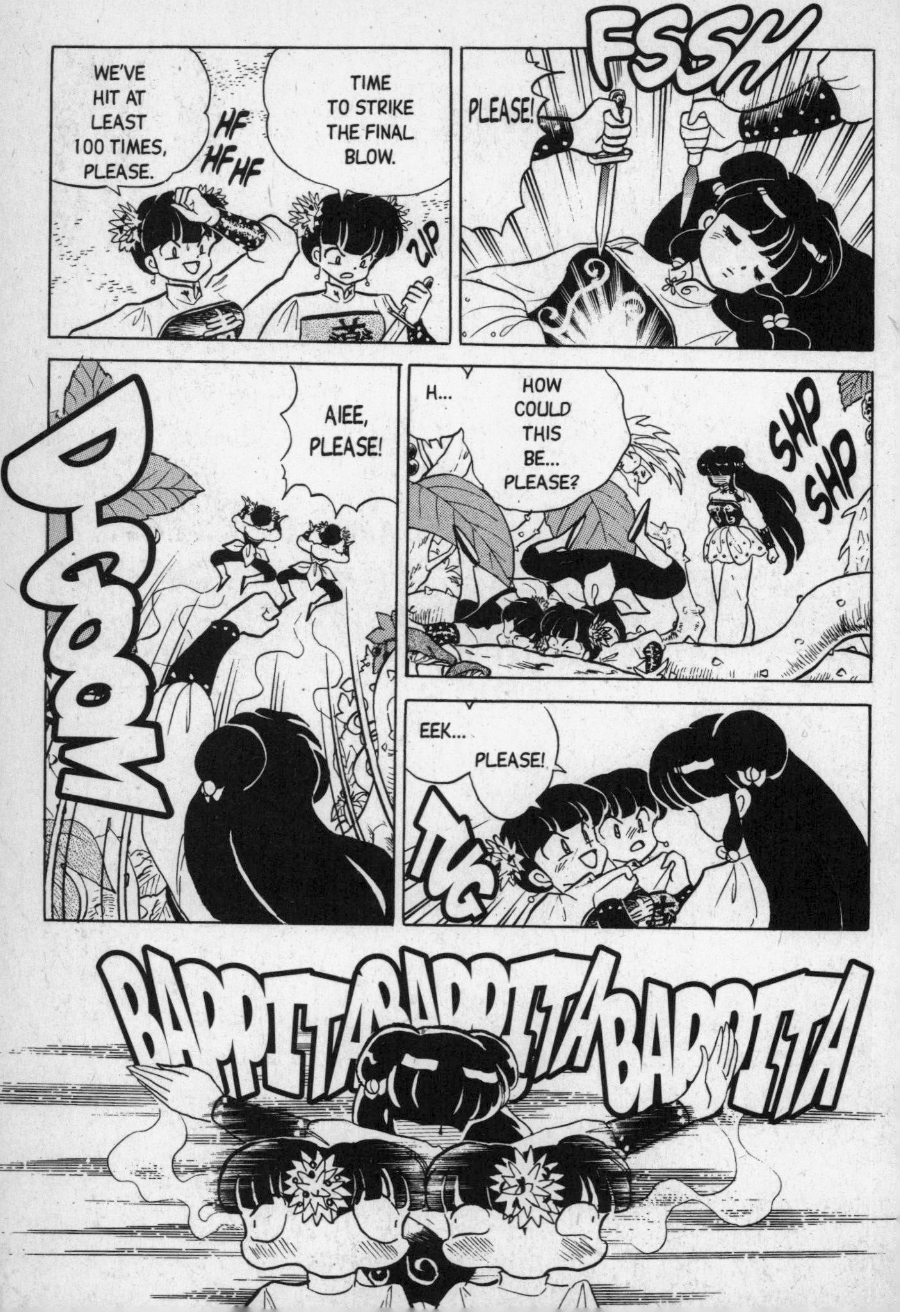
WE'VE HIT AT LEAST 100 TIMES, PLEASE.
HF HF HF
TIME TO STRIKE THE FINAL BLOW.
ZIP
FSSH
PLEASE!
DGOOM
AIEE, PLEASE!
H...
HOW COULD THIS BE... PLEASE?
SHP SHP
EEK... PLEASE!
TUG
BAPPITA BAPPITA BAPPITA

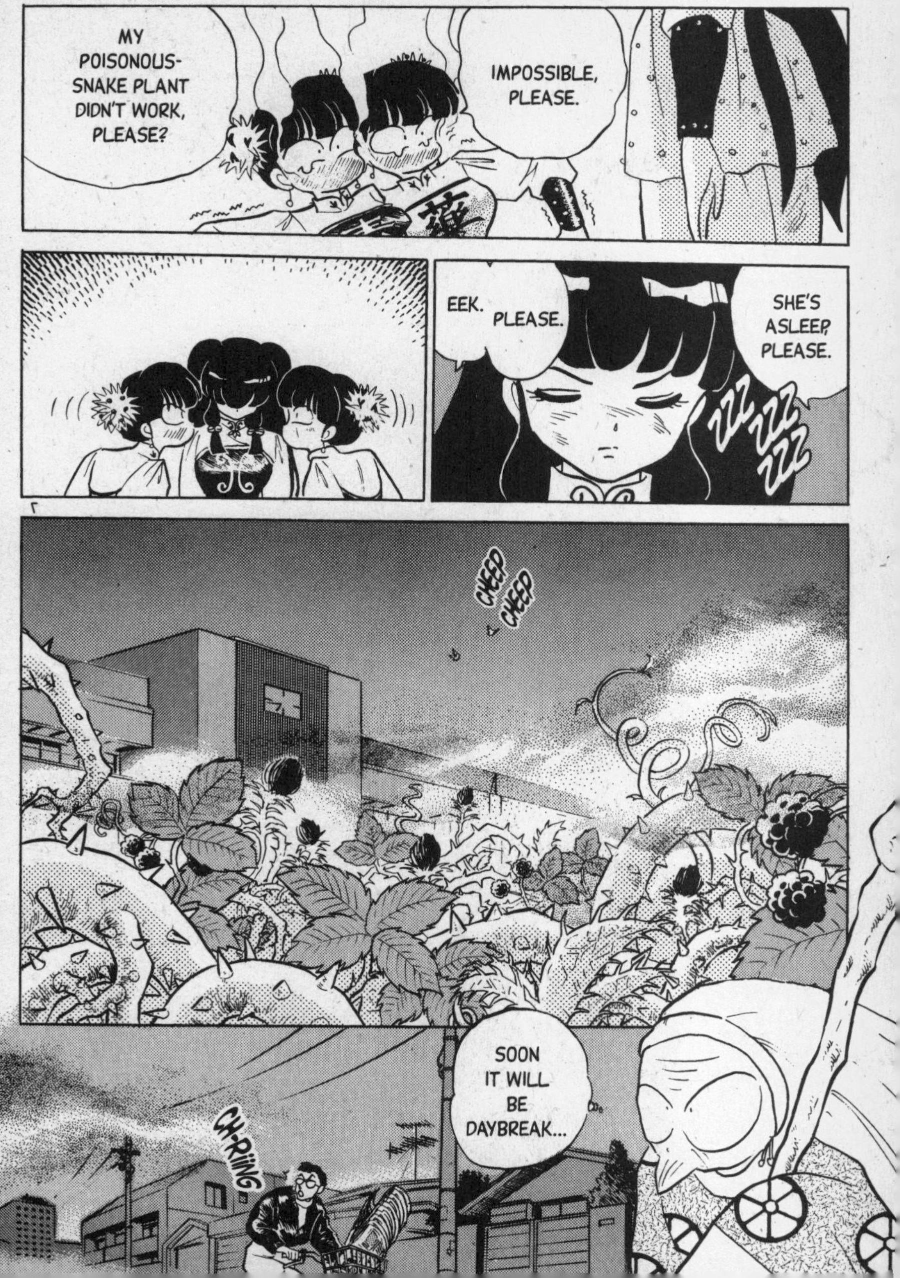
MY POISONOUS-SNAKE PLANT DIDN'T WORK, PLEASE?
IMPOSSIBLE, PLEASE.
EEK.
PLEASE.
SHE'S ASLEEP, PLEASE.
ZZZ ZZZ ZZZ
CHEEP CHEEP
CH-RIING
SOON IT WILL BE DAYBREAK...

CHEEP

BOOF

HYGRRRRR

EH?

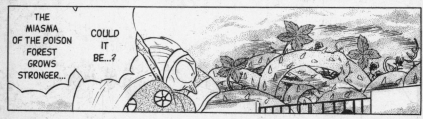

THE MIASMA OF THE POISON FOREST GROWS STRONGER...

COULD IT BE...?

BOOF

THE POISON POLLEN...

SHOOP

BOOF

YEAH! EVEN IF THEY'RE POISONOUS MONSTER PLANTS, THEY'RE STILL PLANTS!

NATURALLY, THEY GET STRONGER IN THE MORNING!

SHF

GOTTA HURRY AND GET OUT OF THIS FOREST...

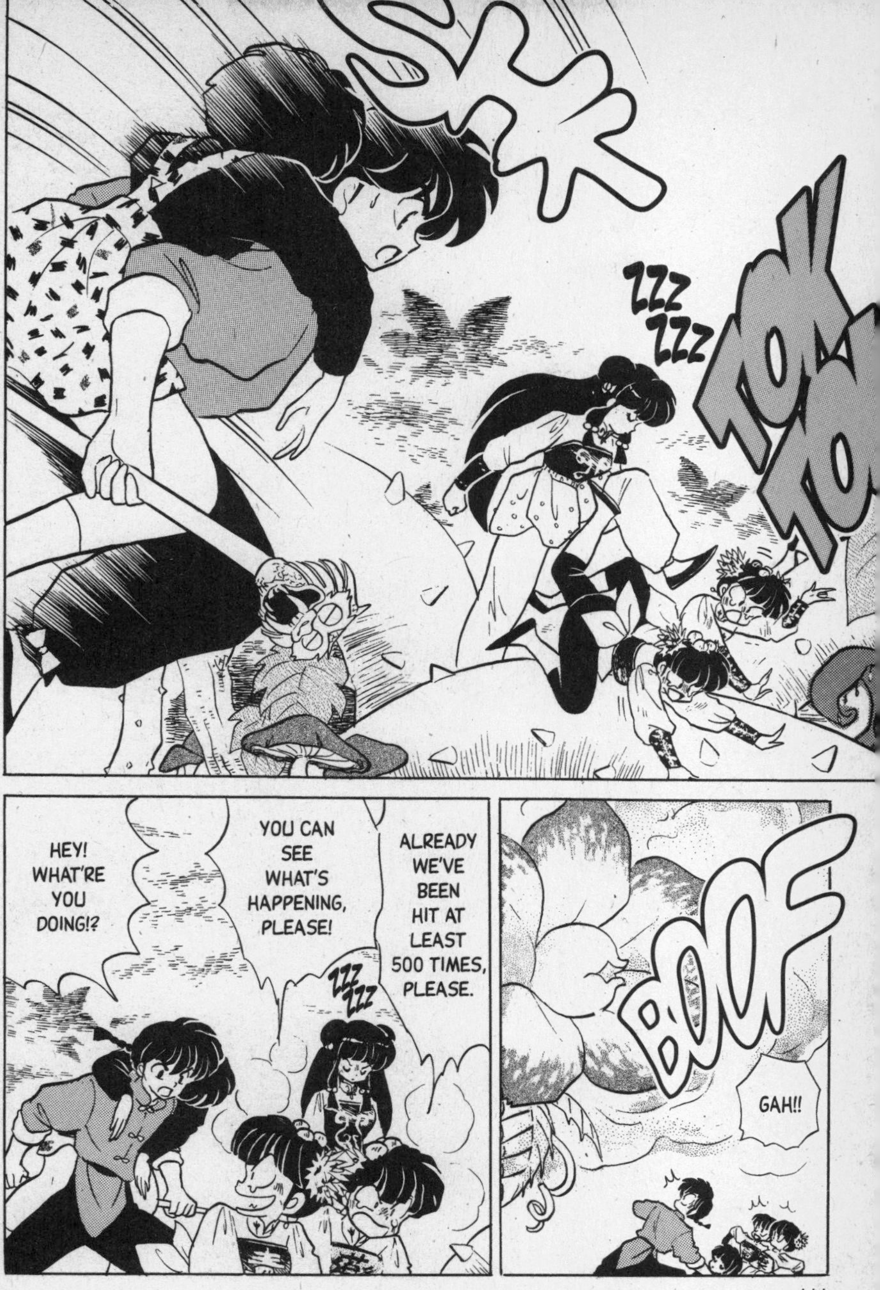
ZZZ
ZZZ
TOK
TOK
HEY! WHAT'RE YOU DOING!?
YOU CAN SEE WHAT'S HAPPENING, PLEASE!
ALREADY WE'VE BEEN HIT AT LEAST 500 TIMES, PLEASE.
ZZZ
ZZZ
BOOF
GAH!!

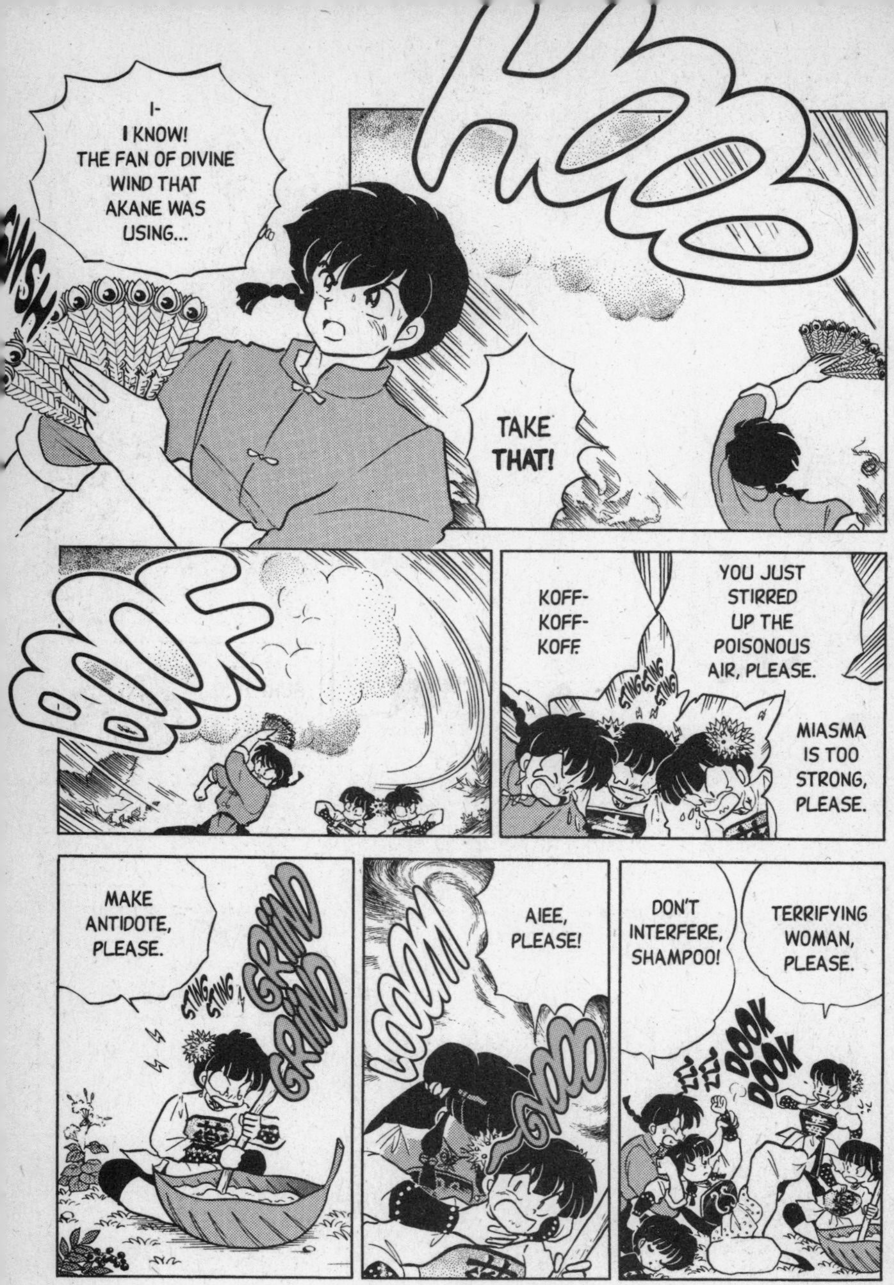
I-
I KNOW! THE FAN OF DIVINE WIND THAT AKANE WAS USING...
TAKE THAT!
KOFF-KOFF-KOFF.
YOU JUST STIRRED UP THE POISONOUS AIR, PLEASE.
STING STING STING
MIASMA IS TOO STRONG, PLEASE.
MAKE ANTIDOTE, PLEASE.
STING STING
GRIND GRIND
AIEE, PLEASE!
DON'T INTERFERE, SHAMPOO!
TERRIFYING WOMAN, PLEASE.
DOOK DOOK

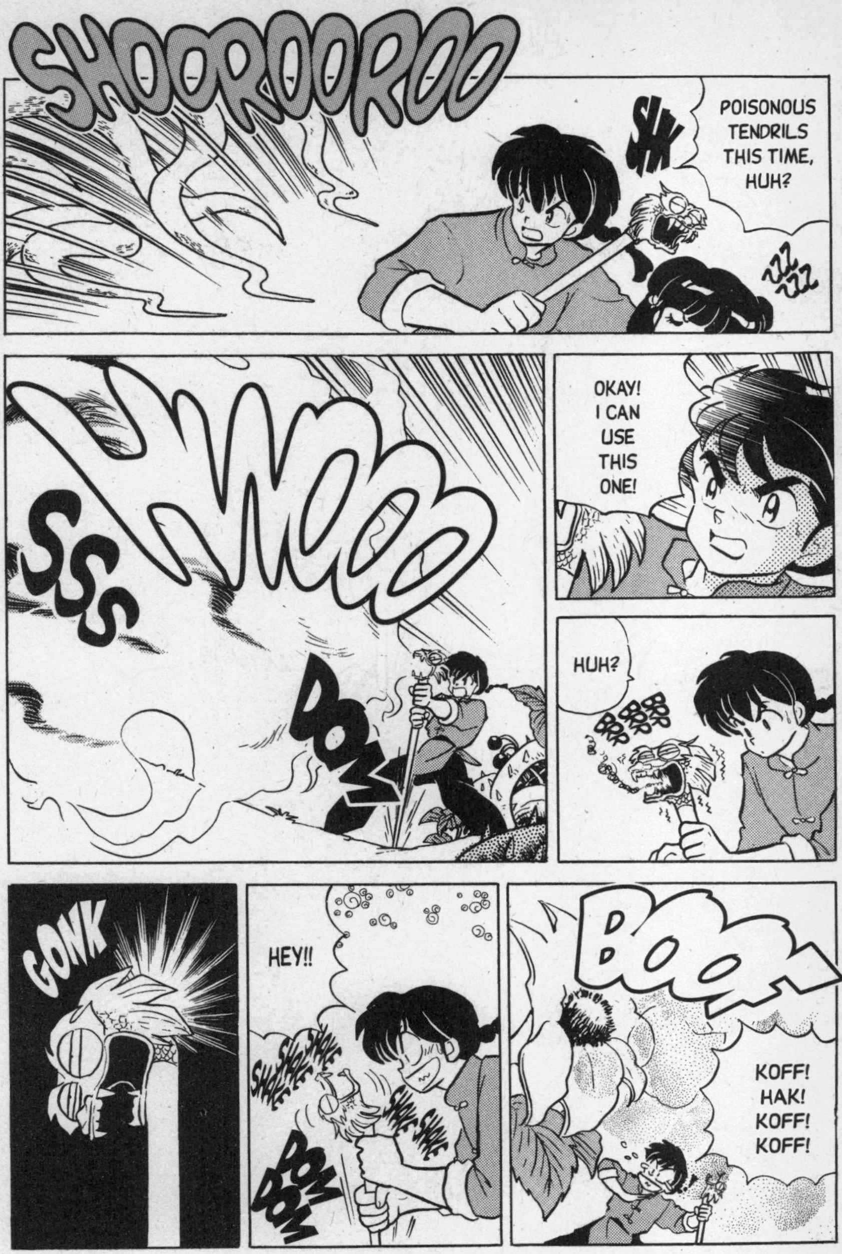
SHOOROOROO
SHK
POISONOUS TENDRILS THIS TIME, HUH?
ZZZ ZZZ
SSS
DOM
OKAY! I CAN USE THIS ONE!
HUH?
GONK
HEY!!
SHAKE SHAKE SHAKE SHAKE
SHAKE SHAKE
DOM DOM
KOFF! HAK! KOFF! KOFF!

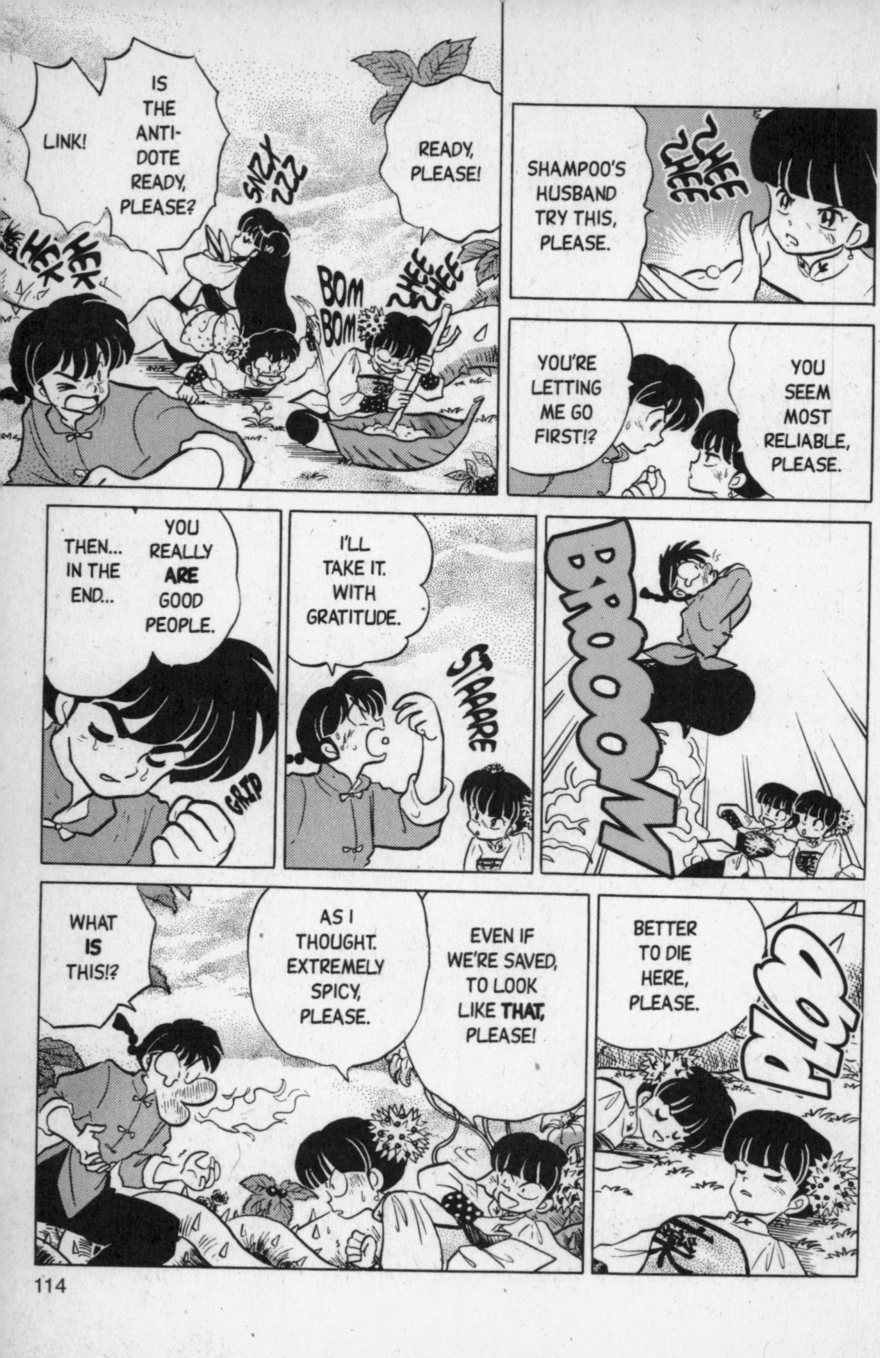
LINK!
IS THE ANTI-DOTE READY, PLEASE?
HEK HEK
BOM BOM
SHEE SHEE
READY, PLEASE!
SHAMPOO'S HUSBAND TRY THIS, PLEASE.
SHEE SHEE
YOU'RE LETTING ME GO FIRST!?
YOU SEEM MOST RELIABLE, PLEASE.
THEN... IN THE END...
YOU REALLY **ARE** GOOD PEOPLE.
GRIP
I'LL TAKE IT. WITH GRATITUDE.
STAAARE
BROOOOM
WHAT **IS** THIS!?
AS I THOUGHT. EXTREMELY SPICY, PLEASE.
EVEN IF WE'RE SAVED, TO LOOK LIKE **THAT**, PLEASE!
BETTER TO DIE HERE, PLEASE.
PLOP

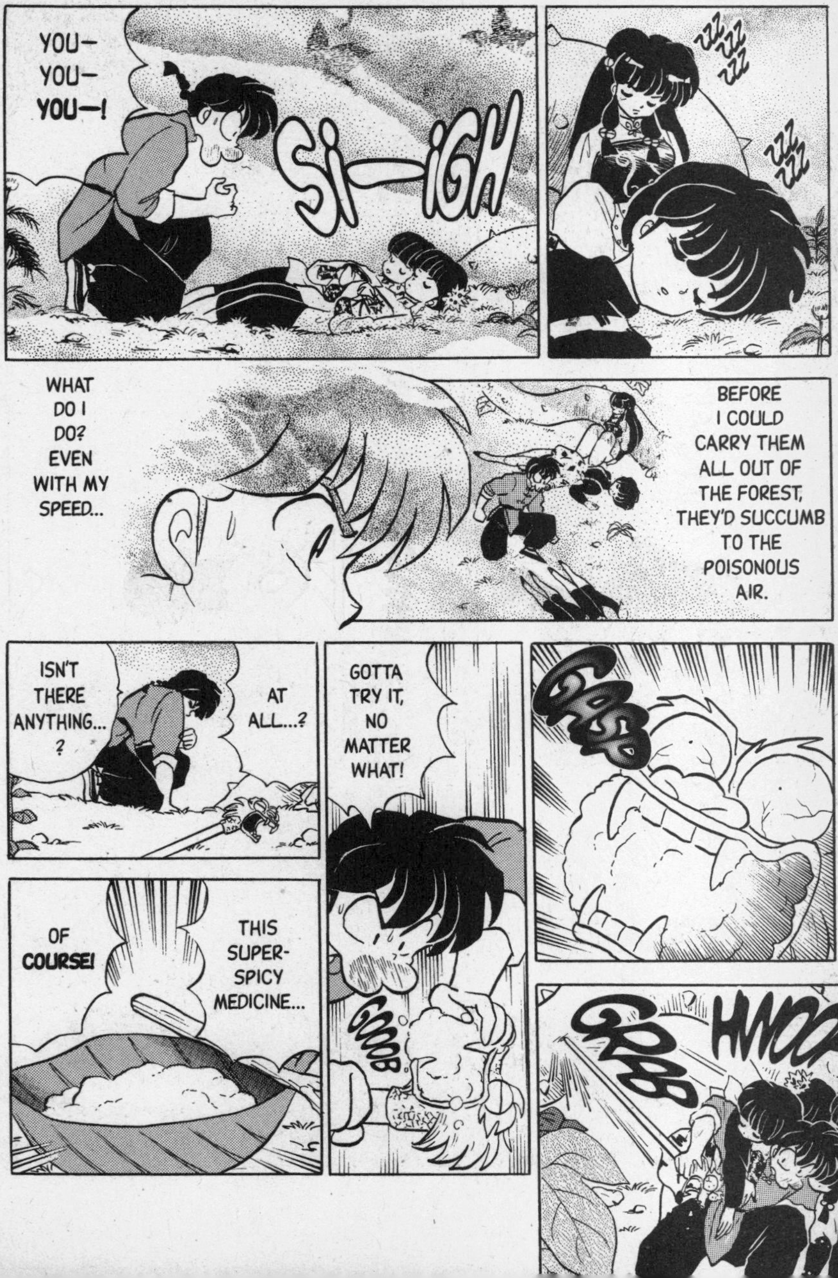
YOU—
YOU—
YOU—!
SI—IGH
ZZZ ZZZ ZZZ
ZZZ ZZZ
WHAT DO I DO? EVEN WITH MY SPEED...
BEFORE I COULD CARRY THEM ALL OUT OF THE FOREST, THEY'D SUCCUMB TO THE POISONOUS AIR.
ISN'T THERE ANYTHING... ?
AT ALL...?
OF COURSE!
THIS SUPER-SPICY MEDICINE...
GOTTA TRY IT, NO MATTER WHAT!
GASP
GRAB
HWOOP

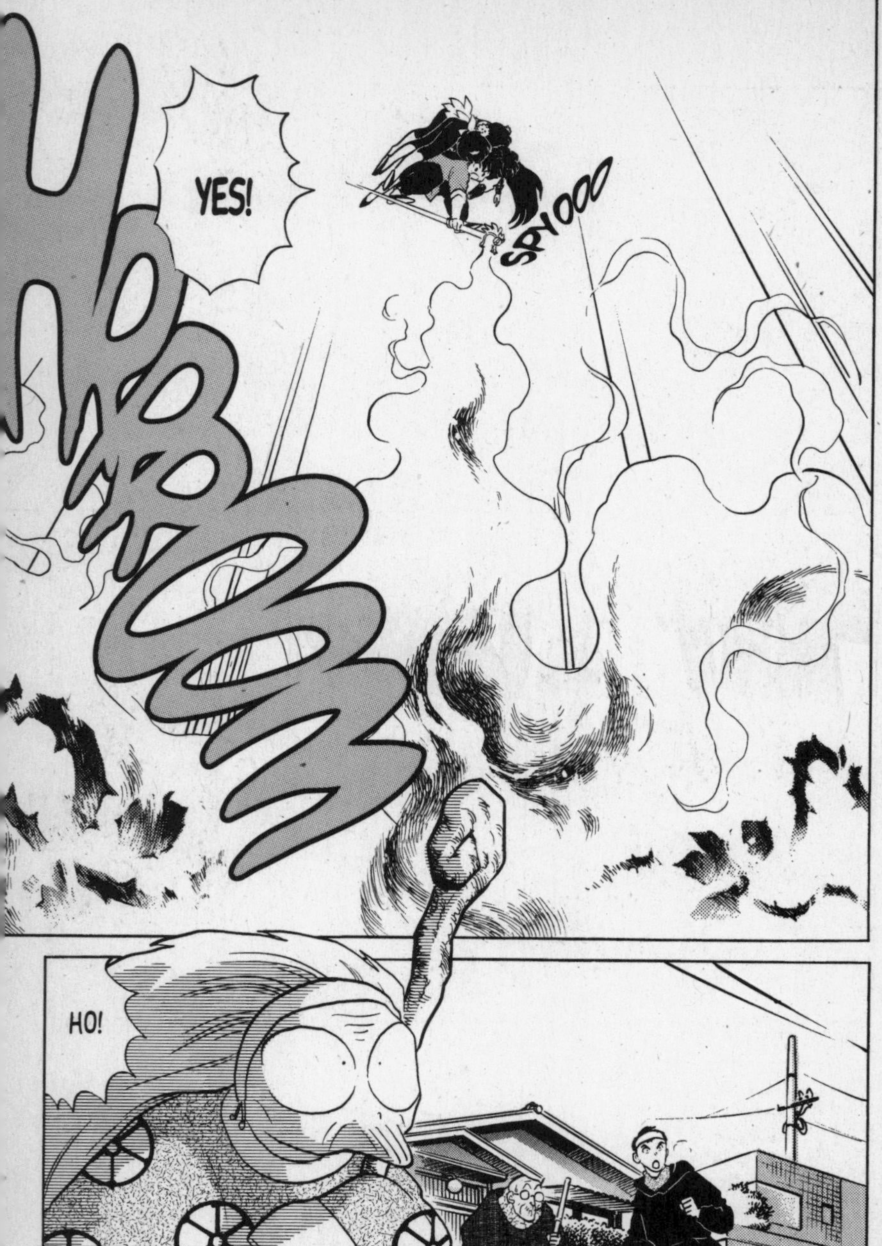
YES!
SPYOOO
HO!

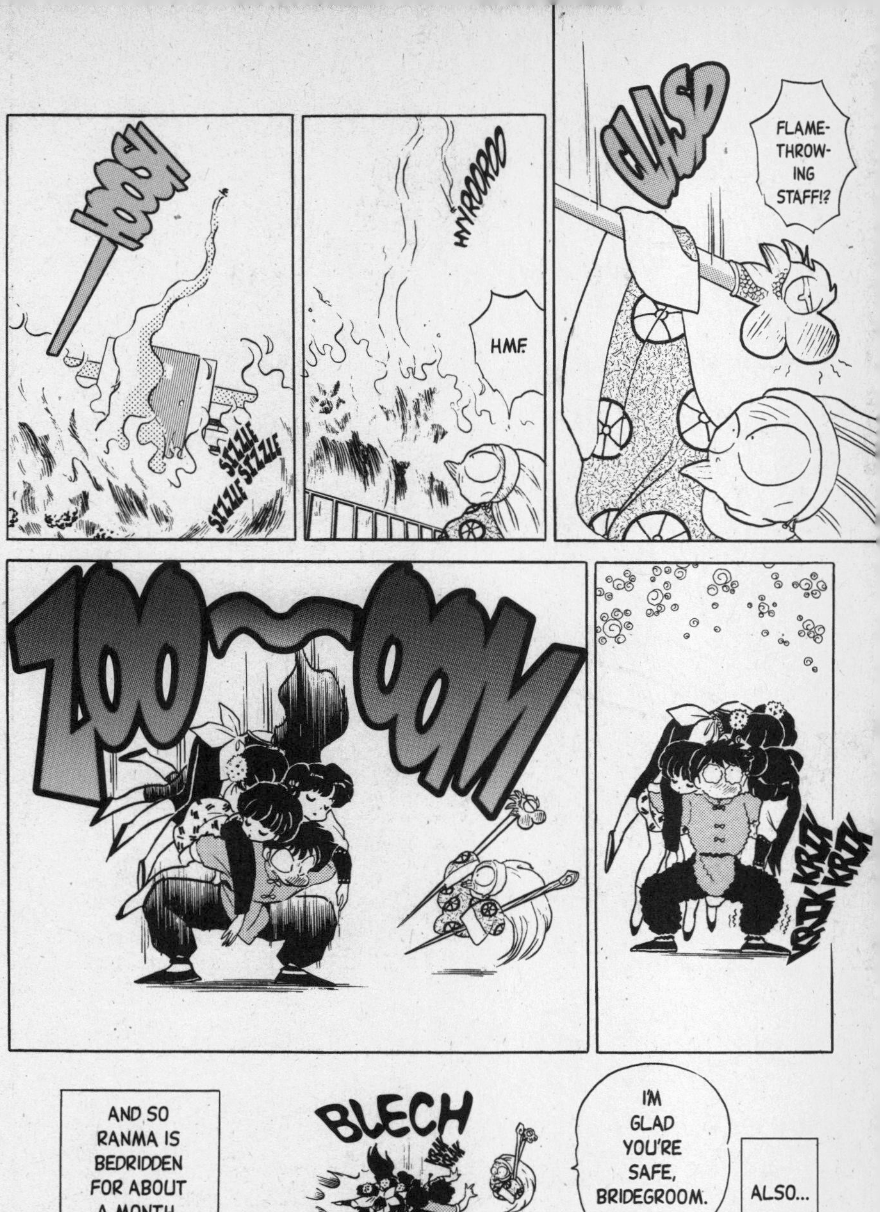
SIZZLE
SIZZLE SIZZLE
HMF.
FLAME-THROWING STAFF!?
ZOO~OOM
AND SO RANMA IS BEDRIDDEN FOR ABOUT A MONTH.
BLECH
I'M GLAD YOU'RE SAFE, BRIDEGROOM.
ALSO...

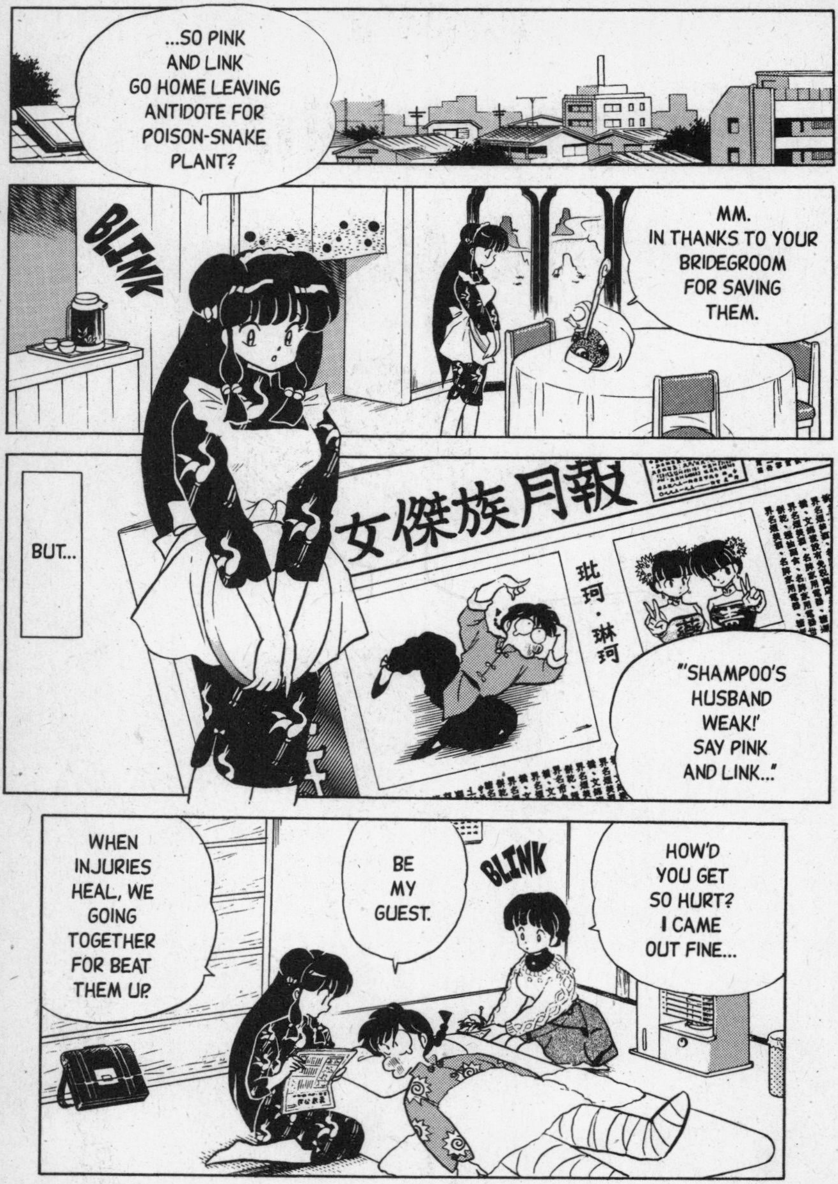
...SO PINK AND LINK GO HOME LEAVING ANTIDOTE FOR POISON-SNAKE PLANT?
BLINK
MM. IN THANKS TO YOUR BRIDEGROOM FOR SAVING THEM.
BUT...
女傑族月報
"'SHAMPOO'S HUSBAND WEAK!' SAY PINK AND LINK..."
WHEN INJURIES HEAL, WE GOING TOGETHER FOR BEAT THEM UP?
BE MY GUEST.
BLINK
HOW'D YOU GET SO HURT? I CAME OUT FINE...

PART 8

EVIL AND THE BEAN

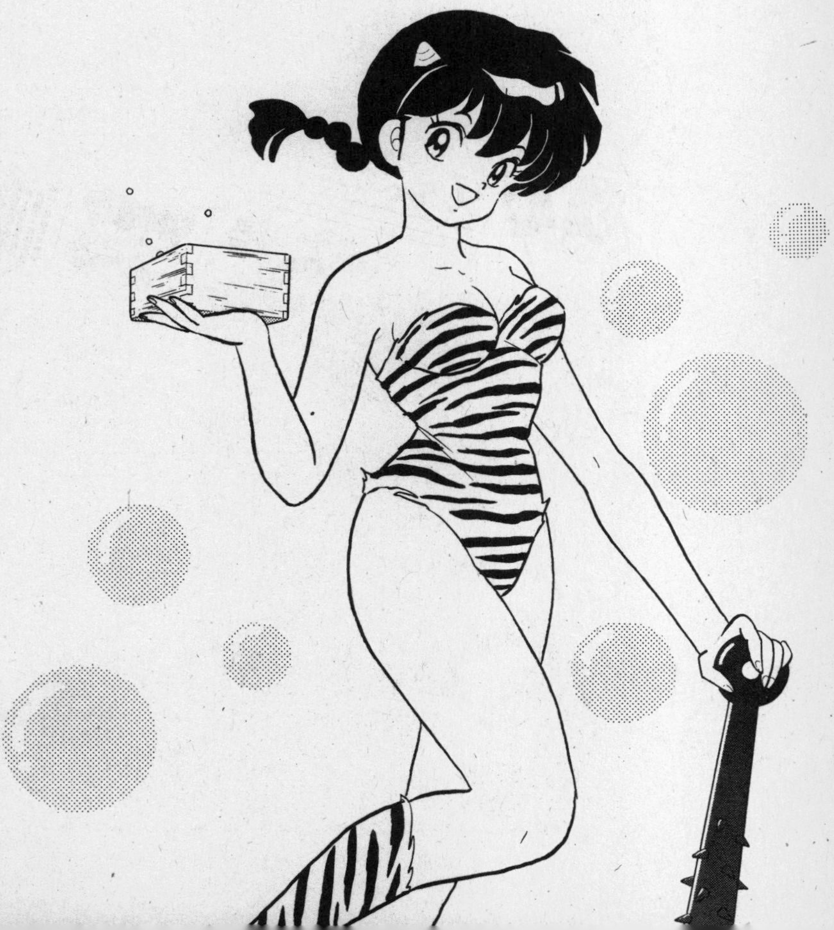

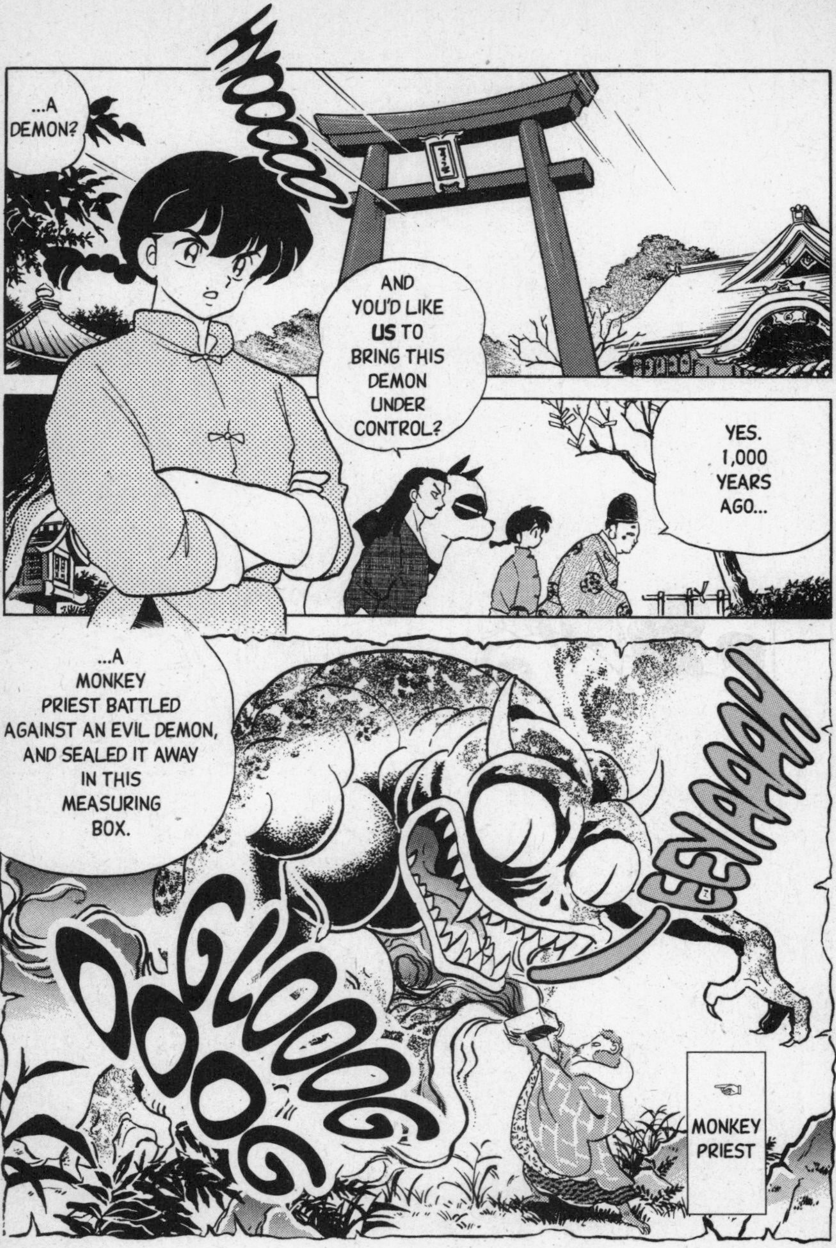
...A DEMON?
AND YOU'D LIKE US TO BRING THIS DEMON UNDER CONTROL?
YES. 1,000 YEARS AGO...
...A MONKEY PRIEST BATTLED AGAINST AN EVIL DEMON, AND SEALED IT AWAY IN THIS MEASURING BOX.
MONKEY PRIEST

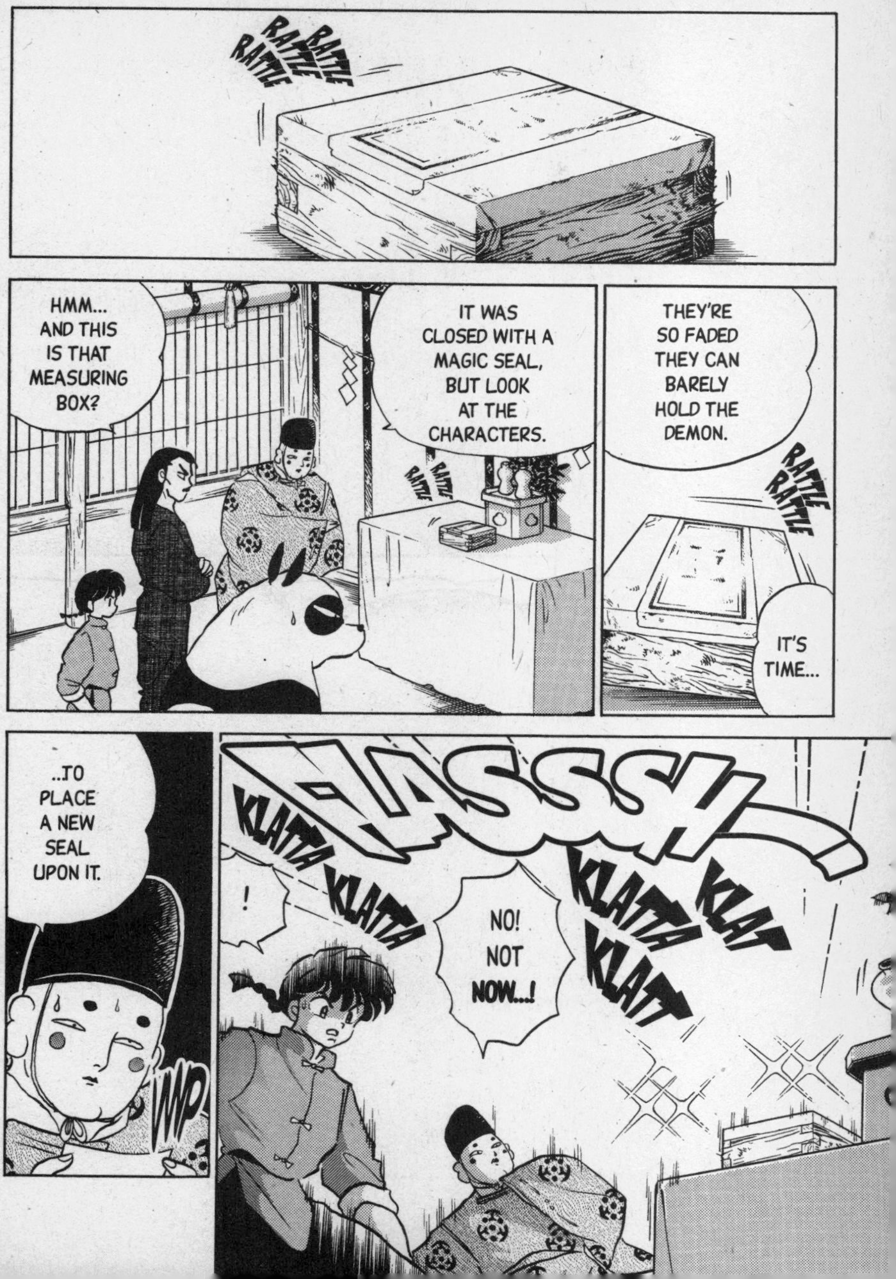
RATTLE RATTLE RATTLE
HMM... AND THIS IS THAT MEASURING BOX?
IT WAS CLOSED WITH A MAGIC SEAL, BUT LOOK AT THE CHARACTERS.
RATTLE RATTLE
THEY'RE SO FADED THEY CAN BARELY HOLD THE DEMON.
RATTLE RATTLE
IT'S TIME...
..TO PLACE A NEW SEAL UPON IT.
WIP
FASSSH
KLATTA KLATTA
!
NO! NOT NOW...!
KLATTA KLATT KLAT

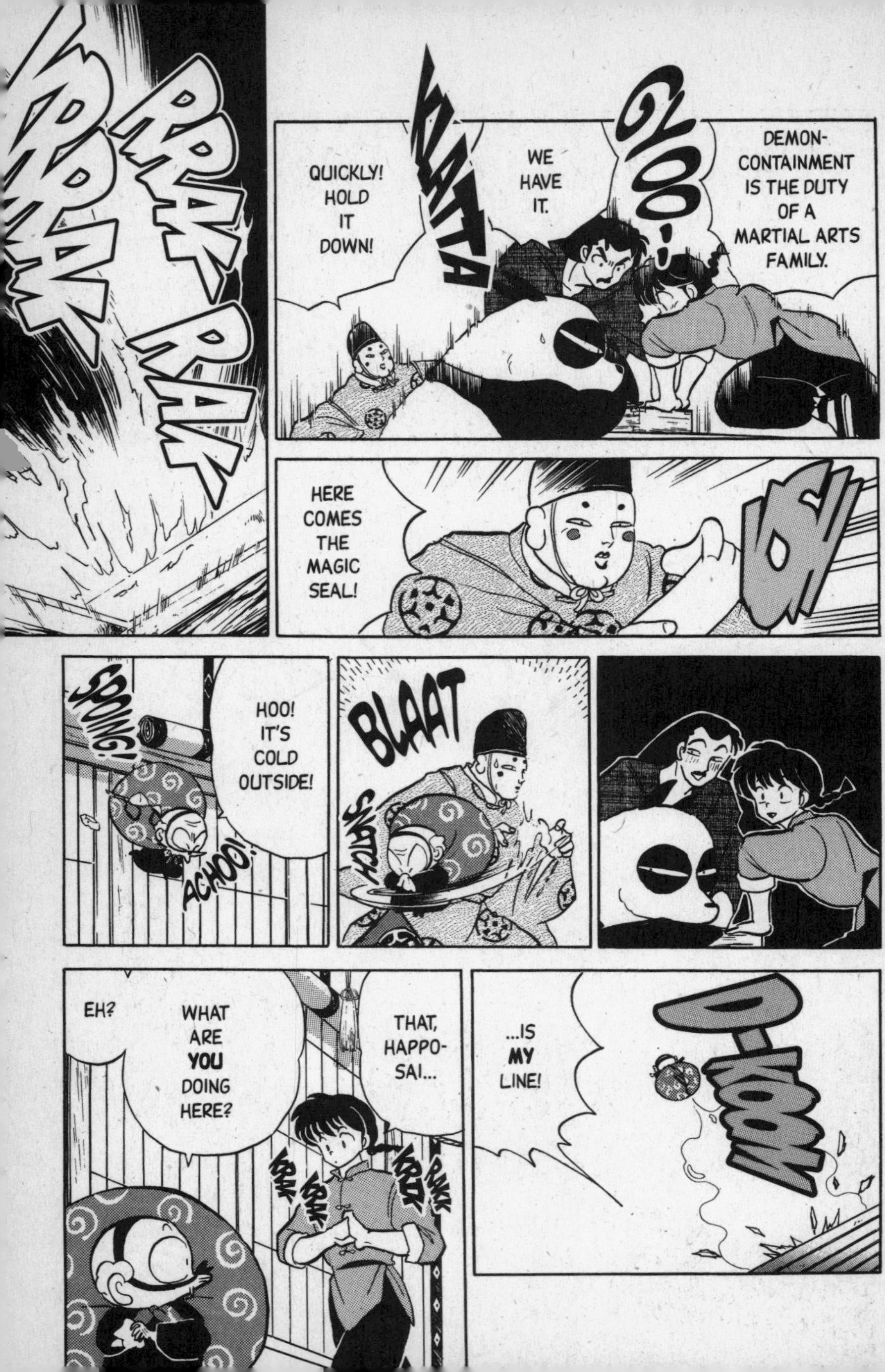
KRRAK
RRAK-RAK
QUICKLY! HOLD IT DOWN!
KLATTA
WE HAVE IT.
GYOO!
DEMON-CONTAINMENT IS THE DUTY OF A MARTIAL ARTS FAMILY.
HERE COMES THE MAGIC SEAL!
SPOING!
HOO! IT'S COLD OUTSIDE!
ACHOO!
BLAAT
SNATCH
EH?
WHAT ARE **YOU** DOING HERE?
THAT, HAPPO-SAI...
KRAK
KRAK
KRICK
KRAKK
...IS **MY** LINE!
DTOOM

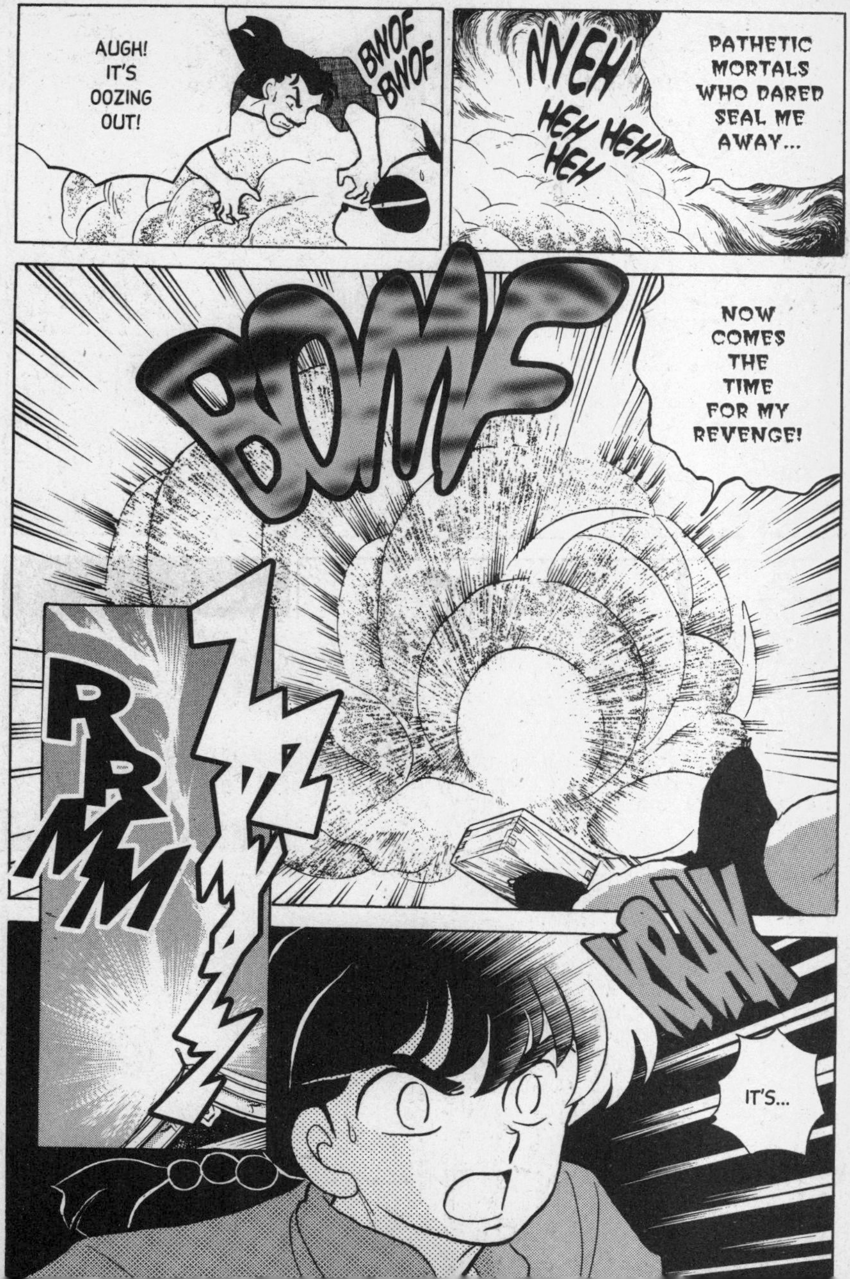
AUGH! IT'S OOZING OUT!
BWOF BWOF
NYEH HEH HEH HEH
PATHETIC MORTALS WHO DARED SEAL ME AWAY...
BOMF
NOW COMES THE TIME FOR MY REVENGE!
RRMM
IT'S...

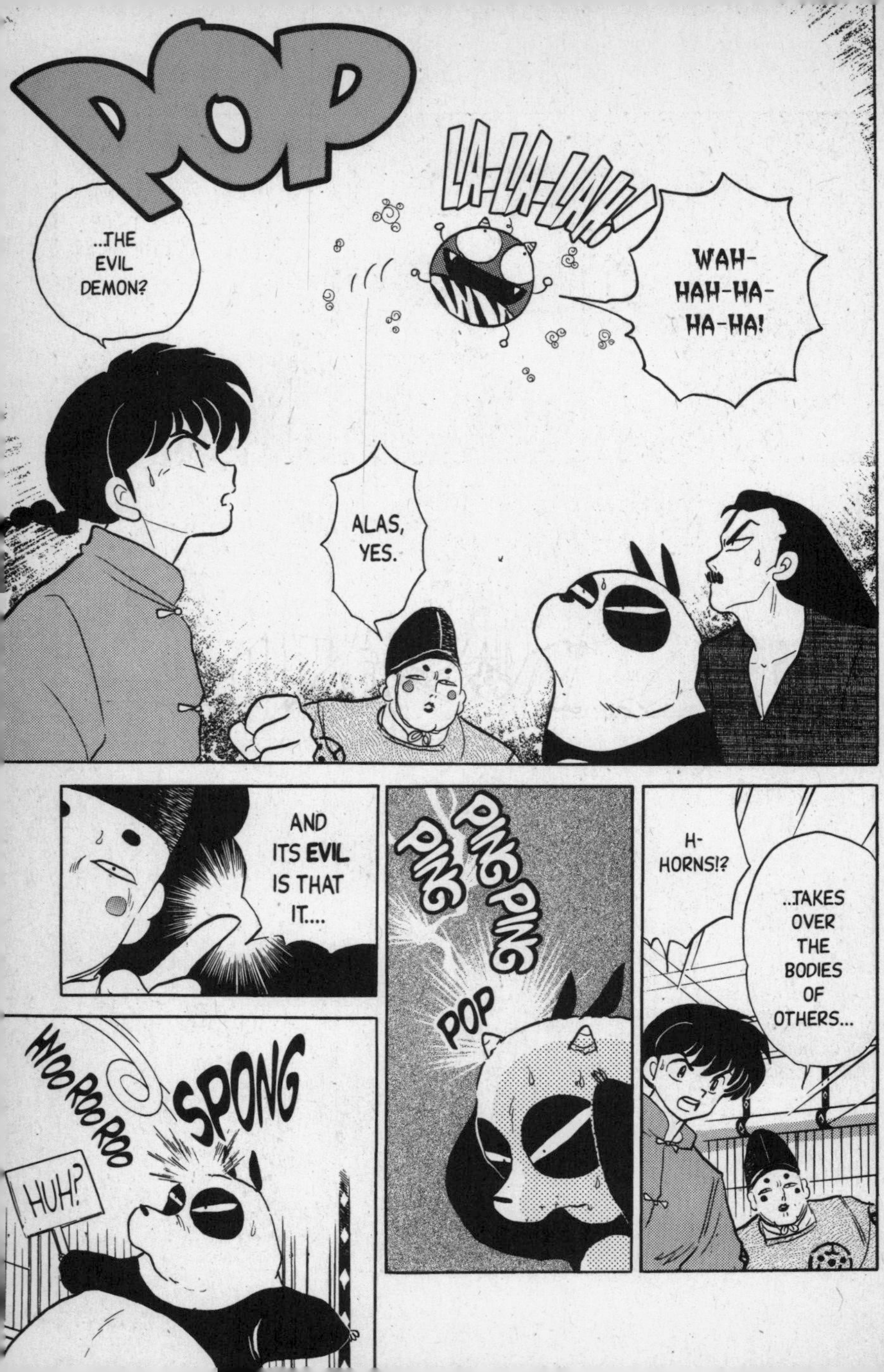
POP
...THE EVIL DEMON?
LA-LA-LAH!
WAH-HAH-HA-HA-HA!
ALAS, YES.
AND ITS EVIL IS THAT IT....
HYOO ROO ROO
SPONG
HUH?
PING PING PING PING
POP
H- HORNS!?
...TAKES OVER THE BODIES OF OTHERS...

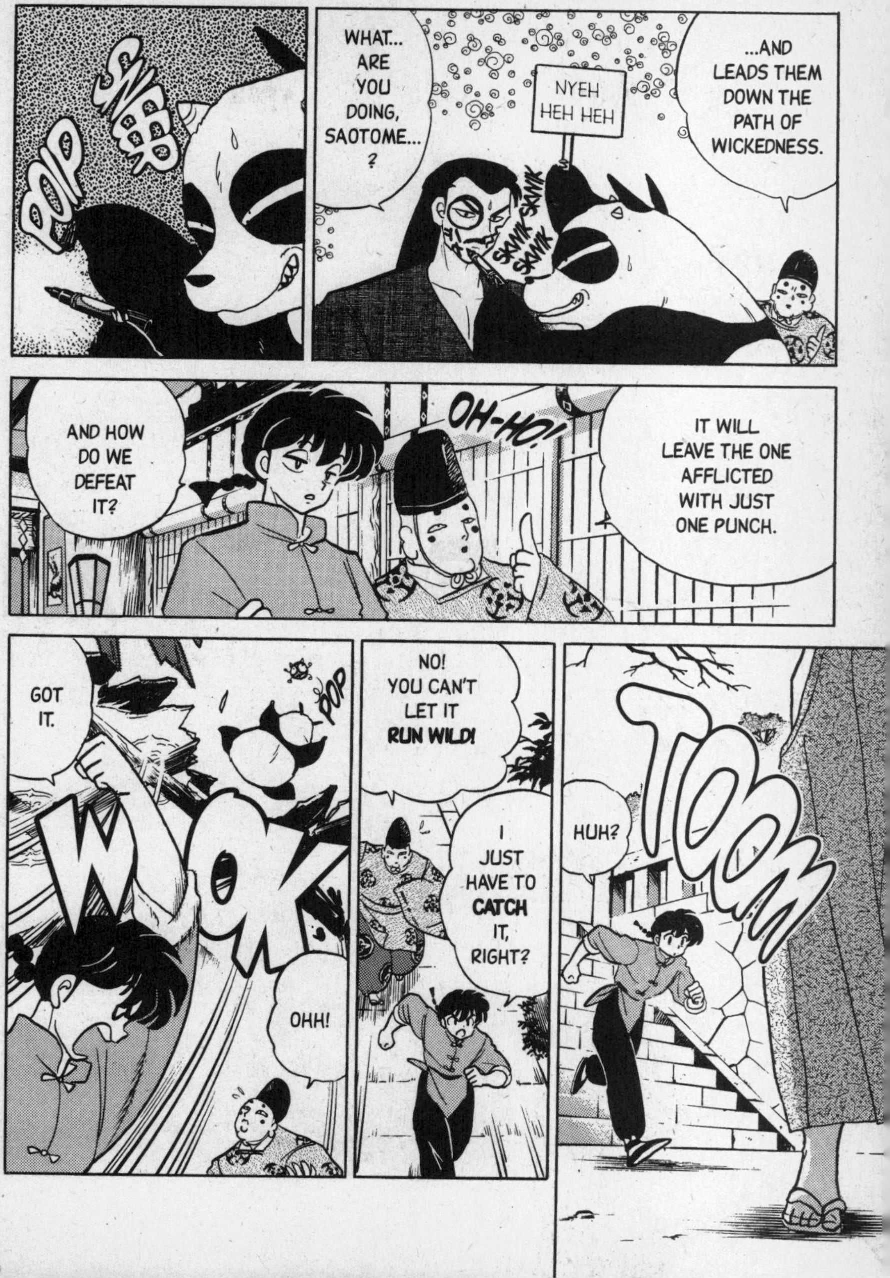
POIP
SWEEP
WHAT... ARE YOU DOING, SAOTOME...?
NYEH HEH HEH
SKWIK SKWIK
SKWIK SKWIK
...AND LEADS THEM DOWN THE PATH OF WICKEDNESS.
AND HOW DO WE DEFEAT IT?
OH-HO!
IT WILL LEAVE THE ONE AFFLICTED WITH JUST ONE PUNCH.
GOT IT.
POP
WOK
OHH!
NO! YOU CAN'T LET IT **RUN WILD!**
I JUST HAVE TO **CATCH** IT, RIGHT?
HUH?
TOOM

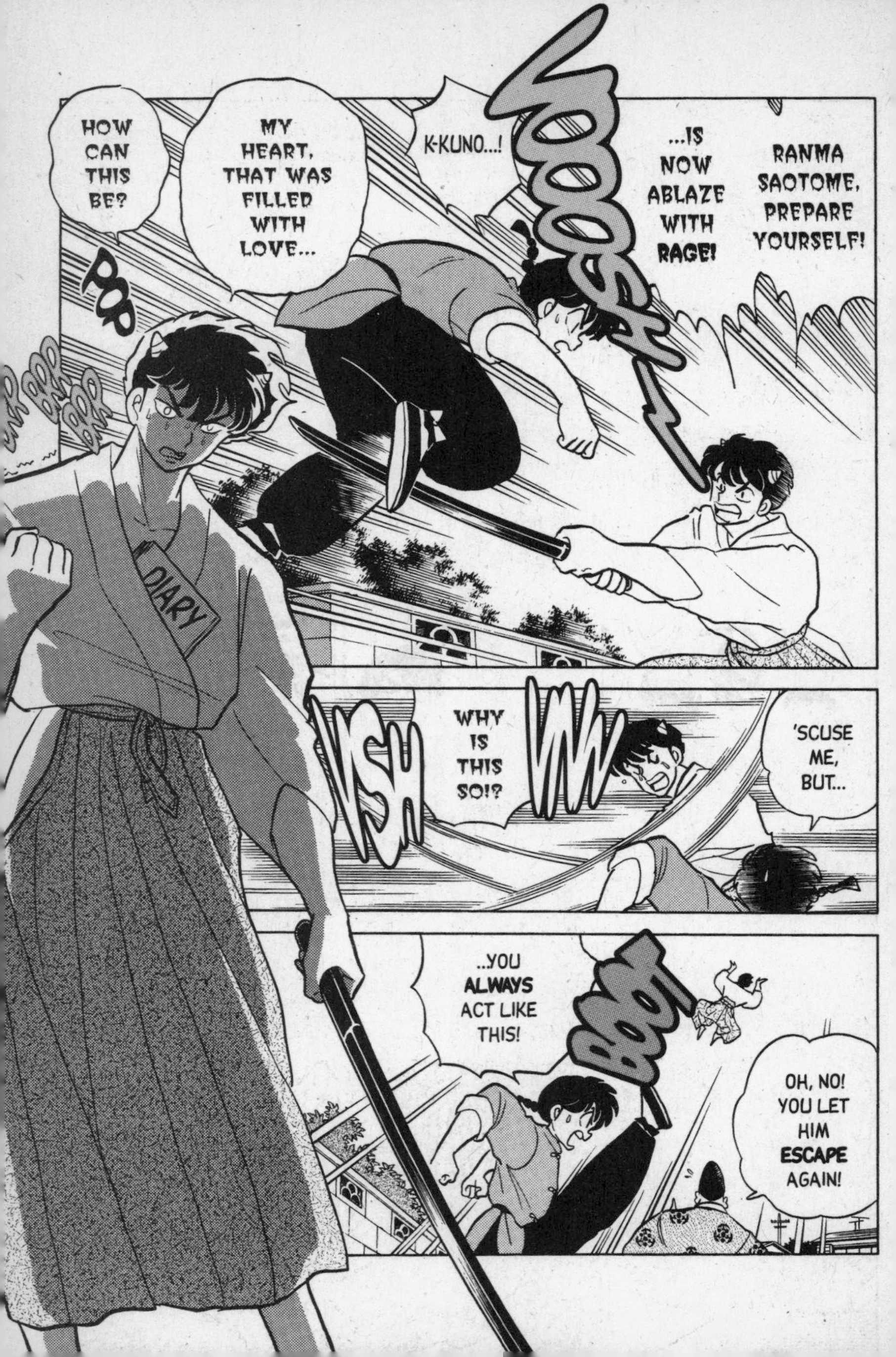
HOW CAN THIS BE?
MY HEART, THAT WAS FILLED WITH LOVE...
K-KUNO...!
VOOOSH
...IS NOW ABLAZE WITH RAGE!
RANMA SAOTOME, PREPARE YOURSELF!
POP
WHY IS THIS SO!?
'SCUSE ME, BUT...
...YOU **ALWAYS** ACT LIKE THIS!
BOOT
OH, NO! YOU LET HIM **ESCAPE** AGAIN!
DIARY

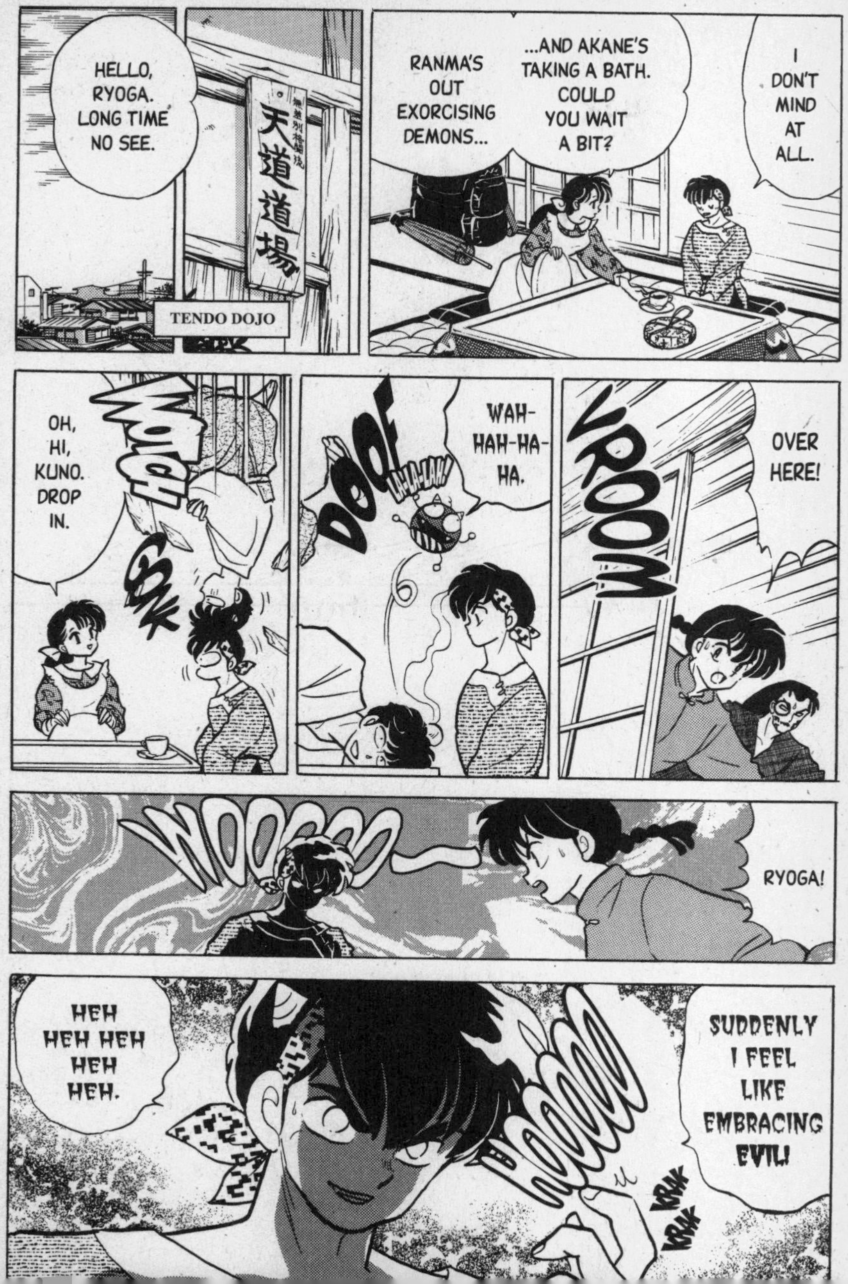
HELLO, RYOGA. LONG TIME NO SEE.
天道道場
TENDO DOJO
RANMA'S OUT EXORCISING DEMONS...
...AND AKANE'S TAKING A BATH. COULD YOU WAIT A BIT?
I DON'T MIND AT ALL.
OH, HI, KUNO. DROP IN.
GONK
DOOF
LA-LA-LAH!
WAH-HAH-HA-HA.
VROOM
OVER HERE!
RYOGA!
HEH HEH HEH HEH HEH.
SUDDENLY I FEEL LIKE EMBRACING EVIL!
KRAK
KRAK

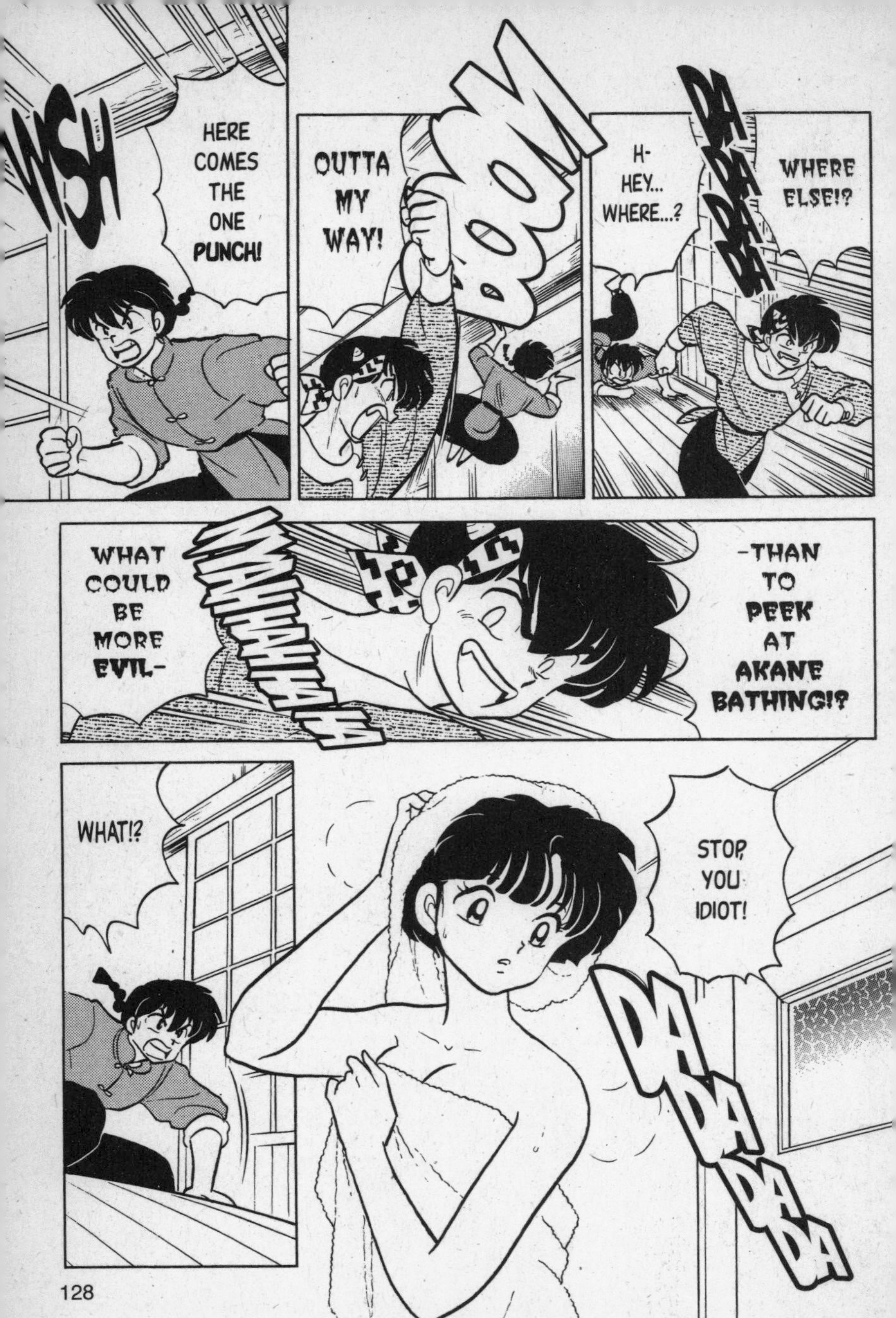
WISH
HERE COMES THE ONE PUNCH!
OUTTA MY WAY!
DADADADA
H- HEY... WHERE...?
WHERE ELSE!?
WHAT COULD BE MORE EVIL-
-THAN TO PEEK AT AKANE BATHING!?
WHAT!?
STOP, YOU IDIOT!
DADADADA

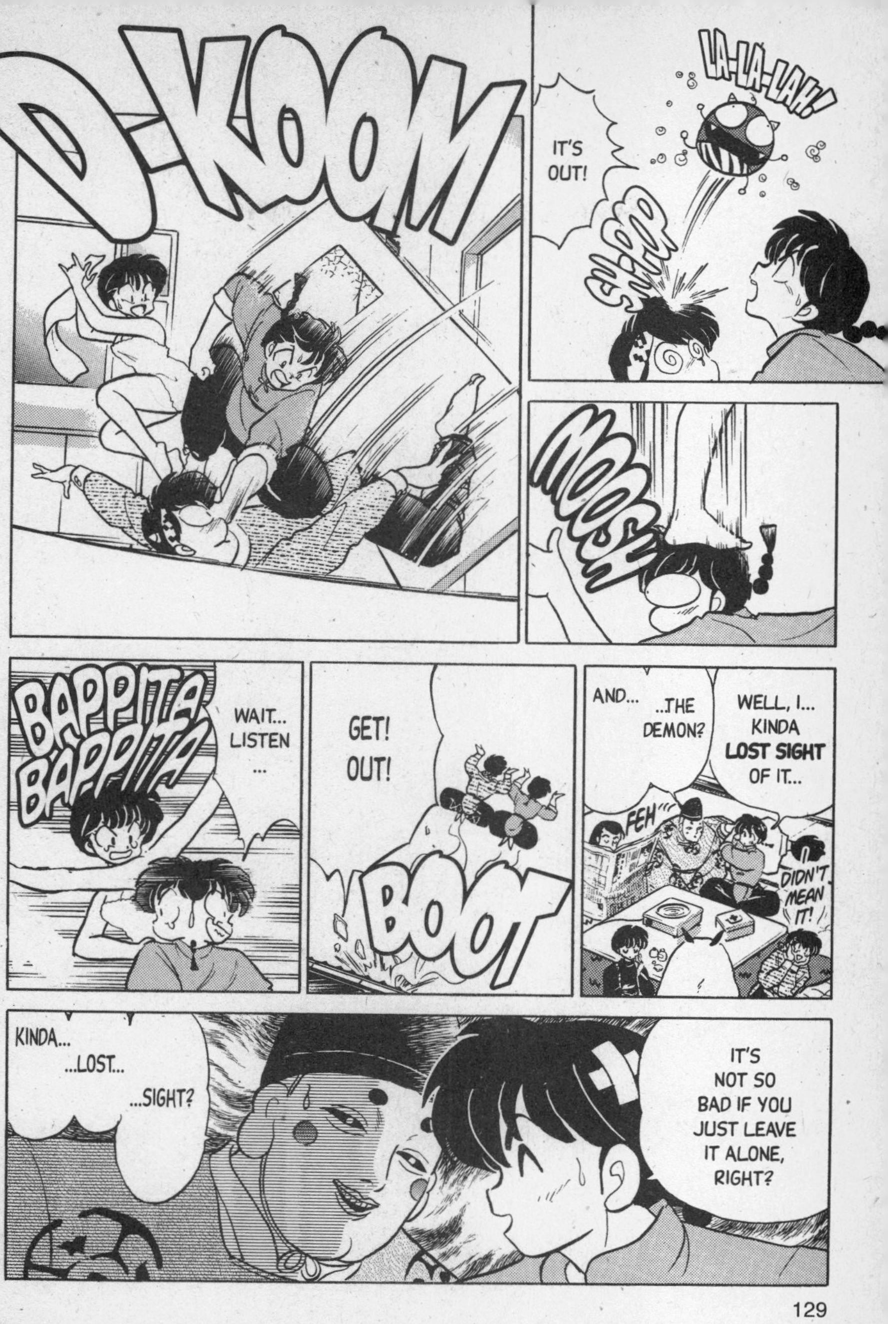
D-KOOM
IT'S OUT!
LA-LA-LAH!
MOOSH
BAPPITA BAPPITA
WAIT... LISTEN ...
GET! OUT!
BOOT
AND...
...THE DEMON?
WELL, I... KINDA **LOST SIGHT** OF IT...
FEH
I DIDN'T MEAN IT!
KINDA... ...LOST... ...SIGHT?
IT'S NOT SO BAD IF YOU JUST LEAVE IT ALONE, RIGHT?

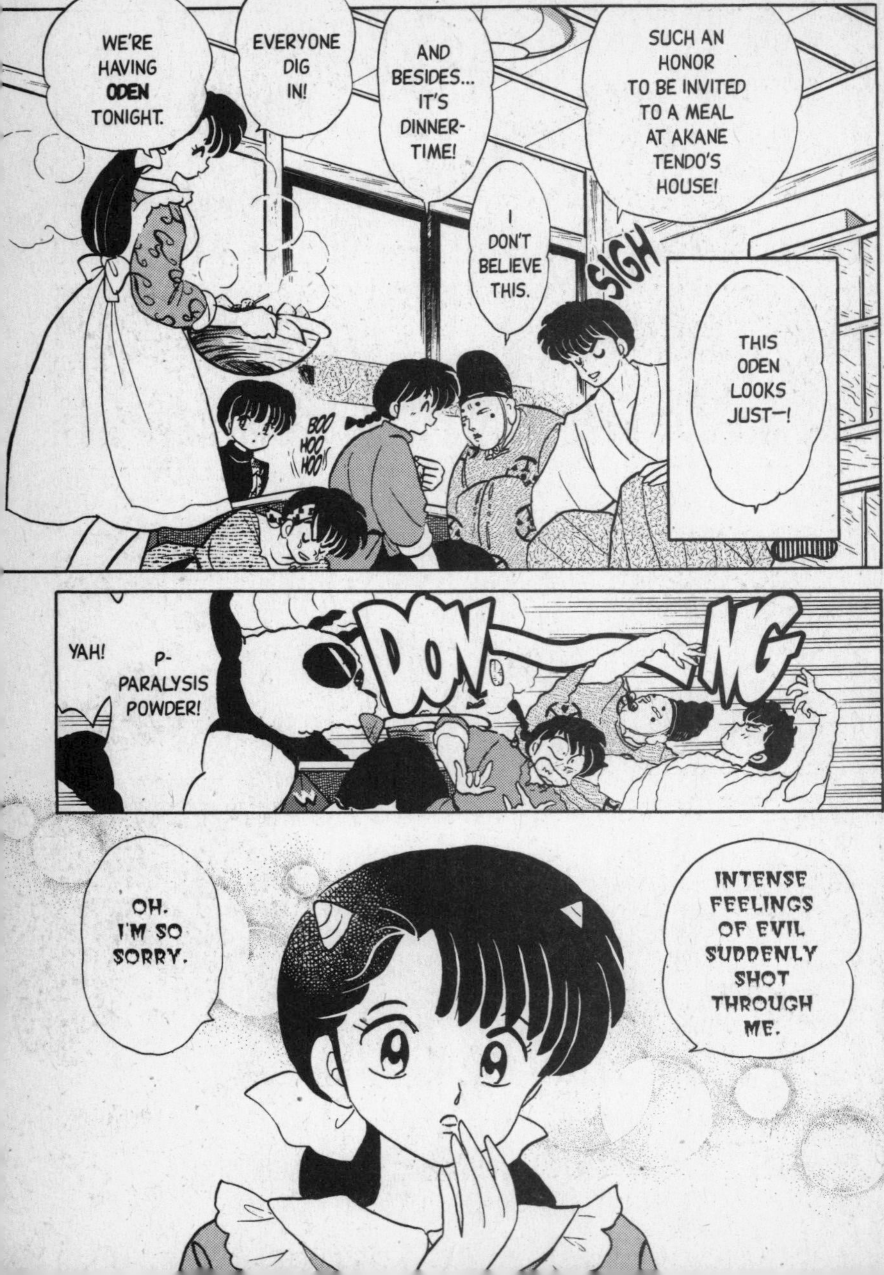

WE'RE HAVING **ODEN** TONIGHT.
EVERYONE DIG IN!
AND BESIDES... IT'S DINNER-TIME!
I DON'T BELIEVE THIS.
SUCH AN HONOR TO BE INVITED TO A MEAL AT AKANE TENDO'S HOUSE!
SIGH
BOO HOO HOO
THIS ODEN LOOKS JUST—!
YAH!
P-PARALYSIS POWDER!
DONNG
OH. I'M SO SORRY.
INTENSE FEELINGS OF EVIL SUDDENLY SHOT THROUGH ME.

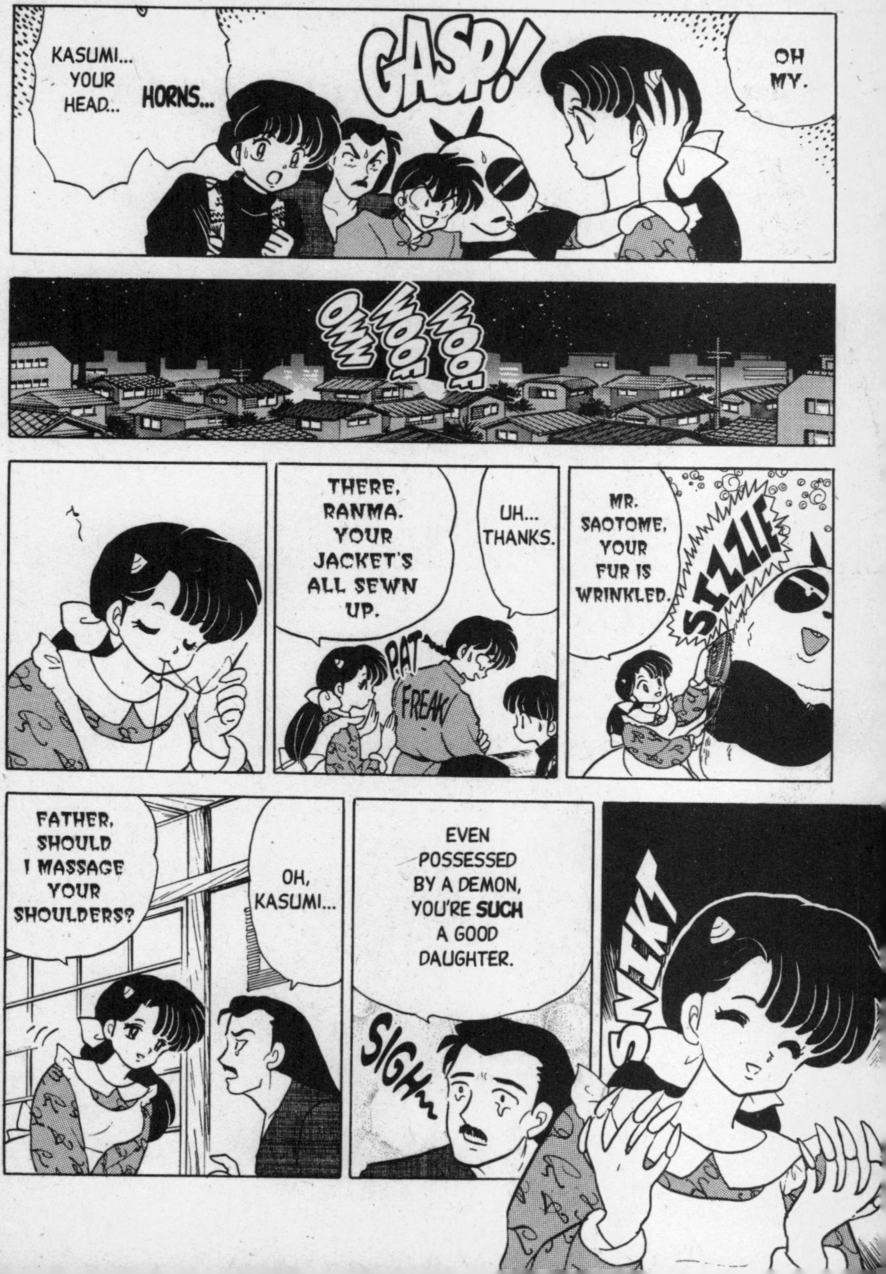
KASUMI... YOUR HEAD... HORNS...
GASP!
OH MY.
WOOF WOOF OWW
THERE, RANMA. YOUR JACKET'S ALL SEWN UP.
UH... THANKS.
PAT
FREAK
MR. SAOTOME, YOUR FUR IS WRINKLED.
SIZZLE
FATHER, SHOULD I MASSAGE YOUR SHOULDERS?
OH, KASUMI...
EVEN POSSESSED BY A DEMON, YOU'RE SUCH A GOOD DAUGHTER.
SIGH
SNIKT

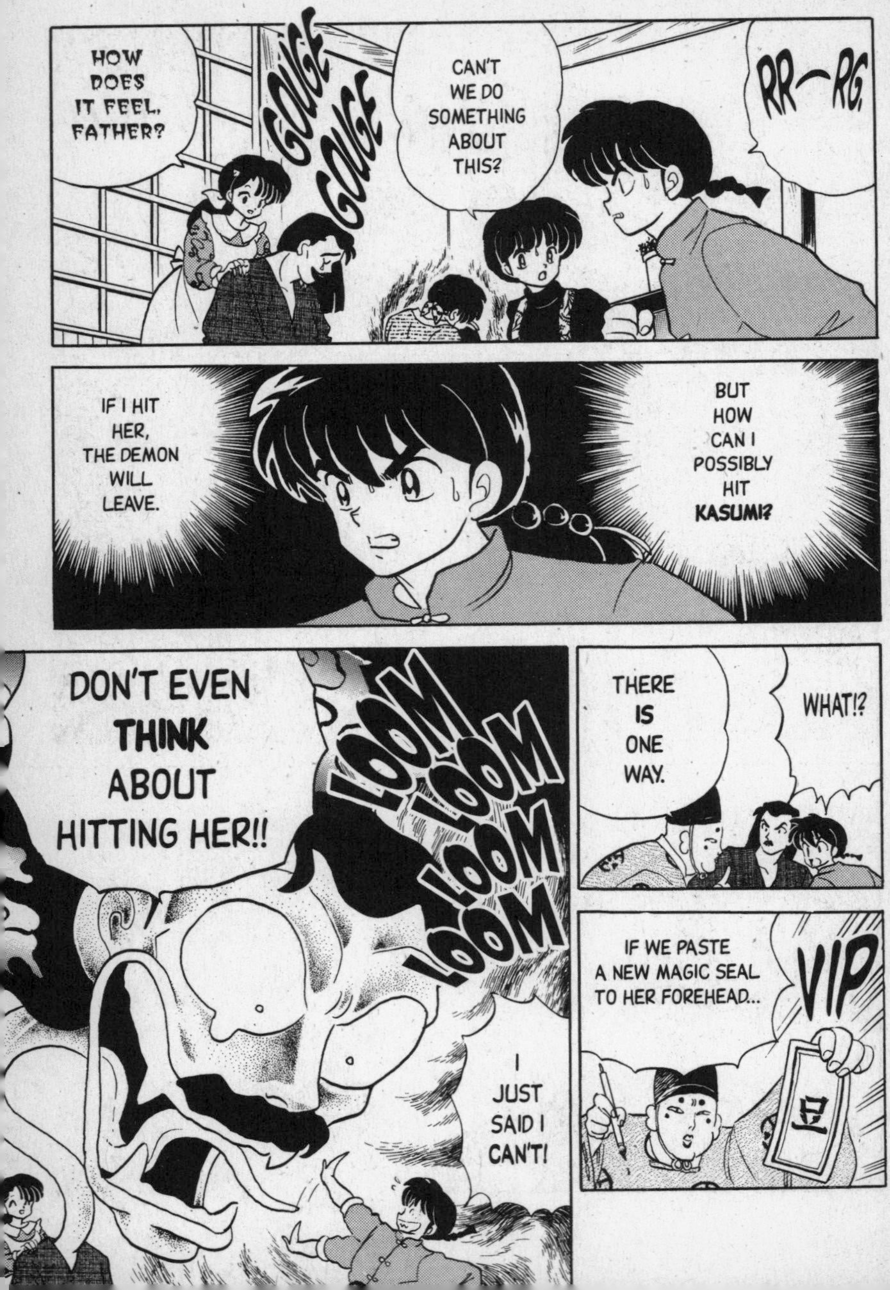

HOW DOES IT FEEL, FATHER?
GOUGE GOUGE
CAN'T WE DO SOMETHING ABOUT THIS?
RR—RG.
IF I HIT HER, THE DEMON WILL LEAVE.
BUT HOW CAN I POSSIBLY HIT **KASUMI?**
DON'T EVEN **THINK** ABOUT HITTING HER!!
LOOM LOOM LOOM LOOM
I JUST SAID I CAN'T!
THERE **IS** ONE WAY.
WHAT!?
IF WE PASTE A NEW MAGIC SEAL TO HER FOREHEAD...
VIP

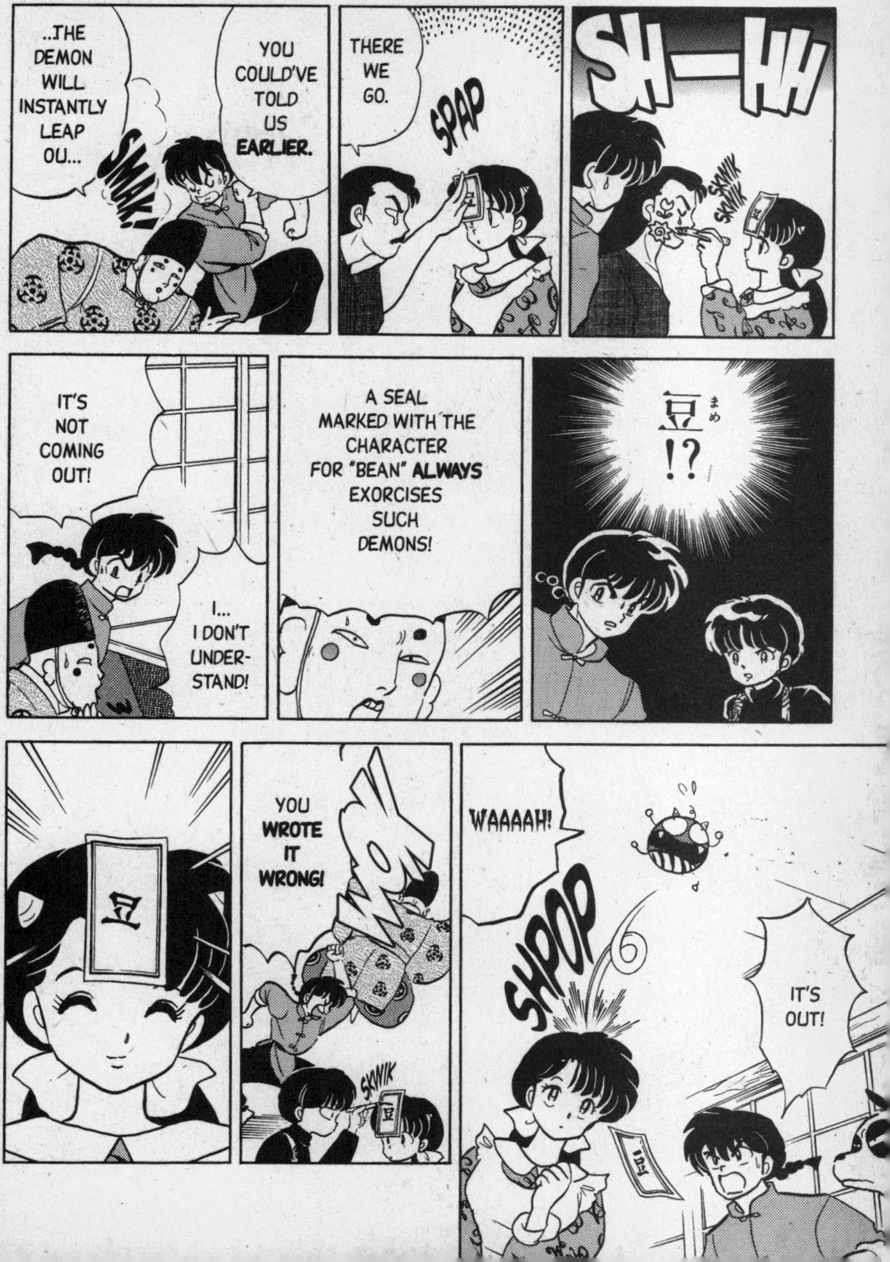

...THE DEMON WILL INSTANTLY LEAP OU...
YOU COULD'VE TOLD US EARLIER.
SMAK!
THERE WE GO.
SPAP
SH—HH
SKWIK SKWIK
IT'S NOT COMING OUT!
I... I DON'T UNDER-STAND!
A SEAL MARKED WITH THE CHARACTER FOR "BEAN" ALWAYS EXORCISES SUCH DEMONS!
まめ
豆!?
豆
YOU WROTE IT WRONG!
SKWIK
豆
WAAAAH!
SHPOP
IT'S OUT!

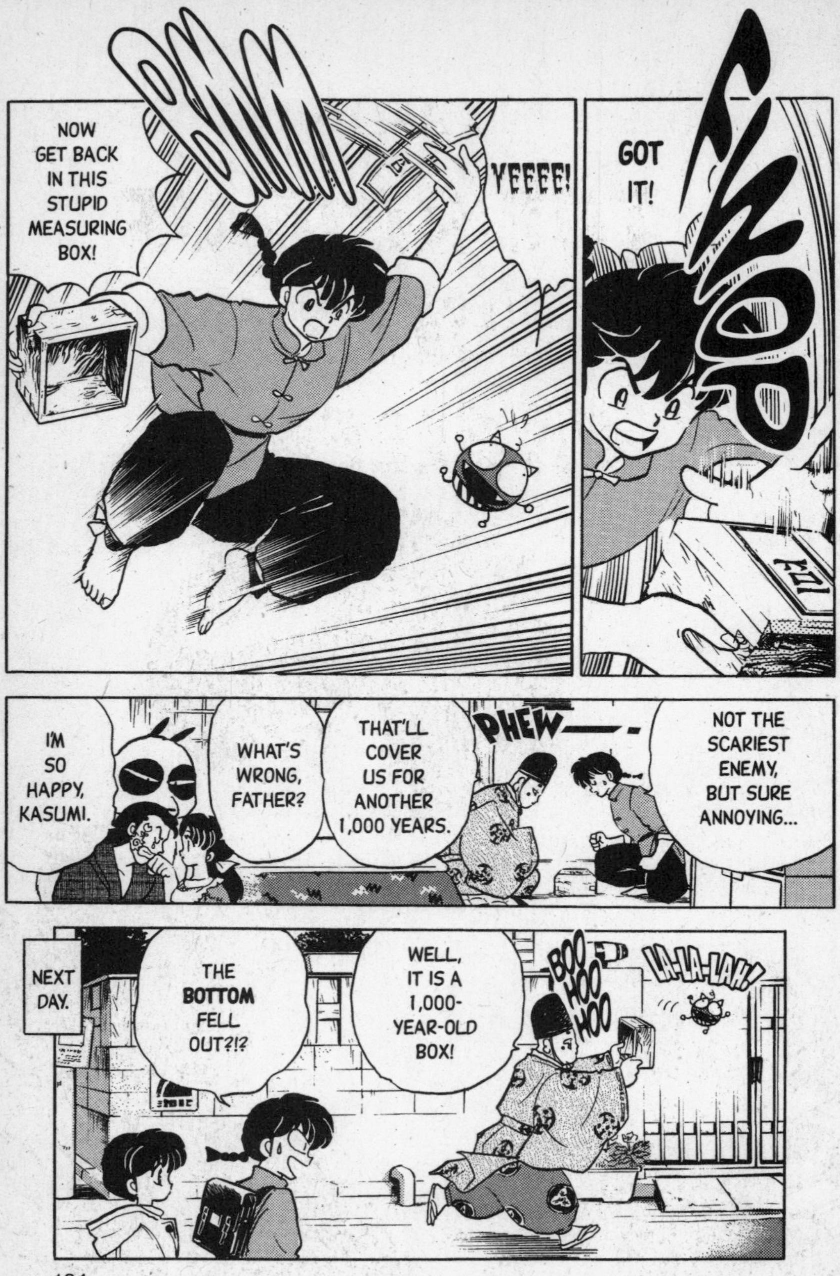
NOW GET BACK IN THIS STUPID MEASURING BOX!
YEEEE!
GOT IT!
I'M SO HAPPY, KASUMI.
WHAT'S WRONG, FATHER?
THAT'LL COVER US FOR ANOTHER 1,000 YEARS.
PHEW—
NOT THE SCARIEST ENEMY, BUT SURE ANNOYING...
NEXT DAY.
THE **BOTTOM** FELL OUT?!?
WELL, IT IS A 1,000-YEAR-OLD BOX!
BOO HOO HOO
LA-LA-LAH!

PART 9

THE KING OF POVERTY'S CHALLENGE

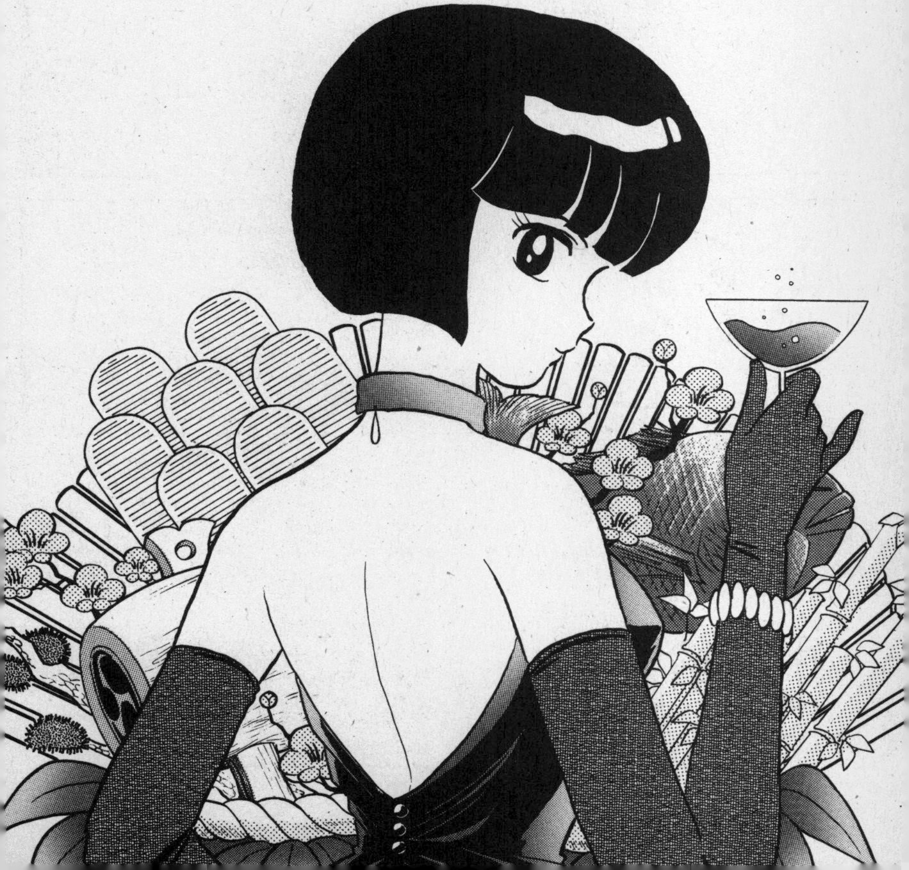

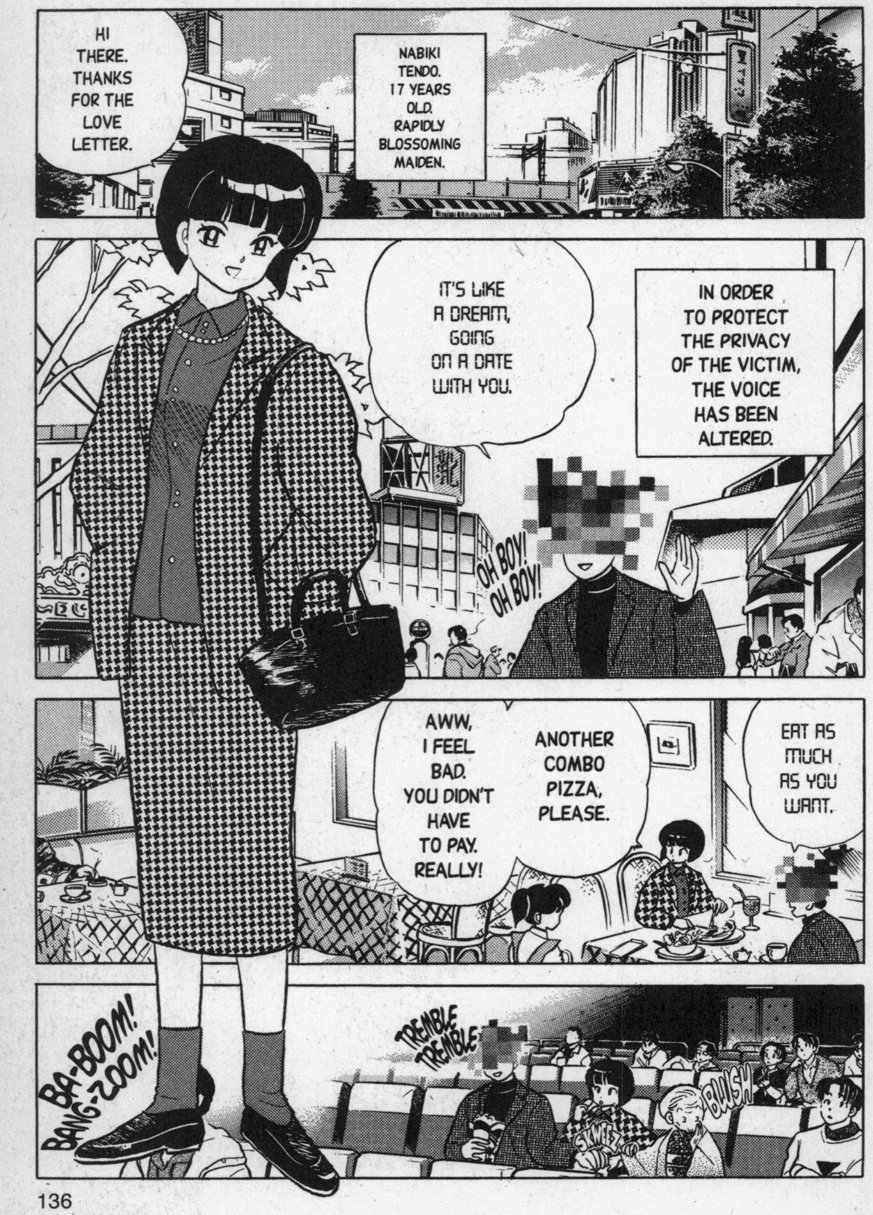
HI THERE. THANKS FOR THE LOVE LETTER.
NABIKI TENDO. 17 YEARS OLD. RAPIDLY BLOSSOMING MAIDEN.
IT'S LIKE A DREAM, GOING ON A DATE WITH YOU.
OH BOY! OH BOY!
IN ORDER TO PROTECT THE PRIVACY OF THE VICTIM, THE VOICE HAS BEEN ALTERED.
AWW, I FEEL BAD. YOU DIDN'T HAVE TO PAY. REALLY!
ANOTHER COMBO PIZZA, PLEASE.
EAT AS MUCH AS YOU WANT.
BA-BOOM! BANG-ZOOM!
TREMBLE TREMBLE
SKWEEZ
BLUSH

OOO, THIS IS SO CUTE!

I'LL B-BUY IT FOR YOU!

THANKS FOR TODAY. BYE!

UM... MISS TENDO... WHEN CAN I SEE YOU AGAIN?

SORRY, BUT I DON'T THINK WE SHOULD SEE EACH OTHER.

WHAT!?

B-BUT... I SPENT ALL THAT MONEY...

WELL... I SUPPOSE IT WAS WORTH...

OH, THIS WONDERFUL **LOVE LETTER** YOU GAVE ME...?

Miss Nabiki Tendo

I'VE MADE TONS OF COPIES.

WANNA BUY 'EM BACK?

...HOW MUCH!?

NABIKI TENDO. 17 YEARS OLD. BLOSSOMING BUT NOT NAIVE.

HA!

PNG PNG PNG

"NABIKI SENSE" TINGLING...

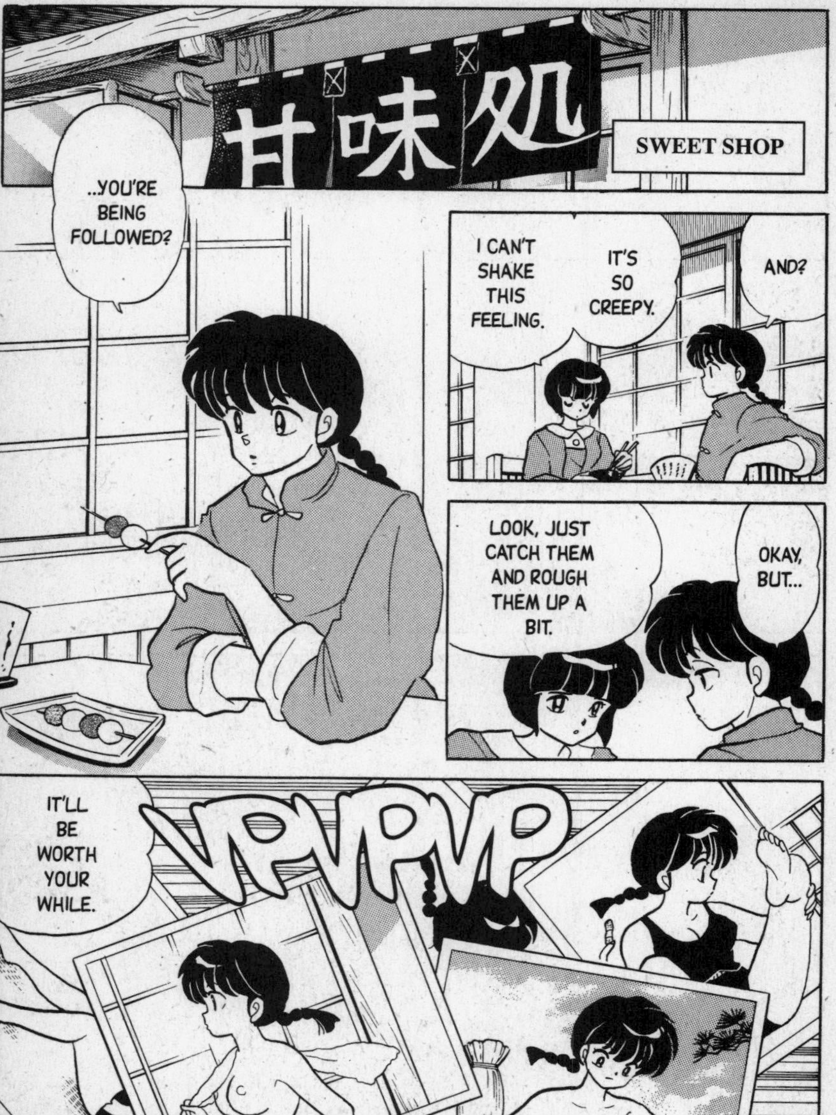

甘味処
SWEET SHOP
...YOU'RE BEING FOLLOWED?
I CAN'T SHAKE THIS FEELING.
IT'S SO CREEPY.
AND?
LOOK, JUST CATCH THEM AND ROUGH THEM UP A BIT.
OKAY, BUT...
IT'LL BE WORTH YOUR WHILE.
VPVPVP

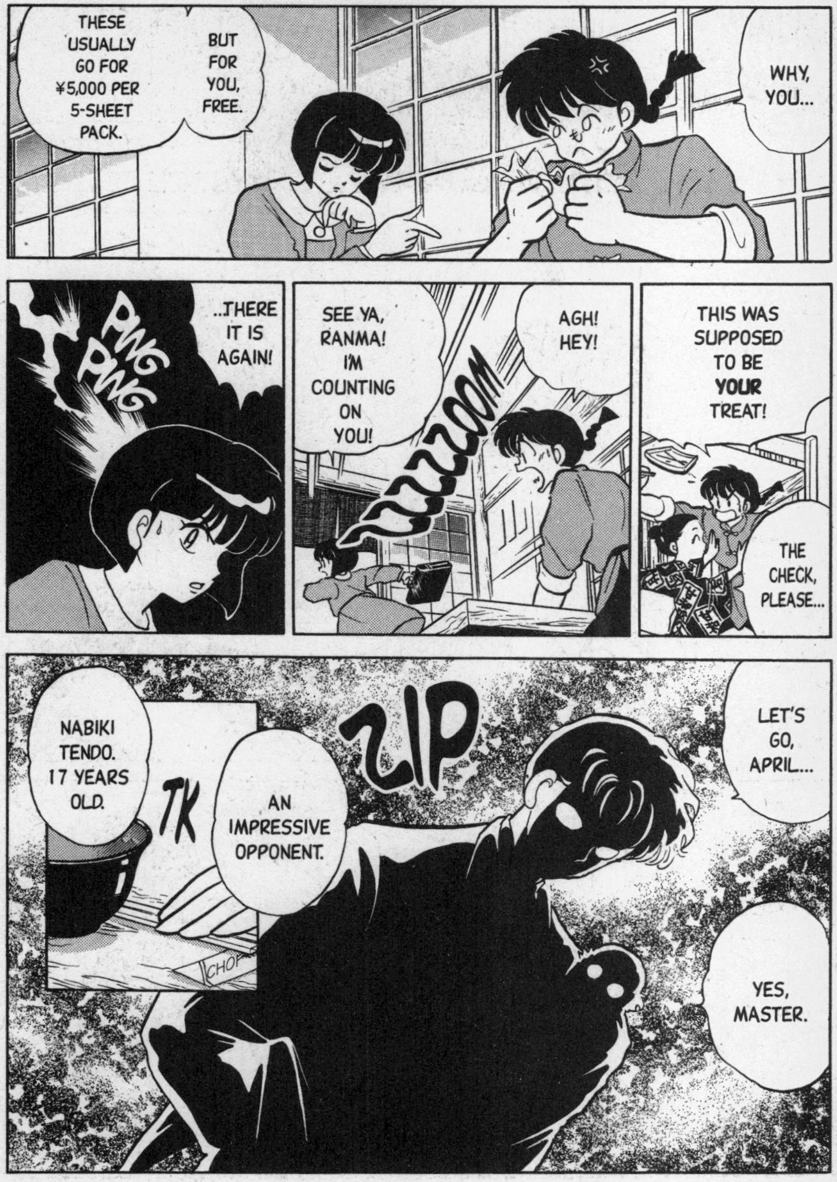
THESE USUALLY GO FOR ¥5,000 PER 5-SHEET PACK.
BUT FOR YOU, FREE.
WHY, YOU...
PWNG PWNG
...THERE IT IS AGAIN!
SEE YA, RANMA! I'M COUNTING ON YOU!
VZZZOOM
AGH! HEY!
THIS WAS SUPPOSED TO BE YOUR TREAT!
THE CHECK, PLEASE...
NABIKI TENDO. 17 YEARS OLD.
TK
AN IMPRESSIVE OPPONENT.
ZIP
LET'S GO, APRIL...
YES, MASTER.

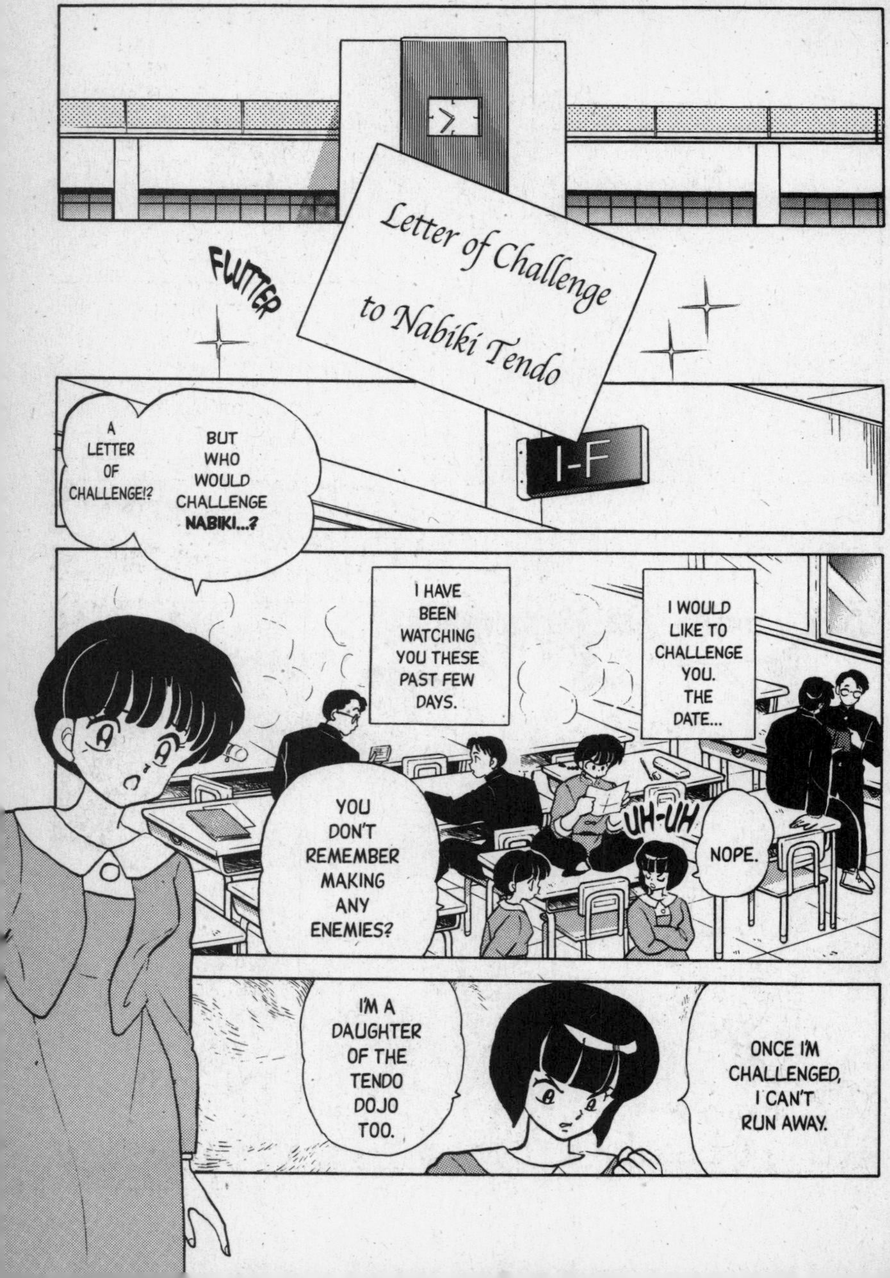
FLUTTER
Letter of Challenge to Nabiki Tendo
A LETTER OF CHALLENGE!?
BUT WHO WOULD CHALLENGE NABIKI...?
I-F
I HAVE BEEN WATCHING YOU THESE PAST FEW DAYS.
I WOULD LIKE TO CHALLENGE YOU. THE DATE...
YOU DON'T REMEMBER MAKING ANY ENEMIES?
UH-UH
NOPE.
I'M A DAUGHTER OF THE TENDO DOJO TOO.
ONCE I'M CHALLENGED, I CAN'T RUN AWAY.

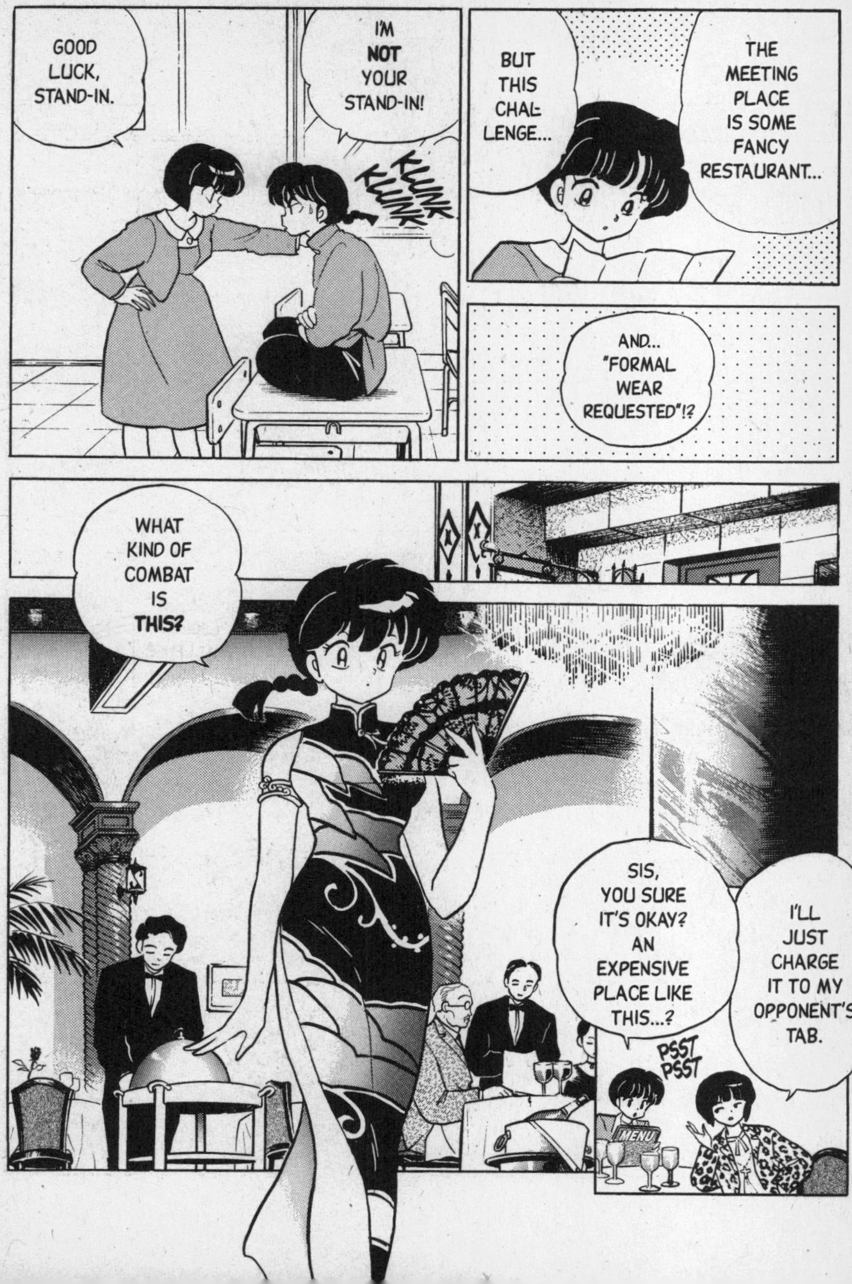
GOOD LUCK, STAND-IN.
I'M NOT YOUR STAND-IN!
KLUNK KLUNK
BUT THIS CHAL-LENGE...
THE MEETING PLACE IS SOME FANCY RESTAURANT...
AND... "FORMAL WEAR REQUESTED"!?
WHAT KIND OF COMBAT IS THIS?
SIS, YOU SURE IT'S OKAY? AN EXPENSIVE PLACE LIKE THIS...?
I'LL JUST CHARGE IT TO MY OPPONENT'S TAB.
PSST PSST
MENU

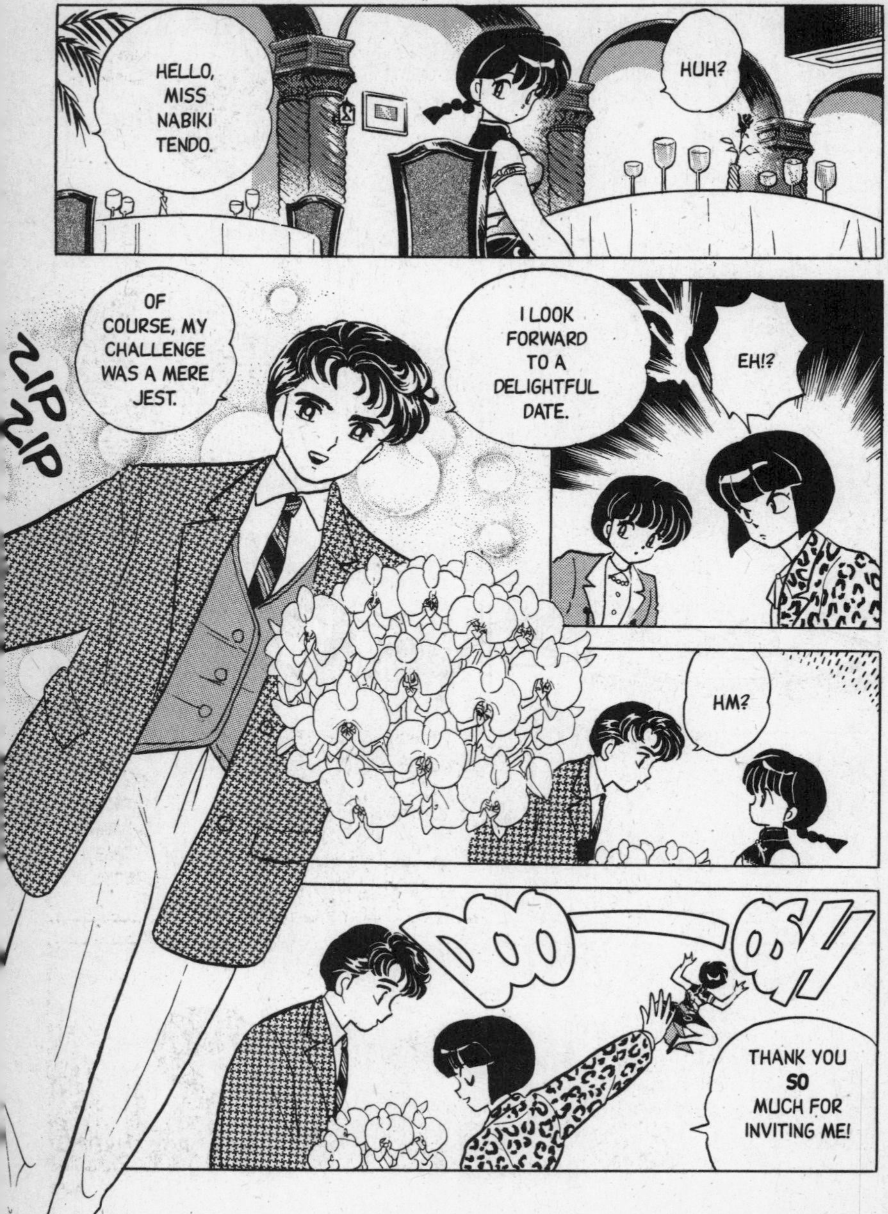
HELLO, MISS NABIKI TENDO.
HUH?
ZIP ZIP
OF COURSE, MY CHALLENGE WAS A MERE JEST.
I LOOK FORWARD TO A DELIGHTFUL DATE.
EH!?
HM?
DOO—OSH
THANK YOU **SO** MUCH FOR INVITING ME!

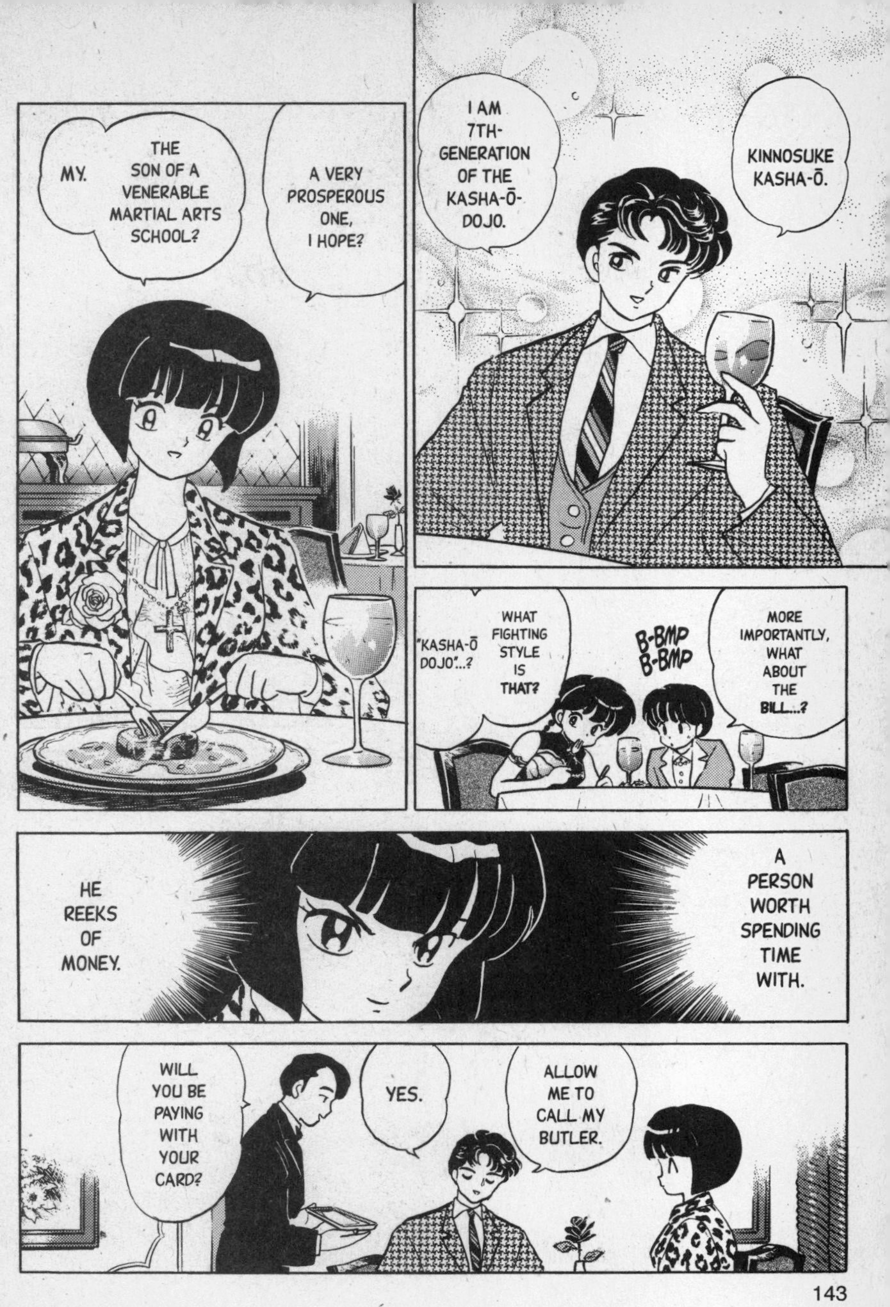
MY.
THE SON OF A VENERABLE MARTIAL ARTS SCHOOL?
A VERY PROSPEROUS ONE, I HOPE?
I AM 7TH-GENERATION OF THE KASHA-Ō-DOJO.
KINNOSUKE KASHA-Ō.
"KASHA-Ō DOJO"...?
WHAT FIGHTING STYLE IS THAT?
B-BMP B-BMP
MORE IMPORTANTLY, WHAT ABOUT THE BILL...?
HE REEKS OF MONEY.
A PERSON WORTH SPENDING TIME WITH.
WILL YOU BE PAYING WITH YOUR CARD?
YES.
ALLOW ME TO CALL MY BUTLER.

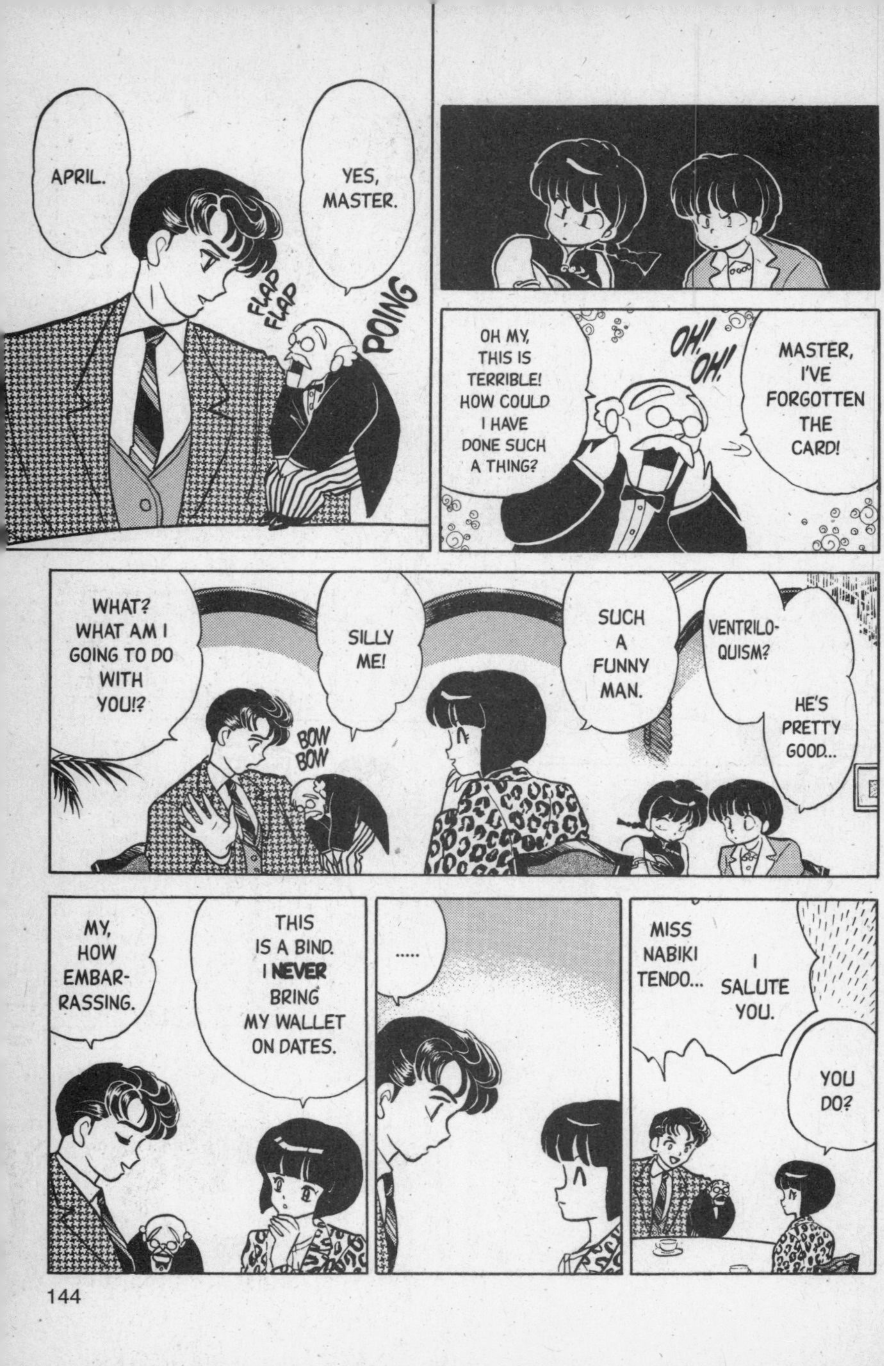

APRIL.
YES, MASTER.
FLAP FLAP
POING
OH MY, THIS IS TERRIBLE! HOW COULD I HAVE DONE SUCH A THING?
OH! OH!
MASTER, I'VE FORGOTTEN THE CARD!
WHAT? WHAT AM I GOING TO DO WITH YOU!?
SILLY ME!
BOW BOW
SUCH A FUNNY MAN.
VENTRILO-QUISM?
HE'S PRETTY GOOD...
MY, HOW EMBAR-RASSING.
THIS IS A BIND. I **NEVER** BRING MY WALLET ON DATES.
.....
MISS NABIKI TENDO...
I SALUTE YOU.
YOU DO?

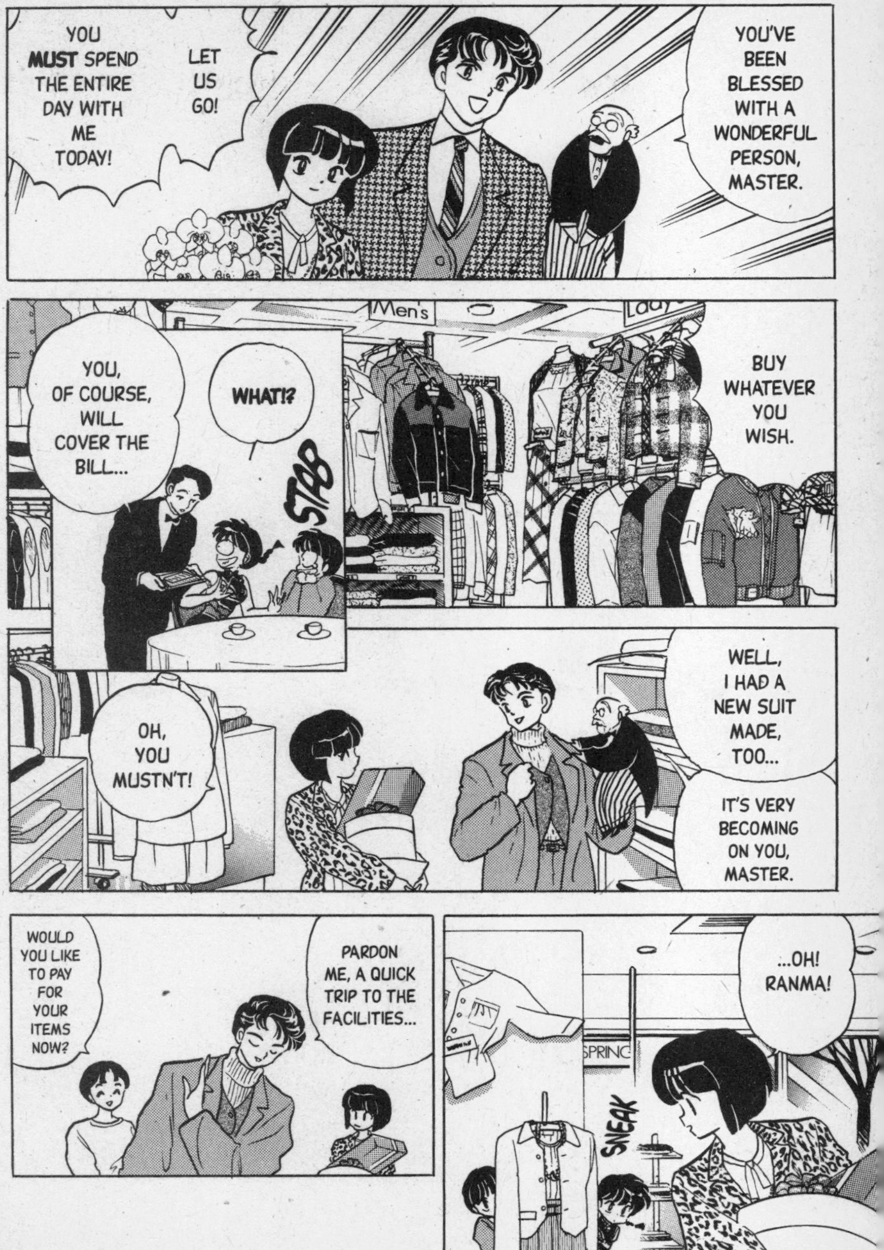
YOU **MUST** SPEND THE ENTIRE DAY WITH ME TODAY!
LET US GO!
YOU'VE BEEN BLESSED WITH A WONDERFUL PERSON, MASTER.
YOU, OF COURSE, WILL COVER THE BILL...
WHAT!?
STAB
Men's
BUY WHATEVER YOU WISH.
OH, YOU MUSTN'T!
WELL, I HAD A NEW SUIT MADE, TOO...
IT'S VERY BECOMING ON YOU, MASTER.
WOULD YOU LIKE TO PAY FOR YOUR ITEMS NOW?
PARDON ME, A QUICK TRIP TO THE FACILITIES...
...OH! RANMA!
SPRING
SNEAK

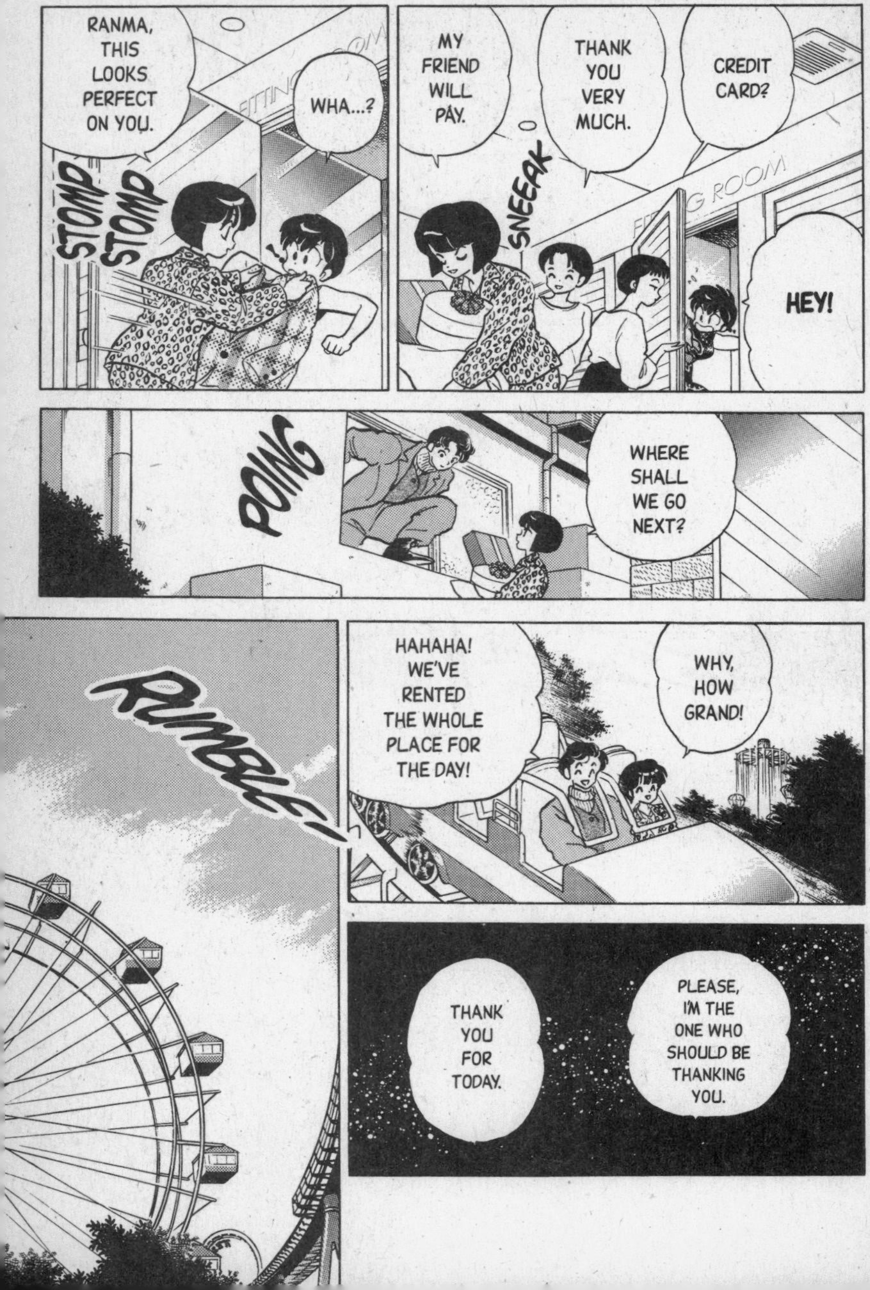
RANMA, THIS LOOKS PERFECT ON YOU.
WHA...?
STOMP STOMP
FITTING ROOM
MY FRIEND WILL PAY.
THANK YOU VERY MUCH.
CREDIT CARD?
SNEEAK
FITTING ROOM
HEY!
POING
WHERE SHALL WE GO NEXT?
RUMBLE!
HAHAHA! WE'VE RENTED THE WHOLE PLACE FOR THE DAY!
WHY, HOW GRAND!
THANK YOU FOR TODAY.
PLEASE, I'M THE ONE WHO SHOULD BE THANKING YOU.

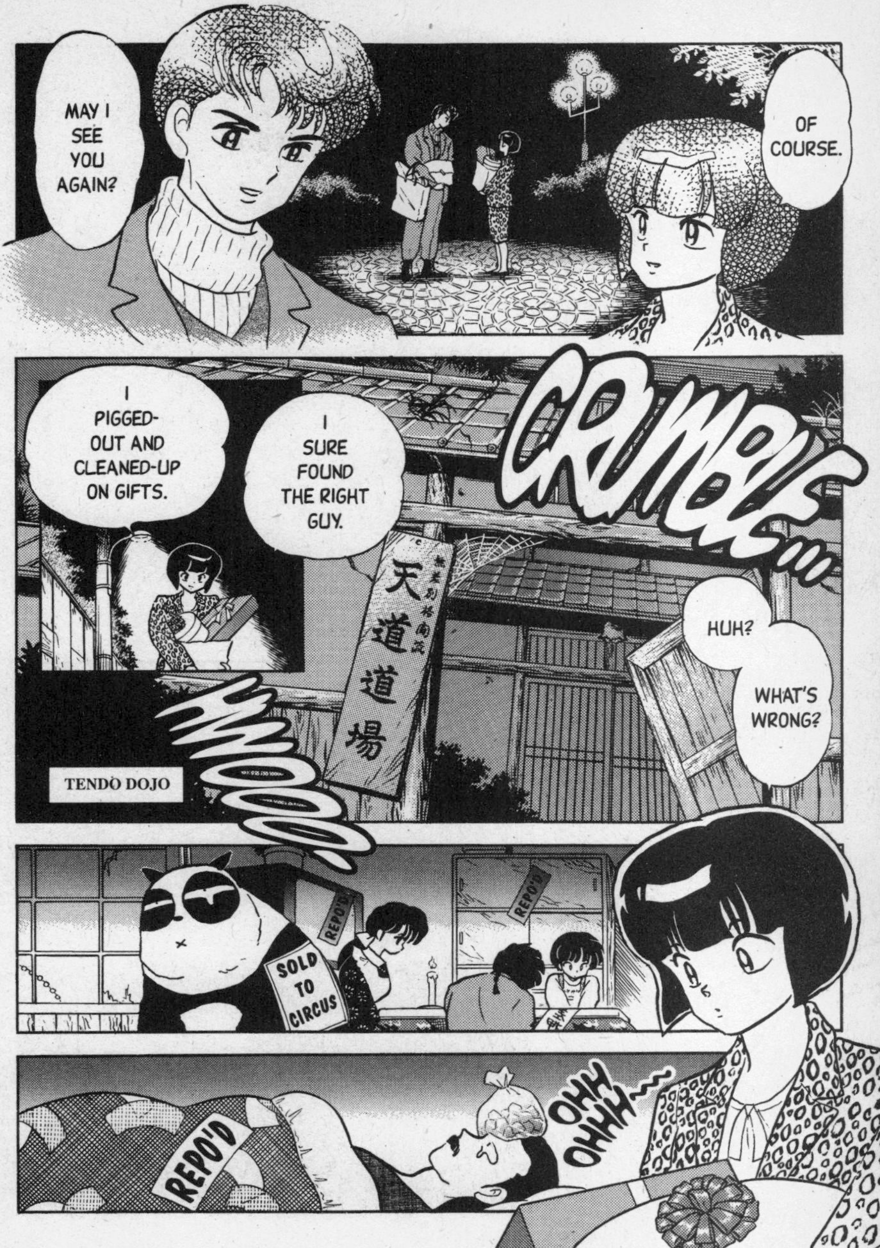
MAY I SEE YOU AGAIN?
OF COURSE.
I PIGGED-OUT AND CLEANED-UP ON GIFTS.
I SURE FOUND THE RIGHT GUY.
CRUMBLE...
天道道場
HUH?
WHAT'S WRONG?
TENDO DOJO
REPO'D
SOLD TO CIRCUS
REPO'D
REPO'D
OHHH OHHH~~

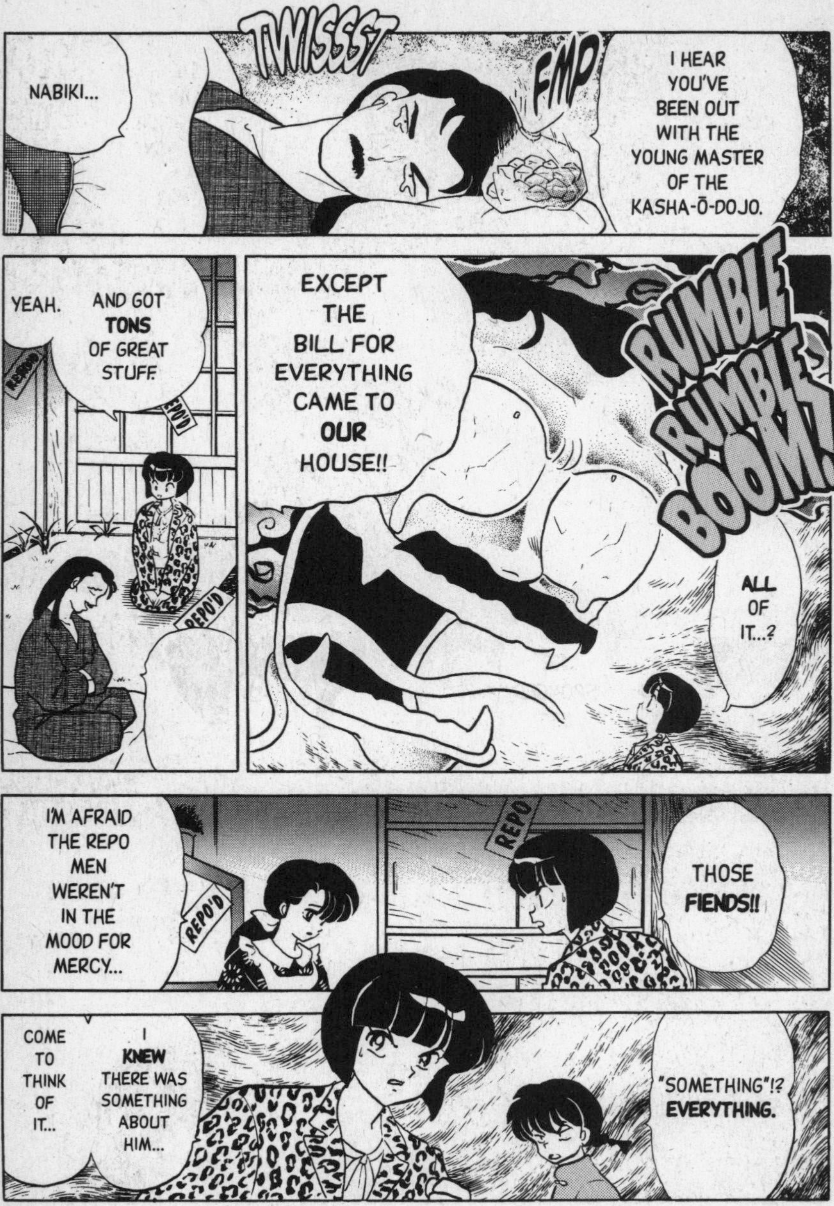
NABIKI...
TWISSST
FMP
I HEAR YOU'VE BEEN OUT WITH THE YOUNG MASTER OF THE KASHA-Ō-DOJO.
YEAH.
AND GOT TONS OF GREAT STUFF.
REPO'D
REPO'D
REPO'D
EXCEPT THE BILL FOR EVERYTHING CAME TO OUR HOUSE!!
RUMBLE RUMBLE BOOM!!
ALL OF IT...?
I'M AFRAID THE REPO MEN WEREN'T IN THE MOOD FOR MERCY...
REPO'D
REPO
THOSE FIENDS!!
COME TO THINK OF IT...
I KNEW THERE WAS SOMETHING ABOUT HIM...
"SOMETHING"!? EVERYTHING.

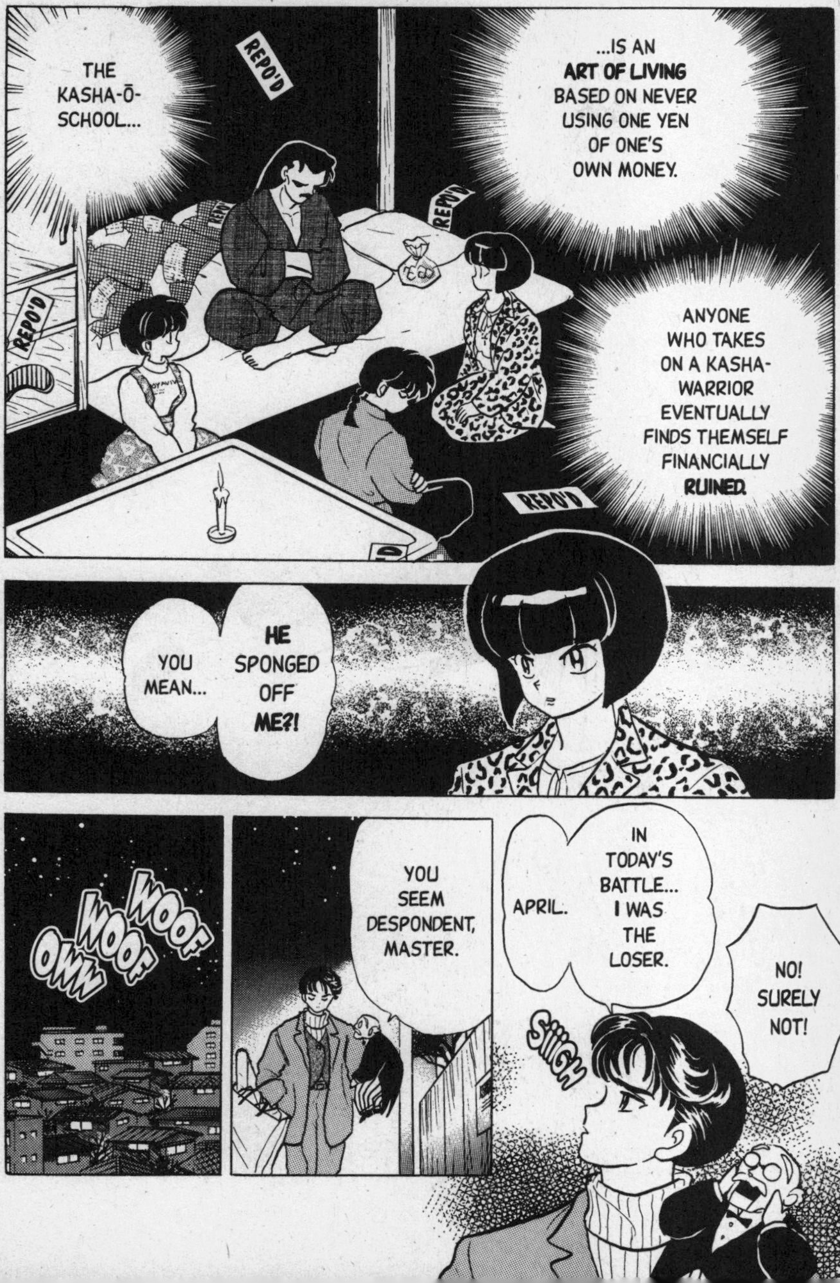
THE KASHA-Ō-SCHOOL...
REPO'D
REPO'D
REPO'D
REPO'D
REPO'D
...IS AN ART OF LIVING BASED ON NEVER USING ONE YEN OF ONE'S OWN MONEY.
ANYONE WHO TAKES ON A KASHA-WARRIOR EVENTUALLY FINDS THEMSELF FINANCIALLY RUINED.
YOU MEAN...
HE SPONGED OFF ME?!
WOOF WOOF OWW
YOU SEEM DESPONDENT, MASTER.
APRIL.
IN TODAY'S BATTLE... I WAS THE LOSER.
SIGH
NO! SURELY NOT!

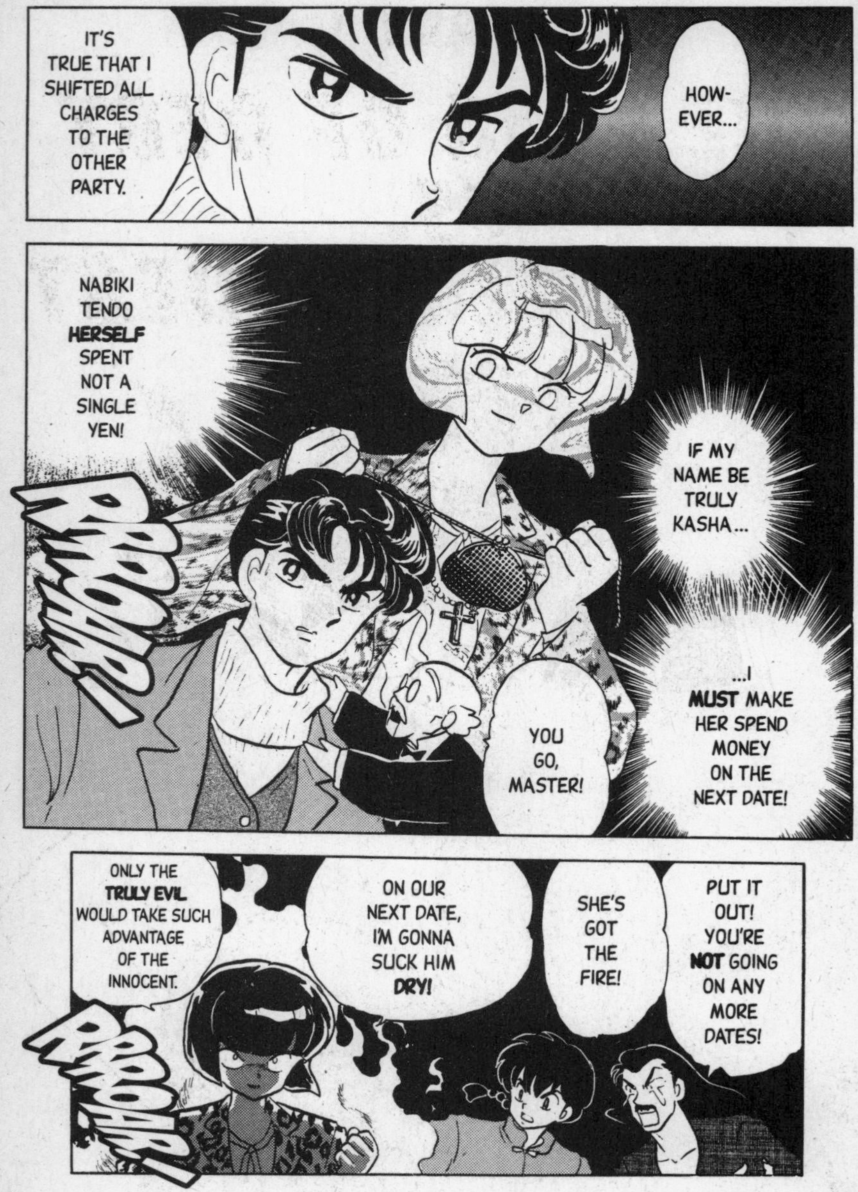
IT'S TRUE THAT I SHIFTED ALL CHARGES TO THE OTHER PARTY.
HOW-EVER...
NABIKI TENDO **HERSELF** SPENT NOT A SINGLE YEN!
RRROAR!
IF MY NAME BE TRULY KASHA...
YOU GO, MASTER!
...I **MUST** MAKE HER SPEND MONEY ON THE NEXT DATE!
ONLY THE **TRULY EVIL** WOULD TAKE SUCH ADVANTAGE OF THE INNOCENT.
RRROAR!
ON OUR NEXT DATE, I'M GONNA SUCK HIM **DRY!**
SHE'S GOT THE FIRE!
PUT IT OUT! YOU'RE **NOT** GOING ON ANY MORE DATES!

PART 10

THE KING OF DEBT VS. THE QUEEN OF DEBT

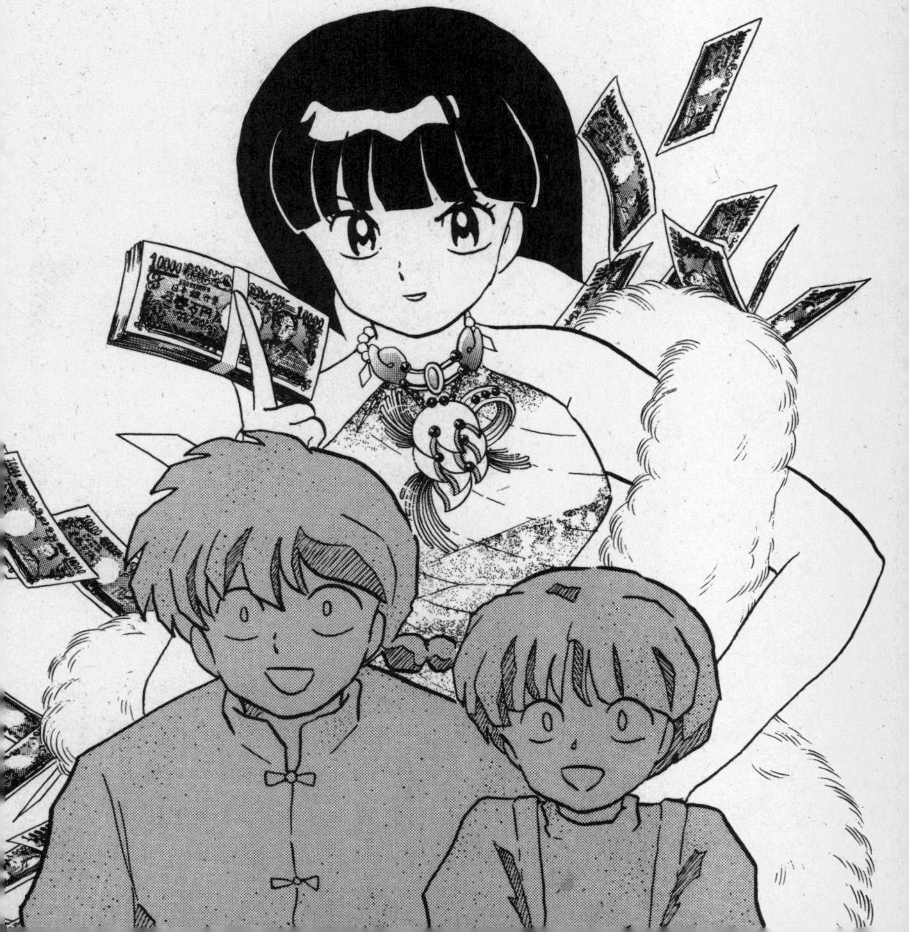

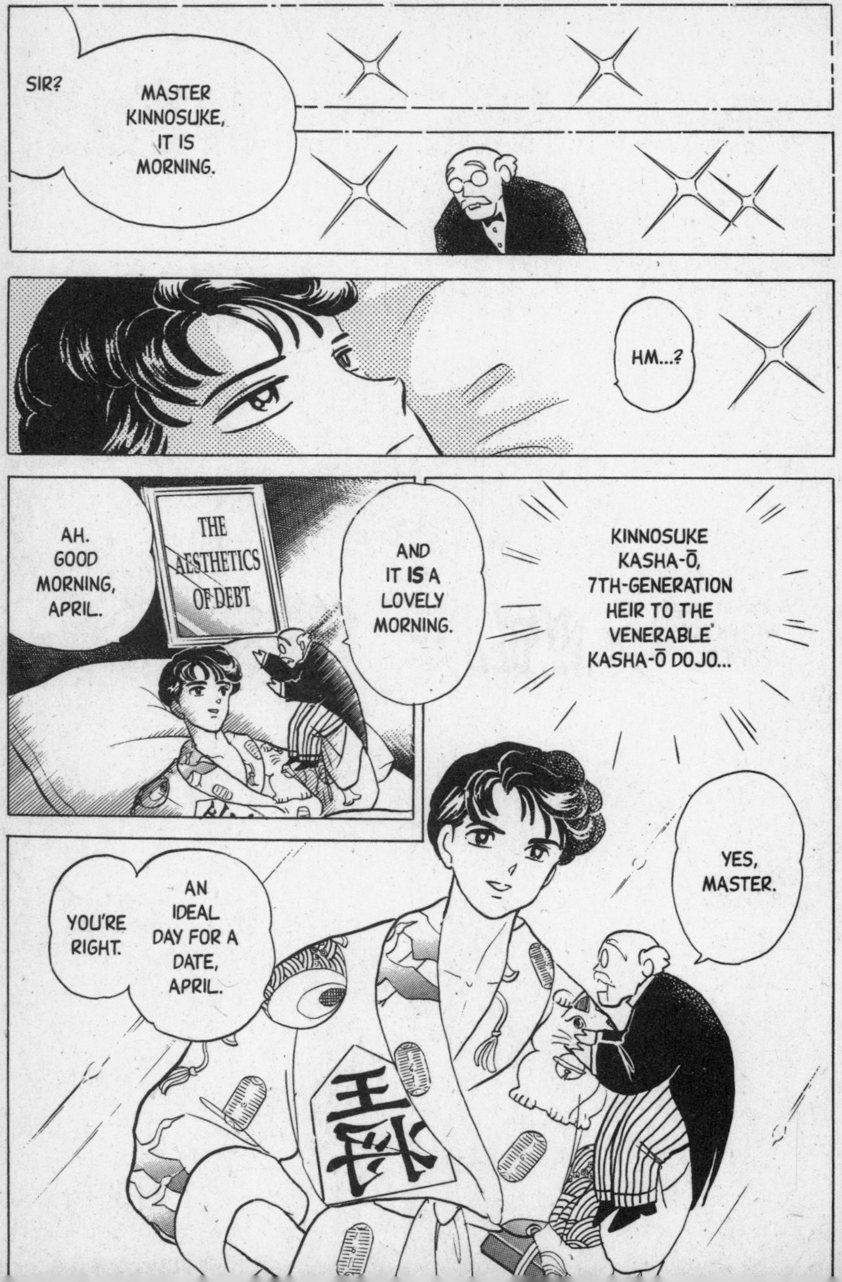

SIR?
MASTER KINNOSUKE, IT IS MORNING.
HM...?
AH. GOOD MORNING, APRIL.
THE AESTHETICS OF DEBT
AND IT **IS** A LOVELY MORNING.
KINNOSUKE KASHA-Ō, 7TH-GENERATION HEIR TO THE VENERABLE KASHA-Ō DOJO...
YOU'RE RIGHT.
AN IDEAL DAY FOR A DATE, APRIL.
YES, MASTER.

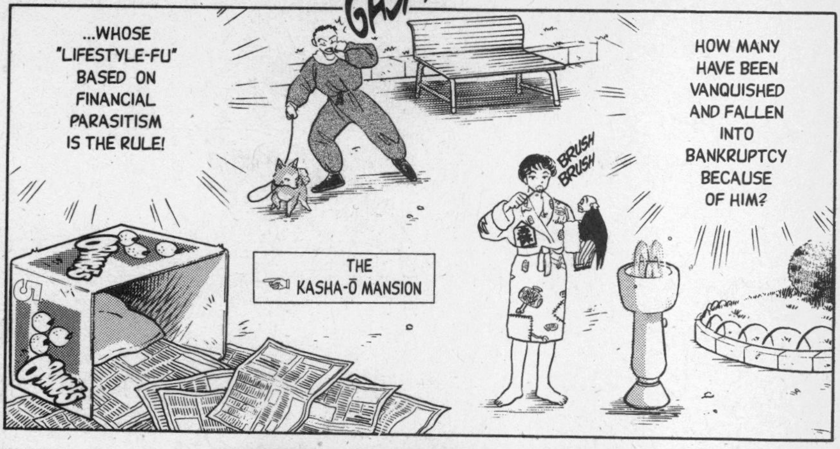
...WHOSE "LIFESTYLE-FU" BASED ON FINANCIAL PARASITISM IS THE RULE!
GASP!
BRUSH BRUSH
THE KASHA-Ō MANSION
HOW MANY HAVE BEEN VANQUISHED AND FALLEN INTO BANKRUPTCY BECAUSE OF HIM?

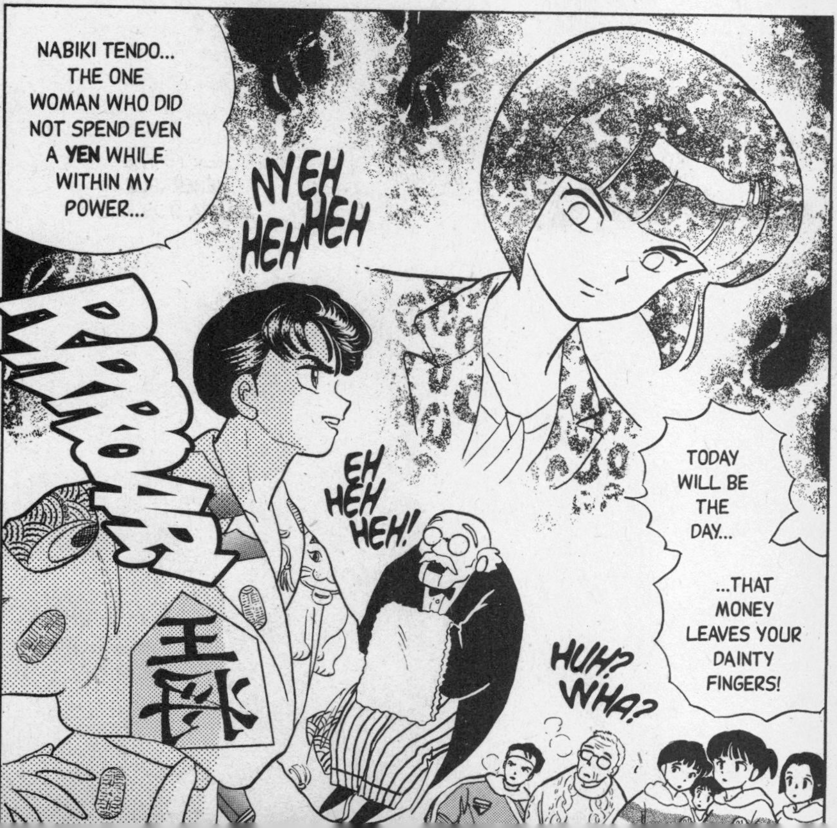
NABIKI TENDO... THE ONE WOMAN WHO DID NOT SPEND EVEN A YEN WHILE WITHIN MY POWER...
NYEH HEH HEH HEH
EH HEH HEH HEH!
TODAY WILL BE THE DAY...
...THAT MONEY LEAVES YOUR DAINTY FINGERS!
HUH? WHA?

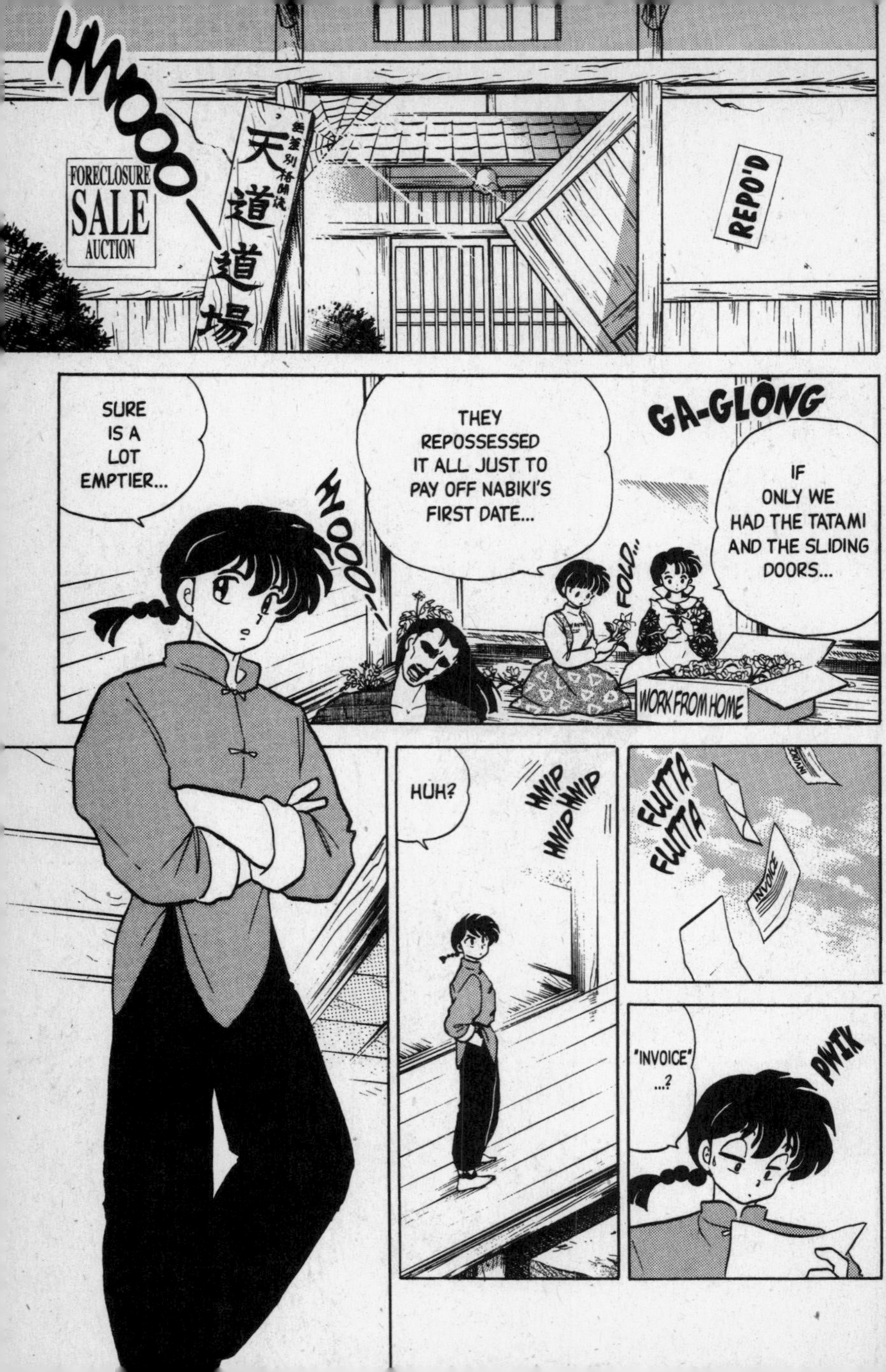
HWOOO—
FORECLOSURE
SALE
AUCTION
天道道場
REPO'D
SURE IS A LOT EMPTIER...
HWOOO—
THEY REPOSSESSED IT ALL JUST TO PAY OFF NABIKI'S FIRST DATE...
FOLD...
GA-GLÔNG
IF ONLY WE HAD THE TATAMI AND THE SLIDING DOORS...
WORK FROM HOME
HUH?
HWIP HWIP HWIP
FLUTTA FLUTTA
INVOICE
"INVOICE" ...?
PWIK

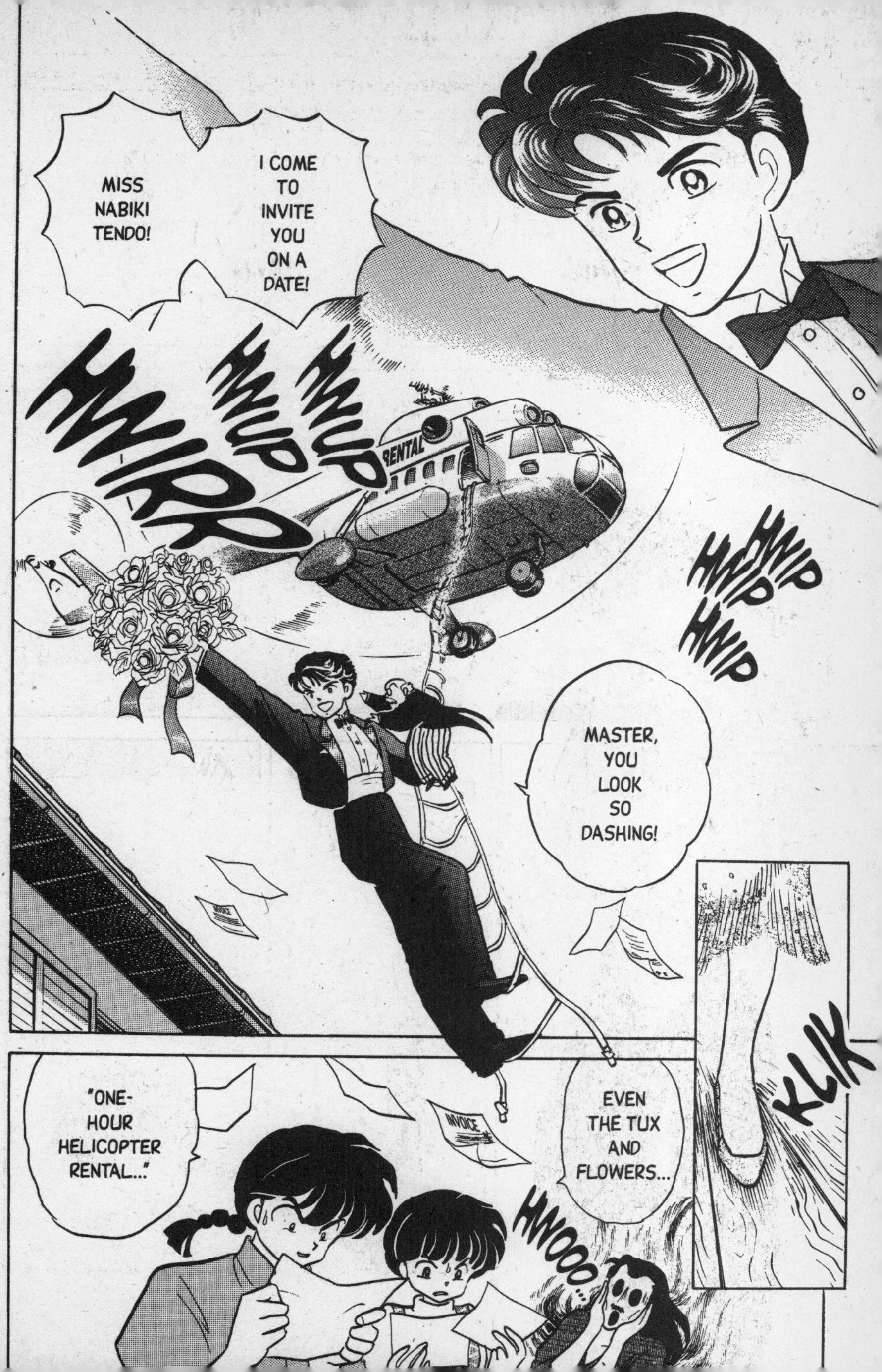
MISS NABIKI TENDO!
I COME TO INVITE YOU ON A DATE!
HWIRR
HWUP HWUP
RENTAL
HWIP HWIP HWIP
MASTER, YOU LOOK SO DASHING!
INVOICE
"ONE-HOUR HELICOPTER RENTAL..."
EVEN THE TUX AND FLOWERS...
HWOOO...
KLIK

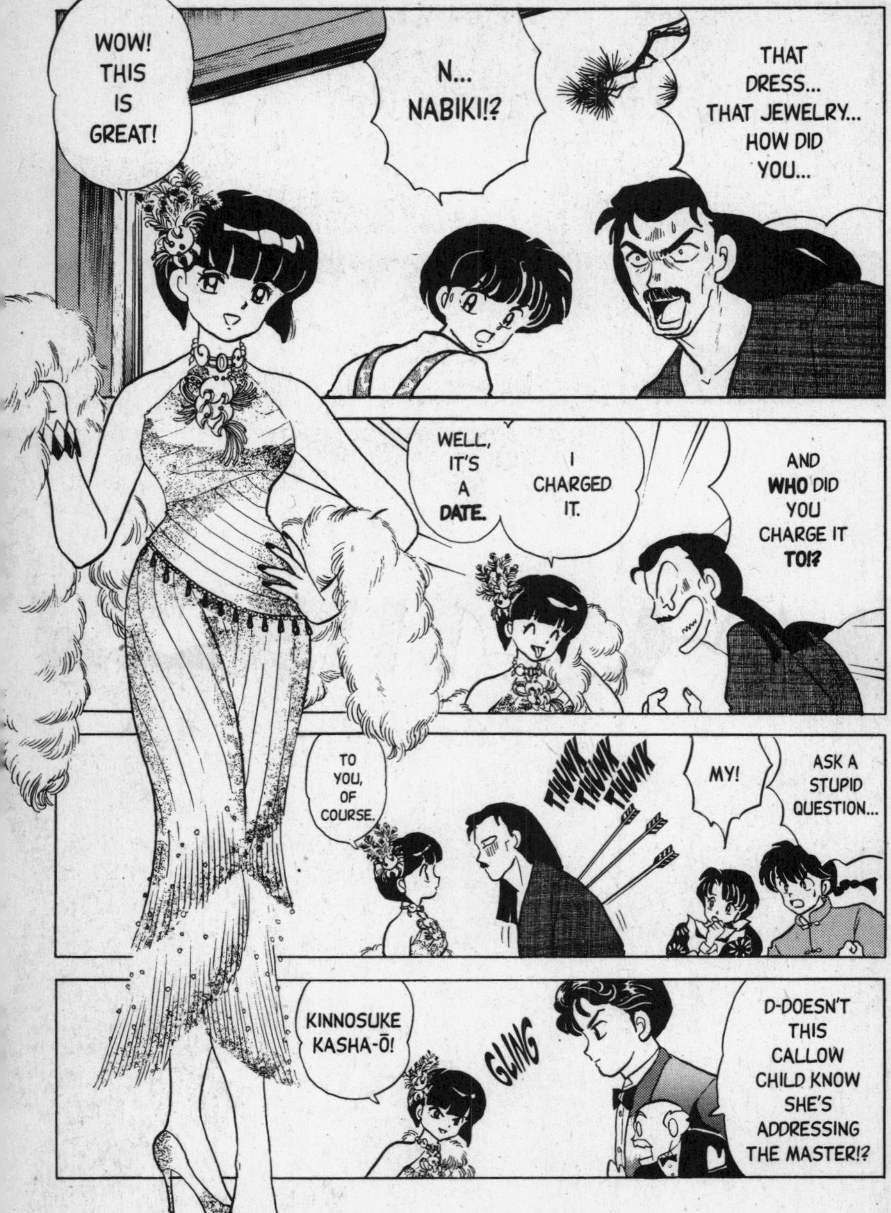
WOW! THIS IS GREAT!
N... NABIKI!?
THAT DRESS... THAT JEWELRY... HOW DID YOU...
WELL, IT'S A DATE.
I CHARGED IT.
AND WHO DID YOU CHARGE IT TO!?
TO YOU, OF COURSE.
THUNK THUNK THUNK
MY!
ASK A STUPID QUESTION...
KINNOSUKE KASHA-Ō!
GLING
D-DOESN'T THIS CALLOW CHILD KNOW SHE'S ADDRESSING THE MASTER!?

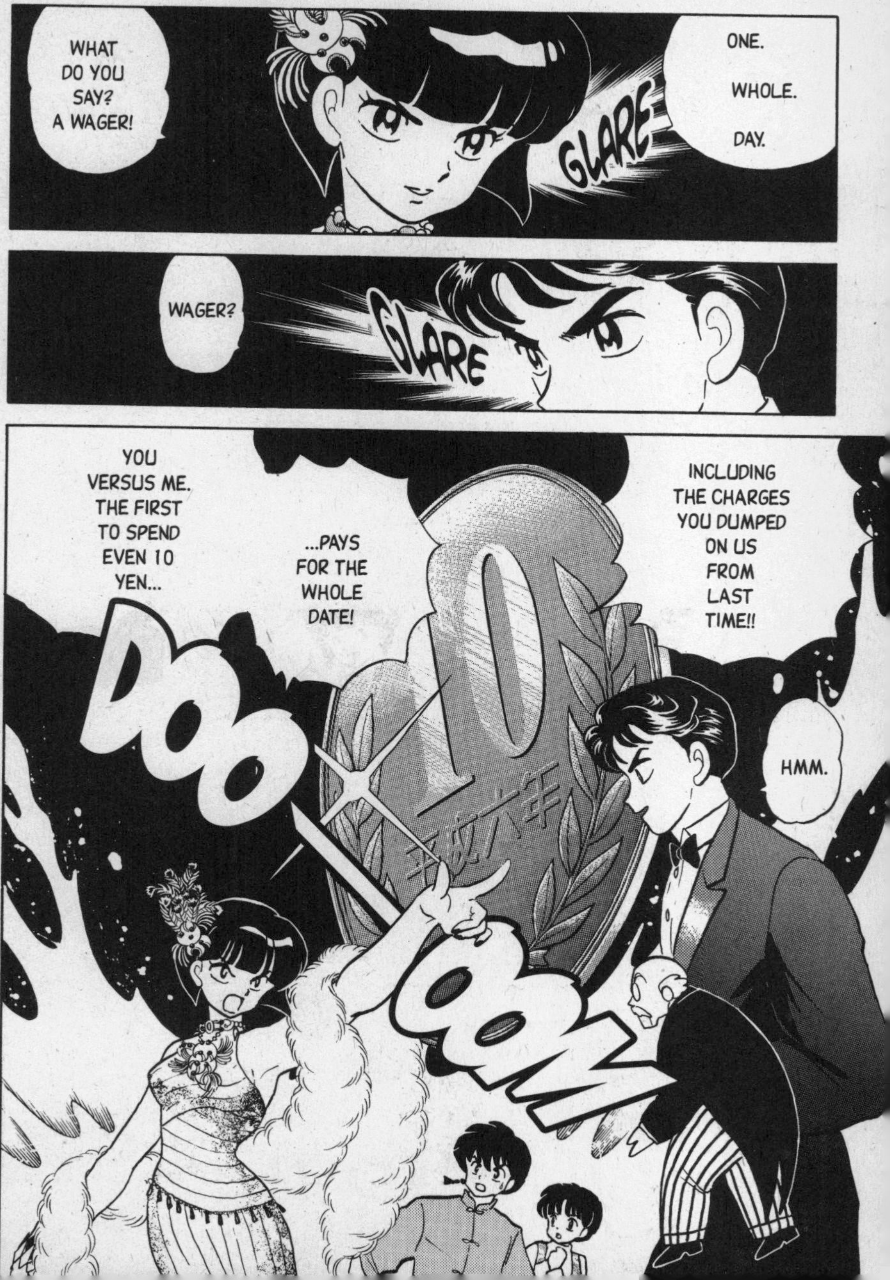
WHAT DO YOU SAY? A WAGER!
GLARE
ONE. WHOLE. DAY.
WAGER?
GLARE
YOU VERSUS ME. THE FIRST TO SPEND EVEN 10 YEN...
...PAYS FOR THE WHOLE DATE!
DOO
INCLUDING THE CHARGES YOU DUMPED ON US FROM LAST TIME!!
HMM.
OOM!

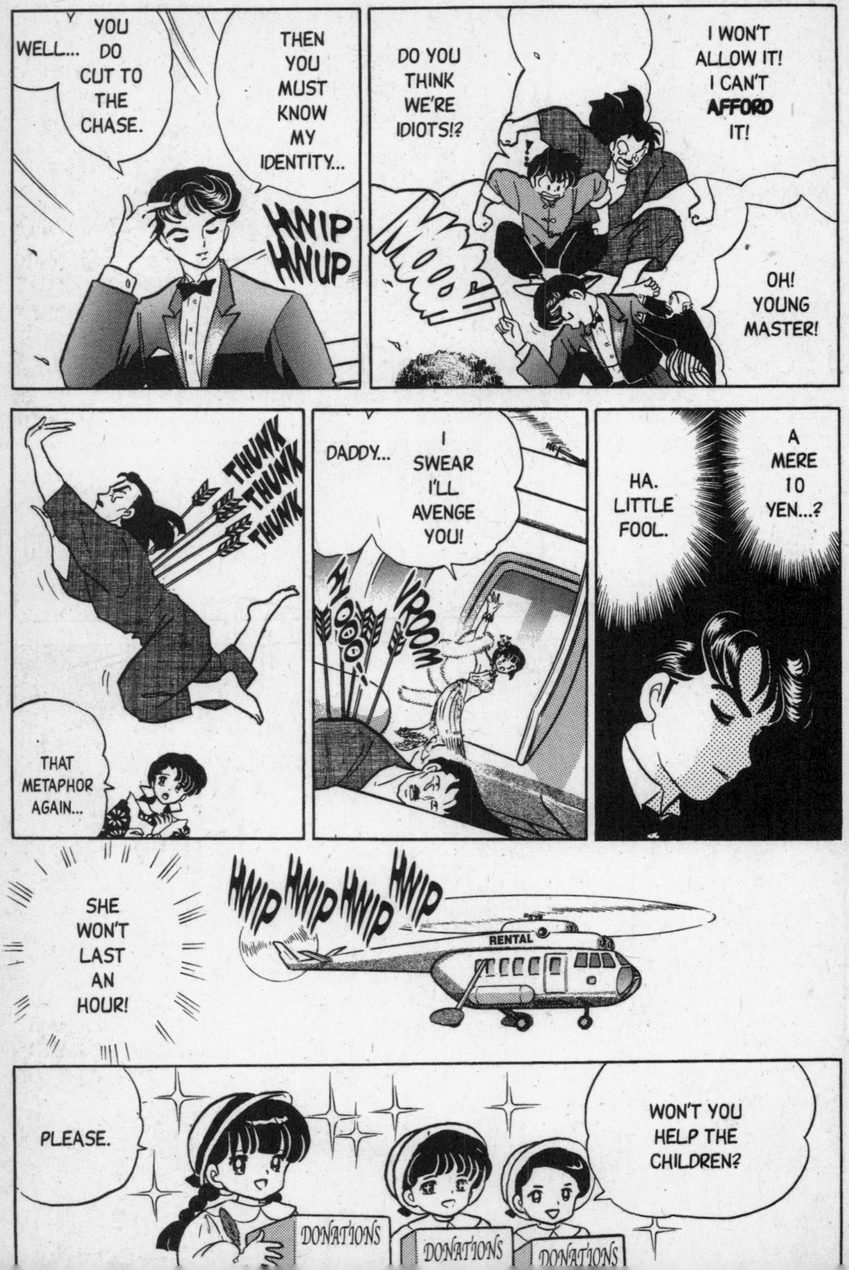
WELL... YOU DO CUT TO THE CHASE.
THEN YOU MUST KNOW MY IDENTITY...
HWIP HWUP
DO YOU THINK WE'RE IDIOTS!?
I WON'T ALLOW IT! I CAN'T AFFORD IT!
WOOOO
OH! YOUNG MASTER!
THUNK THUNK THUNK
THAT METAPHOR AGAIN...
DADDY...
I SWEAR I'LL AVENGE YOU!
HYOOO!
VROOM
HA. LITTLE FOOL.
A MERE 10 YEN...?
SHE WON'T LAST AN HOUR!
HWIP HWIP HWIP HWIP
RENTAL
PLEASE.
WON'T YOU HELP THE CHILDREN?
DONATIONS
DONATIONS
DONATIONS

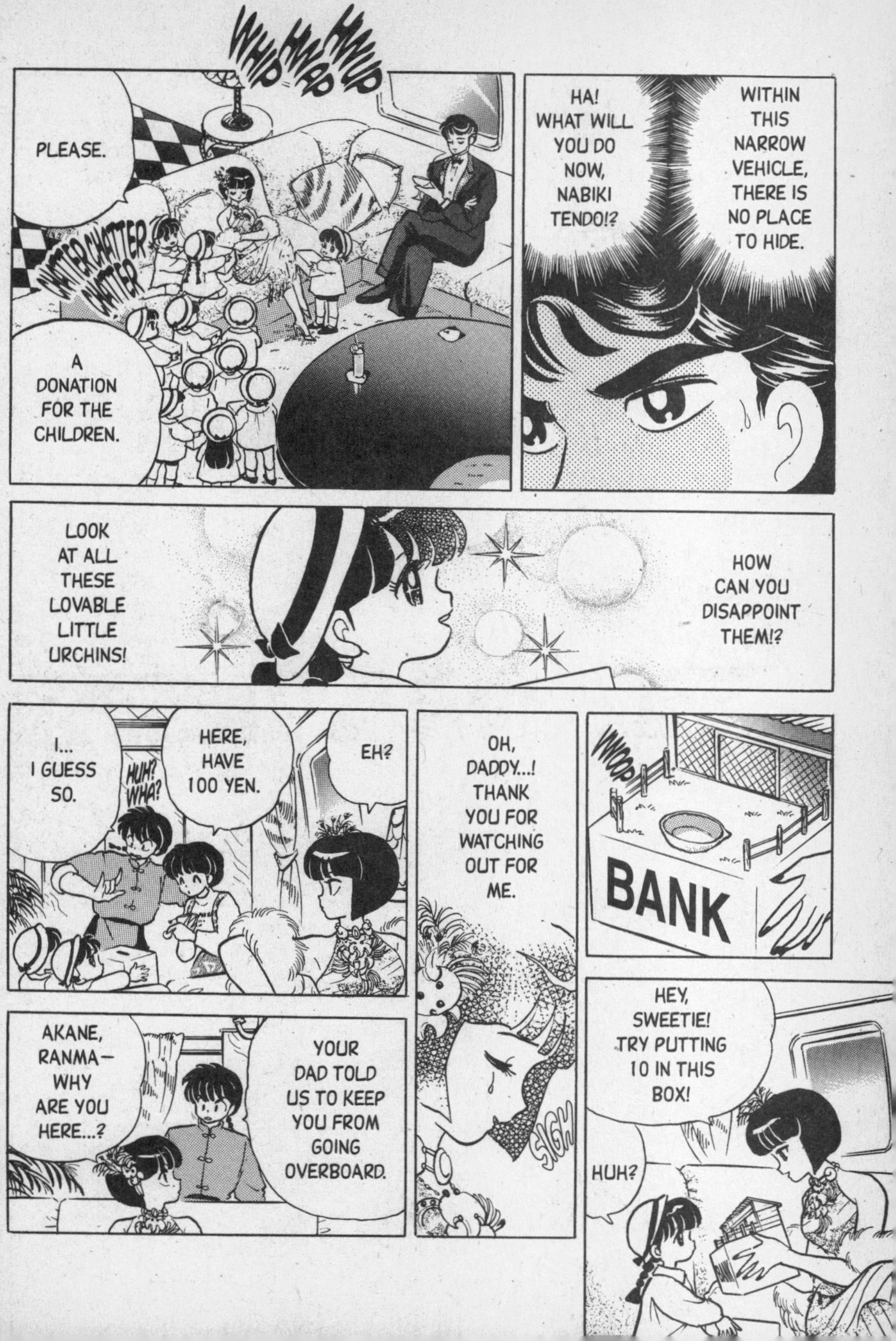
WHIP HWAP HWUP
PLEASE.
CHATTER CHATTER CHATTER
A DONATION FOR THE CHILDREN.
HA! WHAT WILL YOU DO NOW, NABIKI TENDO!?
WITHIN THIS NARROW VEHICLE, THERE IS NO PLACE TO HIDE.
LOOK AT ALL THESE LOVABLE LITTLE URCHINS!
HOW CAN YOU DISAPPOINT THEM!?
I... I GUESS SO.
HUH? WHA?
HERE, HAVE 100 YEN.
EH?
OH, DADDY...! THANK YOU FOR WATCHING OUT FOR ME.
SIGH
VWOOP
BANK
AKANE, RANMA— WHY ARE YOU HERE...?
YOUR DAD TOLD US TO KEEP YOU FROM GOING OVERBOARD.
HEY, SWEETIE! TRY PUTTING 10 IN THIS BOX!
HUH?

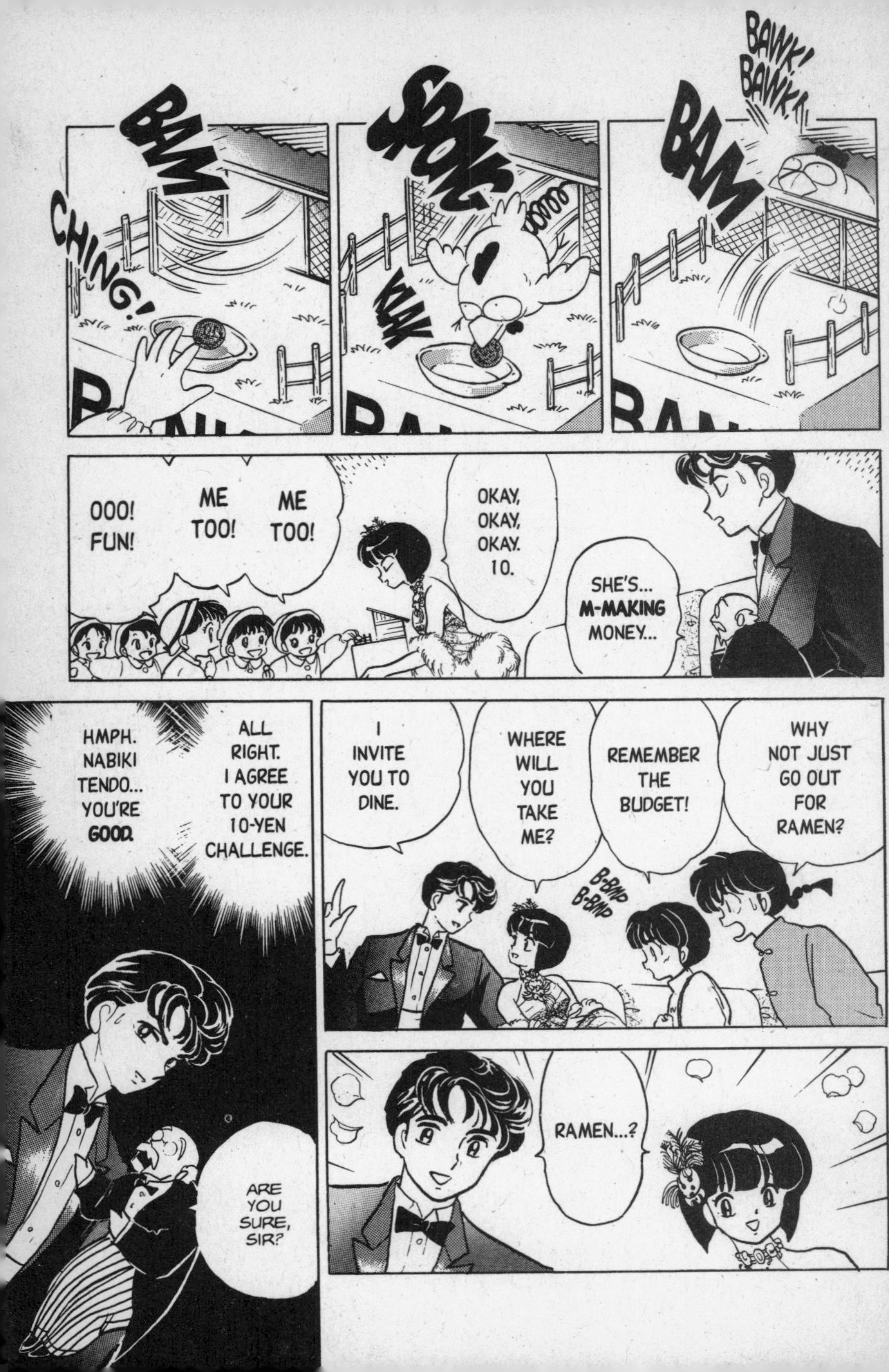
BAM
CHING!
SPONG
KLAK
BAWK! BAWK!!
BAM
OOO! FUN!
ME TOO!
ME TOO!
OKAY, OKAY, OKAY. 10.
SHE'S... M-MAKING MONEY...
HMPH. NABIKI TENDO... YOU'RE GOOD.
ALL RIGHT. I AGREE TO YOUR 10-YEN CHALLENGE.
ARE YOU SURE, SIR?
I INVITE YOU TO DINE.
WHERE WILL YOU TAKE ME?
REMEMBER THE BUDGET!
WHY NOT JUST GO OUT FOR RAMEN?
B-BINP B-BINP
RAMEN...?

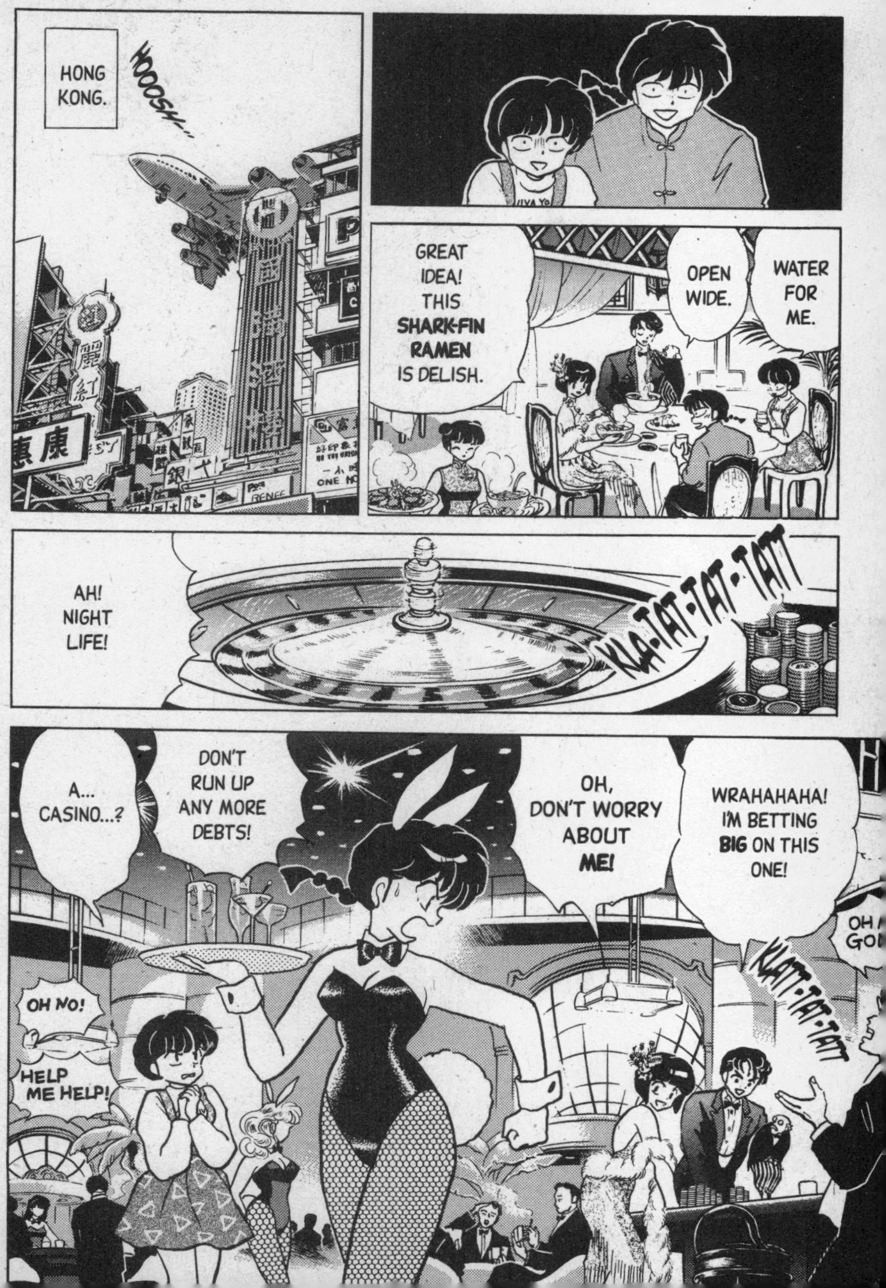
HONG KONG.
HOOOSH...
GREAT IDEA! THIS SHARK-FIN RAMEN IS DELISH.
OPEN WIDE.
WATER FOR ME.
AH! NIGHT LIFE!
KLA-TAT-TAT-TATT
A... CASINO...?
DON'T RUN UP ANY MORE DEBTS!
OH, DON'T WORRY ABOUT ME!
WRAHAHAHA! I'M BETTING BIG ON THIS ONE!
KLATT-TAT-TATT
OH NO!
HELP ME HELP!

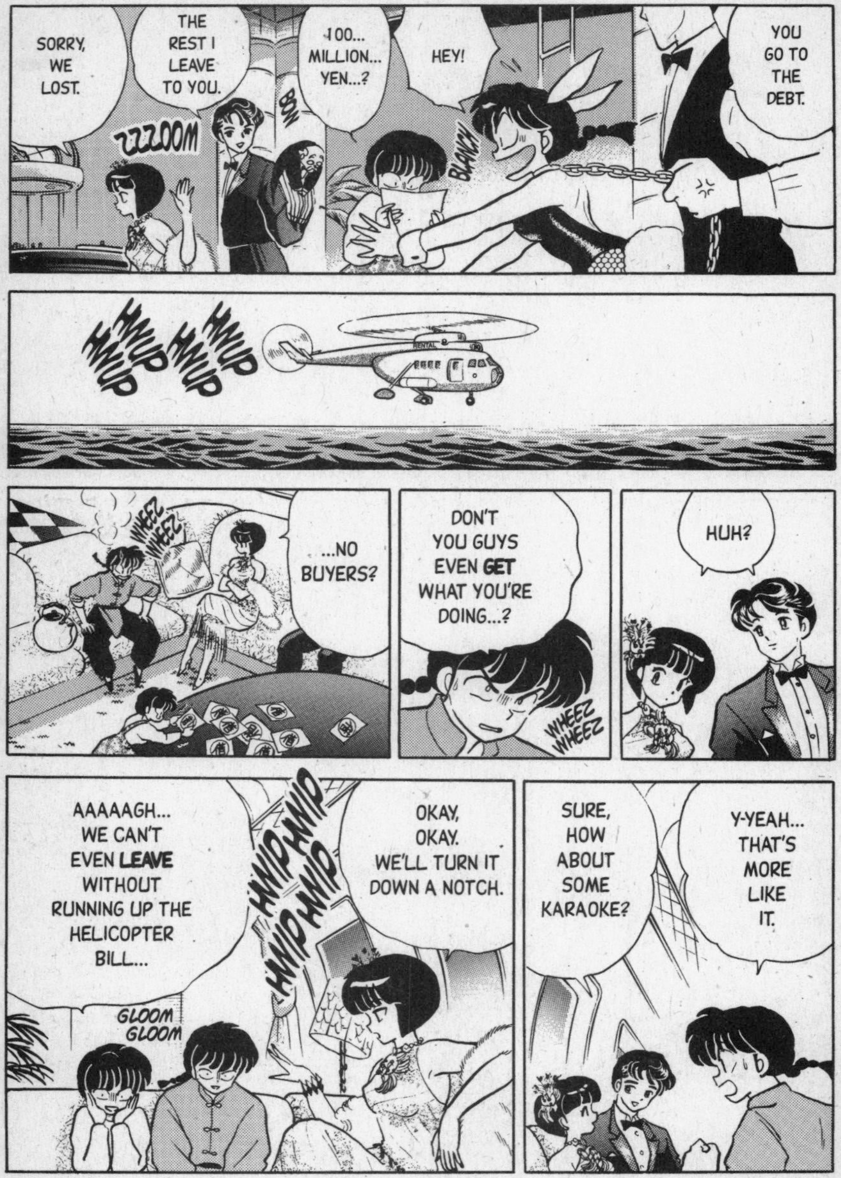
SORRY, WE LOST.
ZZZOOM
THE REST I LEAVE TO YOU.
BOW
100... MILLION... YEN...?
HEY!
BLANCH
YOU GO TO THE DEBT.
HWUP HWUP
HWUP HWUP
RENTAL
WHEEZ WHEEZ
...NO BUYERS?
DON'T YOU GUYS EVEN **GET** WHAT YOU'RE DOING...?
WHEEZ WHEEZ
HUH?
AAAAAGH... WE CAN'T EVEN **LEAVE** WITHOUT RUNNING UP THE HELICOPTER BILL...
GLOOM GLOOM
HWIP HWIP HWIP HWIP
OKAY, OKAY. WE'LL TURN IT DOWN A NOTCH.
SURE, HOW ABOUT SOME KARAOKE?
Y-YEAH... THAT'S MORE LIKE IT.

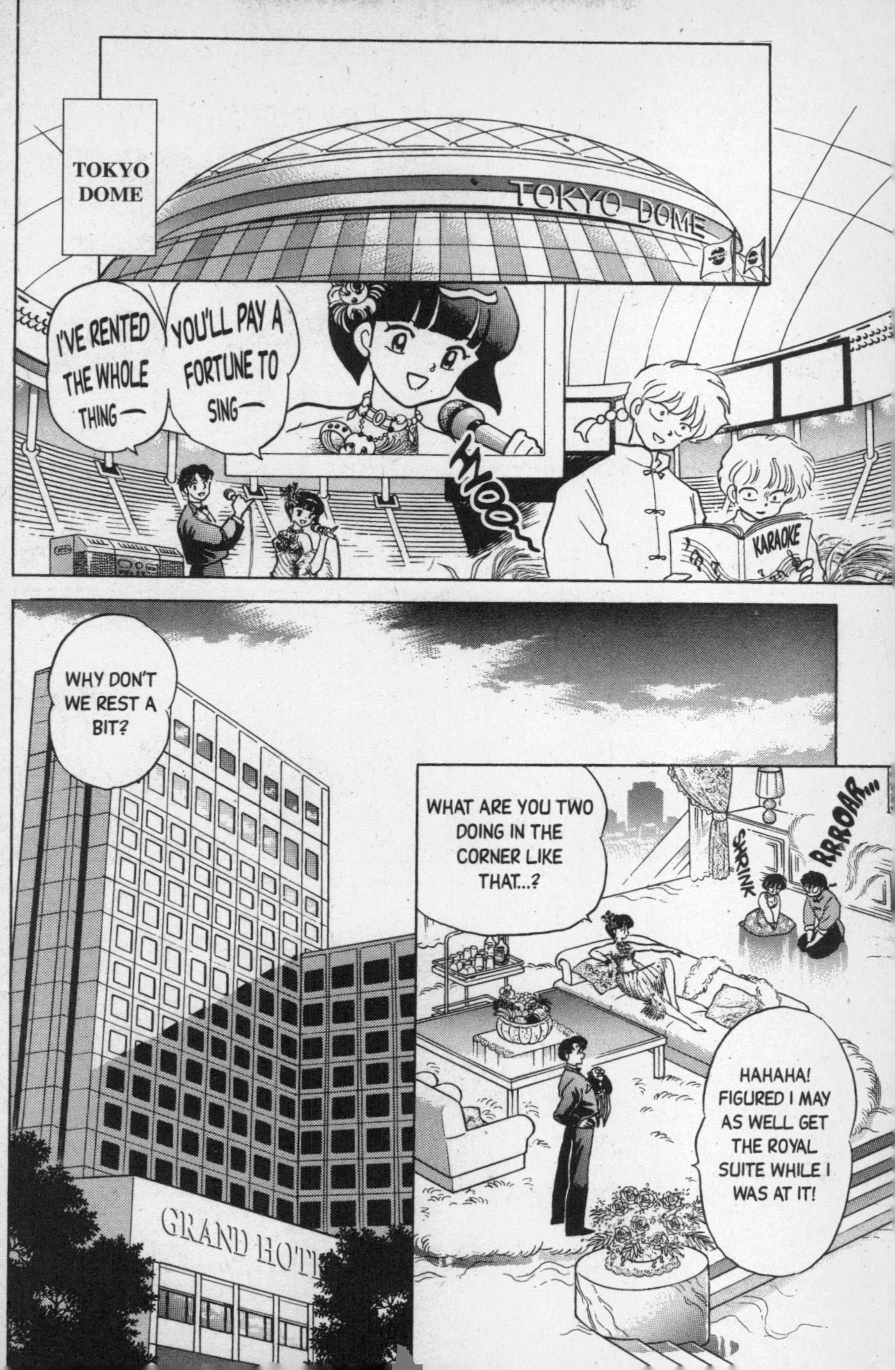
TOKYO DOME
TOKYO DOME
I'VE RENTED THE WHOLE THING—
YOU'LL PAY A FORTUNE TO SING—
HNOO~
KARAOKE
WHY DON'T WE REST A BIT?
GRAND HOT
WHAT ARE YOU TWO DOING IN THE CORNER LIKE THAT...?
SHRINK
RRROAR...
HAHAHA! FIGURED I MAY AS WELL GET THE ROYAL SUITE WHILE I WAS AT IT!

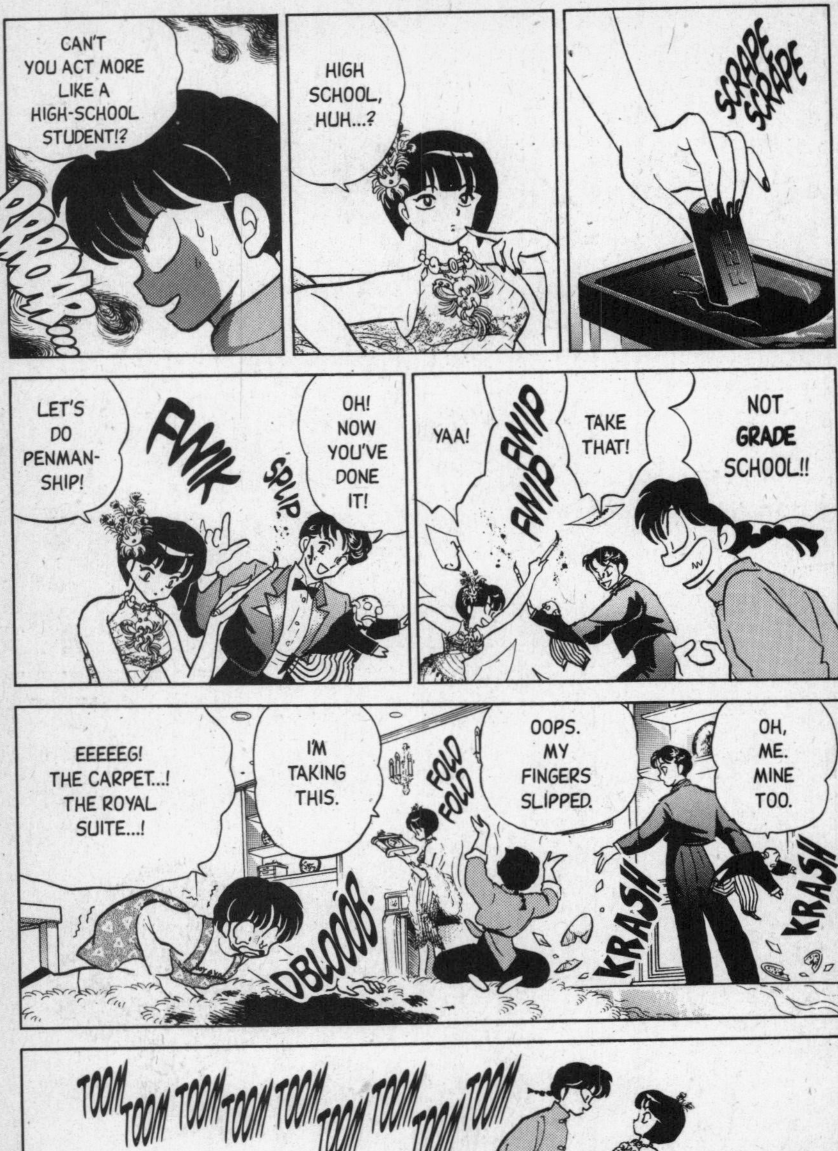
CAN'T YOU ACT MORE LIKE A HIGH-SCHOOL STUDENT!?
RRROWR...
HIGH SCHOOL, HUH...?
SCRAPE SCRAPE
LET'S DO PENMANSHIP!
FWIK
SPLIP
OH! NOW YOU'VE DONE IT!
YAA!
FWIP FWIP
TAKE THAT!
NOT GRADE SCHOOL!!
EEEEEG! THE CARPET...! THE ROYAL SUITE...!
I'M TAKING THIS.
FOLD FOLD
OOPS. MY FINGERS SLIPPED.
OH, ME. MINE TOO.
DBLOOOB
KRASH
KRASH
TOOM TOOM TOOM TOOM TOOM TOOM TOOM TOOM TOOM

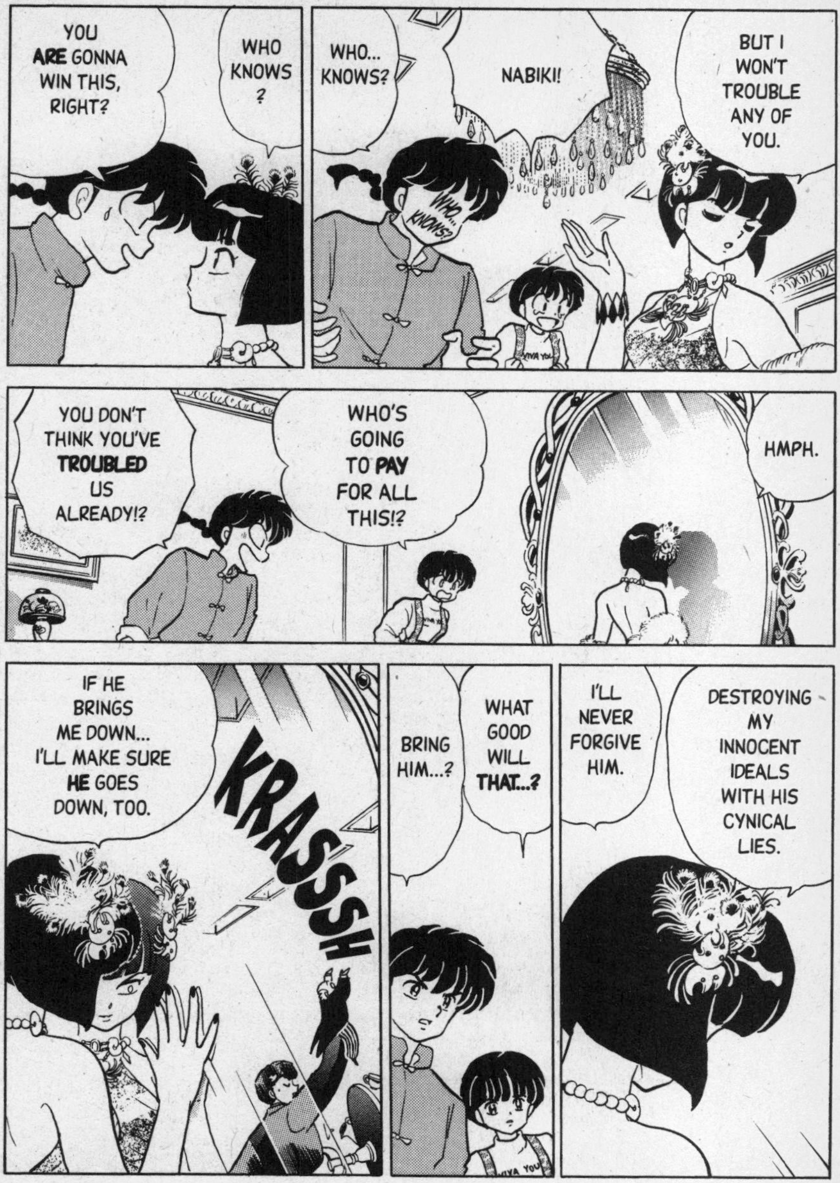
YOU ARE GONNA WIN THIS, RIGHT?
WHO KNOWS ?
WHO... KNOWS?
WHO... KNOWS?
NABIKI!
BUT I WON'T TROUBLE ANY OF YOU.
YOU DON'T THINK YOU'VE TROUBLED US ALREADY!?
WHO'S GOING TO PAY FOR ALL THIS!?
HMPH.
IF HE BRINGS ME DOWN... I'LL MAKE SURE HE GOES DOWN, TOO.
KRASSSH
BRING HIM...?
WHAT GOOD WILL THAT...?
I'LL NEVER FORGIVE HIM.
DESTROYING MY INNOCENT IDEALS WITH HIS CYNICAL LIES.

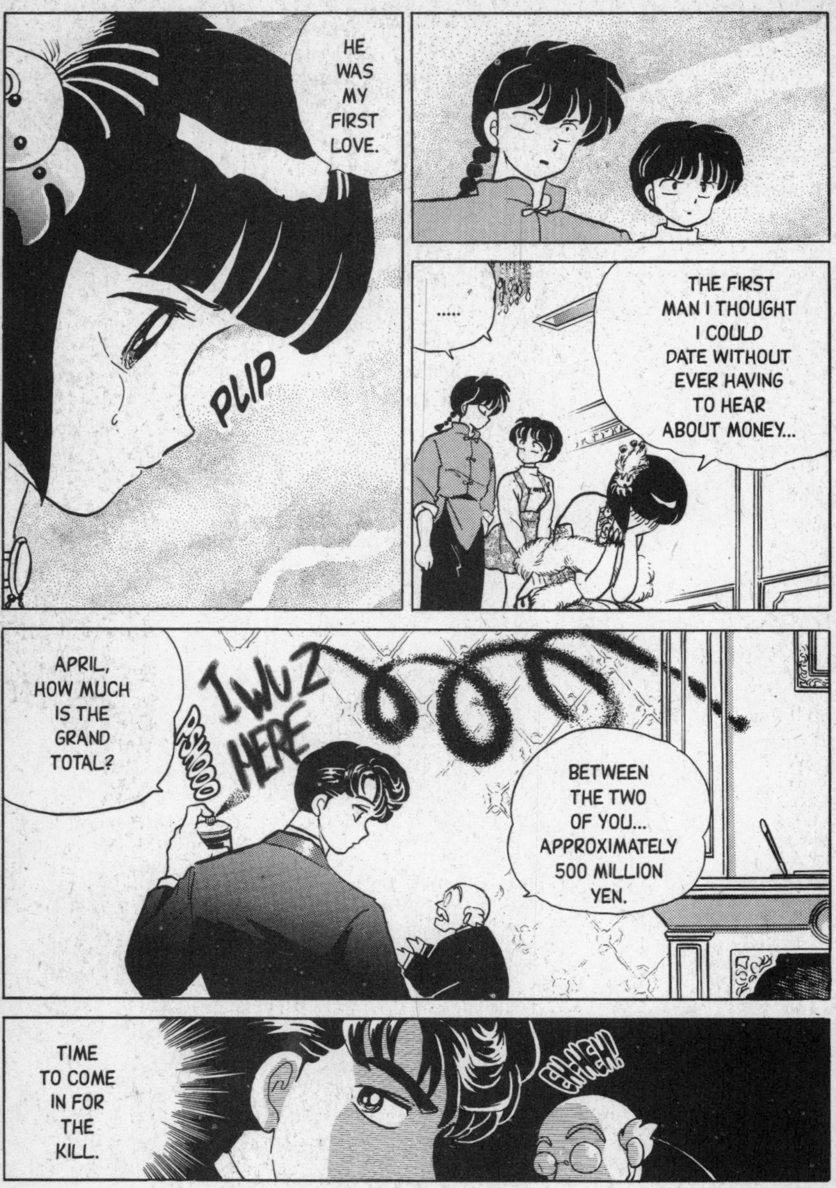
HE WAS MY FIRST LOVE.
PLIP
.....
THE FIRST MAN I THOUGHT I COULD DATE WITHOUT EVER HAVING TO HEAR ABOUT MONEY...
APRIL, HOW MUCH IS THE GRAND TOTAL?
PSHOOO
I WUZ HERE
BETWEEN THE TWO OF YOU... APPROXIMATELY 500 MILLION YEN.
TIME TO COME IN FOR THE KILL.
GHHEH!

PART 11

FOR THE LOVE OF TEN YEN

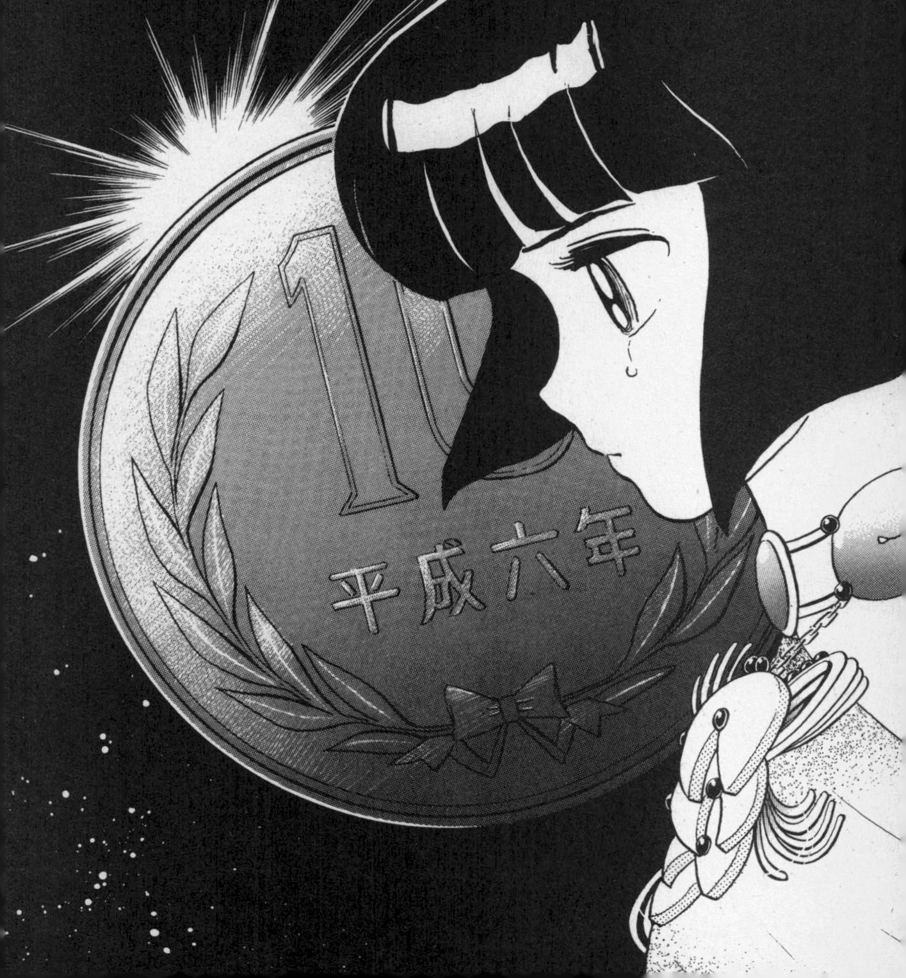
平成六年

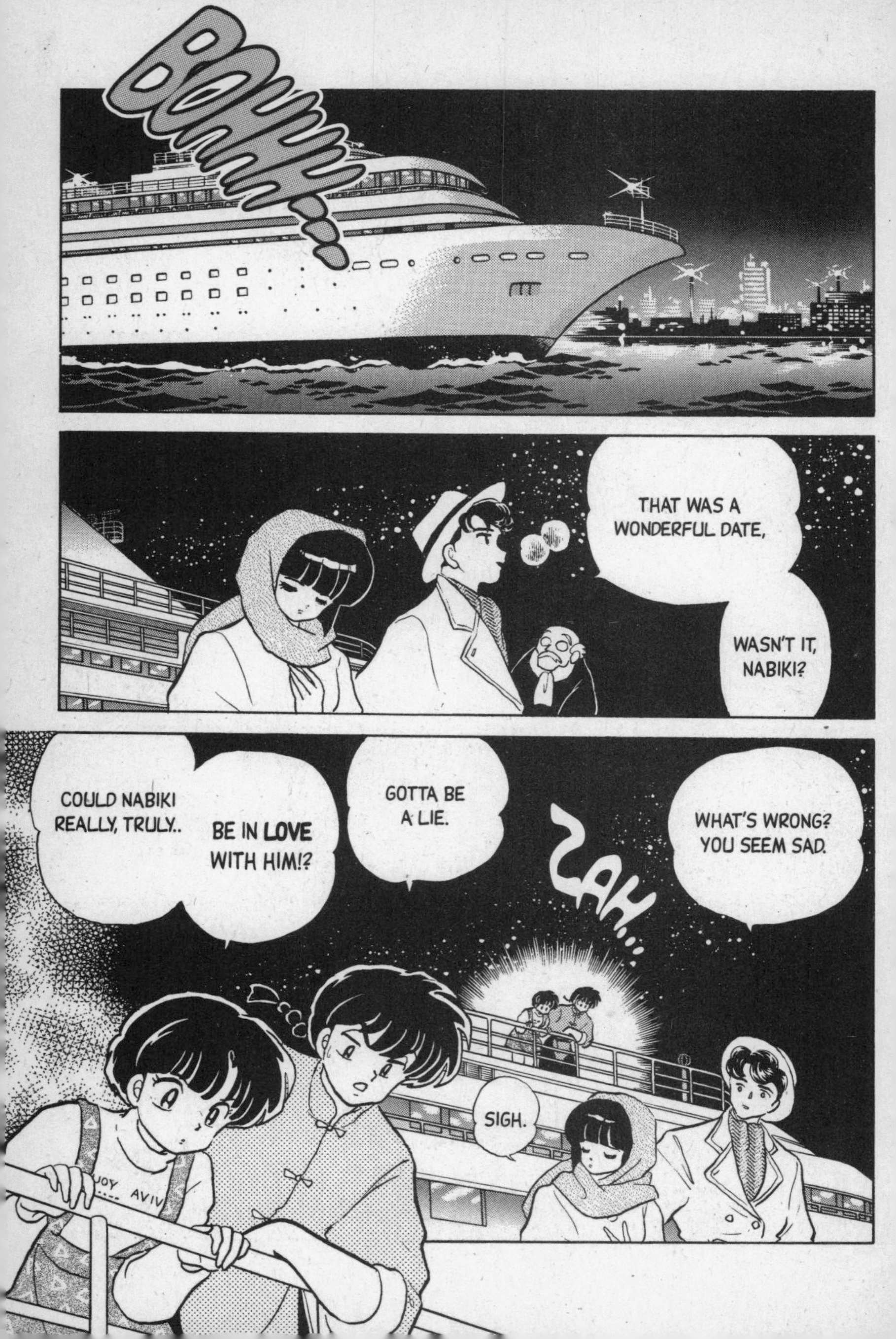
BOHHH...
THAT WAS A WONDERFUL DATE,
WASN'T IT, NABIKI?
COULD NABIKI REALLY, TRULY..
BE IN LOVE WITH HIM!?
GOTTA BE A LIE.
ZAH...
WHAT'S WRONG? YOU SEEM SAD.
SIGH.

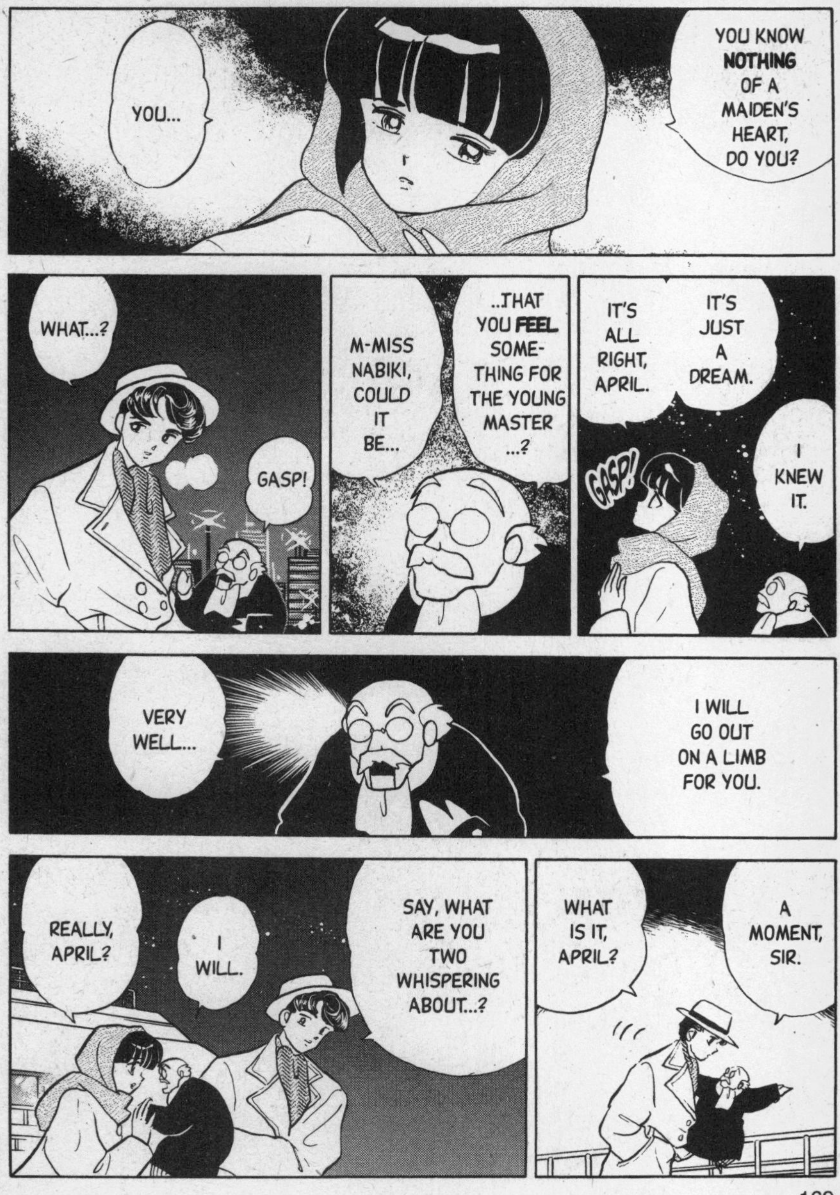
YOU...
YOU KNOW **NOTHING** OF A MAIDEN'S HEART, DO YOU?
WHAT...?
GASP!
M-MISS NABIKI, COULD IT BE...
...THAT YOU **FEEL** SOME-THING FOR THE YOUNG MASTER ...?
IT'S ALL RIGHT, APRIL.
IT'S JUST A DREAM.
GASP!
I KNEW IT.
VERY WELL...
I WILL GO OUT ON A LIMB FOR YOU.
REALLY, APRIL?
I WILL.
SAY, WHAT ARE YOU TWO WHISPERING ABOUT...?
WHAT IS IT, APRIL?
A MOMENT, SIR.

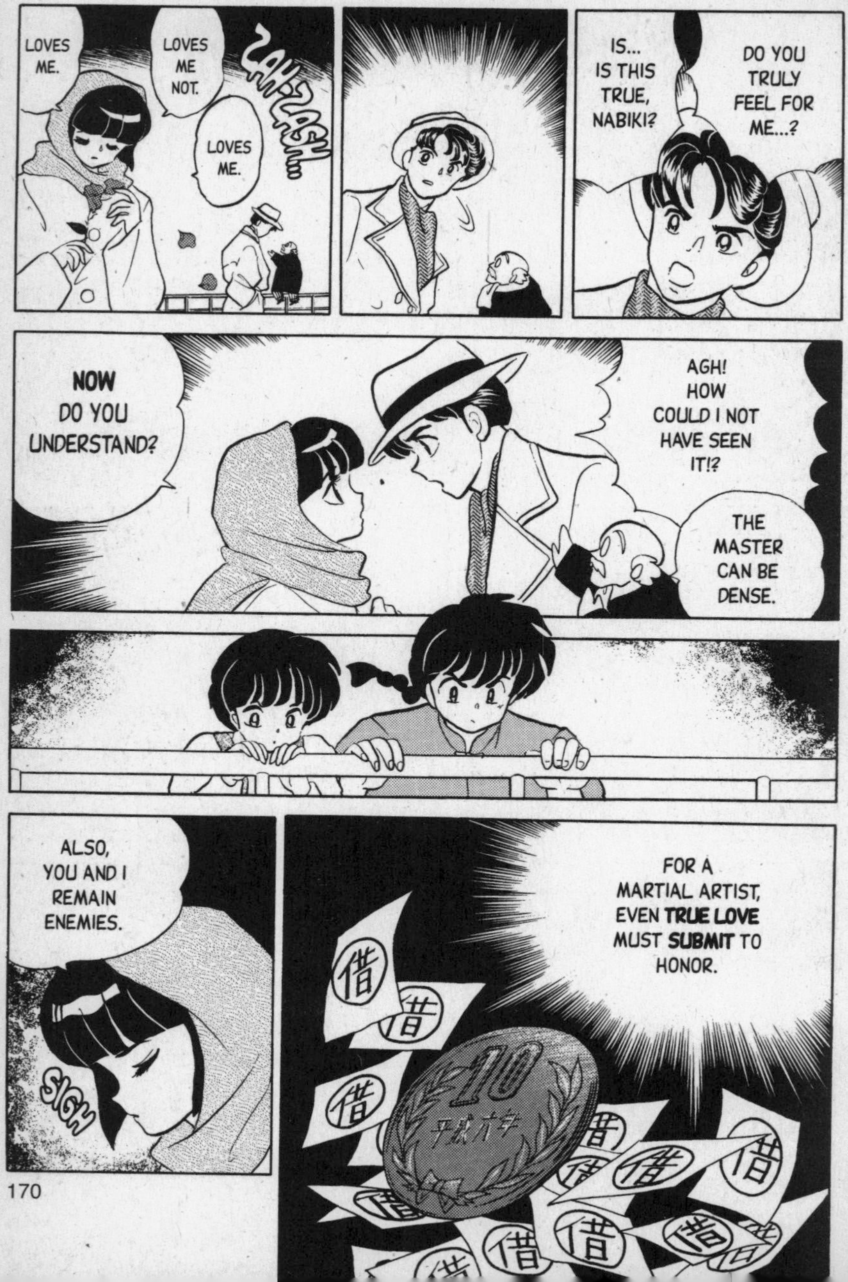
LOVES ME.
LOVES ME NOT.
LOVES ME.
IS... IS THIS TRUE, NABIKI!?
DO YOU TRULY FEEL FOR ME...?
NOW DO YOU UNDERSTAND?
AGH! HOW COULD I NOT HAVE SEEN IT!?
THE MASTER CAN BE DENSE.
ALSO, YOU AND I REMAIN ENEMIES.
SIGH
FOR A MARTIAL ARTIST, EVEN **TRUE LOVE** MUST **SUBMIT** TO HONOR.

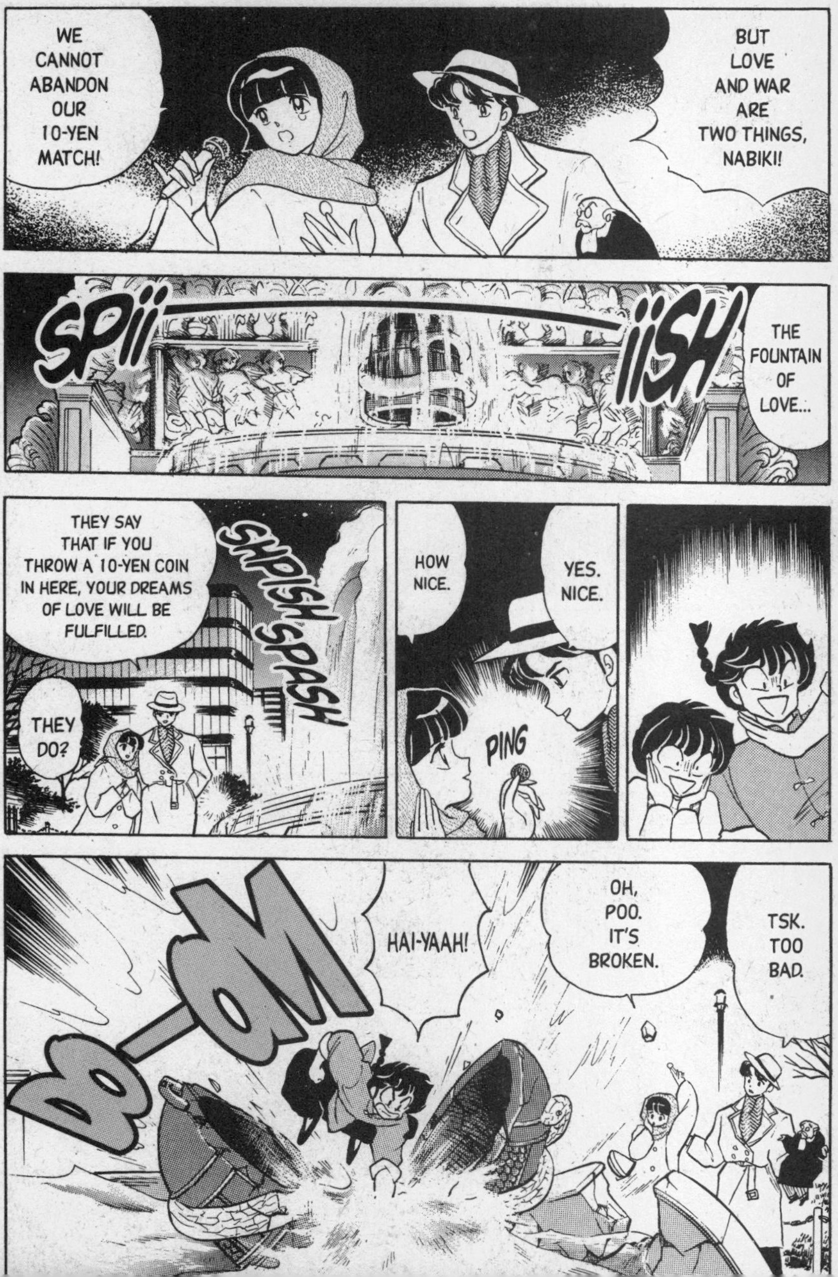
WE CANNOT ABANDON OUR 10-YEN MATCH!
BUT LOVE AND WAR ARE TWO THINGS, NABIKI!
SPIIIISH
THE FOUNTAIN OF LOVE...
THEY SAY THAT IF YOU THROW A 10-YEN COIN IN HERE, YOUR DREAMS OF LOVE WILL BE FULFILLED.
SHPISH SPASH
THEY DO?
HOW NICE.
YES. NICE.
PING
BOOM
HAI-YAAH!
OH, POO. IT'S BROKEN.
TSK. TOO BAD.

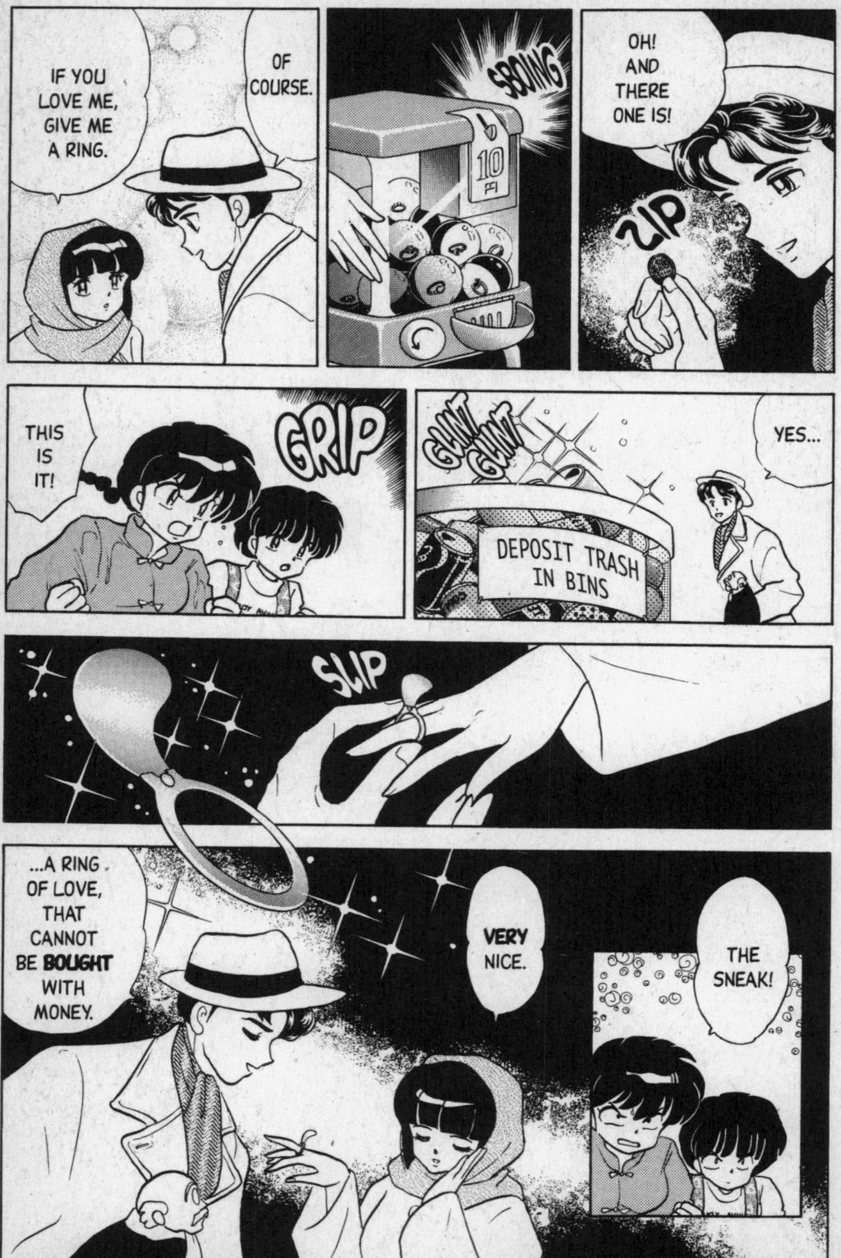
IF YOU LOVE ME, GIVE ME A RING.
OF COURSE.
SBOING
10
OH! AND THERE ONE IS!
ZIP
THIS IS IT!
GRIP
GLINT GLINT
DEPOSIT TRASH IN BINS
YES...
SLIP
...A RING OF LOVE, THAT CANNOT BE **BOUGHT** WITH MONEY.
VERY NICE.
THE SNEAK!

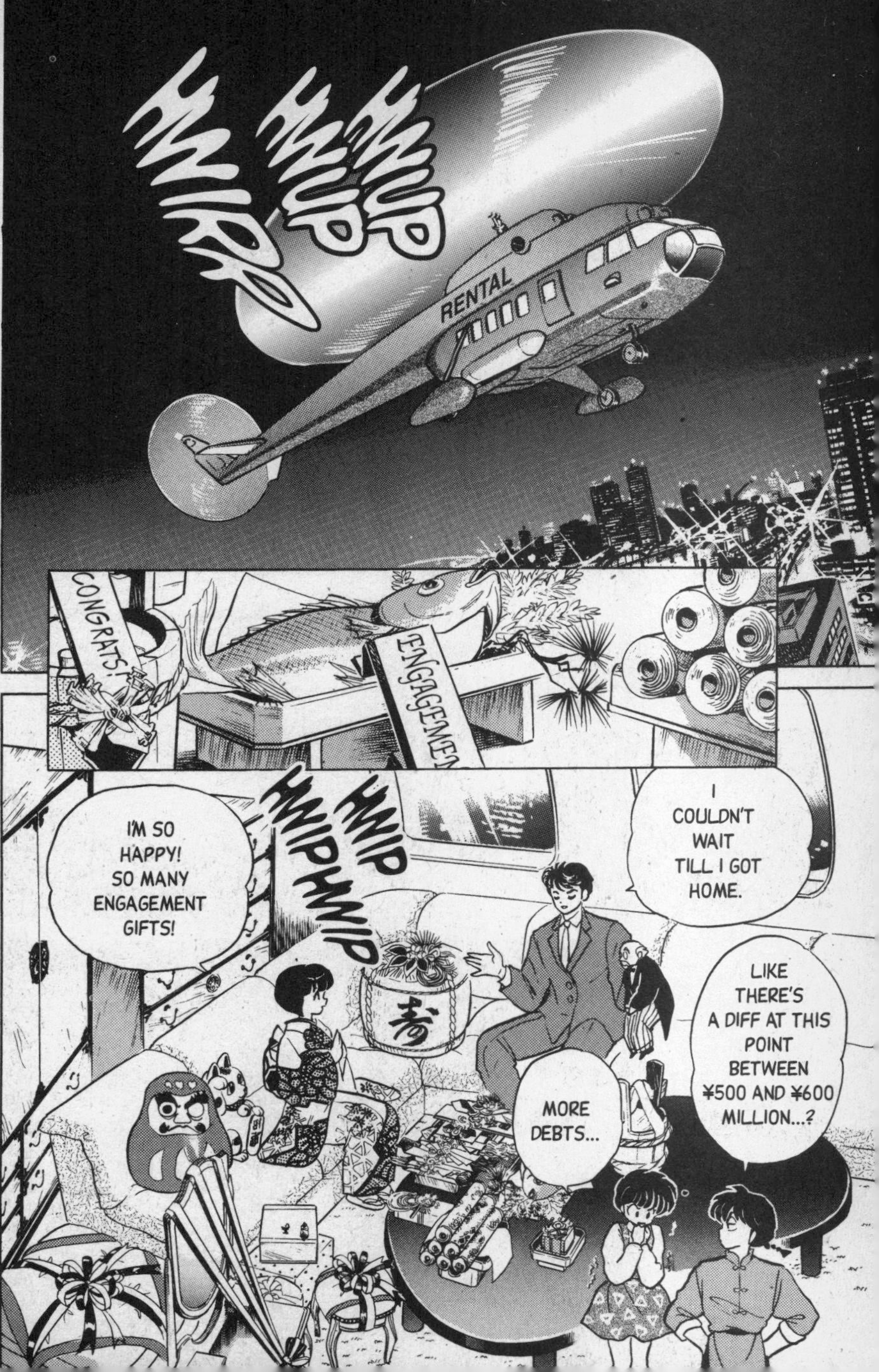
HWIP
HWUP
HWUP
RENTAL
CONGRATS!
ENGAGEMEN
I'M SO HAPPY! SO MANY ENGAGEMENT GIFTS!
HWIP HWIPHWIP
I COULDN'T WAIT TILL I GOT HOME.
MORE DEBTS...
LIKE THERE'S A DIFF AT THIS POINT BETWEEN ¥500 AND ¥600 MILLION...?

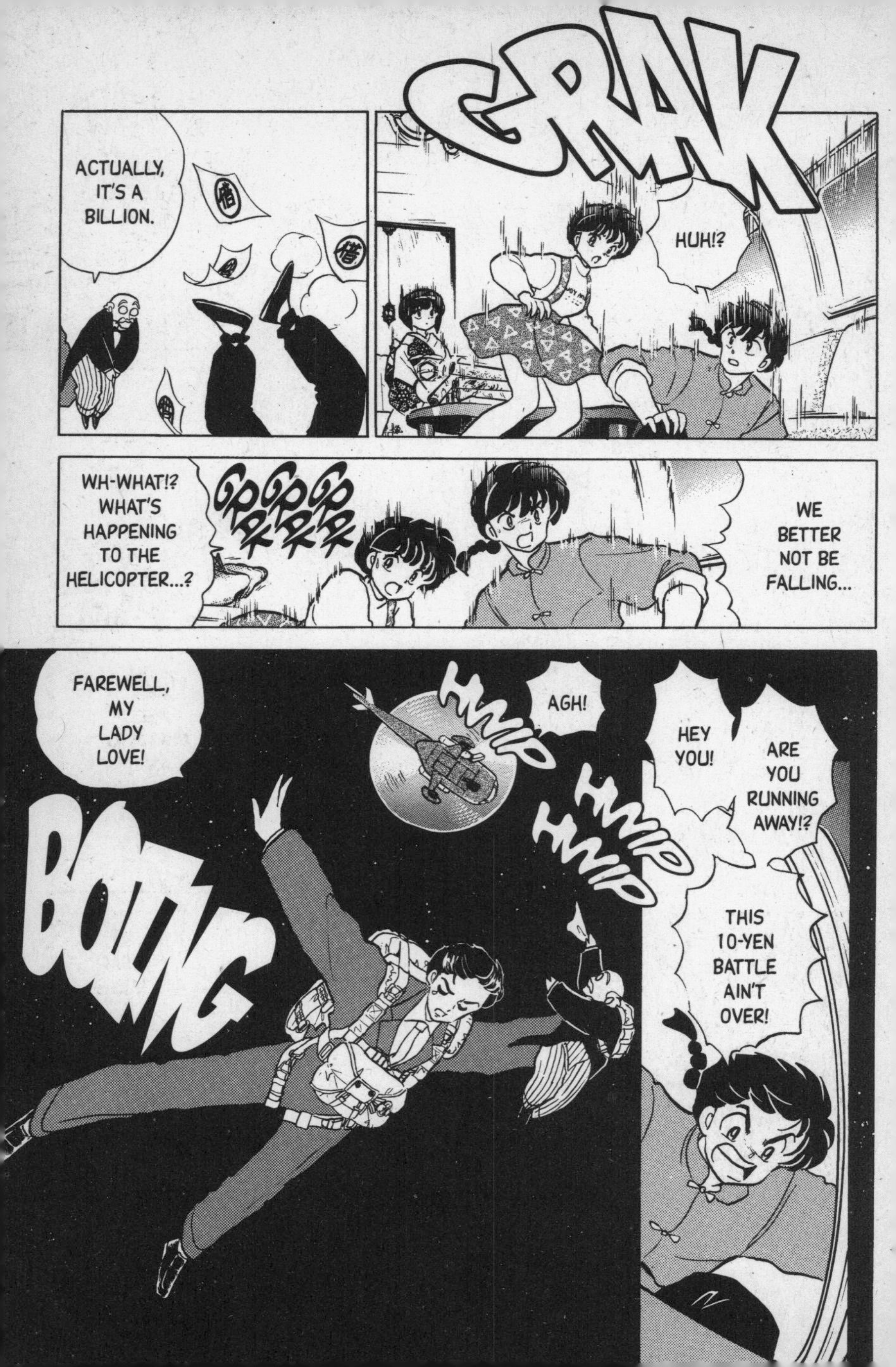
ACTUALLY, IT'S A BILLION.
CRAK
HUH!?
WH-WHAT!? WHAT'S HAPPENING TO THE HELICOPTER...?
GRAK GRAK GRAK
WE BETTER NOT BE FALLING...
FAREWELL, MY LADY LOVE!
BOING
HWIP
AGH!
HWIP HWIP
HEY YOU!
ARE YOU RUNNING AWAY!?
THIS 10-YEN BATTLE AIN'T OVER!

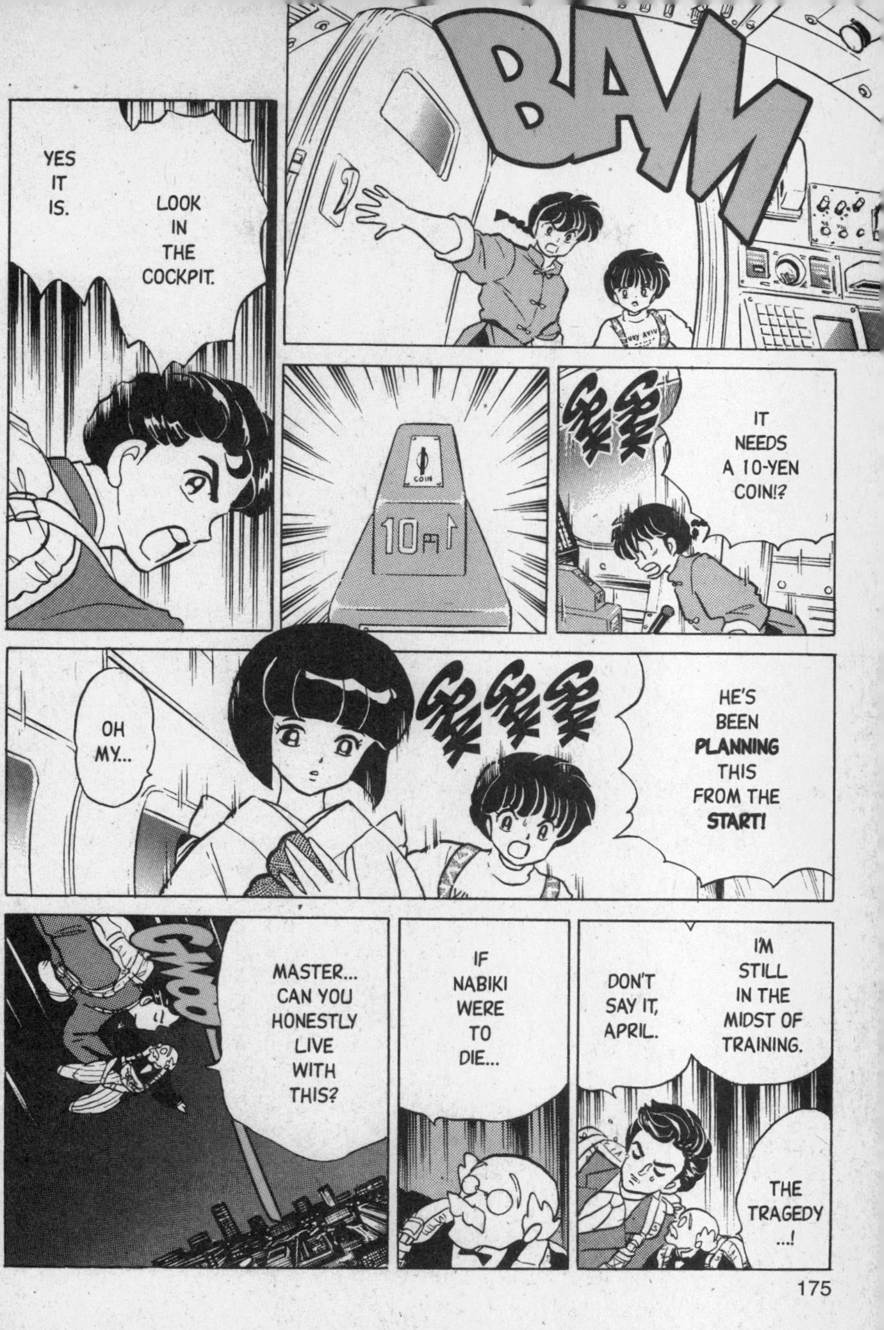
YES IT IS.
LOOK IN THE COCKPIT.
BAM
10円
COIN
GRAK GRAK
IT NEEDS A 10-YEN COIN!?
OH MY...
GRAK GRAK GRAK
HE'S BEEN **PLANNING** THIS FROM THE **START!**
MASTER... CAN YOU HONESTLY LIVE WITH THIS?
IF NABIKI WERE TO DIE...
DON'T SAY IT, APRIL.
I'M STILL IN THE MIDST OF TRAINING.
THE TRAGEDY ...!

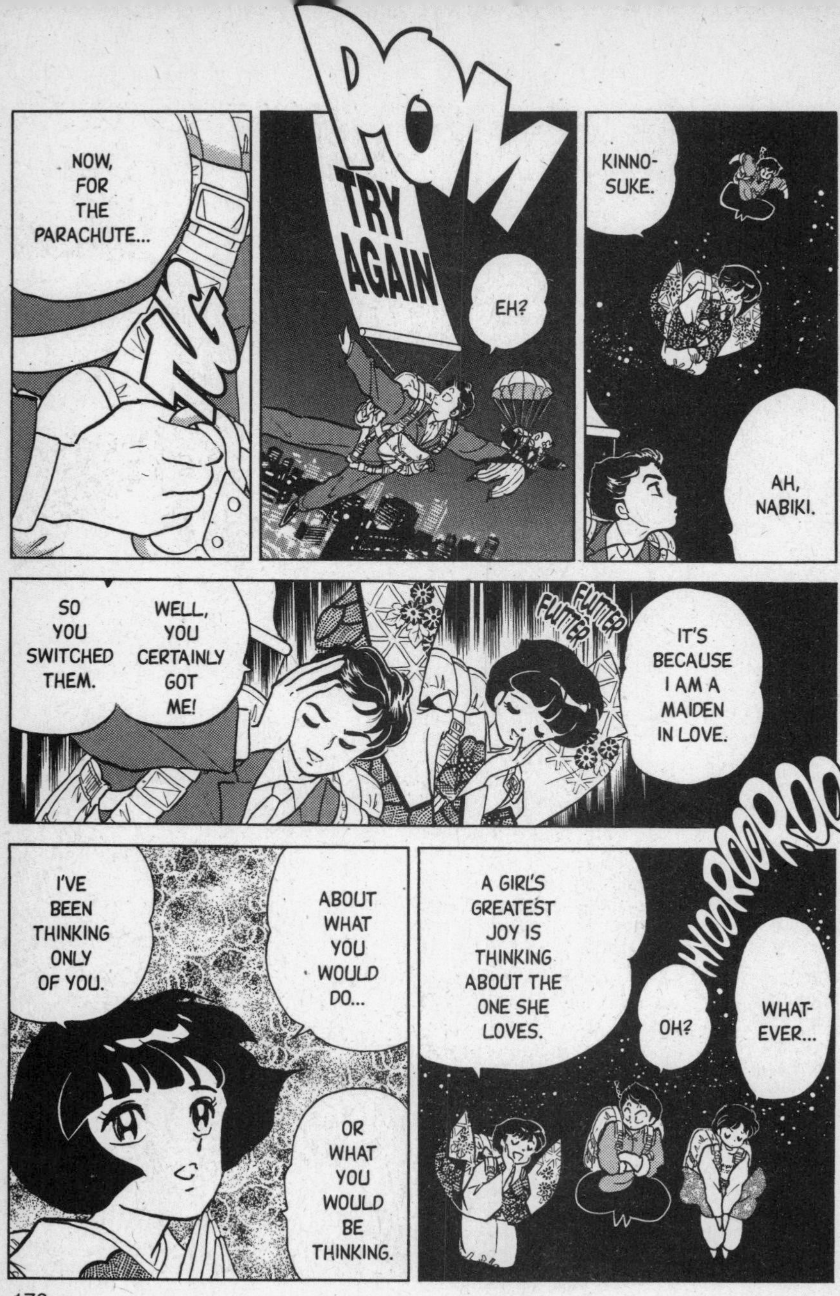
NOW, FOR THE PARACHUTE...
POM
TRY AGAIN
EH?
KINNO-SUKE.
AH, NABIKI.
SO YOU SWITCHED THEM.
WELL, YOU CERTAINLY GOT ME!
FLUTTER FLUTTER
IT'S BECAUSE I AM A MAIDEN IN LOVE.
HYOOROOROO
I'VE BEEN THINKING ONLY OF YOU.
ABOUT WHAT YOU WOULD DO...
OR WHAT YOU WOULD BE THINKING.
A GIRL'S GREATEST JOY IS THINKING ABOUT THE ONE SHE LOVES.
OH?
WHAT-EVER...

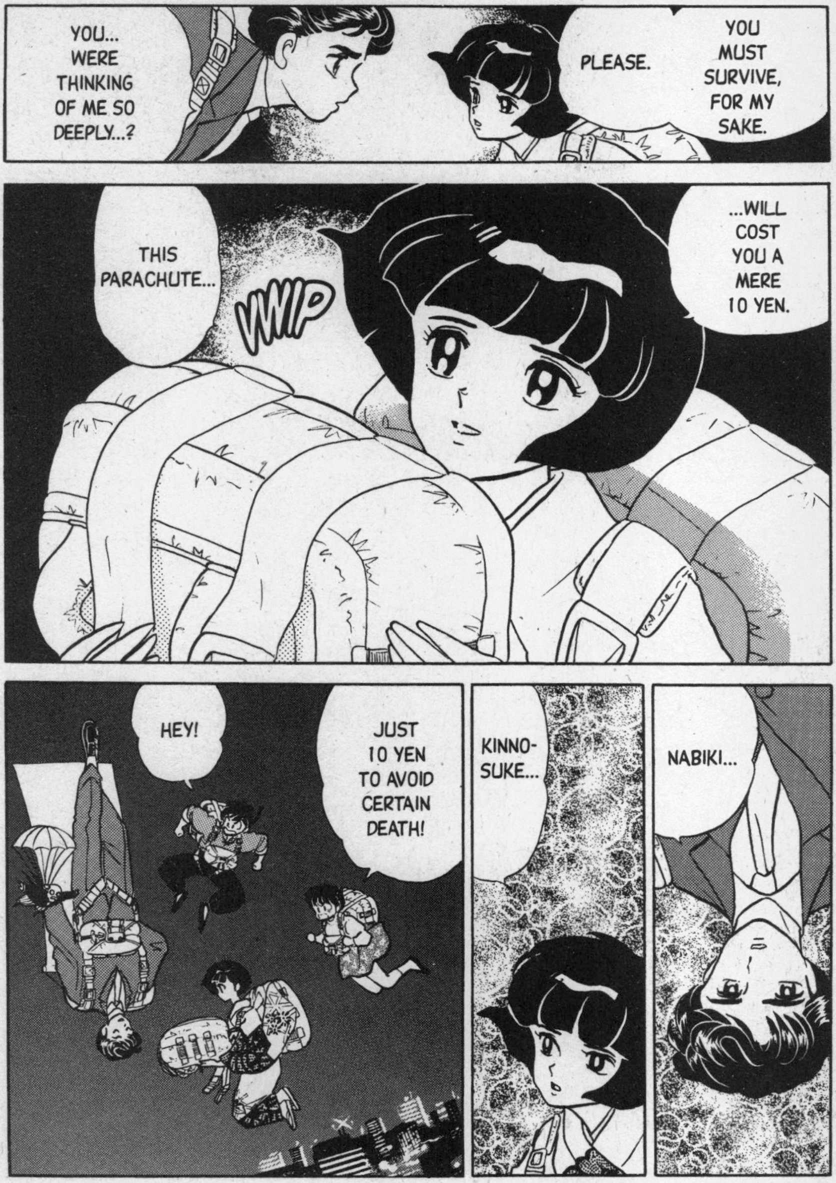
YOU... WERE THINKING OF ME SO DEEPLY...?
PLEASE.
YOU MUST SURVIVE, FOR MY SAKE.
THIS PARACHUTE...
VWIP
...WILL COST YOU A MERE 10 YEN.
HEY!
JUST 10 YEN TO AVOID CERTAIN DEATH!
KINNO-SUKE...
NABIKI...

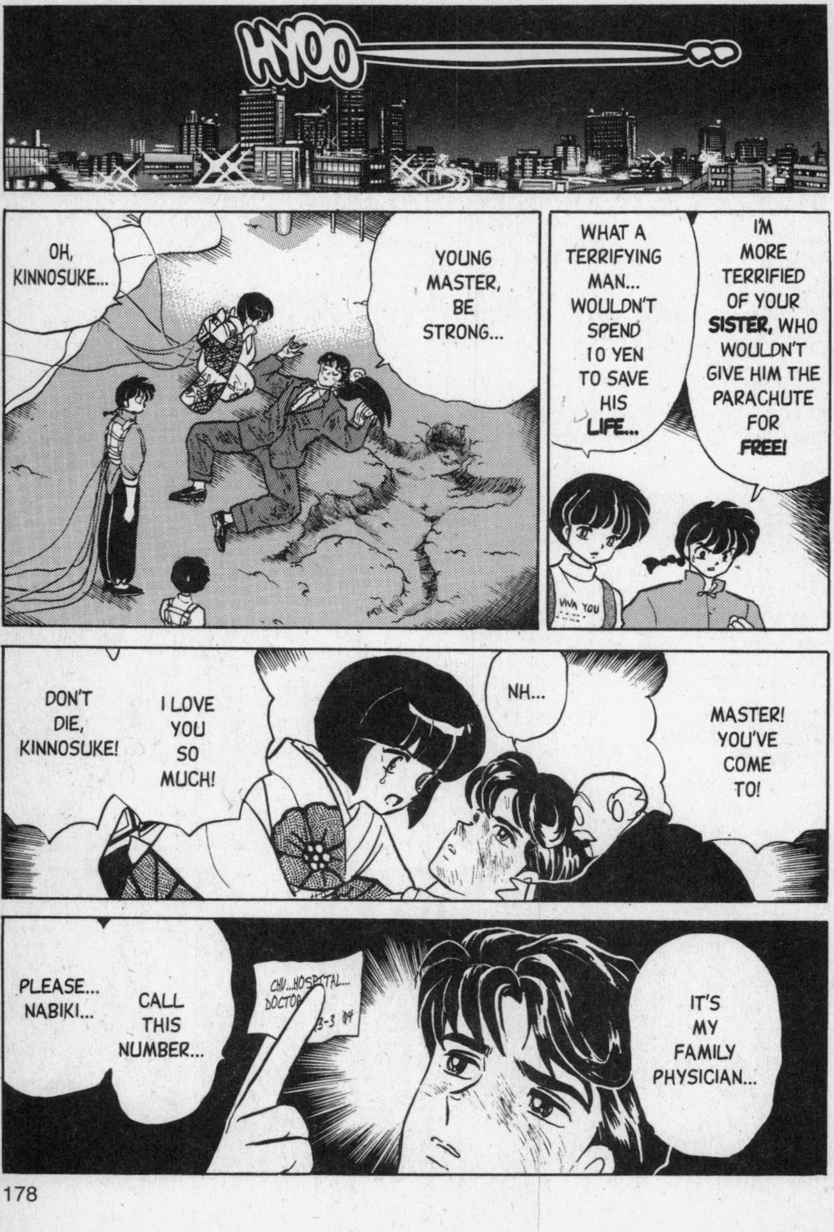
HYOO
OH, KINNOSUKE...
YOUNG MASTER, BE STRONG...
WHAT A TERRIFYING MAN... WOULDN'T SPEND 10 YEN TO SAVE HIS **LIFE...**
I'M MORE TERRIFIED OF YOUR **SISTER,** WHO WOULDN'T GIVE HIM THE PARACHUTE FOR **FREE!**
VIVA YOU
DON'T DIE, KINNOSUKE!
I LOVE YOU SO MUCH!
NH...
MASTER! YOU'VE COME TO!
PLEASE... NABIKI...
CALL THIS NUMBER...
CHU...HOSPITAL...
IT'S MY FAMILY PHYSICIAN...

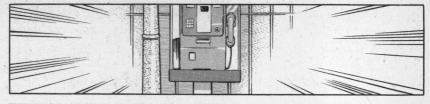

A PHONE CALL!?

WAIT A MINUTE-!!

GON——NG

VERY WELL!

MISS NABIKI...

DIG DIG

PLEASE USE THIS.

ZIP

BUT APRIL, THIS IS **KINNOSUKE'S** 10-YEN COIN!

IF IT MEANS THE YOUNG MASTER'S LIFE...

K-CHNK

SHE WON!?

HELLO?

W... WAIT...

KRAK SNAP

DRAGGG

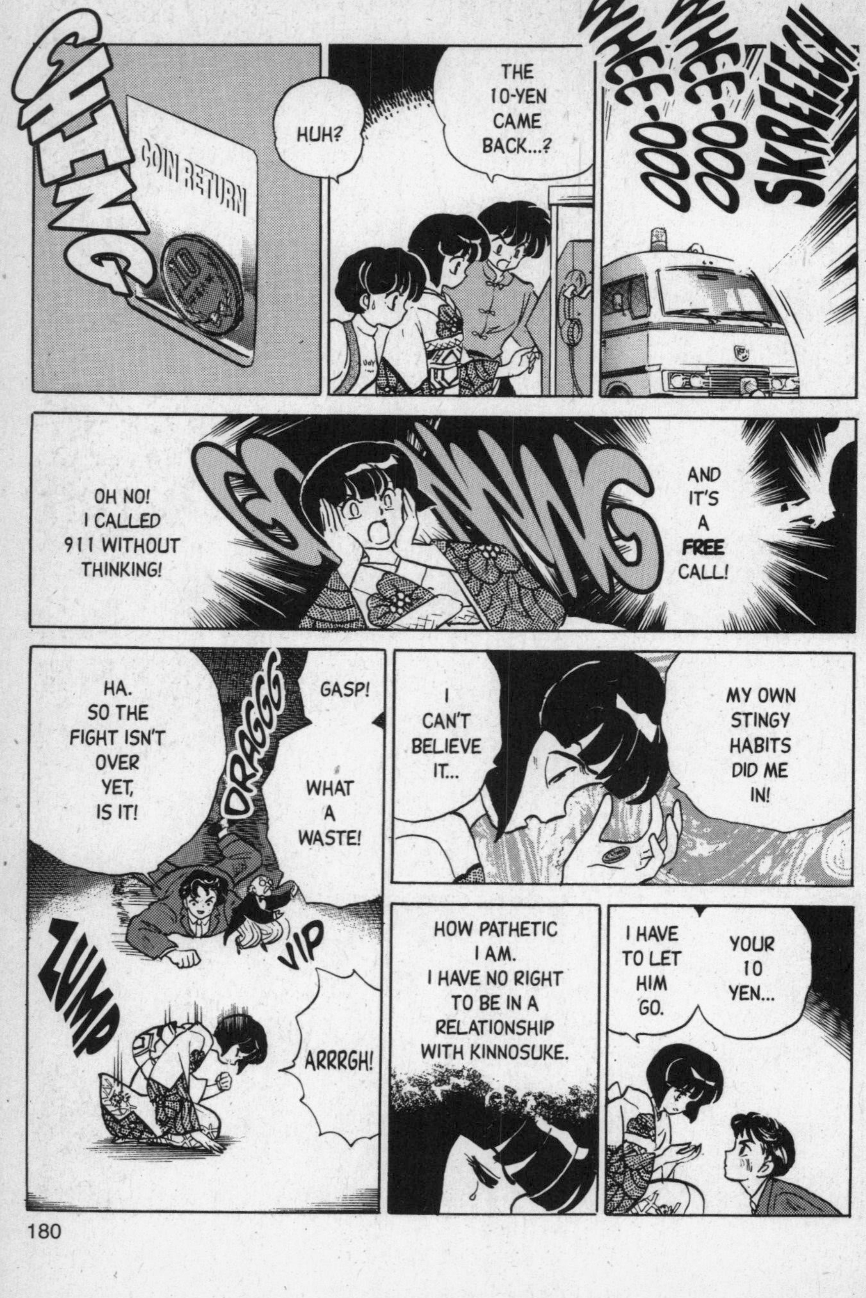

CHENG
COIN RETURN
HUH?
THE 10-YEN CAME BACK...?
WHEE-OOO
WHEE-OOO
SKREEECH
OH NO! I CALLED 911 WITHOUT THINKING!
AND IT'S A **FREE** CALL!
HA. SO THE FIGHT ISN'T OVER YET, IS IT!
DRAGGG
GASP!
WHAT A WASTE!
ZUMP
VIP
ARRRGH!
I CAN'T BELIEVE IT...
MY OWN STINGY HABITS DID ME IN!
HOW PATHETIC I AM. I HAVE NO RIGHT TO BE IN A RELATIONSHIP WITH KINNOSUKE.
I HAVE TO LET HIM GO.
YOUR 10 YEN...

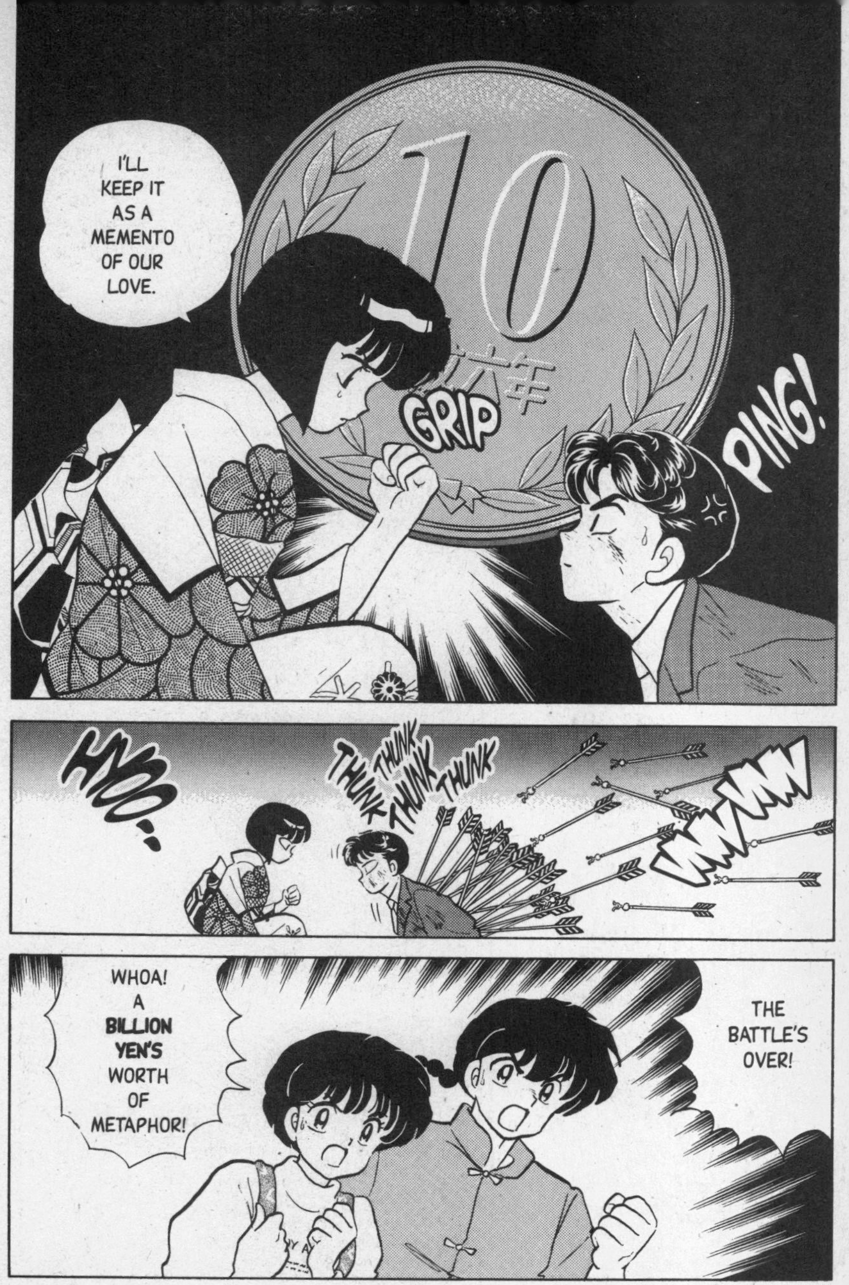
I'LL KEEP IT AS A MEMENTO OF OUR LOVE.
GRIP
PING!
HYOO...
THUNK
THUNK
THUNK
THUNK
WHOA! A **BILLION YEN'S** WORTH OF METAPHOR!
THE BATTLE'S OVER!

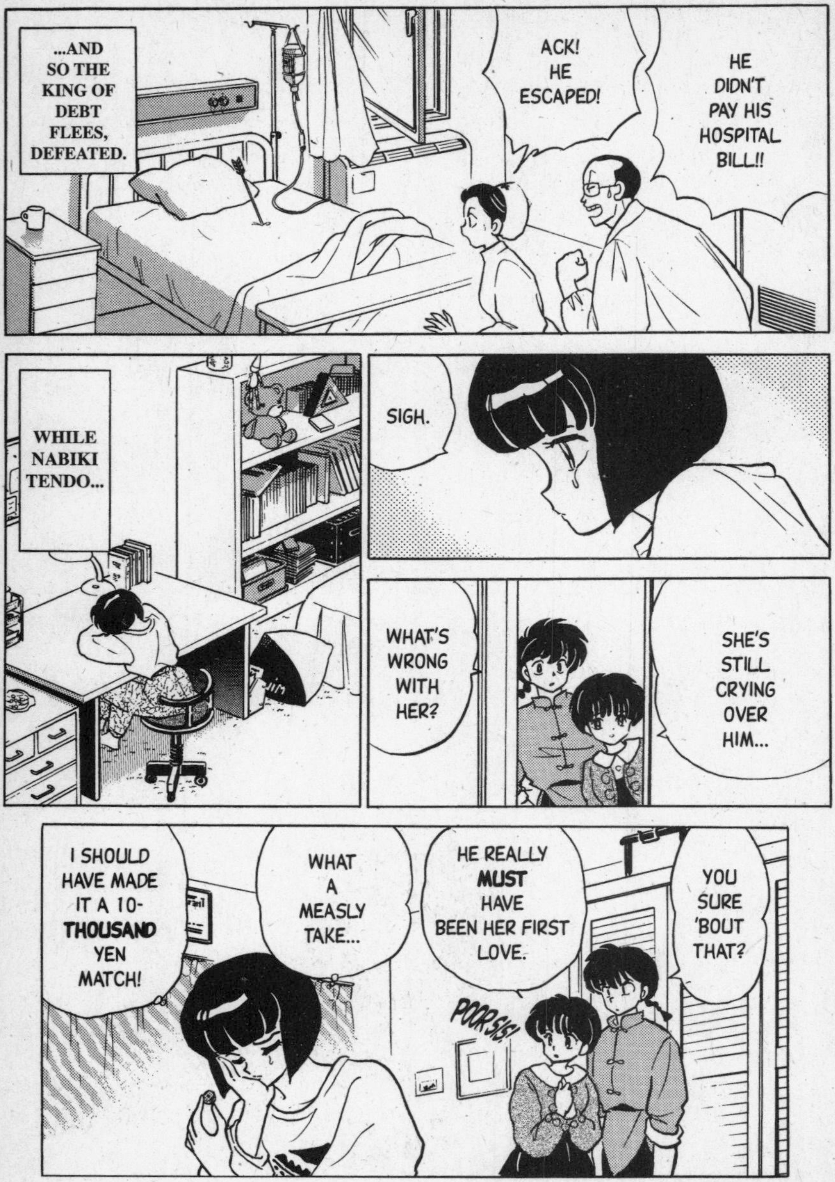
...AND SO THE KING OF DEBT FLEES, DEFEATED.
ACK! HE ESCAPED!
HE DIDN'T PAY HIS HOSPITAL BILL!!
WHILE NABIKI TENDO...
SIGH.
WHAT'S WRONG WITH HER?
SHE'S STILL CRYING OVER HIM...
I SHOULD HAVE MADE IT A 10-THOUSAND YEN MATCH!
WHAT A MEASLY TAKE...
HE REALLY MUST HAVE BEEN HER FIRST LOVE.
YOU SURE 'BOUT THAT?
POOR SIS!

THE END

About Rumiko Takahashi

Born in 1957 in Niigata, Japan, Rumiko Takahashi attended women's college in Tokyo, where she began studying comics with Kazuo Koike, author of CRYING FREEMAN. She later became an assistant to horror-manga artist Kazuo Umezu (OROCHI). In 1978, she won a prize in Shogakukan's annual "New Comic Artist Contest," and in that same year her boy-meets-alien comedy series URUSEI YATSURA began appearing in the weekly manga magazine SHÔNEN SUNDAY. This phenomenally successful series ran for nine years and sold over 22 million copies. Takahashi's later RANMA 1/2 series enjoyed even greater popularity.

Takahashi is considered by many to be one of the world's most popular manga artists. With the publication of Volume 34 of her RANMA 1/2 series in Japan, Takahashi's total sales passed one hundred million copies of her compiled works.

Takahashi's serial titles include URUSEI YATSURA, RANMA 1/2, ONE-POUND GOSPEL, MAISON IKKOKU and INUYASHA. Additionally, Takahashi has drawn many short stories which have been published in America under the title "Rumic Theater," and several installments of a saga known as her "Mermaid" series. Most of Takahashi's major stories have also been animated, and are widely available in translation worldwide. INUYASHA is her most recent serial story, first published in SHÔNEN SUNDAY in 1996.

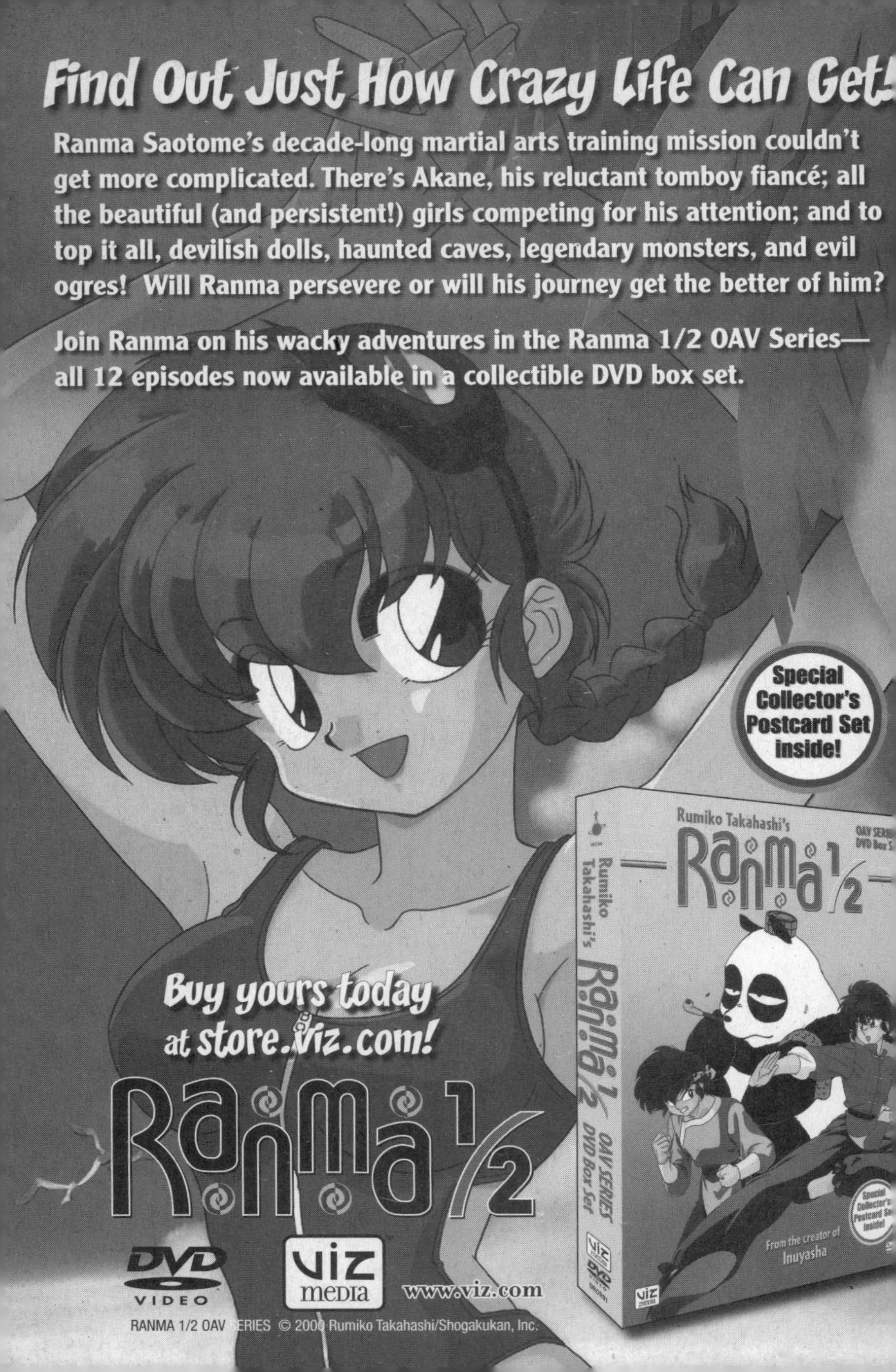

Find Out Just How Crazy Life Can Get!
Ranma Saotome's decade-long martial arts training mission couldn't get more complicated. There's Akane, his reluctant tomboy fiancé; all the beautiful (and persistent!) girls competing for his attention; and to top it all, devilish dolls, haunted caves, legendary monsters, and evil ogres! Will Ranma persevere or will his journey get the better of him?
Join Ranma on his wacky adventures in the Ranma 1/2 OAV Series—all 12 episodes now available in a collectible DVD box set.
Special Collector's Postcard Set inside!
Rumiko Takahashi's
Ranma 1/2
Rumiko Takahashi's Ranma 1/2 OAV SERIES DVD Box Set
From the creator of Inuyasha
Buy yours today at store.viz.com!
Ranma 1/2
DVD VIDEO
viz media
www.viz.com
RANMA 1/2 OAV SERIES © 2000 Rumiko Takahashi/Shogakukan, Inc.

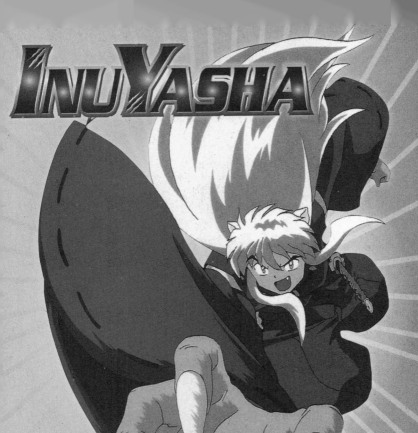

InuYasha

Read the action from the start with the original manga series

Full color adaptation of the popular TV series

Art book with cel art, paintings, character profiles and more

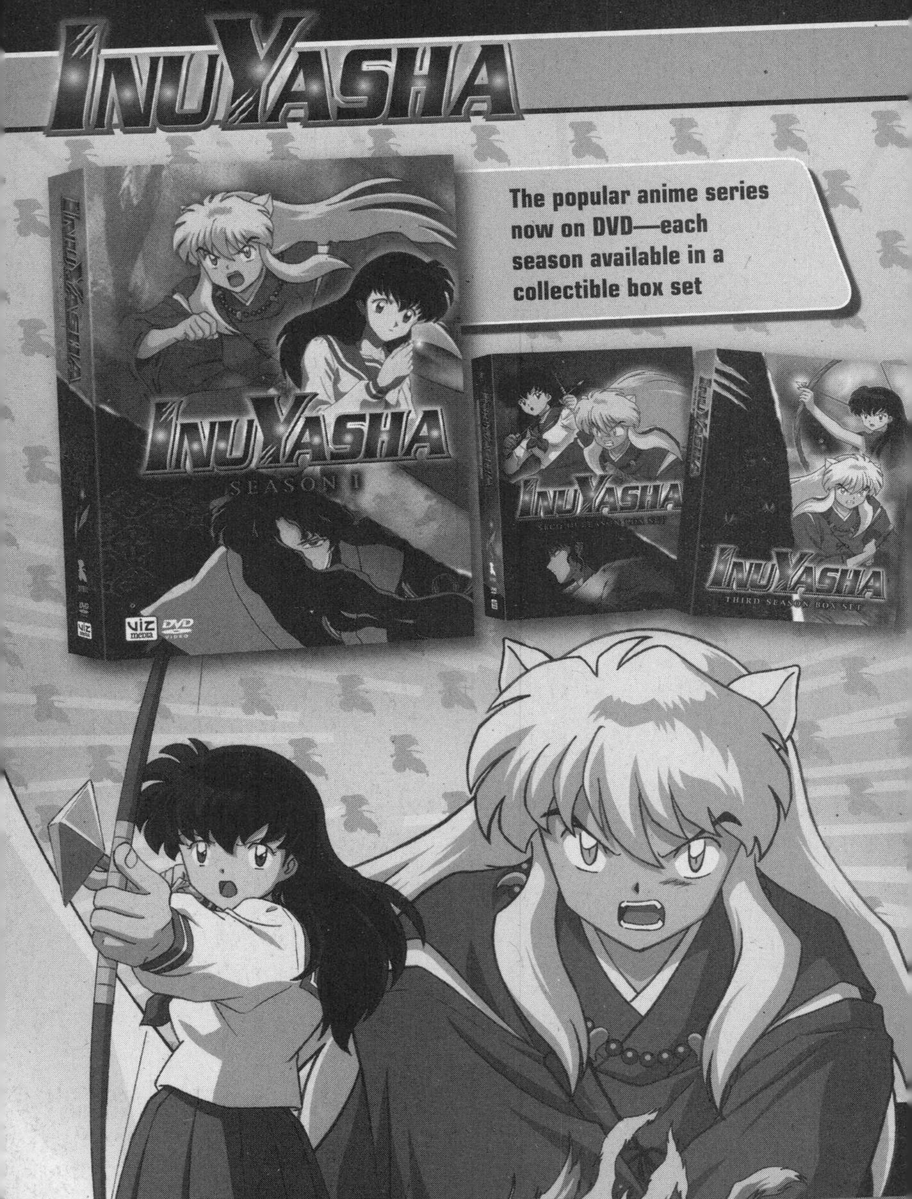
INUYASHA
The popular anime series now on DVD—each season available in a collectible box set
INUYASHA
SEASON 1
INUYASHA
INUYASHA
THIRD SEASON BOX SET

TV SERIES & MOVIES ON DVD!

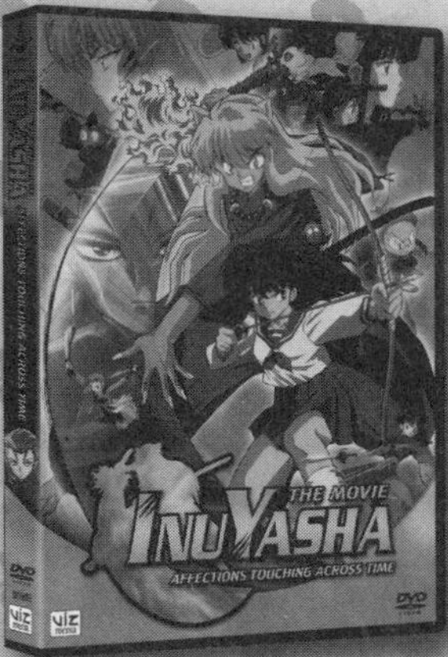
THE MOVIE
INUYASHA
AFFECTIONS TOUCHING ACROSS TIME

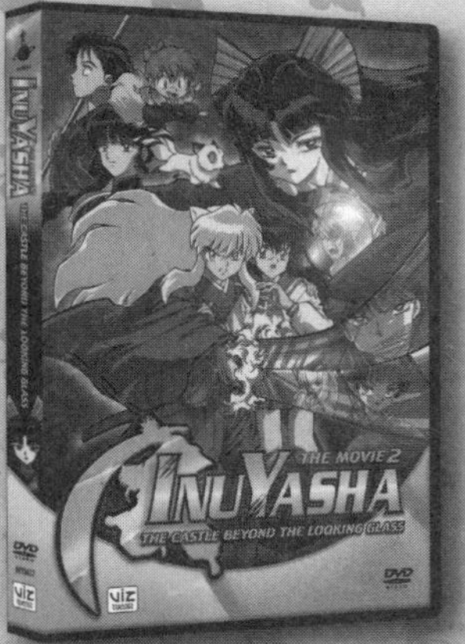
THE MOVIE 2
INUYASHA
THE CASTLE BEYOND THE LOOKING GLASS

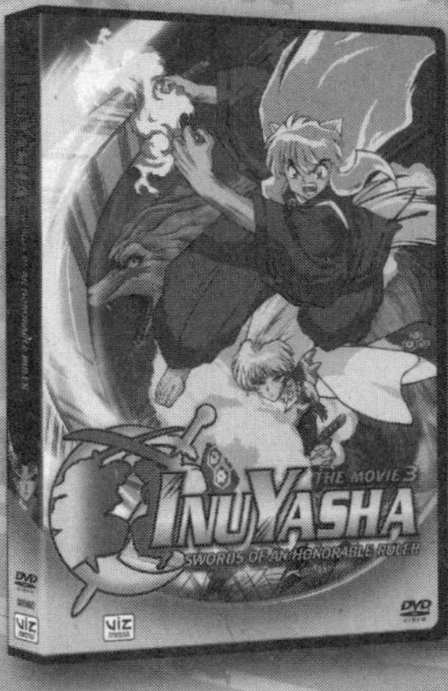
THE MOVIE 3
INUYASHA
SWORDS OF AN HONORABLE RULER

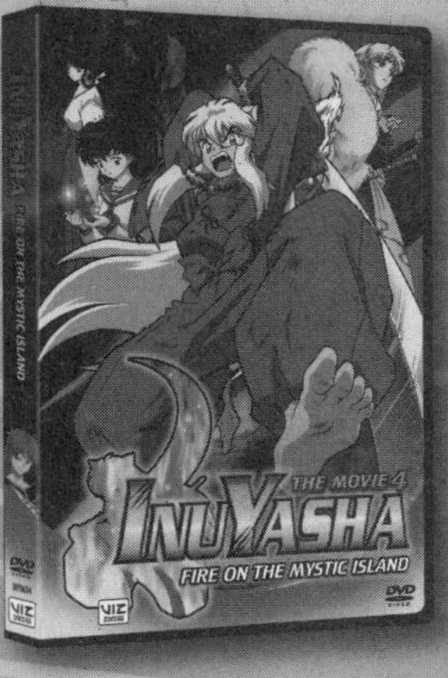
THE MOVIE 4
INUYASHA
FIRE ON THE MYSTIC ISLAND

See more of the action in Inuyasha full-length movies

viz media

www.viz.com
inuyasha.viz.com